I0868139

GENDER, SEPARATIST POLITICS, AND EMBODIED NATIONALISM IN CAMEROON

AFRICAN PERSPECTIVES

Kelly Askew and Anne Pitcher
Series Editors

Gender, Separatist Politics, and Embodied Nationalism in Cameroon
Jacqueline-Bethel Tchouta Mougoué

The Postcolonial Animal: African Literature and Posthuman Ethics
Evan Maina Mwangi

Developing States, Shaping Citizenship: Service Delivery and Political Participation in Zambia
Erin Accampo Hern

African Print Cultures: Newspapers and Their Publics in the Twentieth Century,
edited by Derek R. Peterson, Emma Hunter, and Stephanie Newell

Unsettled History: Making South African Public Pasts,
by Leslie Witz, Gary Minkley, and Ciraj Rassool

Seven Plays of Koffi Kwahulé: In and Out of Africa,
translated by Chantal Bilodeau and Judith G. Miller
edited with Introductions by Judith G. Miller

The Rise of the African Novel: Politics of Language, Identity, and Ownership,
by Mukoma Wa Ngugi

Black Cultural Life in South Africa: Reception, Apartheid, and Ethics,
by Lily Saint

Nimrod: Selected Writings,
edited by Frieda Ekotto

Gender, Separatist Politics, and Embodied Nationalism in Cameroon

Jacqueline-Bethel Tchouta Mougoué

University of Michigan Press
Ann Arbor

Copyright © 2019 by Jacqueline-Bethel Tchouta Mougoué
All rights reserved

This book may not be reproduced, in whole or in part, including illustrations, in any form (beyond that copying permitted by Sections 107 and 108 of the U.S. Copyright Law and except by reviewers for the public press), without written permission from the publisher.

Published in the United States of America by the
University of Michigan Press
Manufactured in the United States of America
Printed on acid-free paper
First published October 2019

A CIP catalog record for this book is available from the British Library.

Library of Congress Cataloging-in-Publication Data

Names: Mougoué, Jacqueline-Bethel Tchouta, 1983– author.
Title: Gender, separatist politics, and embodied nationalism in Cameroon / Jacqueline Mougoue.
Description: Ann Arbor : University of Michigan Press, 2019. | Series: African perspectives | Includes bibliographical references and index. |
Identifiers: LCCN 2019019139 (print) | LCCN 2019022361 (ebook) | ISBN 9780472074136 (hardback) | ISBN 9780472054138 (paper)
Subjects: LCSH: Women—Political activity—Cameroon—History—20th century. | Women—Cameroon—History—20th century. | Women—Identity. | Nationalism—Cameroon—History—20th century. | Cameroon—Politics and government—20th century. | BISAC: HISTORY / Africa / Central. | SOCIAL SCIENCE / Women's Studies.
Classification: LCC HQ1236.5.C17 M68 2019 (print) | LCC HQ1236.5.C17 (ebook) | DDC 305.4096711/0904—dc23
LC record available at https://lccn.loc.gov/2019019139
LC ebook record available at https://lccn.loc.gov/2019022361

Publication of this volume has been partially funded by the African Studies Center, University of Michigan.

For my mother, Marcie Sidonie Tchouta Mougoué
Mami za si zo ma mbuani ntam ndua shuapu sie
(In Fe'fe', also known as Bafang: "Mother, rest in peace in the Lord's house")

CONTENTS

Digital materials related to this title can be found on the Fulcrum platform via the following citable URL: https://doi.org/10.3998/mpub.9955202

ACKNOWLEDGMENTS

One day at a scholarly conference in Washington, DC, I tried to bargain as if I were in an African market. The worker at the booth struggled to convince me that the books being sold at the booth were just for show and that I would have to place an order to get one. Among the works was Pamela Feldman-Savelsberg's newly released book. I had never met her, but I had long admired her work, which shaped my curiosity and knowledge about gender in Cameroon. I was desperate to have this second book, and I offered to pay twice the asking price, exclaiming, "Please, I need this new book immediately!" From behind me I heard a soft whisper, "I am Pamela and I have never heard someone be so passionate about my work before!" I turned around to behold Pamela, who offered me her own sample copy on the spot. We got to talking, and the relationship that she and I eventually forged is one of many vital supportive relationships in my life. Publishing my first book with the University of Michigan Press, who published Pamela's first, is an enormous honor.

The women I study fostered camaraderie and wove emotional relationships, and so have those in my life, offering support beyond academia in many aspects of life. Cameroonians in both Cameroon and the diaspora facilitated the research for this book. I am grateful to the women who shared their memories of West Cameroon in the 1960s and early 1970s, opening their homes to me and providing the vivid narratives that are the backbone of this book. Profound thanks to chief archivist Primus Forgwe and his staff at the National Archives of Cameroon in Buea. At the University of Buea, I am deeply indebted to Walter Gam Nkwi, who welcomed me as colleague and friend, and Professor Joyce Endeley, Dorothy Forsac-Tata, and Helen Linonge-Fontebo, who provided an African feminist intellectual community. The staff at the National Archives in Yaoundé, especially Nevian Fonkwa, provided guidance and support. Annie Kamani, Eileen Manka Tabuwe, and Frida Bate served as my research assistants and interlocutors. In the United States, I am deeply indebted to Esmeralda Kale, Marie-Thérèse Guessou, and Mariana Endeley-Matute.

My dissertation committee helped me build the intellectual scaffolding of this work, serving as advisors and friends and championing me in my work. For thirteen years Alicia Decker has been the best mentor I could have had. She has provided key insights into my work, encouraged me to push my intellectual and creative boundaries, and offered warm friendship, helping me to grow as a scholar, mentor, and person. Whitney Walton brightened my holidays with Christmas cards, and Ellen Gruenbaum and Jay O'Brien acted in loco parentis when I was a graduate student at Purdue University, bringing me along as a third wheel on their outings and treating me like a daughter. Konrad Tuchscherer at St. John's University also served on my committee and my work is the better for his contribution.

I am indebted to individuals who read the manuscript at various stages. Alicia, Joan Supplee, Kate Epstein, Whitney, Ellen, Konrad, Walter, and the anonymous scholars who reviewed this book read the full manuscript and offered impeccable insights on both content and writing. Aili Tripp, Jennifer ("Jenna") Johnson-Hanks, Barbara Cooper, Nwando Achebe, Oyèrónkẹ́ Oyěwùmí, Mary Jo Maynes, James Sweet, Isabel Hofmeyr, Elizabeth ("Betsy") Schmidt, Susan Andrade, Harmony O'Rourke, Oluwakemi Balogun, Leslie James, Emma Hunter, Katie Jarvis, Jill Kelly, and Leslie Ballard read parts of the manuscript and made vital suggestions. Stephen D. Allen is the best writing partner I could have asked for. At Baylor I thank Beth Allison Barr, Daniel Barish, Elesha Coffman, Deirdre Fulton, Kim Kellison, Barry Hankins, Andrea Turpin, René Coker-Prikryl, and members of my philosophy writing group. Baylor graduate students Samuel Kelley, Samuel Young, and Lynneth Miller have been key readers as well, and Lynneth's help with the bibliography was vital. The challenging, but productive, feedback I received from Meredith Terretta and other peer reviewers on articles based on the same research inspired me to improve the book's content and arguments.

Financial support for research and writing made this book possible, including the Purdue Research Foundation (PRF) Research Grant, the Bernadotte E. Schmitt Grant from the American Historical Association, and the Libraries Grant-in-Aid at the University of Wisconsin–Madison. Baylor gave me tremendous support in the form of numerous research grants and leave including the Arts and Humanities Faculty Research Program Award and the Institute for Oral History Faculty Research Fellowship. The University of Michigan Press has been fantastic, including Ellen Bauerle, series editors Anne Pitcher and Kelly Askew, Kevin Rennells, and Daniel Otis.

Though substantially revised, an earlier version of chapter 6 appeared as

"Housewives at Husbands' Throats: Recalcitrant Wives and Gender Norms in a West African Nation, 1961–72," *Gender & History* 29, no. 2 (August 2017): 405–22; parts of chapters 2 and 3 were inspired by a publication in *Journal of West African History* ("Intellectual Housewives, Journalism, and Anglophone Nationalism in Cameroon, 1961–1972," *Journal of West African History* 3, no. 2 [2017]: 67–92).

Senior scholars have been vital parts of my wider intellectual community, shepherding me through the intellectual pathways of my work. I am especially indebted to Professors Tripp and Oyěwùmí, whom I first met in graduate school; they were the first senior scholars outside of Purdue to take me and my work seriously, offering critical feedback on the manuscript in its infancy. Other senior scholars who have "adopted" me include Judith Van Allen, Jenna, Benjamin Lawrance, Betsy, Toyin Falola, and Shirley Ardener, who, along with her husband, founded the National Archives of Cameroon in Buea in the 1960s. I thank each and every one of you for your dedication to junior scholars like me as we navigate the complex world of academia.

Social and academic communities have given me support at many levels. I recently made the difficult decision to leave Baylor University for a new opportunity at the University of Wisconsin–Madison. I am deeply grateful for my colleagues at Baylor, especially those in the department of history, who offered tremendous support during my time at the university. Thank you from the bottom of my heart. I also thank my graduate cohort and current faculty at Purdue; individuals I met in the Buffett Institute for Global Studies and the Program of African Studies at Northwestern University during my 2012–13 predoctoral fellow year; and members of the North American Association of Scholars on Cameroon. Jill, Katie, Sarah Hardin, Edgard Sankara, Kofi Asante, Richard Asante, and Laura Ann Twagira cheered me on and sent care packages that brought me joy. Markeysha Davis, thank you for your friendship and for all you taught me as my editor on our undergraduate newspaper. Although she sometimes reminded me that I seemed to have lost my audience as I penned columns on indiscriminate topics—reminding me, for instance, that the opinion column was supposed to be about views on university issues and not my opinions on random African political issues—she nevertheless let me publish my wide-ranging thoughts on any topic I could dream of. Writing about Cameroonian female journalists has brought those memories closer. I also thank Mark D. Delancey for the unending support for my work and being the best craft-beer-drinking partner I know. Allison, Le'Loni, Gary, Susan, Daniele, Marvin, Ashley, Shirley, Aryan, Jennifer, and

Sara have been great friends to me. My friendship with April has provided support spanning continents, including the cherished moment when she and several American expats serenaded me as we rowed through the canals in the Netherlands when I was going through a particularly hard time in my life. Sandra Ciarletta, Elise Edwards, and Reverend Laurie Anne Tuttle, I love all three of you like my sisters. You have radically changed my life and my worldview and have been a light in my life.

This book would not have been written without the love and support of my family and those who are like family in Cameroon, Belgium, France, Canada, and the United States: Christian-Sorel, Shaletta, Jonah, Isaac, Caroline, members of the family of my late grandmother Pauline Tchakounte, Nell Rapport, the Mbatengs, the Tamdjos, the Atangs, the Chins, and the Moys. My family also embodies that of my late mother Marcie Sidonie Tchouta Mougoué, who passed on her spirit, tenacity, and strength to me. I am proud to be her daughter, and her spirit is with me every day. I also thank my dog, Guinness, who endured nightly 3:00 a.m. walks when I finished writing late and grudgingly tolerated the increasingly long interim between his feeding times as the deadline for this book approached.

Finally, various life experiences have forged my hybrid Cameroonian-U.S. identity, adding threads to the fabric of my life and forming a colorful tapestry that spreads over decades, much like what happened to the women who are the focus of this work. From the Detroit poetry clubs, to the vibrant Cameroonian town of Kékem, where my mother is buried, to southern France where I lived and once learned (and forgot) Spanish in Spanish bars, to late-night dinners with friends in Dearborn, Michigan, during Ramadan—these are the overlapping experiences that have shaped and informed the hard but satisfying journey of being an Africanist scholar that served as the backdrop for the writing of this book.

A NOTE ON TERMINOLOGY

In this book, I refer to "Anglophone" Cameroonians. "Anglophone" is an increasingly ambiguous term, as growing debate about who is "Anglophone" and what the term actually means in contemporary scholarship suggests. As a Francophone Cameroonian myself, I have observed a similar phenomenon surrounding debates about who is "Francophone." However, the "Anglophone" term was far less ambiguous in the period this book scrutinizes. Thus, I use the explanation used by most scholars—the ancestors of Anglophone Cameroonians come from the west of the Mungo River, the geographic boundaries between British- and French-controlled Cameroon under the League of Nations mandate. Anglophone Cameroonians during the federal period referred to themselves as West Cameroonians because English-speaking regions comprised the federated state of West Cameroon from 1961 to 1972. Many present-day Anglophone Cameroonians call themselves Southern Cameroonians to emphasize their British administrative legacy and separation from the Francophone majority. I prefer "Anglophone" because it readily applies to Cameroonians before, during, and after British rule, even if it may have fallen into relative disuse more recently.

Typographical corrections were made to original sentences from English-language Cameroonian newspapers from the 1960s and 1970s throughout the book.

ABBREVIATIONS

CDC	Cameroon Development Corporation
CNU	Cameroon National Union
CPNC	Cameroon People's National Convention
CWA	Catholic Women's Association
CWI	West Cameroon Council of Women's Institutes
KNC	Kamerun National Congress
KNDP	Kamerun National Democratic Party
NCCW	National Council of Cameroonian Women
SCNC	Southern Cameroons National Council
SDF	Social Democratic Front
WCNU	Women's Cameroon National Union
WSCA	West Cameroon Federation of Women Social Clubs and Associations

INTRODUCTION

"What the Women of a Nation Are, So Shall the Nation Be"

Gendered Nationalism in Cameroon

In late December 1958, John Ngu Foncha, leader of the Kamerun National Democratic Party (KNDP), was in a serious accident in his Land Rover while campaigning for the 1959 election for premier of the British Southern Cameroons, the region of Cameroon that came under British control when Germany surrendered it after World War I. Having broken both collarbones in the crash, he was forced to wage the last week of his campaign encased in plaster casts. He had been traversing the regions in his trusty Land Rover, campaigning in various English-speaking towns, such as Bamenda, Kumba, Mamfe, and Victoria, against Emmanuel Mbela Lifafa Endeley, the leader of the then-ruling political party, the Kamerun National Congress (KNC).[1] According to Foncha's biographer, Endeley's party "openly jubilated" about the accident, calling on Southern Cameroonians to reject his candidacy since "he was going to die and that people should not vote for a dying man."[2] The statement exaggerated the gravity of Foncha's injuries, but Foncha in his casts could do little to respond. Immobilized, he could not deliver a crucial campaign speech at the recently established Nigerian Broadcasting Corporation (NBC) studio in Buea, the capital city of the British Southern Cameroons. At the time, Foncha was in Widikum, a day's journey from Buea. Foncha asked his wife, Anna Atang Foncha, to get a pen and paper and "play the role of a secretary." He dictated his campaign speech to her, and she personally ensured that Nicholas Ade Ngwa, an education officer in Buea, would secretly receive it so that he could read it on the radio in her husband's stead. NBC radio transmitted the speech to Lagos, Nigeria, and, from there, broadcast it to all regions of the Southern Cameroons. The measure saved Foncha's political career. He defeated Endeley and became the second premier of the British Southern Cameroons in 1959.

The incident occurred during British control of Foncha's region of Cameroon, which lasted from 1922 to 1961. At the end of German rule, a League of Nations mandate put the western part of Germany's colony under British control and the significantly larger eastern part under French rule. Both powers ruled Cameroon as part of their colonial empires. These regions were known as the British Cameroons (partitioned into Northern and Southern Cameroons) and French Cameroun, respectively, and both gained independence gradually over the course of the 1950s. Although the British governed the Southern Cameroons from their administrative headquarters in neighboring colonial Nigeria, the regions were administered separately. Nevertheless, Southern Cameroonians were essentially part of Nigeria, and they elected representatives for the Eastern House of Assembly in Nigeria until the early 1950s.[3] In 1954, Britain, having practiced indirect rule by allowing Africans to keep some administrative and legal power, gave the Southern Cameroons its own legislature, the Southern Cameroons House of Assembly. As premier, John Ngu Foncha led this institution. He and E. M. L. Endeley dominated the political landscape of Southern Cameroons in the 1950s. Foncha's 1959 victory over Endeley made his KNDP the most prominent party as British rule concluded.[4]

At the end of British rule, John Foncha's KNDP advocated for reunification with newly independent French Cameroun, renamed the Republic of Cameroon, led by President Ahmadou Ahidjo. In February 1961, Southern Cameroonians voted for this plan in a plebiscite.[5] Five months later, President Ahidjo called the Foumban Constitutional Conference, nominally to negotiate the constitution of the Federal Republic. Foncha's Anglophone delegation came expecting to negotiate, but they were at a disadvantage, given the far greater size of Francophone Cameroon and Ahidjo's position as representative of an already-independent state. Foncha's arguments for a loose form of federalism availed nothing.[6] The constitution of the Federal Republic of Cameroon largely conformed to the centralized pattern that Ahidjo sought, rather than the loose framework that Foncha and his delegation had envisioned. In October 1961 the two territories together became the Federal Republic of Cameroon, the unified state encompassing the English-speaking West Cameroon State and French-speaking East Cameroon State.[7] John Foncha served simultaneously as prime minister of the West Cameroon State and vice president of the Federal Republic from 1961 to 1970; the federal structure remained, at least in name, for two more years. It was a federation of two states with a central government; each federated state had some level of political autonomy. However, between 1961 and 1972, President Ahidjo increasingly marginalized Anglophone persons, politically, socially, and economically. He banned the multiparty system in 1966, effectively prohibiting all West Cameroonian political parties. His creation of the United Republic of Cameroon, in 1972, effectively subjugated English-speaking regions under his rule.

Scholarly and popular accounts of Anglophone Cameroon's history have generally focused on the activities of male politicians, such as John Foncha. Like Anna Foncha's role in making her husband's key political speech public in 1959, the political roles of Anglophone Cameroonian women have remained largely unknown. This book is about the seemingly invisible women, such as Anna Foncha, in the Anglophone Cameroonian nationalist movement during the federal period, 1961 to 1972. The actions of the wives of political heavyweights, women state bureaucrats, and political activists reveal the roles of women in nationalist endeavors.

Scholars have ignored the role Anna Foncha played in John Foncha's political career. Accounts typically portray her as "play[ing] the role of a secretary." Scholarly interpretations typically mention Anna Foncha as simply John Foncha's wife. Even a 1999 biography of her husband emphasizes her role in his domestic life; most of the material about her appears under section titles such as "Mr. J. N. Foncha Chooses a Wife," and "Mrs. Foncha and the Children Move to Buea."[8] A present-day blog addressing the political history of Anglophone Cameroon asserts that Anna Foncha knew little of political events in the late 1950s and 1960s because "she remained cloistered in the kitchen, while her husband debated state matters with his political colleagues in the parlour."[9] In contrast, I argue that Anna Foncha was probably her husband's top advisor and engaged closely with his political career. A petite woman who had been formally educated at Njinikom in Southern Cameroons and at Teacher Training Centre at Ikot Ekpene in Nigeria, she played a key role in the political trajectory of Anglophone Cameroon that went beyond transcribing her husband's urgently dictated speech in 1958. Anna Foncha was and continues to be a political force in her own right. She founded the Catholic Women's Association (CWA), which today has over 16,000 members around the world. Her presiding over the leading women's organizations in the West Cameroon State, the West Cameroon Federation of Women's Social Clubs and Associations (WSCA) and the West Cameroon

Council of Women's Institutes (CWI), further demonstrates her significance in Cameroonian politics.

This book explores the importance the WSCA and the CWI placed on women's daily actions. It also uses the wide-ranging political activities of Anna Foncha and her various counterparts as a methodological approach, providing entrée into the gendered political history of Anglophone Cameroon more broadly. Using excerpts from the biographies of numerous women such as Anna Foncha as a unifying thread, this book reveals the link between gender, social and political identity, and nationalism, a complex construction in West Cameroon given the multiplicity of ethnic group identifications. The activities of elite Anglophone women often differed from the realm of the political as presented in previous renderings of Cameroon's nationalist politics. Elite Anglophone women slowly entered the formal political structure as civil servants in the late 1950s, accessing political power beyond the traditional women's societies that protected women's agricultural and reproductive fertility. Their activities show both the possibilities that their intelligence, formal education, and social position afforded them and the limitations that their gender imposed on them, illustrating the boundaries that also constrained other women's political participation. Unlike men, female political elites strove to wield social and political power by invoking women's longstanding maternal authority within the home and society to legitimize their importance in varied nationalist activities. In other words, women worked to legitimize their political activities by emphasizing that they "mothered" the well-being of society and ultimately, that of the nation.

By examining the power of women's collective political mobilization and their particular role in creating and carrying out a nationalist campaign laced with separatist undertones—or, as I phrase it, separatist politics—I describe how politically elite women exercised both individual and collective agency when driving social, political, and economic change in women's lives in predominantly patriarchal societies. These formally educated elite women saw themselves as the leaders of nation-building agendas in the West Cameroon State as well. Consequently, they frequently focused on the actions of their formally educated counterparts, primarily women in the professional workforce, housewives, and primary and secondary school-age girls. By focusing on the actions of such women, female journalists and female political elites strove to protect class boundaries even as they sought to improve women's economic, social, educational, and political conditions. Female political elites preserved their own social and political authority by advancing women's rights overall and by attempting to monitor the behavior of women through advice columns, women's organizations, and domestic science courses. As a collective unit, educated elite women advocated for and supported one another, participating in what Pamela Feldman-Savelsberg calls "affective circuits" that precipitate "emotion-laden social networks. . . . whose malleable structure of ties creates conduits that are maintained by ongoing interaction and exchange."[10] By focusing on the political involvement of women such as Foncha, we learn that they formed intimate alliances of emotional support to foster sisterly camaraderie. In building a community of sisterhood in which they worked together to drive particular forms of political discourse and actions, key women political elites fostered hope in politically volatile landscapes in the postcolonial era.

In the period of the Federal Republic, Anna Foncha and her counterparts were part of an Anglophone Cameroonian Christian urban elite that expressed differing European administrative ties, languages, cultures, and geographical boundaries to visualize and imagine, as Benedict Anderson might put it, a West Cameroon "nation." In this period and ever since, the Francophone state has treated English-speaking Cameroonians as potential secessionists, subject to political surveillance as well as, at times, violence.[11] Women in the Federal Republic did not openly criticize the government in Francophone Cameroon as annexationist and hegemonic; they left this to the men. Unlike in many women's organizations, male leadership and membership in political parties at times followed ethnic or regional boundaries. Women such as Foncha—political spouses, civil servants, journalists, and politicians—participated in a subtler ethnic politics that favored a unified Anglophone nationalism that incorporated women from varied ethnic backgrounds. They did so by calling for loyalty and encouraging women to abandon ethnic group affiliations, asking women to instead pursue unity by focusing on female solidarity, a community of sisterhood, and their mutual Anglophone heritage.[12] Nationalist aspirations, as well as personal interests, led female political elites to call on women to unify beyond ethnic group ties. Many politically elite women of the West Cameroon State were of mixed ethnic heritage, and this too may have inspired them to forge a hybrid ethnonationalism that transcended ethnic and cultural boundaries by selectively incorporating varied social and cultural practices, such as indigenous foods and cooking practices from diverse ethnic groups in Anglophone regions of Cameroon. Through "the process of ethnic formation," such women "work[ed] out claims of identity in everyday life."[13]

Anna Foncha (*to the right*) receiving flowers from local women in West Cameroon, ca. 1960s. Image courtesy of National Archives of Cameroon in Buea.

WCNU women leaders in Buea, 1972. (*left to right*) Prudencia Chilla (smiling), Gladys Endeley, Gwendoline Burnley (looking down at paperwork). Image courtesy of National Archives of Cameroon in Buea.

Anna Foncha and her counterparts stressed this subtler ethnic politics as they deployed conservative gender constructs to produce Anglophone separatist nationalism. They advocated for women's political importance by maintaining that women played key roles in the cultural, economic, and social development of the nation as daughters, wives, and mothers. Within this context, female members of the political elite inexorably linked ideal womanhood to nationalist politics by underscoring proper gender norms. While these elite women accessed new spaces of sociopolitical power by monitoring other women's behaviors—their female supporters often recognized their positions as "mothers" of the nation—they also ran the parallel project of genuinely improving women's social, political, and economic lives by calling on women to unify to gain their rights. Women might "emancipate" themselves by participating in Anglophone women's organizations that stressed the rationale for a separatist, national women's identity. Although leaders asserted the apolitical nature of their organizations, those organizations legitimized male-dominated political parties by showing deference and political support. In keeping with this, female political elites drew from the implied power of women's traditional organizations to enforce their will, mobilizing urban women in public rallies and dancing rituals to support male officials. They also called on precolonial traditions of maternalist politics from the Anglophone regions of Cameroon, such as *titi ikoli*, a form of female sanction in which southern coastal Bakweri women collectively mobilized to shame male delinquents and *Takumbeng* (or *Takembeng*), an association of menopausal women in the northwest.[14] As research suggests, the conservative patriarchal cultural constructs that elite women used—establishing themselves as "good" women despite their political activities—to build and maintain Anglophone separatist nationalism were effective. For instance, by claiming to be apolitical, and thus appearing nonthreatening to male-dominated political parties, women's organizations successfully, albeit gradually, developed initiatives and various projects of social reform that expanded their access to formal education, the professional workforce, political careers, and even to organized sports.[15]

Because many texts on Cameroonian history do not differentiate Francophone and Anglophone nationalist movements, they obscure women's efforts to draw cultural distinctions between competing forms of nationalism. Educated political elites commonly referenced the superior morality of Anglophone Cameroonian women. They focused on women's virtue, commonly referencing sexual morality and adherence to household duties, as a fundamental distinction between Anglophone traits and Francophone ones.

Ahidjo's annexationist actions fed their concern about preserving Anglophone cultural values. Within this context, I contend that educated political elites invoked embodied nationalism—a concept that I define as a type of nationalism in which identities can be embodied through performance, emotional expression, and visual representation through, for instance, food, dress, and suitable conduct. Within the *Cameroonian* context, I assert that female educated political elites invoked embodied nationalism to bring visual representations and emotional, or affective, practices of ideal Anglophone womanhood in urban settings. By emphasizing this embodied nationalism, political and economic elites implied that everyday patterns of behavior and comportment—the clothes that women wore, the foods they cooked, their abstention from gossip, and their adherence to appropriate marital behavior—might project a suitable Anglophone Cameroonian persona and esteem locally, nationally, and internationally.

This embodied nationalism became a vehicle for politically elite women to invoke their British heritage and "tradition," mostly derived from the Bamenda (western) Grassfields of Cameroon, to develop tangible markers of a hybrid Anglophone identity through food and dress, such as using the traditional Bamenda male dress to fashion the West Cameroonian national costume for both women and men. These everyday tangible markers—or in the words of Benedict Anderson, "cultural artefacts"—of Anglophone national and cultural identities filtered through an urban setting, shaping a progressive urban ideal womanhood.[16] Yet, formally educated women and women of middle- to upper-middle-class positioning regularly challenged gender norms to shape their own ideas of cosmopolitan womanhood—from the housewife who took her husband to court for failing to provide "food money," to the economically independent young adult women who donned trousers and drank Guinness at bars, much to the dismay of many men, to the female boxer who won a match against her male opponent; after the match, reportedly "still looking fresh," she informed a reporter, "what a man can do, a woman can [do]."[17] In line with this, many urban elite women and men condemned the behaviors of such women who seemingly did not conform to their ideal of Anglophone womanhood in the West Cameroon State, and contrasted this ideal with women in Francophone Cameroon and the West, such as the United Kingdom and the United States. By urging women to subscribe to everyday patterns of behavior and comportment that supported Anglophone nationalist politics, female political elites set Anglophone national identity against a more powerful Francophone state. In doing so, they highlighted similarities among Anglophone persons and ignored social, cultural, and political similarities with their Francophone counterparts. For instance, by imagining Anglophone women as being more devout Christians, more likely to don traditional African attire, and more sexually reserved than their Francophone counterparts, Anglophone women elites actively (re) defined Cameroonian cultural identities. Preserving conservative ideal womanhood, cultural values, and political identity came to be seen as the linchpin of Anglophone unity in English-speaking towns in Cameroon.

Elite women drew from various political ideologies and actions to form a colorful jigsaw puzzle of Anglophone national identity, an assemblage of diverse interlocking pieces drawn from local, national, and global ideas about gender as well as their British administrative heritage. Formally educated women reinterpreted traditional social mechanisms to redraw the boundaries of women's access to traditional modes of authority when confronting conflicting social norms. They drew from sexual mores and social power found in precolonial western Grassfields societies and in Christian missions during European rule. In doing so, they redefined gender norms to change their lived realities. For instance, female journalists established new boundaries to the age-old traditional punishment for marital grievances or improper moral conduct, such as counseling women not to publicly chastise their husbands as long as the husbands continued to extend financial support to their respective families. Additionally, prominent female political figures incorporated oral tradition in numerous forms of print media, and I contend that they took on the role of griots, West African professional storytellers who orally recount history and traditions. But these efforts encompassed tensions and conflicts; the question of which gender norms to preserve and maintain was contentious. Participating in a process Keith Hampton and Barry Wellman term "glocalization," "the combination of global connectivity and local activity," women political elites stayed abreast of women's political conditions in Anglophone countries in Africa, Europe, and the United States.[18] They frequently referenced spirited women's organizations in Nigeria, Sierra Leone, Ghana, and the United Kingdom as models for similar organizations in the West Cameroon State and as a way to be part of a global network. Anna Foncha and others touted these organizations and their role in Anglophone Cameroonian cultural identity and social unity, and thus nationality, as the key to women's empowerment. Josepha Mua, a woman parliamentarian in the West Cameroon Legislative Assembly, for example, wrote in the *Cameroon Times* in 1964 that West Cameroon's women "have been playing a very active part in the world of politics. . . . We are up to the standard of deciding things for ourselves without looking to the men for help."[19] Mua proclaimed: "What the women of a nation are, so shall the nation be."[20]

THEORIZING AND GENDERING SEPARATIST AND SECESSIONIST MOVEMENTS: CAMEROON'S EXCEPTIONALITY

As the 1960s progressed and it became clearer that President Ahidjo was increasingly encroaching on West Cameroonian sovereignty, Anglophone male elites, journalists, and men in the highest echelons of political power at first called for preserving federalism, and later openly questioned whether Anglophone regions could peacefully stay unified with Francophone Cameroon.[21] Scholars and activists have also painted the forced "marriage" of West Cameroon and East Cameroon as a crime against humanity, or Ahidjo's "colonization" of Anglophone persons.[22] As Fonkem Achankeng observes, scholars of English-speaking Cameroon compare their lot to that of Namibia under South African control, Eritrea under Ethiopian control, and Western Sahara, which is presently under Moroccan occupation.[23] The internal colonization of Anglophone Cameroon took place in the broader global context of the 1960s and 1970s, which saw political movements rise against various dominant systems of government, driving secessionist and separatist movements from Canada (Québec), Spain (Basque), China (Tibet), and Nigeria (Biafra). As Brian Girvin argues, secessionist and separatist movements challenge longstanding ideas about democracy, nationalism, and political ideology across the entire world.[24] Yet scant research has addressed separatist and secessionist movements rooted in Africa. As Achankeng concludes, decolonization in Africa is far from complete—and Cameroon is one example of this.[25]

Despite some similarities to Western nations, Africa offers unique perspectives on secessionist and separatist movements due to the differing legacies of European dominance that still shape the national languages, political infrastructures, and economies of each state. Since the 1960s, Anglophone Cameroonians have claimed to be *doubly* colonized (and occupied), by Francophone Cameroon and by France. In an unusual relationship to their former European administrative masters, they used competing ideologies about the legacies of dual European rule to differentiate themselves from their Francophone counterparts in the immediate years following independence. For example, a letter writer objecting to the presence of Francophone Cameroonian soldiers in English-speaking regions in December 1961 said that, "though we are brothers, we should not forget that we were brought up by two different governments, namely English and French."[26] In their work, Miles Larmer and Baz Lecocq assert that contemporary understandings of African political landscapes assume that "official" national identities "are weak or even nonexistent." They note that such "views on the African state, studied in connection with what are generally called 'ethnic conflicts', automatically presume the failure of African national projects, which results from implicitly taking a statist perspective."[27] Such statist perspectives heavily focus on the state's position as having considerable power over economic and social activities. Focusing on nationalist aspirations demonstrates how Anglophone Cameroonian nationalist rhetoric and secessionist and separatist tendencies have never truly faded, which complicates the narrative that posits the "state's failure to become a nation" since independence in Cameroon.[28] I maintain that the existence of competing nationalisms, such as those in other African states, does not mean that Cameroon has failed to become a nation. Instead, the repeated resurgence of Anglophone nationalism and secessionist and separatist intentions speaks to the longevity of challenging narratives about a *monolithic* Cameroonian nationalism.[29] Indeed, narratives of an imagined Anglophone heritage demonstrate the vibrant counter-nationalisms that Anglophone Cameroonians have envisioned in the early postcolonial period.

However, Anglophone political elites have never been unanimous in their views of Francophone rule. A July 1962 letter to the *Cameroon Champion* by an Moris N. Namata argued for a unitary state, saying that federalism was dividing Cameroonians and objecting to loyalty tied to differing cultures and past European administrative rule. Namata concluded, "If the constitution is reviewed and amended for a unitary one, [then] Cameroon would from then [on] continue winning appraisal of her alacrity by the world."[30] A decade later, popular satirical columnist Patrick Tataw Obenson, writing as "Ako-Aya" in the *Cameroon Outlook*, argued in favor of Ahidjo's single-party state, writing partly in Cameroonian pidgin English, an English-based creole language: "Massa ["mister" or "boss"], I glad plenty for this reunification. . . . it has brought peace."[31] Many Anglophone politicians who had condemned Ahidjo's unitary plans decided to preserve what little power they had left rather than fight annexation by the more powerful Francophone state. Contemporary Anglophones debate whether some level of unity benefits them, and many do support separatism—a return to a federal republic—over secession.

Although scholars of Anglophone Cameroonian history have widely addressed the genesis of Anglophone nationalism and struggles for self-determination in the early postcolonial period, they have neglected the role of women.[32] Jill Vickers notes that this is typical: narratives of secessionist movements generally only reference women in relationship to men's violence.[33] Through the lens of embodied nationalism, this book examines the unique strategies women used to maintain political autonomy, preserve suitable representations of Anglophone cultural identity, and drive separatist politics differently from their male counterparts in the Federal Republic of Cameroon. Although federalism did not lead to the secession of the West Cameroon State and Ahidjo exerted overcentralized control in the Federal Republic—one scholar even going as far as identifying the federal period as "more shadow than reality"—the federal period *did* provide fertile grounds on which elite political women planted ideologies about a distinct Anglophone identity.[34] Analyzing the activities of elite political women illustrates how they used various global ideologies to grow, or bring to fruition, social and political unity in a diverse nation. As chapter 2 describes, Anna Foncha and other CWI leaders looked to the infrastructures of Anglophonic women's organizations—in Ghana, the United Kingdom, and the United States—to tie themselves to a wider Anglophone community in Africa and on the global stage, reaffirming their Anglophone heritage against a Francophone one. Political elites also overtly and unambiguously called on their British heritage in events such as British Week, which climaxed in a Miss British beauty contest, as chapter 4 will describe. Marginalizing or erasing such efforts by women obscures a crucial underpinning of contemporary separatist and secessionist movements. Anglophone women's separatist endeavors to articulate ideas about suitable gender codes of behavior within political, domestic, and community spaces complicate traditional Africanist scholarship by illuminating the unique gendered political experiences of Anglophone Cameroonian women. In emphasizing their narratives, we learn much about how the legacy of foreign rule and intracolonization by a hegemonic "other" can influence contesting ideas about nationalism and political identity.

In highlighting the strategies women used to navigate a turbulent political setting, this work illustrates how elements of embodied nationalism might extend beyond Cameroon and even outside of Africa, resonating on a broader and global scale. Using Anglophone Cameroon as a case study may provide unique insight into women's roles in separatist and secessionist projects across the world, such as in Quebec, Puerto Rico, and Tibet. In Tibet, for example, the Miss Tibet annual beauty pageant is held in India and has become a space to debate proper comportment and the embodiment of Tibetan nationalism and separatist ideologies.[35] Such examples suggest that embodied nationalism often emerges as a channel for tangible markers of national and cultural identity in political, social, or religious movements where individuals seek to claim and preserve authority and agency across time and space.

GENDER AND NATIONALISM IN AFRICAN HISTORICAL STUDIES

In tracing the history of nationalism as imagined and embodied by Anglophone Cameroonians, this book expands a substantial body of research that has complicated wide-ranging concepts about gender—social and cultural ideas that define the state of being female or male. Oyèrónkẹ́ Oyěwùmí explains that "gender is socially constructed [and] that the social differences between males and females are located in social practices, and not simply in biological facts."[36] While acknowledging that gender involves relations between and among people of different genders, this book mostly focuses on constructions of gender norms as they pertain to women, highlighting how women respond to various expectations of gender norms differently than their male counterparts when shaping political identities and leading nationalist undertakings. Nira Yuval-Davis asserts that women become the symbolic bearers of "the collectivity's identity" because of societal beliefs that they possess the authentic voice of their culture.[37] Thus, ideas about dominant gender codes of behavior for women contribute to beliefs that women, not only the bureaucracy, give nations life, from a biological, cultural, and symbolic point of view.[38]

Three themes are central to the book's main argument. Using gender as a vehicle of analysis to traverse three literal and figurative spaces—women's collective mobilization, discursive arenas, and seemingly mundane everyday activities and rituals—this work examines how elites endeavored to monitor women's political and social actions in the Federal Republic of Cameroon. While this work examines women's formal political participation by analyzing the collective activities of women's organizations in the West Cameroon State, it also considers how women embody nationalism through daily actions, such as eschewing gossip and donning trousers only in proper settings (the subject of chapters 5 and 7). Moreover, by drawing inspiration from the western Grassfields to, for instance, fashion the national costume, this embodied nationalism extended beyond elite women and reached to the everyday urban population. Focusing on women's collective mobilization, discursive arenas (specifically advice columns), and everyday activities illuminates the colorful interlocking cultural pieces that formed the Anglophone "nation."

Women's Collective Mobilization

I draw from the work of numerous scholars to examine how ideas about gender profoundly affected women's access to political power in colonial and postcolonial states. Scholarship on African women's political activities demonstrates that diverse social, cultural, and political women's associations have powerfully shaped political actions and nationalist agendas in twentieth-century Africa. Through various women's organizations and ritual associations—which are common throughout West Africa, from Cameroon to the coast of Guinea—African women have reinforced their agricultural, economic, and reproductive authority to further their influence in nationalist struggles. In French Cameroun, the women's wing of the Marxist nationalist party, the Union des Populations du Cameroun (UPC), was among the most powerful.[39] Like their Anglophone counterparts, the leaders of the Union Démocratique des Femmes Camerounaises (UDEFEC) sought to bridge divides by mobilizing women from various sectors of society. As Meredith Terretta points out, UDEFEC "women joined together . . . reclaiming . . . patterns of women's access to power that predated European occupation."[40] Terretta argues that "[t]he era of nationalism provided an opportunity for rural women to revisit and reshape" spheres they had dominated before French rule, such as their reproductive and agricultural authority.[41]

Similar to their Francophone Cameroonian and West African counterparts, Anglophone Cameroonian women drew from their long-standing economic and agricultural authority to advance their social and political significance in nationalist struggles. In the final three years of British rule, women in the Bamenda (western) Grassfields of Cameroon, John and Anna Foncha's home territory, revolted against the interference of British administrators in agriculture, which women had traditionally dominated. The period of this uprising is known as the Anlu Rebellion. The women of the Anlu, a centuries-old women's organization that usually acted against people who breached moral codes, targeted British officials and local African men who they believed supported British officials' attempt to interfere with women's agriculture by "requiring all women farmers to use a new crop implementation strategy."[42] Further, responding to rumors that Endeley's KNC planned to sell their land to the Igbo people, one of the largest ethnic groups in neighboring Nigeria, they gave support to John Foncha's KNDP that proved crucial.[43] Neglecting their regular domestic and agricultural duties, they participated in Anlu as a way to disturb local political power from 1958 to 1961. The women's "tactics included stripping naked in front of men," who "considered the sight of the vagina in public to be a bad portent"; entering schools singing obscene songs; and storming the classrooms of teachers they believed had backed Endeley's KNC.[44] Female leaders during the Anlu Rebellion invoked women's agricultural rights in mobilizing women in the movement and drawing support for the KNDP.

Anlu called on a tradition of maternalist politics to enforce their will during British rule, as did female members of the political elite in the early years of Cameroon's independence. While Anna Foncha and many of her counterparts were not involved in the Anlu Rebellion, they would refurbish the "wife and mother" tropes to foster women's collective mobilization, drawing, for example, from women's traditional maternal authority in the Bamenda (western) Grassfields tradition, thus underpinning their social and political importance throughout the 1960s. Female political elites focused on their domestic duties as wives and mothers by encouraging women to hold public rallies and support the KNDP government.

While both nationalist efforts focused on women's "natural" duties as wives and mothers, the political discourse and actions of the 1960s differed. Formal education was often a de facto qualification for entering the leadership ranks of women's organizations. Further, these educated female political elites reinterpreted the boundaries of women's political participation, drawing from both local and international ideas about gender norms. Moreover, unlike Anlu, which is only temporarily active to address serious grievances, Anna Foncha and her counterparts strove to progressively achieve women's long-term political participation while remaining deferential to male authority.

The Anlu tradition resembles practices that give many women, particularly older women, power across Africa. Women's collective mobilization continued in the postcolonial period, as women engaged in similar efforts across ethnic, geographic, and class boundaries to fuse their social and political unity and strength. These groups often focused on their roles as mothers in homes and society and couched their political actions as apolitical to avoid being seen as threatening to the male-dominated postcolonial state.[45] As Ifi Amadiume contends, the interconnectedness of motherhood, women's unity, and political power is not new in Africa: "Female solidarity in the African context is fundamentally associated with the culture of matriarchy and the ideology of motherhood. . . . matriarchy—that is, African women's construct of motherhood—was a means of institutional and ideological empowerment."[46] Like the women who participated in the Federation of South African Women during the period of apartheid that Meghan Healy-Clancy studies, elite Anglophone Cameroonian women similarly "talked about their public activism as emanating from an idealized private sphere in order to make themselves legible as social actors." Also, comparably, because "[m]otherhood became a potent political discourse," it informed the concept of a "public motherhood" that allowed women to legitimatize their public activism and political actions.[47]

Elite women throughout Cameroon presented themselves as "good" women as long as they deferred to their husbands at home. Here they differed from politically elite Muslim women in Tanzania and Guinea. These Muslim women defied their husbands to support radical Africanist and socialist nationalist parties, and in some cases were divorced as a result or resorted to divorce to mobilize for the political parties.[48] In Anglophone Cameroon, leaders of women's organizations asserted that women could only "liberate" themselves and make social, economic, and political advances if they participated in women's organizations and adhered to dominant ideas about gender norms at home and in male-dominated West Cameroonian societies.

Scholars of women's movements have explored how best to identify African women's organizations that seek women's social, political, and economic advancement. For instance, scholars of the Anlu Rebellion, such as Eugenia Shanklin and Henry Kam Kah, assert that although the uprising was primarily a movement against British rule, it was also a women's movement because it defended women's agricultural rights.[49] Filomina Chioma Steady, on the other hand, asserts that the Sierra Leone Women's Movement, an association active since British rule, "was the first truly African feminist association in Freetown [the capital]" because it was the first organization to "advocate for greater participation of women in national politics and public life."[50] But while some women's movements may have feminist agendas, seeking gender equality in various areas, scholars of African gender studies assert the need to place such actions within a larger African context. Shireen Hassim calls on scholars to recognize a distinction between "feminine" and "feminist" women's movements: "both . . . mobilise women on the basis of the roles conventionally ascribed to women, such as their reproductive and domestic responsibilities [but] feminist movements seek to challenge those roles and articulate a democratic vision of a society in which gender is not the basis for a hierarchy of power."[51] As Hassim argues, however, some modern women's organizations in South Africa seek to eschew complete autonomy to avoid being "marginalized from national political processes"; by doing so, they "may make enormous gains through the patronage of other political organizations."[52] Similarly, in the 1960s West Cameroon State, the leaders of women's organizations looked to politically powerful male institutions such as the KNDP and later the Francophone government for financial and political support for their economic and social projects.

Notwithstanding my African feminist interjection in this work, I am careful not to forcibly inject contemporary ideas about feminism into the past, choosing instead to privilege how women envisioned their political and social realities at that time in the past. The women on whom this book focuses did not openly identify as feminists. This probably reflects a suspicion of feminism that was common in Africa, an apprehension that reflects a sense that feminism is based on social conditions and values "not indigenous to Africa."[53] As Juliana Makuchi Nfah-Abbenyi affirms, "Often, when an African woman is associated with feminism or directly labeled as a 'feminist,' such labeling incongruously defines her as Western, meaning that she is either condemned or not credited for what she is or does because she is said to be deviant or simply imitating Western women (a negative statement)."[54] Perhaps this is why Prudencia Chilla, a female parliamentarian during the 1970s, a cofounder of the CWA, and the first Anglophone woman to publish an autobiographical novel, *Promise*, never openly identified as feminist albeit the feminist undertones of her novel. However, I am also unwilling to identify Anna Foncha and other politicians' wives as simply engaging in what Hussaina Abdullah terms "wifeism," institutionalizing their roles as politicians' wives, or to merely label them as femocrats—a term that Amina Mama defines as women who have few ideas of their own and draw most of their power from being married to politically powerful men.[55] They exerted great agency in developing initiatives and policies when endeavoring to, and succeeding in, improving women's social, economic, and political lives in the Federal Republic. Moreover, their statements and actions "illustrate that they perceived the limits of patriarchy" even as they engaged in what some gender studies scholars call "feminist action," a process by which "participants explicitly place value on challenging gender hierarchy and changing women's social status, whether they adopt or reject the feminist label."[56] They strove to progressively improve women's lives, challenging select gender norms while still maintaining and preserving a patriarchal order. Ultimately, because women political elites perceived Anglophone identity and nationalism to be in crisis, that dilemma was transferred not into a feminist movement, but into what was primarily a gendered nationalist movement and secondarily a women's movement.

Embodied Nationalism: Politicizing the Everyday

Scholarship illustrates that everyday rituals can become highly politicized, connected to issues of nationalism, social anxiety, and individual and collective agency. In 1995, Michael Billig coined the term "banal nationalism" to identify nationalist elements of seemingly benign, everyday, unnoticed representations of the nation, such as the flag; "[d]aily, the nation is indicated, or 'flagged', in the lives of its citizenry." As Billig avers, such banal expressions of nationalism reflect ideologies that powerfully facilitate the process by which nations are politically and culturally reproduced.[57] While Billig applied his definition of banal nationalism to long-established states in the West, such as the United States and the United Kingdom, scholars such as Igor Cusack contend that "this 'banal' flagging of the nation also appears in the recently established nations"; Cusack extends the concept to his work on national cuisines in Equatorial Guinea.[58] I too extend this idea to Anglophone Cameroon while simultaneously invoking and applying the concept of embodied nationalism.[59] It is a concept that I understand as being informed by Billig's characterization of banal nationalism, combined with Elisabeth Militz's and Carolin Schurr's definition of "affective nationalism" and, finally, integrated with Evelyn Brooks Higginbotham's concept of the "politics of respectability." Militz and Schurr assert that the nation can be "represented and embodied" through a type of affective nationalism in which "the nation emerges in moments of encounter between different bodies and objects through embodying, sharing, enjoying or disliking what feels national."[60] Militz and Schurr reference celebrated contemporary Azerbaijani dances as one way in which "people feel a sense of national belonging through everyday practices such as a national style of dancing." Through affective connections, varied individuals around the world, such as the Azerbaijani people, strive to preserve visual and emotional representations of national identities. Higginbotham argues that between 1880 and 1920 in the United States, black women in black Baptist churches emphasized a "politics of respectability that equated public behavior with individual self-respect and with the advancement of African Americans as a group." They stressed temperance, refined etiquette, and sexual virtue as a way to increase the self-respect of African Americans and obtain "a measure of esteem from white America."[61] In Anglophone Cameroon, everyday conduct, cookery, and dress were three key sites where ostensibly unnoticed daily routines were politicized and expressed through an embodied nationalism that quietly flagged larger ideas about nationalism, identity, and suitable public decorum and esteem on local, national, and global stages. Political elites invoked varied embodied emotional practices in public rallies and dancing rituals to support both male and female officials. Leading newspapers frequently published photos of, for instance, Anna Foncha performing diverse local dances with a surrounding crowd of female supporters during tours of West Cameroon. Anna Foncha and her supporters fostered sentiments of national belonging when they collectively performed popular local dances.

Political wives and women journalists also held women's public behavior as key to successful nation-building endeavors. In line with this belief, they condemned women who gossiped as lazy, wasting time that should be spent on fulfilling patriotic duties: participating in political rallies or attending the meetings of women's organizations. Chapter 5 explores condemnation of gossip as a way of talking about the failure to be "good" moral Christian women citizens and community members. While praising women's education and entrance into the workforce, elite women argued that formally educated women should still adhere to traditional gender hierarchies, for example, by respecting male authority in marriages. Thus, ideas about the respectability and proper comportment, such as emotional restraint of married women who publicly acted aggressively toward their husbands or husbands' mistresses, as chapter 6 shows, were also intimately tied to larger ideas about suitable Anglophone gendered public behavior and reverence. Chapter 4 reveals a similar dynamic in relation to urban young-adult women who participated in state-supported beauty pageants and strived to model Anglophone cultural identity through bodily performance and varied aesthetic and sartorial practices.

Cookery was also a way to facilitate the formation of national identities on the African continent. Specifically focusing on Ethiopia, James McCann asserts that "food and cooking [can be] both the symbol and the substance of a national identity." As he observes of Ethiopia's endeavor to form national cuisines, such activities are political processes, conducted with a key awareness of an international audience.[62] Chapter 3 describes how women's everyday tasks became politicized as food and cookery were used to assemble key ingredients of an Anglophone national culture. What women cooked at home and in public celebrations came to be seen as an important way to unobtrusively flag a distinct and authentic Anglophone national and cultural identity. But as Pamela Feldman-Savelsberg shows, cooking also plays a significant role in social reproduction in that it reaffirms women's and men's "natural" gender roles and relations by, for instance, emphasizing a wife's duty to cook food for her husband and family.[63] Hence, the importance of women's cooking reflected a patriarchal system in which women subscribed to a view of ideal womanhood and morals by being subservient to men. Further, women's adherence to prevailing ideas about authentic and traditional African food symbolized the refashioning of patriarchy along indigenous lines. In doing so, they claimed an African authenticity that their Francophone counterparts supposedly lacked—focusing on indigenous recipes in their cookbooks and stressing women's traditional, subordinate status in patriarchal societies.

Dress, an intimate fabric of social values that reveals threads of identity, can also powerfully shape embodied nationalisms and foster sentiments of national belonging. As Heather Marie Akou asserts, "[d]ress, as a basic necessity of life, offers many opportunities for individuals to build a sense of community through modifying and/or supplementing their bodies. . . . [a]s an extension for the body, dress can 'speak' much more loudly and continuously."[64] Marie Grace Brown comparably argues that, "[a]s an extension of the body's surface, clothing conveys status, values, and belonging. But fabric is more fluid than flesh; as a result, clothing styles and adornment are far more adaptive and responsive to rapid social and political change."[65] If dress reflects "social and political change," then in 1960s Anglophone Cameroon, the politics of dress reflected anxieties about the performances of a larger Anglophone identity that was respectable, moral, and tied to larger Christian identities. Linking women's dress rituals to modernity, morals, respectability, and cultural identity additionally highlights how urban elites in West Cameroon participated in a discourse that was common in colonial and postcolonial sub-Saharan Africa and in many other countries in the Global South at the time.[66] Added to the West/African binary, the Anglophone/Francophone binary figured miniskirts, hot pants, and slacks—also disdained by many urbanites in Tanzania and Kenya for example—as challenging and contesting Anglophones' claim to a respectable identity in opposition to the morally (sexually) lax and un-Christian Francophone women. I focus on slacks, which challenged male authority in different ways than did miniskirts. While individuals condemned miniskirts as Westernized and immodest, they recognized them as feminine attire. The critics practiced what Tanya Lyons calls "single-trouser nationalism"—a form of nationalism occurring "in a patriarchal state, where women are expected to be the symbols of the nation in long skirts, and men are supposed to wear the pants."[67] In conformity with this visual paradigm, newspaper advice columnists at times accused women who donned slacks of literally wanting to challenge gender norms by "wearing the pants" in their marriages and exhibiting masculine traits in public. As chapter 7 illustrates, anxiety over women wearing slacks mirrored concern about formally educated women usurping male authority and gender norms in perceived spaces of respectability, such as churches and prestigious members-only private venues.

Female "Print Griots" and Nationalist Rhetoric in Newspapers

Much scholarly work has highlighted newspaper content as an important historical source illuminating changing political identities and nationalist discourse.[68] As Benedict Anderson contends, print can facilitate "the possibility of a new form of imagined community" by fostering national consciousness and a sense of belonging.[69] Scholars of Anglophone Cameroonian history have underlined the social and political importance of male journalists such as Patrick Tataw Obenson, described as a "Cameroonian pioneer in daring journalism and social commentary in Cameroon," who boldly criticized the highest governing authorities during the 1960s and 1970s.[70] However, few scholars have given equal attention to the nationalist role of female writers in a period of rising nationalism throughout 1950s and 1960s Africa. As Susan Andrade explains, "[e]arly female writers' representation of politics rarely involved explicitly nationalist or syndicalist themes. Partly for this reason, writing by women has been considered apolitical—which means concerned only with domestic issues—and certainly not part of the national narrative." Yet, as Andrade asserts, "rigorously scrutiniz[ing] women's writing in public political terms" illuminates the varied ways in which African women's writings *have* been political.[71] In West African print culture, it was mostly male journalists who openly debated political issues while women journalists were relegated to domestic pieces. West Cameroon had such columns in most newspapers, and their commentaries addressed issues such as proper behaviors within marriages, courtship and social norms, cosmetics, cookery, and more. Most were more likely to reference women's activities in Anglophone Africa in their columns than those of women in Francophone Africa. West Cameroonian journalists and other educated elites often stayed abreast of Nigerian political and cultural landscapes through the *Daily Times*, *Sunday Times*, and the *West African Pilot*, all Nigerian newspapers that were available in English-speaking Cameroon by the 1950s.[72] It was common for female elites to look to Nigeria as a model, gazing across the border to imitate the social and political activities of their neighbors, as they also had in forming women's associations. Stephanie Newell finds that Anglophone and Francophone novelists and journalists of West Africa have generally been divided from one another, following "different educational, intellectual, and creative paths," finding separate publishers, and participating in separate literary forms.[73]

The relegation of the women's columns to the inside of newspapers in West Cameroon—never on the front pages—might suggest that they were of marginal importance. Jan Whitt points out that US women's advice columns, which also ran on the inside of the paper, were seen as "safeguarding the 'spiritual strength of the nation' or contributing to the 'uplifting of our national life' or 'bringing wholesomeness' into the home of readers."[74] Institutionalized discrimination confined women to the women's pages.[75] Thus, newspapers and their readership "reinforced the idea of separate spheres for men and women. Men ran the world. . . . [w]omen took care of homes and children" and focused on "noncontroversial domestic and social pursuits" in their women's pages.[76] While relegated to the inside of newspapers, Anglophone Cameroonian women's advice columns also included news about women's advancement in politics, organized sports, and higher education in Europe and the United States, as well as historical pieces about West Cameroon's past. While their columns in many ways resembled "Dear Dolly," a column penned by a rotating team of men that appeared in *Drum* magazine and was popular throughout English-speaking Africa, all of my research suggests that Anglophone women's columns were written by individual, formally educated women.[77] The use of pseudonyms with familial terms gave them a position of authority and warmth that lent power to their valorization of Anglophone Cameroonian identity and women's social and political improvements. At the time, just as political wives publicly asserted that they prioritized wifehood and motherhood, West Cameroonian women journalists avoided an overtly political tone, finding nonthreatening ways to infuse political content. Most adopted pseudonyms that gave them additional protection. Ultimately, the custom of writing under pseudonyms allowed women journalists to shape ideas about Anglophone Cameroonian nationalism and to distinguish themselves from the hegemonic Francophone state in alternative spheres of influence.

In addition to capturing the political nature of female journalists' writings, this book recovers the intellectual nature of Anglophone Cameroonian writings, journalism for instance, which narratives on West African intellectual traditions do not typically include. Ibrahim Seaga Shaw argues that African values shape journalism practice on the continent and that "the African journalism model [is] grounded in oral discourse, creativity, humanity and agency."[78] With this in mind, I expand the definition of "griots" in this work, just as scholars have expanded the term to refer to musicians in urban areas of the 1960s United States.[79] I make an observation similar to one Marie-Soleil Frère makes about the role of journalists in French-speaking Africa in the early 1990s, which is that Anglophone Cameroon female journalists resembled traditional griots in three key ways: through their (oral) discursive narrative style which was "very close to the oral style of the griot"; their role as "express[ing] the people's frustrations"; and "occupy[ing] an 'in between' position in society because, at the same time, they belong to the social group they are speaking or writing for, while being looked at as a different 'cast' practising the power of public speech."[80] While both women and men can be griots—professional storytellers, poets, and musicians—"there is nevertheless a general absence of discussion about griottes [female griots] in much scholarship on the African oral tradition."[81] But closer examination reveals that Anglophone Cameroonian women journalists, as (what I term) "print griots," reimagined Africa's past through anecdotes and stories passed down to them from family, friends, and other community members, embedding themselves within a broader West African culture in which griots were professional storytellers about the past. Karin Barber contends that Africa has "a vast domain of cultural production which cannot be classified as either 'traditional' or 'elite', as 'oral' or 'literate', as 'indigenous' or 'Western' in inspiration, because it straddles and dissolves these distinctions."[82] Women journalists in West Cameroon were formally educated in Western-style schools, but their literary approach was a mixture of indigenous and international ideas about the literary process, thus dissolving various cultural distinctions. Through their historical reporting, they reinterpreted and reshaped Africa's past, using traditional practices of storytelling to carve out new spaces of authority, not only within their societies but within broader realms of intellectualism. By invoking, for example, women's political power as queens in the precolonial era, as chapter 2 shows, they traced a straight line from women's essential roles in history to their continuing social importance in 1960s urban Cameroon. But at times they published response letters in which men challenged these historical interpretations, which suggests that they were a threat.[83] In spite of their limitations, these newspaper sources provide a powerful view of a set of debates over changing Anglophone Cameroonian cultural identities that no other source offers. They anticipate outcomes that Anna Foncha once predicted at a Women's Day rally on March 31, 1965: "the voice of the Cameroon woman must and will be heard in all corners of the globe. The time has come when we must make our contribution so that when history is written, the Cameroonian women will have an Honourable place in its pages."[84]

CHAPTER 1

Tracing the "Golden Age" of Anglophone Cameroon

Gender, Nationalism, and Political Identity

One bright morning in 1968, Gwendoline Etonde Burnley was working at her desk at home in the cosmopolitan seaside city of Victoria in the southern West Cameroon State when she received an alarming phone call. The ominous call would darken her day. She had been a civil servant for almost a decade, and she knew, she told an interviewer, "that political meetings were going on. In fact, there was an important meeting in Yaoundé where all the top political people on this side, that is West Cameroon, went." She could barely hear the person on the line, but it became clear that "they wanted to put me on the CNU [Cameroon National Union] list for the National Assembly [meaning the Federal National Assembly that comprised of representatives from the West Cameroon Legislative Assembly and the East Cameroon Legislative Assembly] and I said I was grateful for the consideration but was not interested."[1] Even more alarming than the phone call was what she heard on the radio. While eating dinner with her family later, she heard her name called as among those who had been formally appointed to government positions. Her objections to being recommended for a political post in President Ahidjo's newly single-party state had fallen on deaf ears. "I burst out crying," she told the author of the book, *Women of the Reunification*. "Honestly, I was so upset. My husband tried to talk to me [and said that] 'we are in a different setup now; if you make a false move, they would think you don't want to serve your country.'" It was clear that refusing Ahidjo's request might be dangerous. Burnley was quite surprised, and even more upset when she "later found out that there was a lot of disagreement on the other proposed names and the president Ahidjo had said they should find a woman and most of the people there [in Yaoundé] suggested my name." Burnley had expected to support another female candidate for the position: "We women [presumably in the Women's Cameroon National Union (WCNU)] had discussed it and we had said it would be good to look for somebody [serving in the West Cameroon Legislative Assembly] that would be an advantage to. Those of us who were in [the] nongovernmental organization had decided that we would try and promote one of the women who was interested."[2] Burnley would serve four years in the West Cameroon Legislative Assembly until its dissolution, and her service in Ahidjo's CNU continued until 1983. In a more recent interview she described her induction as "'my conscription' into politics," but she says, "[I] developed enthusiasm when I realized how effective I could be."[3] What had started as an ill-omened phone call one afternoon in 1968 would lead to a bright and prominent political career.

How had a woman like Burnley caught the eye of the male politicians serving in the West Cameroon Legislative Assembly who had recommended her for the position in the Federal National Assembly? How did Ahidjo's government incorporate women into governance, and how does this compare to the practices of John Foncha's Kamerun National Democratic Party (KNDP) government? How did Burnley navigate the politically turbulent landscape of West Cameroon in the late 1960s as Ahidjo's hegemony grew? This chapter, and the next, contemplate these questions to map out the historical landscape in which Anglophone women maintained political power in the Anglophone western state of the Federal Republic of Cameroon from 1961 to 1972.

THE CONSCRIPTION AND RISE OF GWENDOLINE BURNLEY

Gwendoline Burnley was born Gwendoline Martin on February 29, 1932, in Buea, to parents of Creole origin, reflecting the diversity of the western coast of Cameroon.[4] They were descendants of slaves who had been freed after the abolition of slavery in the Danish West Indies; they were left on an island off the coast of West Africa around 1846 and later that year settled in the area soon to be named Victoria (renamed Limbe in 1982).[5] The settlers were called the Freetown Krios because they were descendants of manumitted individuals from Freetown Sierra Leone, as historian Ian F. Hancock notes, "Krio settlers with names like 'Burnley' and 'Martin' had high prestige as Christians, teachers, clerks and their descendants are among the most prosperous families in Anglophone Cameroon."[6] Burnley's parents were formally educated and were civil servants during British rule and in the federal period. Her father was an education officer for the British administration who, on retirement, entered politics and served as secretary for Endeley's Kamerun National Congress (KNC) party.[7] Her mother was a primary school teacher and later opened her own nursery school in Victoria. They had six daughters, all of whom achieved undergraduate degrees in Nigeria, England, or the United States; some of them earned advanced degrees.[8] Gladys Silo Endeley, the sister-in-law of John Foncha's main political rival and a key political figure, was Gwendoline Burnley's maternal aunt. Gwendoline, the eldest of the sisters, attended both primary school and secondary school in Nigeria. She and her aunt Gladys both earned their bachelor's degrees in 1958, Gwendoline from Durham University in the UK where she was secretary of the African Society and "invited prominent Africans to speak" to members.[9] Burnley later took a one-year post-graduate diploma course in social welfare at Den Haag (the Hague) University in the Netherlands and returned to Cameroon in 1959 and worked as an education officer for the Southern Cameroons government, teaching at the Government Teacher's Training College in Kumba.[10] She and Robert Efesoa Burnley, an agricultural officer in the Southern Cameroons government, who had personally witnessed the unfolding of the Anlu Rebellion in Bamenda in 1958, began courting her while she was teaching in Kumba in her early twenties.[11] They married at Ebenezer Baptist Church in Victoria in December 1959.[12] The couple had six children, and Burnley continued to serve as a civil servant in various positions.[13] Her appointment to the West Cameroon Legislative Assembly in 1968 was the culmination of years of "apolitical" political activities.

Burnley, like a few other Anglophone Cameroonian women, sought to foster Anglophone nationalism and to improve women's lives even as they navigated the political landscape in which Ahidjo increasingly subjugated Anglophone personhood. At the time Ahidjo appointed her, she had been active in women's organizations for years, along with other politically elite women. These organizations served an important function in furthering the welfare of their communities and provided a key training ground for Burnley's political skills. In spite of her familial affiliation with Anna Foncha's husband's greatest rival, she and Anna Foncha were close allies in raising money and organizing the building of hospitals and schools in the period of the Federal Republic. As Burney would acknowledge to one of her biographers, it was her association with prominent women such as Foncha that "thrust her into the limelight."[14] In spite of her expectation that the position in the West Cameroon Legislative Assembly would go to someone else, she recognizes that her engagement in women's organizations gave the impression that she had a keen interest in politics. That is, she credits the affective relationships and the sisterly camaraderie fostered by women's associations. Through intimate alliances in which politically elite women supported one another's social reform projects, they changed women's lives. While I will argue that Burnley's claims to be apolitical were not strictly accurate, her association with Anna Foncha suggests that women were willing to work across party lines to unite and advance women's lives socially and economically.

Burnley was a powerful political advocate for women's social and political rights and equality even during British rule. When teaching at the Government Teacher's Training College in Kumba, she vigorously protested and petitioned against the inclusion of the term "woman" preceding her "education officer" title. She remembers saying to colleagues, "men . . . are called education officers, so, why am I being called woman education officer?"[15] At the same time, her biography indicates that when she was a civil servant for the West Cameroon State, "[s]he did not take part in or organize political meetings." Instead, she focused on "educating other less privileged women by going around the country with other Western-educated women giving talks. . . . on pertinent topics, organizing baby shows [educational programs for mothers], and sharing information on issues affecting the health of the family and community at large."[16] Her activities as a community activist and a civil servant for the West Cameroon government made her well known. Another biographer describes her relationship with Anna Foncha as highly advantageous, because the older woman gave Burnley key support in her campaign "for the promotion of women's education and women's social and economic empowerment."[17] Burnley and Foncha worked together in the early 1960s to organize leadership training for the leaders of women's groups throughout West Cameroon, which ultimately led to the formation of the CWI, one of the most powerful women's political groups in the country.[18] These activities led directly to Burnley's political career.[19]

Undeniably, Burnley was a political force in both KNDP-ruled West Cameroon and in the United Republic under Ahidjo's CNU. Her savvy approach to achieving progressive goals in a conservative era of politics allowed her to improve women's lives and be appointed into Ahidjo's CNU political structure. Following her conscription, she was the only woman among the twenty-nine members of the West Cameroon Legislative Assembly. She served as secretary of the West Cameroon Bureau, a position of power, until the dissolution of the Assembly in 1972. Having dissolved the Assembly and made other constitutional changes that minimized Anglophone political power, Ahidjo appointed Burnley to his CNU, where she served as one of 5 women among the 120 members. While she described hesitation about serving in Ahidjo's government, Burnley would serve as a member of Cameroon's parliament, the National Assembly, from 1973 to 1983.

Burnley campaigned in Francophone Cameroon to keep her position in the National Assembly in the 1970s and 1980s. She recalls: "People were not used to the way I talked; they talked in a kind of lingua franca [implying a dialect using French grammar but with significant English vocabulary] that people would understand. I was mixing my own grammar with pidgin [Cameroonian Creole]. . . . [and] wear[ing] [a] *kabba* [a traditional Cameroonian free-flowing dress mostly worn for casual events]. I tied my headscarf in a funny way." She was doubly marginalized as an Anglophone woman, and parliament was even more uncomfortable. She admitted to the author of *Women of the Reunification* that at first, she had trouble asking to take the floor in the male-dominated parliament. "They [her male colleagues] used to laugh at me," she recalled, but remarked with tenacity and humor, "but I learnt how to laugh at them also."[20] Certainly, the life of Gwendoline Burnley serves as a powerful example of how Anglophone Cameroonian women navigated political landscapes, preserving Anglophone political identity while making social and economic changes in women's lives in the federal period and beyond. Her life story and her approach to a conservative concept of politics and ideal womanhood, like those of Anna Foncha, make more sense when we consider the historical context of Anglophone Cameroon.

FROM EUROPEAN RULE TO THE FEDERAL REPUBLIC

The panoply tapestry that comprises Anglophone Cameroon's history, and the lives of individuals such as Gwendoline Burnley, reflects the country's general diversity. Popularly termed "Africa in miniature" because it offers all of the diversity of climate, culture, and geography of the entire continent, Cameroon is located at the junction of west and central Africa, neighboring the Gulf of Guinea and the Atlantic Ocean coastlines. Cameroon is bordered by Nigeria to the west, Chad to the north, and the Central African Republic to the east. Gabon, Equatorial Guinea, and the Republic of Congo are to the south. Cameroon contains as many as 270 different ethnic groups.[21] Cameroon's name originates from the Portuguese word for shrimp, *camaroes*, because an ambitious Portuguese fifteenth-century explorer, Fernando Pó, mistook the abundant prawns of the estuary of the Wouri River for shrimp, dubbing it *Rio do Camarões* ("shrimp river"). Germany adopted the name Kamerun when it colonized the area in 1885. Germany's defeat in World War I led to an arrangement in which France controlled the bulk of the territory as French Cameroun, but Britain controlled a smaller western portion, the Northern and Southern Cameroons. The United Nations approved the trusteeship agreements for Britain and France to govern the regions as trust territories in late 1946, and both gained independence gradually over the course of the 1950s. The British Southern Cameroons government was headquartered in Nigeria, and subjects in the territory elected representatives for the Eastern House of Assembly in Nigeria during the early 1950s.[22] In 1954, the Southern Cameroons House of Assembly began to meet in Buea under the premier, first E. M. L. Endeley and then John Ngu Foncha. Formal independence followed seven years later.

French Cameroun became an autonomous state with a parliament and a prime minister in 1960 while British rule still hung on to the west.[23] While many African and Asian countries achieved independence from European colonial rulers during this period of global decolonization, the British Southern Cameroons achieved formal independence by *voting* to join neighboring countries that had already achieved independence. British Cameroonians were never given the option to vote for outright independence and achieve independence like most of their counterparts on the continent and in Asia. The United Nations organized a plebiscite on February 11, 1961 that would mark the severing of the British sector from Europe.[24] Separate votes gave Northern Cameroonians and Southern Cameroonians a choice between union with Nigeria and union with former French Cameroun on a federal basis. Many Anglophone Cameroonian political elites today allege that British or French officials rigged the plebiscite votes in Northern Cameroons partly to appease Nigerian politicians, and that in any case, independence from both Nigeria and the new Republic of Cameroon should have been on the ballot.[25] As it was, the Muslim-majority British Northern Cameroons became part of Nigeria. The British Southern Cameroons, Christian-dominated and consisting of the modern-day Northwest and Southwest Regions, became West Cameroon within the Federal Republic of Cameroon.[26]

In 1961, the East Cameroon State had an area of 432,000 square kilometers and a population of around 3.2 million people, about 78 percent of the country. The West Cameroon State consisted of approximately 800,000 people and an area of 43,500 square kilometers.[27] The East and West Cameroon States had separate capitals, in Yaoundé and Buea, respectively. John Ngu Foncha and E. M. L. Endeley continued to dominate the political landscape in Buea. Foncha, a teacher by profession, was of royal lineage in the *fondom* (kingdom) of Nkewn in the Bamenda (western) Grassfields, in northwest Cameroon.[28] He led the KNDP, founded in 1955. Most of the KNDP leadership were originally from the western Grassfields, and the party had difficulty fostering credibility in southern coastal regions. Endeley was part of the Bakweri ethnic group from the coastal forest area, who settled on the slopes of Mt. Cameroon in southwest Cameroon. A medical doctor by training, he was the son of the Bakweri Paramount Chief at Buea.[29] He was the leader of the KNC, established in 1952 (Foncha, once part of the KNC, broke away to form the KNDP).[30] The KNC had advocated uniting with Nigeria (some scholars have asserted that Endeley's marriage to a Nigerian Yoruba woman influenced the party's stance), while the KNDP advocated unification with French Cameroun, perhaps in part because of widespread anti-Nigerian sentiments in Southern Cameroons that arose because Nigerian Igbos had come to dominate trade during British rule.[31] The KNC argued that reunification with French Cameroun would change Southern Cameroonians' lives completely, requiring them to adopt French language and submit to a different form of governance.[32] Neither party had the political will to advocate for the independence of the British Southern Cameroons. Scholars of Cameroonian history argue that political disunity facilitated the hobbling of West Cameroon's autonomy within the Federal Republic.[33]

By contrast, Ahidjo was the firm leader of East Cameroon. He was elected president early in his political career, on January 1, 1960, and would remain in office until he voluntary retired in 1982. Pro-France Ahidjo was elected to the Assembly of the French Union in Paris in 1953 before serving as the vice prime minister and prime minister of Cameroon in the late 1950s. In December 1958, a series of secret economic, military, and administrative treaties with France, bolstered French support for Ahidjo's leadership while furthering France's neocolonial ties to independent Cameroon. Ahidjo would maintain close political, economic and military ties with France during his regime; early on, he called on French troops to oppress Union des Populations du Cameroun (UPC) dissidents who challenged his rule.[34]

The constitution of the Federal Republic was determined at the Foumban

Women in the British Southern Cameroons wearing the Kamerun National Congress cloth while rallying in support of the KNC, ca. 1950s. Image courtesy of National Archives in the United Kingdom.

A KNDP women's-wing march, early 1960s. The CWI would become the de facto KNDP women's wing by 1962. Image courtesy of National Archives of Cameroon in Buea.

Constitutional Conference from July 17 to 21 in 1961, the February plebiscite having united the former British Southern Cameroons with the Republic of Cameroon. John Foncha led the twenty-five-member Anglophone delegation, who met with twelve Francophones.[35] Nerius Namaso Mbile, who was elected into the Eastern House of Assembly in Nigeria during the 1950s and later served in the West Cameroon Legislative Assembly, described the Anglophone delegation's anticipation in his 2011 memoir:

> [A]t last the time had arrived for us now reasonably united on this purpose in West Cameroon, to tackle the politicians of the East in a conference that would define our constitutional relation. Here, we would confront the "brothers" [from] across the Mungo [River] in a battle to test our wits and our experience in constitution making. Indeed, against the background of having attended four Constitutional Conferences, three in London and one in Lagos, several of us in the West Cameroon contingent felt confident to be more than a match for our Francophone counterparts. . . . In men like [E. M. L.] Endeley, [John Ngu] Foncha, [Salomon Tandeng] Muna, [Peter] Motomby [Woleta], [Augustine Ngom] Jua, my humble self to name only these, [was the feeling of excitement of] wrestlers, on hearing the drums and music of their popular sport.[36]

The Mungo River was once the geographic border between British- and French-controlled Cameroon; Mbile suggests the Anglophones were an invading army. His comparison of the Anglophone delegation to warriors and athletes invokes their virility, which was soon challenged. Foncha's delegation expected to have a key role in negotiating the terms of the constitution, and they were shocked and insulted when Ahidjo handed them a version of the constitution the morning of the first day of the conference and invited them to make comments on the draft.[37] As historians point out, even the international community framed Ahidjo's actions as trickery: Pierre Messmer, a French high commissioner in French Cameroun and a consultant to Ahidjo, asserted "that he and others knew at the time" that the meeting was a sham and Ahidjo's plans purely annexationist. The Francophone representatives had, in fact, spent months drafting "the constitution with the assistance of French constitutional law experts" in Yaoundé.[38] Ultimately, Foncha's delegation made few changes, and Ahidjo's government had considerable power throughout both federated states.[39]

Rumors abounded that Ahidjo co-opted Foncha by promising to make him vice president even before the Foumban conference, and that Foncha had known about the predrafted constitution.[40] Residents of the region of Southern Cameroons where Foncha grew up had composed a song after the 1961 plebiscite: "Foncha has walloped Endeley. Foncha has walloped Endeley. If Foncha hadn't been there, Endeley would have sold us." But by the 1990s, the song concluded, "If Foncha hadn't trounced Endeley, we wouldn't have been sold."[41] Since the events at the Foumban conference, Foncha's political opponents increasingly considered his KNDP party to be corrupt.[42] But Anglophone Cameroon was clearly at a political disadvantage from the very start because it was not yet independent and was smaller and less economically developed. Foncha and his delegation may have had few options.

Ahidjo's regime massacred, imprisoned, condemned to death, or forced into exile political dissidents, strategies inherited from the French administration, particularly in the terminal stages of French rule. Meredith Terretta enumerates the tactics of Ahidjo's administration in the early years of independence—"heavy-handed violence, interrogations, imprisonment, 'disappearings,' resettlement and concentration camps, public beatings, intrusive intelligence gathering, and propaganda campaigns" and explains that Ahidjo's regime retained these tactics along with close links with France, which helped him to violently suppress those who challenged his power.[43] Resistance included insurgents with the nationalist Marxist UPC, who fired bullets on Ahidjo's inauguration ceremony and condemned him as a French puppet.[44] During the early years of Ahidjo's regime, a French-Cameroonian military force massacred at least 300,000 people, and the UPC leaders who survived went into exile.[45] Certainly, targets included both Francophone and Anglophone persons, regardless of the geographic location. A December 1966 incident between two ethnic groups, the Tombel Massacre, suggests Ahidjo's heavy hand: violence erupted between the Francophone Bamiléké people and the Anglophone Bakossi people in Tombel, a town in the Southwest Region of Cameroon. In subduing the conflict, Ahidjo's government massacred over 230 Bamiléké indigents. It also imprisoned 140 Bakossi Anglophones in a later trial.[46]

Thus, while political oppression was never limited to Anglophones, they have always been particular targets. For their part, Anglophones describe the violence of the Ahidjo regime generally as proof of the inherent cultural and political differences between Anglophone and Francophone persons. Anthony Yana Zumafor, a former civil servant for the West Cameroon State during the 1960s, for example, implied in a 2015 interview that British influence has given them moral and political superiority over Cameroonians who had a legacy of French rule: "we were brought up in strictly . . . English Victorian ethics, morals, principles, moral norms and you know sense of duty, dedication to work, honesty . . . on the whole 90% of the British Cameroonians were men of honor, people of honor. . . . As Southern Cameroonians . . . we were brought up the Anglo-Saxon way." Although Zumafor's statistics might be questionable, his use of "Anglo-Saxon" nevertheless serves to embed Anglophone Cameroon in a larger English-speaking world that has been influenced by English customs. On the other hand, in his assessment, French Cameroonians "were brought up in the spirit of violence, brutality, [and] non-respect for the human dignity. You had corporal punishments openly against workers. . . . Until today we don't understand that method of governance."[47] A series of letters to Anglophone newspapers in the 1960s similarly illustrates standpoints about perceived differing governing approaches of Anglophone and Francophone governments. One letter demonstrates how Ahidjo's administration regularly stationed military in Anglophone regions to visually assert his political authority. Shortly after the 1961 reunification, the gendarmerie, from East Cameroon, was quartered in all the administrative divisions of the territory, causing panic and apprehension among West Cameroonians. For instance, a December 1961 *Cameroon Champion* letter titled "Authorities Should Intervene" said West Cameroon could "not live happily with" their "brothers" in East Cameroon because of the behavior of the gendarmes.[48] The letter's writer, B. Waha, charged that rather than keeping the peace, the gendarmes disrupted it, that they were "left wanton and loose," getting drunk and fighting with one another and "intimidat[ing] the people of West Cameroon." The letter accused the soldiers of taking "the path of mischief, laziness and dishonesty."[49] Residents of West Cameroon had been used to the presence of British and Nigerian police forces during British rule. However, many residents, such as B. Waha, charged that Ahidjo's military presence in Anglophone regions proved that unity with Francophones was impossible.

Ahidjo's tactics to unify the country were not all violent, though they generally fostered resentment. For instance, his regime legally compelled West Cameroonians to drive on the right side of the roadway, as East Cameroonians always had, and to adopt the metric system.[50] In practice, subjugation to Francophone culture involved subjugation to France. As Richard Joseph observed in 1976, France "maintained an economic and cultural stranglehold on its former colonies, backed by a significant military presence. Far from being decolonised, the former French colonies have experienced an increase in French economic entrenchment in the post-independence era. . . . The first pillar on which France rested its neo-colonial structure was monetary in nature."[51] Anglophone political elites have cited these economic, political, and military French ties as evidence of double colonization, by Francophone Cameroon and by France. Although Ahidjo promised in a July 1960 speech in Tiko (during a three-day official visit to the Southern Cameroons) that he was "not going into the French community,"[52] formal connections between the Republic of Cameroon and the French Community violated a joint declaration Ahidjo signed with Foncha in October 1960 that the reunified Cameroon would not be part of either "the French Community or the British Commonwealth." In flagrant violation of the joint declaration, Ahidjo "signed a series of cooperation agreements and treaties with France" in the early 1960s and formally dissolved agreements Foncha had made with the British Commonwealth. Consequently, the Federal Republic of Cameroon became firmly part of the French Community.[53]

Ahidjo's agreements with France were the basis of France's military and political support of Ahidjo's regime, and they gave France preferred trade status. These agreements enriched France, which, acting like a bank, required Cameroon to convert money paid to France into francs and transfer it to the French treasury. As Joseph asserted, these earnings "increased steadily during the 1960s."[54] In exchange, France gave Ahidjo a considerable commitment of French troops; as Joseph writes, "As late as 1971 . . . a majority of senior Army officers in Cameroon were still French nationals."[55] France had at least 10,000 service men from their armed forces in Africa at the time. While the cooperation accords Ahidjo had signed with France in November 1959 did not include a mutual defense agreement, Ahidjo used French troops to suppress the insurgency in Cameroon through much of the 1960s. By suppressing the UPC rebellion with the assistance of the French troops, Ahidjo strived to foster political stability so as to acquire the foreign assistance that was needed to bolster his rule as well as foster Cameroon's economic development.[56] Joseph also identifies the involvement of the French secret services in maintaining Ahidjo's power.[57]

If France's meddling allowed Ahidjo to maintain control of the country, his economic ties with France threatened the livelihood of the West Cameroon State. The end of Britain's Commonwealth Preference for West Cameroon in the early 1960s, for example, had a negative economic impact. On September 30, 1963, the British parliament removed its Commonwealth Preference for West Cameroon, a crucial engine of the West Cameroon economy, particularly regarding the banana industry.[58] It is also likely that the British removed the preference because West Cameroon had to adhere to the import-licensing and exchange-control policies of East Cameroon; maintaining East Cameroon's preferential trade status would divert West Cameroon purchases away from the United Kingdom.[59] The general economic disparity between the federal states during Ahidjo's regime rendered West Cameroon economically marginalized. As Emmanuel Chiabi argues, "during federalism, the government prioritized industrialization in East Cameroon more than in West Cameroon" resulting in "more capital accumulation in the East than it did for the farmers or planters of the West."[60] Even a male letter writer from Victoria to the *Cameroon Telegraph* who believed that the unification of the British Southern Cameroons with French Cameroun had brought "the green atmosphere of peace, the subtle palms of freedom and harmony, the meek whispers of brotherly love," pointed to "the bitter parity in economic investment in the two federated states." He boldly writes, "I stoop to wonder why West Cameroon always occupies the reserve seat in economic development plans. In fact, she is denied the blanket. . . . West Cameroon is always given the beggar's ration." He contends that if "the appropriate circles continue to by-pass West Cameroon when taking economic and social development decisions," there will be "economic backwardness" in the federated state.[61]

Ahidjo further consolidated his power following his March 1965 reelection. In 1966, his regime banned the multiparty system and created a single-party state, part of a sweeping trend in the rise of one-party states in 1960s and 1970s Africa that took place in such states as in Ghana and Tanzania.[62] Ahidjo effectively consolidated his power by prohibiting all West Cameroonian political parties and openly signifying his decision to overthrow Anglophone political autonomy.[63] Nonetheless, some West Cameroonian politicians embraced the prevailing order to regain "positions of power and influence" in the Federal Republic. Civil servants supported the federalization of state services, which they believed would increase their salaries and the level of support the government could offer.[64] In 1966, the Ahidjo government enacted the first press law which forced many papers to closure because of censorship, including newspapers in West Cameroon.[65] Carlson Anyangwe asserts that "[t]he editor and publisher of every newspaper were required, under pain of imprisonment, to submit dummies of their papers to the [prefect] for censorship before publication. So invidious and pervasive was the censorship that the contents of newspapers read more like government press releases." Anyangwe further discloses that newspaper editors in Anglophone towns, such as Victoria and Bamenda, tried to expose the censorship to the public: "[w]hen dummies returned from the [prefect] with sentences or paragraphs or whole articles crossed out the editor would publish the paper as is, with those crossings. . . . In that way the public got to know that Ahidjo's local censor had been at work and that the regime had something to hide."[66] By censoring newspapers, Ahidjo sought to solidify his authority and public image, even in the media.

Ahidjo was reelected in 1970, and after silencing the last of the UPC "guerrilla movement with the execution of Ernest Ouandié," a key UPC nationalist leader who opposed Ahidjo's rule, on January 15, 1971, he turned his focus to altering the country's governance structure.[67] The loss of West Cameroonian independence became formal on May 20, 1972, when Ahidjo called for a referendum in which West Cameroonians might vote for or against a unitary state. He called on them to dissolve the federal structure, condemning it as a barrier to economic development and national unity.[68] It seems possible that the discovery of oil in the northern region of West Cameroon in 1967 drove Ahidjo's actions.[69] The civil war in Nigeria provoked by the Igbo's secessionist tendencies in 1967 may have been a factor as well; Ahidjo feared the secessionist movement would encourage Anglophone Cameroonian political elites to follow suit.[70]

Ample evidence suggests that the 1972 referendum was rigged, just as Anglophone activists suggest that the 1961 plebiscite was. The army suppressed student protests. Students and faculty at the Cameroon College of Arts, Science and Technology in Bambili, in northwest Cameroon, reported that they received only "yes" ballots. Officers in "villages where people had all gone to their farms" and were unlikely to return to the village to vote gave vote tallies of 99.9 percent, suggesting that they falsified the votes. The remainder were probably intimidated into casting their nonsecret ballots in favor of a united republic. Salomon Tandeng Muna, who succeeded John Foncha as the third prime minister of the federated state of West Cameroon in 1968, admitted in a radio interview in 1990 that he knew many Anglophones opposed plans for a united republic but that he never said so because he knew Ahidjo would have him killed. The president claimed that overwhelming support of the draft constitution he advanced for the fully unified republic justified the "immediate establishment, of the United Republic of Cameroon," dissolving the federal structure in favor of a governmental structure in which the central (Francophone) government had more power.[71]

THE START OF THE "GOLDEN AGE": ANGLOPHONE NATIONALISM AND PRINT CULTURE

Anglophone elites had rightly feared the hegemonic and annexationist plans of the Francophone state throughout the federal period, and they fiercely sought to construct a robust Anglophone nationalism. This drew on efforts already in places; scholars maintain that the ferment of Anglophone Cameroonian nationalism and political identity really started in Nigeria in the early 1950s. Anthony Ndi dated the roots of Anglophone Cameroonian nationalism to the Eastern Nigerian Regional Crisis of 1953, when the Eastern Region of Nigeria threatened to secede from the country. Until that point, "there were hardly any Southern Cameroonian political parties with truly nationwide appeal."[72] He identified a "Golden Period" of Anglophone Cameroon as its independence from Britain grew and it maintained a distinction from Francophone Cameroon; this period began the year the UN approved the trusteeship agreements that gave the Southern Cameroons significant autonomy as trust territories in 1946 and ended with the dissolution of the federal system in 1972. He points to "constitutional and socio-economic and political changes originating in Nigeria of which the territory [British Southern Cameroons] was an integral part [including]. . . . the representation of British Southern Cameroons in the legislative assemblies at Enugu and Lagos in Nigeria" in the late 1940s and early 1950s.[73] Piet Konings also attributes strong nationalism to Anglophone Cameroon following World War II, saying that "the Anglophone elite initially demonstrated a large degree of unity." He asserts that the administration of the UN trust territory of the Southern Cameroons as "a mere appendage of Nigeria" as well as "eastern Nigerian domination of the Southern Cameroonian economy" were rallying points for male Anglophone Cameroonian political elites. He notes that the leaders of some of these Anglophone political parties considered the possibility of unifying with Francophone Cameroon as a way "for the Southern Cameroons to escape from its subordinate position in the British-Nigerian colonial system and Igbo domination."[74] Thus, scholars perceive a sense of inter-African colonization in this period as well, which persists in Anglophone Cameroon to this day; Anglophone Cameroonian politicians elected into the Eastern House of Assembly in Enugu felt that Nigerians had colonized them. Just as later they would feel doubly colonized by the Francophone Cameroon government and the French, they felt doubly colonized by the British and Nigerians.

Unity broke down beginning in the mid-1950s, however. Personality differences between Endeley and Foncha reinforced ethnic and regional differences and divisions among the population. Endeley's KNC party supported unification with Nigeria, while Foncha's KNDP sought a loose federal republic with French Cameroun.[75] Both envisioned greater political autonomy than West Cameroon would experience under the Federal Republic. Endeley believed the creation of the Southern Cameroons House of Assembly in 1954 as protecting Anglophone Cameroonians from Nigerian domination and giving them a greater political voice. He argued that economic stagnation would soon end. He also pointed out that unity with French Cameroun, KNDP's plan for post-independence, would expose them to the costs, economic and otherwise, of the struggle for independence underway between French authorities and the armed rebellion that the UPC was engaged in.[76]

While the achievement of regional status that Endeley trumpeted gave the Southern Cameroons their own Assembly in 1954, the joint British legacy with Nigeria would continue to be complex. In this context, print culture played a crucial role in facilitating the spread of nationalism and political parties. Despite their ambivalence toward Nigeria, many Anglophone elites looked to Nigeria to shape progressive ideas and nationalist aspirations in newspapers. The most significant contribution to press development in the British Southern Cameroons came from Nigeria, specifically from the Zik Press newspaper chain owned by Nnamdi Azikiwe, a nationalist leader who founded newspapers in Ghana and Nigeria in the 1940s and later served as president of Nigeria. The *West African Pilot*, one of Zik's papers, had a special correspondent for Cameroon, Emmanuel Epie, who was a resident in Lagos but visited Cameroon frequently. Several Nigerian papers were available in Southern Cameroons before independence, and Nigerian newspapers were the training ground for many Anglophone Cameroonian journalists who became prominent in West Cameroon after independence.[77]

Nigerian newspapers stoked the desire to set up private presses to champion Southern Cameroonian political priorities and articulate patriotic aspirations against the background of the rise of nationalism throughout Africa.[78] In 1960, as the end of British rule approached, the Kamerun National Congress, renamed the Cameroon People's National Convention (CPNC), founded the *Cameroon Champion*, and the KNDP founded the *Cameroon Times*. Throughout the federal period, the papers would feature speeches and activities of the parties backing them. The papers facilitated the construction of a distinct Anglophone nationalism and political identity that was separate from their Francophone counterparts, demarcating space for competing nationalist ideologies and movements in Cameroon. Ndi's assertion of a "Golden Age" partially reflects the vibrancy of the multiparty system under these two parties and the autonomy.[79]

The larger Anglophone print culture traversed the Atlantic. As Anthony Yana Zumafor, a former civil servant for the West Cameroon government in the 1960s, told me, referring the 1950s and 1960s:

> we were exposed to the enlightenment of which existed in Nigeria . . . and the Gold Coast in Sierra Leone and the Gambia. So, we were part of British West Africa, and we got news [from that] reading culture. . . . Our newspapers came from Britain, from Nigeria, at times from Ghana, from the Gold Coast. . . . [W]e got reading materials from the United States. . . . So, our outlook and attitude to the media, was Anglo-Saxon. . . . you had a plethora of newspapers from Nigeria and you chose your own newspaper which you loved very much. I remember at the age of 18, my newspapers from Nigeria were the *Daily Times of Nigeria* . . . the *Sunday Times of Nigeria*, the next one was, the *West African Pilot*.[80]

Several Anglophone Cameroonian journalists in the 1960s had worked for the *West African Pilot*, which ran the leading newspaper women's column in 1940s and 1950s Nigeria.[81] Zumafor further recalls,

> *Drum Magazine* [an Anglophone publication distributed throughout Africa from its South African headquarters] . . . that was also my favorite. It carried the emotions, the feelings, you know, the aspirations and concerns of women. And the most famous columnist . . . was ["Dear] Dolly["]. And in the 1950s and 1960s you had the explosion of . . . love relationships between men [and] women, and the rest of the kind and so forth, and they would complain to Dolly and they would write to Dolly, and Dolly would write back. . . . the Anglo Saxon of Africa world all wrote to Dolly.[82]

Indeed, "Dear Dolly" was wildly popular throughout the continent. It was team-written by male journalists, but it probably had a significant influence on the women who wrote the advice columns of Anglophone Cameroonian newspapers in West Cameroon.

"Dear Dolly" and others also had a significant influence on readers' expectations in 1960s West Cameroon. In a dynamic similar to the one Derek Peterson and Emma Hunter identify in their work on print culture in colonial

Africa, newspaper editors created women's columns in response to readers' letters.[83] In February 1964, Ruff Wanzie announced that due to public outcry,[84] the *Cameroon Times* would reintroduce the "Women's Forum," explaining:

> [This] is a new era for women. . . . The women's column is a challenge to women to express their views, activities, to be happy and show that they can compete with men in all fields of work. You are free to criticize, educate, and build up matters to help our women and prepare our girls morally for the future. Through this column your activities, reports of plays, dances, women's trades, speeches organized and delivered by women are made known to the public. The column paves a way for our women to prove the worth of their education to the men who keep on menacing them by looking low on their interests and the general struggle of women striving to get back their rights.[85]

Shortly thereafter, Josepha Mua, a woman parliamentarian in the West Cameroon Legislative Assembly, supported the paper's decision: "I am very grateful to the editor of the *Cameroon Times* for reintroducing the women's column to teach, stir and bring our women up to date. . . . in the . . . next issue I should be writing on myself in the world of politics, my ambitions and achievements when representing women's interest in the House of Assembly [West Cameroon Legislative Assembly]."[86] Readers called for other papers to follow suit. A letter to the *Cameroon Telegraph* in 1968 chided, "It may be you have forgotten that you were delivered by a woman and . . . your daily meals are prepared by a woman. Please for courtesy sake, give us a column in your journal."[87] Likewise, a 1970 letter to the editor of the *New Cameroon* called for a women's column and evidenced the influence of a broader Anglophone culture when it said that women had "been described as 'regular readers' by organizations like the London Union of Journalists."[88] Editors gave readers what they had requested. Although rare, some readers asked editors to remove the women's columns for perceived immoral reasons, such as a 1962 letter to the editor of the *Cameroon Champion* proposing that journalist Auntie Clara's "immoral articles" in her women's advice column be replaced by local news or even by a "Beaufort [beer] advertisement." The writer suggests that "sparking youths could write strait [*sic*] to [Dear] Dolly in *Drum* Magazine" instead of to Auntie Clara.[89] The suggestion that advertisements for alcoholic beverages replace a women's column were unusual, and on the whole, readers seemed receptive to the women's advice columns. Newspaper columns are one space in which female journalists, as "print griots," would guest-feature female political elites and visiting foreign female economic elites, such as those from India,[90] to shape ideal womanhood and Anglophone political identities within urban settings.[91]

WOMEN, EDUCATION, AND POLITICS

While there are indeed great social, economic, and cultural differences between understood Anglophone and Francophone identities, women faced similar economic, educational, and social plights in West Cameroon and East Cameroon. British administrative policies and mission dogmas about gender strongly informed West Cameroon's notion of ideal womanhood in the early post-independence period. In the latter part of British rule in the Southern Cameroons, women were marginalized rather than mostly excluded from formal political structures, while women in French-ruled Cameroon were mostly excluded.[92] As Emmanuel Konde points out, this has more to do with the behavior of the European administrations in the waning days of formal rule than any other factor. The French government, and later Ahidjo's government, did not acknowledge the legitimacy of the UPC in any respect thus making it more difficult for women affiliated with the UPC to participate in politics in 1960s East Cameroon. The British government, on the other hand, recognized both the KNC and the KNDP, during the end of its rule, and this resulted in women being marginalized instead of mostly excluded at the end of British rule and during the 1960s.[93]

Once new political autonomy was granted in 1954, Southern Cameroons House of Assembly undertook the writing of new electoral regulations.[94] The new regulations, which took effect in December 1957, granted women the right to vote, the right to stand as candidates for elective office, and the right to serve as representatives in the parliament.[95] Two women served in the Assembly before the federal period, Dorcas Idowu from 1957 to 1959 and Josepha Mua from 1959 to 1961. However, they had been appointed as Special Members for Women's Interests rather than elected and therefore had limited power; their mandate was to focus on women's social and political issues. Mua, however, was propelled into the limelight when she cast the deciding vote in the Southern Cameroons House of Assembly on whether Southern Cameroons should join newly independent French Cameroun. Like Foncha, Mua was afraid that "West Cameroon would be swallowed up and would disappear" if they united with Nigeria. She noted that reunification with French Cameroun was "going back home to our brothers." But, as her biographer notes, Mua later regretted the decision "as she blamed the West and East Cameroun union for rampant corruption and the erosion of Anglo-Saxon values. . . . and failed to take into consideration . . . the impact of neo-colonization on Cameroonian system today."[96] In French-ruled Cameroon, women had to seek election. Julienne Ngoumou, the unsuccessful first female candidate to run for a seat in French Cameroun's Territorial Assembly in 1952, paved the way for Julienne Keutcha, a kindergarten teacher who became the first woman elected to the National Assembly of the Republic of Cameroon in 1960.[97] In general, the British government, more than its French counterpart, explicitly advocated for women's inclusion in its administration and incorporating them into public life, particularly in the declining years of European rule.[98]

Nonetheless, during the period of European rule, women in both Anglophone and Francophone regions were subordinate at home. While the period of European rule had not invented the subjugation of women in these regions, they had given it particular flavor in each of their domains. In the Southern Cameroons, many Christian values regarding the roles of women reflected the efforts of various Christian (Protestant) missions from Europe, the United States, and the West Indies that were active during British rule. Christianity was promoted by Protestant groups such as the Jamaica Baptist Missionary Society and the English Baptist Missionary Society, active from the mid- to late 1880s; the German Missionary Society (later the Basel Mission Society), a Christian missionary society founded in Germany and active in Cameroon from the late 1880s to the mid-1900s; and the American Presbyterian Mission and the North American Baptist Mission. Missionaries who took up the education of girls under British rule throughout Africa were mindful of the importance of training women to become "domestic" by taking on Western gender norms, an extension of the educational norms taught to women educated in the United Kingdom and the United States.[99] Tabitha Kanogo asserts that in colonial Kenya, "[m]issions endeavored to produce moderately literate girls steeped in Christian ideals and suitable as wives for Christian men. The girls were introduced to educational syllabi designed to cultivate their domestic skills for their roles as wives and mothers . . . . [i]n the great scheme of things, missions anticipated that the majority of women would not pursue careers."[100] Nakanyike Musisi makes similar observations in her work on missionary education in early twentieth century Uganda: "[t]he education they offered . . . did not go beyond preparing women for the domestic life. . . . Practical domestic work combined with religious education to build character heavily outweighed the time given to academic studies."[101]

Nancy Wood Folkerts, for example, who carried out her mission under the North American Baptist Mission and served with her husband mostly in Bamenda from 1959 to 1972, explained in an interview how she facilitated literacy programs alongside weekly Bible meetings and how the mission offered post-natal services for Cameroonian women.[102]

In French Cameroun, the Catholic Church, for example, played a significant role since German rule, although Catholic missionaries were also active in areas that would later comprise the Northwest Region, particularly Bamenda, where Anna Foncha hailed from.[103] For instance, "[t]he earliest and most widely operated educational institutions for African women in French-administered Cameroon were known as 'fiancée schools' or the '*Sixa*,' which French missionaries promoted as 'ecoles professionnelles' for Christian marriage." Women in the Sixa, many of whom were single for varied reasons "received religious instruction and lessons on household management until they were baptised, married or remarried."[104] Christian missionaries' emphasis on domesticity in both British and French territories firmly situated "good" women as wives and mothers who focused on cooking, housekeeping, and childcare. Their goal was to create "good" Christian wives and mothers who were "prepared to remain in the home and instill Christian values in their children."[105] The same values shaped perceptions of respectability of women throughout Cameroon. A woman's fertility, piety, submissiveness, chastity, care of her "children, and effective household management defined and shaped her respectability" and adherence to proper gender norms.[106]

Mission education shaped hybrid identities among mission-educated female students during British rule and in the federal period. But as Karen Tranberg Hansen argues about the diverse encounters African women had with Western notions of domesticity during colonialism, "Western-derived ideas about domesticity were often culturally redefined and put to different uses as the Africans selected some aspects of the model and discarded others."[107] For instance, Kanogo asserts that although "colonial administrators, indigenous patriarchal authorities, and missionaries sought increased control over the central elements of Kenyan women's lives", nevertheless "women adopted negotiated solutions, outrightly violated conventional norms, or adopted novel responses to intractable problems."[108] In the Belgian Congo, Nancy Rose Hunt describes "new colonial middle figures—evangelical teachers, nursing men, and midwives—[as being] key to the altercation of bodily practice and to the creolization and transcoding that were necessarily involved."[109] In British Southern Cameroons, mission-educated students also formed hybrid identities shaped by their mission-education and diverse local cultural norms. As Melinda Adams asserts in her work on women's participation in public life in the British Southern Cameroons: "women were not just passive recipients of missionary and colonial doctrine, they were also active agents who reinterpreted and reshaped these messages. . . . women frequently subverted these domestic ideologies, taking what was useful and leaving the rest behind."[110] Women, for instance, used their skills they learned in domestic science classes to access new independent economic resources.

Women's societies existed in both the British Southern Cameroons and French Cameroun further informing many mission-educated women's social and political activities. The Anglophones had the Young Ladies Improvement Society in Victoria, the Women's Progressive Society in Kumba, and the Ladies' Dramatic Society in Buea.[111] The Francophones had L'Union Feminine Civique et Sociale (UFCS), a French organization based in Paris with a chapter in Douala; the UDEFEC, the women's wing of the UPC; L'Union des Femmes Camerounaises (UFC), an organization with close connections with the anti-UPC L'Évolution Sociale Camerounaise, although it was officially autonomous; La Jeunesse Feminine Camerounaise, an autonomous, indigenous, local organization. Both the French and British governments promoted women's associations that did not challenge their authority—thus, the groups were explicitly apolitical, just as they would be after independence.[112] After independence, John Ngu Foncha's wife, Anna, and E. M. L. Endeley's sister-in-law, Gladys, and Gladys's niece, Gwendoline Burnley, would be highly active in ensuring the continuation of Anglophone Cameroonian women's organizations.

African women in many colonial societies also exercised forms of collective power through traditional women's societies and engaged in anticolonial protests, and there were commonalities and continuities in the postcolonial period. The Anlu Rebellion of 1958–1961 that helped propel John Foncha and the KNDP to power was part of a significant tradition in which women exerted authority over men who violated moral codes or encroached on women's traditional authority, as the British administration had sought to do by enforcing a new crop implementation strategy. The Anlu Rebellion was a movement that resisted European rule in that it challenged and subverted British authority, but it also explicitly and successfully defended women's agricultural and social rights.[113]

Anglophone Cameroon had other traditional women's societies with similar authority that mobilized women socially and politically. Among the

Bakweri people of the southwestern region there was *titi ikoli*, a movement in which women assembled together to shame male offenders, and in the northwest the Takumbeng only accepted women after menopause. Such traditional women's organizations helped maintain social decorum and shamed any male who broke social rules. As an example, Takumbeng appeared naked, invoking cultural beliefs that the vagina was a powerful tool to express serious grievances. Women used this "vaginal power" to shame men who are like their "sons." The "sons" feared that seeing a "mother's" genitalia might bring them bad luck and death. The age of the women was intricately linked to the shaming process; the older the woman, the greater her ability to function as an elder maternal relation.[114]

Such traditional women's associations provided a foundation for women's collective mobilization during the federal period. Owing a good deal of its success to the Anlu in the early postcolonial era, the KNDP continued to make use of the long history of mobilizing women's collective protests. Also, elite women's use of "wife and mother" tropes were powerful supports for Anglophone separatist intentions, as they drew from women's traditional authority in the western Grassfields. In addition, women's access to "traditional" protests against men who had brokered social norms in the precolonial and colonial era were sometimes reinterpreted in the early post-independence era, with circumstances and allowances shifting to fit the times.

Just as women's positions in the Southern Cameroons House of Assembly between 1957 and 1960 provided an alternative to full political participation, women's organizations during the 1960s and early 1970s created moral and nationalist role models, delegating to women the political role of instilling cultural values and gender norms in other women. While West Cameroon mostly continued to marginalize women from the modern political structures established during British rule, women's organizations gave them the opportunity to prove their political worthiness by adhering to ideal womanhood and prevailing gender norms. As Nira Yuval-Davis asserts, women's citizenship within a nation is usually of a dual nature, combining the rights and responsibilities of all adult citizens with the "rules, regulations, and policies which are specific to them."[115] The leaders of women's organizations in West Cameroon were aware of the differing political rules that society applied to them. Women's clubs in West Cameroon, revised versions of women's societies that existed during European rule, thus became an arena in which to practice, perform, and display to the male-led state that members adhered to notions of ideal womanhood. The leaders of West Cameroon's women's organizations perceived it as their responsibility to lead and teach less-educated women to preserve gender norms and nationalism within domestic and nationalist spaces. Even with increased participation in political activities and entry into the professional workforce, "good" women continued to uphold their household responsibilities and extend respect to their husbands and other male figures. Susan Geiger and Elizabeth Schmidt offer examples of Muslim women in the same period in Tanzania and Guinea who engaged in politics despite their husbands' willingness to divorce them for doing so, but this was less common in Anglophone Cameroon, perhaps because it did not have the radical Africanist socialist nationalist parties of those countries in the 1950s and 1960s.

Involvement in women's associations, as well as formal education, were de facto prerequisites for working in government for women in Cameroon during the federal period. Experience in women's organizations probably gave politically active women training in leadership skills.[116] The biographer of Gladys Silo Endeley, the first vice president of the Women's Cameroon National Union (WCNU) and president of the Fako Divisional Section, as well as being E. M. L. Endeley's sister-in-law, avows that Endeley "was [a] champion [at] creating [women's] meetings and clubs of various sorts. Her style was based on women's differences from men: women felt they had a superior morality; they lacked self-interest and had a sense of politics as an educative and moral crusade."[117] During the federal period, though, political participation involved co-optation. Ahidjo, for example, co-opted Delphine Tsanga, a leader in the National Council of Cameroonian Women (NCCW), into his Cameroon Union (a precursor to Ahidjo's Cameroon National Union) much as he would conscript Gwendoline Burnley into the West Cameroon Legislative Assembly.[118] These female parliamentarians were all Christian; the first female politician from the predominately Muslim Far North Region took office in 1973. Marginalization did not necessarily mean irrelevance; Burnley and Tsanga were particularly prominent in women's organizations throughout the 1960s and 1970s.[119]

WOMEN IN URBAN WEST CAMEROON

The political activities of formally educated elite women such as Burnley unfolded in Anglophone towns throughout West Cameroon. The urban population in all of Cameroon was at most 20 percent of the population throughout the 1960s, and at most 31 percent by the end of the 1970s.[120] While the findings of a 1964 demographic survey of West Cameroon do not indicate the exact percentages of rural and urban women, we do know the approximate distribution of the population in all of the divisions of West Cameroon in 1964; 834,260 individuals lived in the "rural zone," whereas 98,199 individuals inhabited large towns such as Bamenda, Buea, Tiko, Kumba, Mamfe, and Victoria.[121] Although urban dwellers comprised of 47,830 residents of West Cameroon's smaller towns such as Muyuka, Tombel, Wum, and Kumbo, the majority of individuals in the federal period lived in rural areas. This urban-rural divide was not evenly distributed geographically, however. In northern West Cameroon, where Bamenda is, 91.8 percent lived in rural places (8.1 percent lived in small or large towns). In the southern part, near Buea, only 67.3 percent did (21.8 percent lived in small or large towns). Thus, the area of the western Grassfields was significantly more rural than the southern region.[122]

While the 1964 demographic survey does not indicate the status of urban women in Anglophone Cameroon at the time, such as upper-class women or "working-class" women (those in the professional workforce), government pamphlets and other print sources from the period give us some sense of their economic and educational positions, or in other professional settings, such as in banks or as teachers. For example, a 1975 pamphlet by the women's wing of Ahidjo's CNU, *Visages de la Femme Camerounaise* (Faces of the Cameroon Woman) suggests that most urban women in all of Cameroon worked in the commerce and industry sectors; their rural counterparts generally worked in crop agriculture and sellers in markets or in food production.[123] Many women in the West Cameroon State worked for the Cameroon Development Corporation (CDC), an agroindustrial company that was and remains the second-largest employer in Cameroon, or for the tea plantations that the CDC owned at the time and which almost all of which were, according to the 1964 demographic survey of the West Cameroon State, located in southern West Cameroon.[124] Many formally educated women of middle- to upper-middle-class worked for the CDC offices as accountants or in other professional capacities. Virginia DeLancey's and Piet Konings's work on tea estates in Anglophone Cameroon shows that many women of lower socioeconomic status found employment in the CDC as plantation laborers during and after British rule.[125] Formally educated urban women throughout Cameroon worked in all sectors of the workforce, such as public service, commerce, and industry (comprising 16.6 percent of industry workers).[126]

Women were 13 percent of bank workers and insurance workers, 10 percent of restaurant workers, and 6.72 percent of teachers in private schools and shop assistants; 0.3 percent were in the public sector, which includes general administration, army, police, education, health, water and electricity corporations, posts and telegraphs, and radio and press.[127] Some of these women comprised the political elite in their roles as civil servants. It is these urban women who comprised the elite educated grouping referenced in this work. To be clear, few women received enough formal education to work in the professional workforce in West Cameroon. The 1964 demographic survey of the West Cameroon State shows that the majority of adult women, 86.3 percent, engaged in occupations in the informal sector, including agriculture, local trade, and crafts skills.[128]

Gender inequality was the norm, and men continued to achieve higher levels of formal education than women throughout Cameroon, reflecting the persistence of traditional gender roles and the general societal prejudice against formally educating women.[129] In 1961 in East Cameroon, the number of girls attending school reached 151,529, 35.5 percent of the total in the primary school age group; during the 1968–69 school year their numbers increased to 289,445, 42.4 percent of the total in the primary school age group.[130] In 1964 West Cameroon, male teenagers between the ages of fifteen and nineteen were five times as likely to have a primary education as girls their own age, although even boys within this age group had only a 34.6 percent rate of participation. Secondary education rates were not quite as skewed, but only 2.3 percent of teenage girls had technical, secondary, or higher education.[131] Thus, the formally educated women who drove the Anglophone culture at the time were a small minority. The Federal University of Cameroon, the first university of higher education in Cameroon, founded in 1961, admitted both Anglophones and Francophones; it had only 93 women (out of a total of 1,779 students), or less than 5 percent of the total enrollment in 1968–69 and, at the time, the year of highest female participation during the federal period.[132]

Government documents such as transcribed speeches, newspaper records, and oral interviews suggest that while political and urban elites in Cameroon applauded women's increased access to formal education and the professional workforce, they nevertheless held women to a standard of conservative womanhood. Thus, while the urban women who comprised the educated elite, as well as female political elites, were formally educated, worked mostly in the professional workforce, and often had servants to help with household tasks, they nevertheless remained deferential to male authority and sought to complete domestic duties when at home.

Oral interviews confirmed the strong association between ideal womanhood, motherhood and effective household management and subservience to the husband. Fidelia Ngum, a lively woman who lived in Buea and, in retirement, was a seamstress and also sold food products in a makeshift shop by the roadside to support her family, recalled, "When I got married I know that . . . I can help to do one or two things . . . to take care of my house, my husband . . . as a housewife you have to take care of yourself, take care of your house, take care of your husband, and if God blesses you with kids, take good care of your kids . . . bringing them up in a good way."[133] Columns by female journalists and letters to advice columns further suggested that the "ideal" woman in urban Cameroon was a good cook, honest, trustworthy, cheery, and well-mannered in public.[134] As advice columnist Ruff Wanzie counseled in an August 1964 column entitled "Behave Well, Women," "[w]hen a woman goes out she should aim at what is right and courteous always. Remember your manners are judged in homes, streets, private houses, [dance] balls, social gatherings, functions and in short your manners are judged everywhere." She continued, "Do the correct thing because you are well bred, not because someone is watching you. It is the well-mannered woman who inspires respect and liking. So, you must learn to laugh gently [and] control your temper."[135]

Likewise, perceptions of Anglophone identity shaped women's embodiment of ideal womanhood, both verbally and behaviorally. Anglophone recollections of the federal period reveal the widespread belief that Anglophone women were more authentically African, traditional, and sexually conservative. In contrast, Francophone women were considered sexually loose, with poor public comportment and conduct. For example, Asong Martha Ebey, a retired grocer who was born in Kumba but resided in Buea, recalled that "an Anglophone woman as I see her is straight . . . and steady, courageous." She explains that before leaving the market an Anglophone woman will dress well. She elaborates: "It takes time before an Anglophone woman [will] get into quarrel with you . . . but over there [East Cameroon], it's very very quick. Now like this, common greetings is a problem. They will ask you 'why are you greeting me?' when you ask 'Good morning? Good afternoon.' They don't even care. Some don't even care to greet. And if you are greeting like that it's seems as if you're boring [them]."[136] One woman divulged that she thought that Anglophone and Francophone women had different "movements," or ways of comportment. She explained that Francophone women wore too much Western/French attire—specifically identifying the outfit, "skirt and blouse." Such women said they disliked French clothes and noted that Anglophone women were more likely to wear traditional clothing, such as a *kabba* or *lappa*, which are colorful traditional West African women's attire, whereas, Francophone women were more likely to wear "gowns," or "ready-made" clothing, as one interviewer phrased it.[137] One avowed that Francophones called women who wore wrappers "Biafra,"[138] a slur applied to Anglophones by Francophones since the reunification of Cameroon in 1961, and one that implies a close association with Nigeria and ungratefulness and disloyalty to Cameroon.[139] For this reason, the standard of bodily comportment in Cameroon not only reflected ideal Anglophone conduct, but also solidified the Anglophone Cameroonian elite's claim of moral superiority through their conduct, which was partially shaped by their distinct cultural heritage. As oral interviews have suggested, descriptions such as that proposed by Ebey, reflect the wider belief that Anglophone and Francophone women carried themselves in a visibly different manner.

THE "GOLDEN AGE"

The period that Anthony Ndi describes as Anglophone Cameroon's "Golden Age" was a time "of boundless hope, confidence and justified pride." Ndi asserts that male politicians in Anglophone Cameroon were full "with a sense of mission [and were] like their West African and Nigerian contemporaries." He cites Kwame Nkrumah in Ghana, Léopold Sédar Senghor in Senegal, Ahmed Sékou Touré in Guinea, and several prominent politicians in Nigeria—Nnamdi Azikiwe; Obafemi Awolowo, a Nigerian nationalist; and Abubakar Tafawa Balewa, once prime minster of Nigeria—as examples of "zealous patriots" that Anglophone Cameroonian male politicians were like during the "Golden Age."[140] It seems likely it was that way as much for Anglophone women as for men. In many ways, this period offers a hint of how an independent British Southern Cameroons might have operated. While the legalization of the multiparty system by Ahidjo's successor, Paul Biya, in 1992, led to the reemergence of "Southern Cameroonian" nationalism among self-identified Anglophones, the federal period was a critical time in Anglophone nationalism. Anglophone political elites were more autonomous than at any other time. West Cameroon had more press freedom, numerous private presses, and multiple political parties for most of the federal period, few of which were sustainable in East Cameroon.[141]

It was a time of urbanization. Vibrant, cosmopolitan towns peppered the English-speaking territories of Cameroon during the "Golden Age"—Bamenda, nestled in the Western Highlands (or Bamenda Grassfields); Victoria, a coastal town with black sand beaches; and Buea, capital of the West Cameroon State and former capital of German Kamerun and the Southern Cameroons. Buea and Victoria were growing, fueled by economic developments and activities such as the CDC. In 1964 Buea had a population of 9,171, Victoria, 22,453, Tiko, 9,238, Bamenda, 18,429, and Kumba, 31,140.[142]

Walking through their streets, one would hear Kamtok ("Cameroon-talk"), also called Cameroonian pidgin English, an English-based creole language. "Highlife" music from radios in Victoria and Tiko, as well as Douala, a French-speaking economic hub, set the rhythm; the music blends local African sounds and tunes with Western music. Highlife began in coastal towns in Ghana between 1920 and 1930 and was popular throughout Anglophone West Africa by the 1960s. Makossa music might also set the pace of life; it is an energetic Cameroonian dance music popularized in the 1970s by Manu Dibango.[143] A visitor might also see women in hair salons and men in hotel bars drinking Gold Harp, Guinness, and Becks, and see young men and women dressed in both traditional African and Western-style clothing in dance halls. In the 1960s bell-bottoms, popularly called "*apaga* trousers"—also known as "pattes d'éléphants" ("elephant's feet")— high-heeled shoes termed *salamanda*, miniskirts, and afro wigs were popular. Some locals renamed miniskirts "Don't-Cross-Gutter Skirts" because women were scared to take the wide stride that street gutters required lest they expose their undergarments.[144] While strolling the streets of the rapidly expanding towns, a visitor might smell roasting plantains, grilled fish, and *suya*, a spicy shish kebab popular all over West Africa. The nearby markets would be bustling with women engaged in small trading. They might sell handicrafts, clothing, and other commodities such as corn, yams, cassava, and palm oil. Merchants would include Igbo migrants from neighboring eastern Nigeria. They dominated "the market trade in local foodstuffs and imported goods, as well as the transport industry and the retail and wholesale distribution of palm oil" in Kumba, Tiko, and Victoria by the 1960s.[145]

In Buea, the capital, residents would walk past the Buea government stadium where young men played soccer and political rallies were held. In the background was volcanic Mount Cameroon, shrouded in mist during the

Two women in African outfits (wrappers and head ties) in Buea, 1970. Image courtesy of Walter Gam Nkwi, personal photo collection.

rainy season and visibly magnificent during the dry season. This active volcano has inspired fear and awe among local inhabitants, who weave a tapestry of legends and folklore about Mongo ma Ndemi ("Mountain of Greatness"), its local name, which was coined by the Bakweri people who according to oral traditions originated from the foothills of the mountain.[146] Closer to the slopes of the mountain is a striking white German *Schloss*, the residence of German governors during German rule, and home of the prime minister of the West Cameroon State during the federal period, visual reminders of German colonial rule in the region. These seemingly ordinary scenes and symbols make reference to the diverse cultural, political, and economic mosaic that comprised English-speaking regions. It is in this context that women's implicit and explicit social and political actions complicate the trajectory of Anglophone political history.

Send-off Party for Elizabeth Muna at the Buea Mountain Club, November 1961. Image © MINCOM Cameroon, courtesy of African Photography Initiatives.

The "Golden Age" was a time in which women such as Gwendoline Burnley increasingly accessed political authority in formal political structures. After Ahidjo dissolved the multiparty system in 1966, women, like their male counterparts, endeavored to preserve what little political power they had, even when their fears of the political domination of West Cameroon were realized. Women's political actions during the federal period provided the platform for their continual access to political power after 1972, in the United Republic.

The "Golden Age" was also a time of rapid changes in ideas about gender norms and social values, as women increasingly accessed formal education and the formal work sector throughout Cameroon. In West Cameroon, after completing a course in hotel and catering management in the UK, Judith Mbeng became West Cameroon's first female manager of a hotel in 1966 when she started to manage the Bamenda Ring Way Hotel. In a second groundbreaking example, Gladys Ejomi Martin, Gwendoline Burnley's sister and niece of Gladys Silo Endeley, graduated from the University of Ibadan in Nigeria and became the first female doctor in Cameroon during this period of a hopeful "golden" temporality for women.[147] By advocating for progressive politics throughout the federal republic, female political elites found unique ways to promote women's increased access to social, economic, and political authority. Detailed statistics compiled by various women's organizations at the time confirm that they made real advances in procuring such rights for women, albeit at an incremental pace. Chapters 2 and 3 explore the creation of the West Cameroonian national costume and the designation of Anglophone "national" dishes, which remain touchstones today. These efforts are some of the more obvious examples of women's roles in shaping Anglophone nationalism and political identity, and they arose during the federal period.

Anthony Ndi contends that "Southern [West] Cameroons suffered a ruinous decline beginning with the dissolution of the multi-party system in 1966, reaching its lowest point with the abolition of the federal constitution in 1972. . . . 'So ended our Golden Days of the West Cameroon House of Assembly [West Cameroon Legislative Assembly] in Buea.' . . . Thus the grandiose dream of Southern Cameroonians nursed for twenty-five years at last became 'Paradise Lost.'"[148] But this lost "paradise" that Ndi references was never lost. In many ways, today's male leaders of Anglophone self-determination organizations use the past efforts of these women as a foundation to invoke tangible signifiers of Anglophone nationalism, illustrating the longevity of past cultural relics that continue to shape Anglophone identities. In doing so, they bring to fruition the early nationalist efforts of women such as Gwendoline Burnley; their efforts continue to arouse deep attachments to a long-standing unified and distinct Anglophone identity, allowing advocates to foster, drive, and sustain nationalist aspirations across time and space. In other words, proponents continually use the early efforts of women to fuse commonalities among Anglophones to sustain the vibrant imagery of an Anglophone national "paradise."

CHAPTER 2

Men Must Not "Die Alone in the Task of Nation-Building"

Women's Organizations and Nationalist Activities

"Nowadays it has been noted that most of the women are trying their very best [to participate] in activities. But other women are trying to discourage them in a way of sluggishness,"[1] runs a July 1964 letter to "Women's Special" in the *Cameroon Times*. The exasperated letter writer, identified as Mrs. G. M. N. Lisinge, condemns women who regularly miss the meetings of various women's social clubs and organizations active in urban West Cameroon. Although she applauds women's intentions to "promote society life" by registering as members of women's clubs, she laments that "[t]here are very many examples of sluggish women. . . . for one reason or the other [members who are] always late [to] meetings [are] certainly sluggish." These women, she asserts, are blind to the benefits of networking in women's clubs. Appeals like Lisinge's materialized in speeches at organizational events as well as in newspaper columns. Ruff Wanzie, a civil servant and the wife of a West Cameroonian politician, who also wrote the women's advice column in the *Cameroon Times*, participated in various women's organizations herself and regularly featured editorials supporting such involvement throughout the 1960s.

Lisinge's statements demonstrate how West Cameroonian elite women shaped the political landscape differently than their male counterparts. This chapter examines how, through the activities of women's organizations, formally educated women in urban West Cameroon accessed new spaces of sociopolitical power by fostering a united national identity among women, while also running the parallel project of genuinely improving women's social, political, and economic lives. These women claimed that the organizations they led were essential in driving women's economic and social improvement. In this context, the traits of everyday ideal womanhood were inexorably linked to nationalist politics, underscoring women's important roles as daughters, wives, and mothers. But because beliefs about ideal womanhood were tied to women's domestic duties and active participation in women's clubs, "sluggish", or inactive, women challenged the effort to connect women's political actions to suitable womanhood. Educated women, such as Lisinge, criticized women who wasted time meant for fulfilling domestic duties and participating in women's organizations, for failing to "fight" for women's rights, and ultimately, endangering Anglophone nationhood. They saw participating in women's organizations as a key way for women to subscribe to an ideal womanhood that supported larger Anglophone nationalist politics, even as they claimed the organizations were apolitical.

West Cameroonian political elites were similar to their counterparts throughout Africa, such as in Nigeria, Uganda, and Côte d'Ivoire, in that formally educated women, part of the upper-middle-class, led women's organizations.[2] In these associations, educated women sought to fulfill a perceived responsibility to lead and teach less-educated women how to properly preserve gender norms and nationalism within domestic and nationalist spaces in West Cameroon. Women might "emancipate" themselves by participating in Anglophone women's organizations that stressed the rationale for a separatist, national identity through various projects. In doing so, both male and female political elites held women responsible for their own "emancipation"; "sluggish" women, as Lisinge observes, hampered women's struggle for social and economic advances.

But as the life histories of Anna Foncha and Gladys Silo Endeley illustrate, female political elites used their acute awareness of political conditions in other African and European countries to "emancipate" women, challenging or reaffirming preexisting ideologies about women's political identity and unity in West Cameroon. The transnational relations that women organizations established also shepherded Anglophone Cameroonian women into a global network of exchange and support. But during the federal period, many women's organizations were affiliated with male-led political parties and thus active in nation-building campaigns. The leaders of women's organizations advocated for women's political importance by maintaining that women played key roles in the cultural, economic, and social development of the nation as daughters, wives, and mothers. Reflecting the presence of this dynamic in West Cameroon, Clara Manga, writing as "Auntie Clara" for the

Cameroon Champion, wrote in a November 1962 column that "[t]he future of African society rest[s] on the shoulders of women and the myth of the weaker sex is being replaced by the figure of women as the pillar of the nation."[3] Perceptions such as Manga's stoked the attitude that women were obliged to participate in nationalist activities, thus connecting viewpoints about ideal womanhood and gender norms to citizenship duties.

The fact that educated women sought unity with other educated women as part of the campaign for Anglophone nationalism speaks to their larger role as nationalists and hints at what was partially at stake for these elite West Cameroonian women: the opportunity to garner real social and political power for women, as individuals and as a collective, by supporting the male-dominated Anglophone state. But in Cameroon, as elsewhere, there were limits and challenges to women's political participation. Women claimed their organizations were apolitical to make their activities more palatable and nonthreatening to the patriarchal government. Further, they legitimized their activities by focusing on their symbolic roles as mothers who protected the nation's values and identity, extending an understanding of mothering beyond their homes and into their communities and nationalist activities. But they also underscored their biological functions as mothers by focusing on maternal activities such as building the first preschool in West Cameroon. Within this framework, by emphasizing a seemingly conservative politics, elite women were able to make real systematic changes in women's lives. One way they pursued progressive goals in a conservative context was by defining themselves as "good" women despite their political activities, as long as they continued to defer to their husbands. Ultimately, educated women genuinely saw women's organizations as a crucial way to advance women's social, political, and economic freedoms beyond a "women's rights" discourse that was used rhetorically to legitimatize male-dominated parties and regimes. Indeed, remembering his mother's active role in such organizations, the son of Gladys Silo Endeley recalled that their meetings were "extremely helpful for women's emancipation and evolution as they provided familiar and unthreatening environments for women to gain their political feet and they tended to engage in politics with more confidence" because of these organizations.[4]

But also at stake for female political elites was the opportunity to preserve West Cameroonian cultural values in a hegemonic Francophone republic. As this chapter highlights, while women political elites made bridges across Cameroon's national boundaries, they strove to mostly separate their Anglophone women's organizations from their Francophone counterparts, seeing these organizations as their own spaces in which to define and maintain a distinct Anglophone identity. Although Francophone Cameroon had similar organizations, participation in Anglophone organizations became an element of articulating a distinct womanhood of Anglophone Cameroon. The activities that local women's clubs sponsored, such as the creation of a West Cameroonian national costume, made them a vehicle of nationalism. Such nationalist endeavors allowed women to visually portray what Benedict Anderson calls an "imagined community," in which Anglophone Cameroonians were one people with common ancestry, traditions, and origins in a distinct geographic region with shared British administering legacies and, therefore, English fluency.[5] But, by also focusing on everyday comportment as a signifier of a suitable Anglophone persona, such as donning the national costume when traveling abroad, the leaders of women's organizations invoked an embodied nationalism that prioritized seemingly mundane everyday expressions and representations of an idyllic Anglophone womanhood that traversed international boundaries. Exhortations to support these organizations thus tied women's everyday lives and actions to a wider Anglophonic world.

However, political, cultural, and class divisions threatened these leaders' authority and the nation-building endeavors of the women's organizations, key spaces in which to stress Anglophone separatism through a distinct nationalism. While Lisinge's criticisms of "sluggish" women imply the difficulty of this undertaking, it was Ahidjo's creation of a single-party state in 1966 that posed the biggest threat to the power and autonomy of purportedly apolitical women's organizations. Ahidjo eventually co-opted Anglophone women's organizations into his Cameroon National Union's (CNU) women's wing, just as he did with women's organizations in East Cameroon and with defunct Anglophone and Francophone political parties.

To be clear, women's support of male-dominated political parties in the early period of federalism was not a new phenomenon. In fact, between 1958 and 1961, the Kamerun National Democratic Party (KNDP) had relied on Anlu, the traditional (Bamenda) Grassfields women's association, to build power before independence. The Anlu had successfully prevented a key encroachment on agriculture, their traditional domain, and propelled the KNDP to power in lieu of the rival party, which they believed was allied with British efforts to sell their land to Nigerian Igbos. Although the strategies and approaches may have changed, women's associations and their leaders always found new ways to collectively maintain social and political authority. Their approaches both resonated with traditional women's organizations and protests and embraced new tactics appropriate to the rapidly changing social and political landscape.

THE MOTHERS OF WEST CAMEROON

Anna Foncha and Gladys Silo Endeley were West Cameroon's most prominent members of the female political elite in the federal period. Evidence suggests that they exercised indirect social and political influence, including individually and as their husbands' political advisors and mentors. Historicizing the lives of these women illuminates their individual agency and highlights how past events shaped the ideas and understanding of the world in which such women lived. Excerpts from their life histories clarify not only their individual characters, but the many historical and contemporary power structures that notable female figures have faced across time and space.

Although no book-length treatment of Anna Foncha's life exists, fragments of her life can be pieced together by drawing from the biographies of other political elites, oral interviews, and archival materials. Family and friends described Anna Foncha during the course of her childhood as so extremely weak and fragile that Catechumens (youths training for Catholic confirmation) were ordered by her father to carry her up the hill to the Bamenda Government School on their backs, yet by adulthood she went on to become a stalwart in the field of politics.[6] She was born Anna Nangah Atang on December 23, 1923, in Mankon, a village in Bamenda in the contemporary Northwest Region.[7] She was the eldest daughter of Martin Kushi Atang, a pioneer catechist and founder of St. Joseph's Mission in Mankon.[8] Her mother was Martina Awah Atang from Mbatu, a small village in Bamenda. Described as an intelligent child, Anna received her early education in the modern-day Northwest Region of Cameroon: the Bamenda Government School, the Shisong Catholic school in Kumbo, and Saint Anthony's School in Njinikom.[9] In 1941, after impressing the Nigerian inspector of education with her intellect, he facilitated the process to award Anna a scholarship to attend the Teacher Training Centre at Ikot Ekpene, Nigeria. Anna Foncha would draw from such international experiences throughout her life in shaping her ideas about women's social, economic, and political development in West Cameroon.

John Foncha met Anna Atang in 1941, when she was a student in Njinikom, and began to woo her in 1943 after her return from Ikot Ekpene, Nigeria. As John Foncha's biographer notes about his desire for marriage, "[a]s the years passed by he knew he must get married to a well brought up and educated Catholic girl. It would be unacceptable that a man of his level of learning should have been marred to an unlettered girl. He scouted around and his love fell on Anna." From the moment Anna returned from Ikot Ekpene, John Foncha "would be seen going to the compound of Papa Martin Atang. . . . [soon] news had filtered out that Mr. Foncha intended to get married to Miss Anna Atang."[10] Anna's father was delighted. Although Anna requested that she have more time before getting married, her father insisted she marry right away, fearing that her education would interfere with her marriageability (or her willingness to marry).[11] Just as she adhered to prevailing ideas of womanhood by marrying, John Foncha fulfilled dominant ideas about African manhood by marrying. He paid a bride price, also called "bridewealth"—the payment paid by the male suitor to his wife-to-be's family—in palm wine and cash, according to his biographer, and the two were married in a Catholic wedding in Bamenda on January 15, 1945.[12] They continued to fulfill societal expectations by producing eight children. While John Foncha's biographer underlines the significance of his eight children in building his social status, he fails to underline how Anna Foncha frequently presented herself as a mother first and foremost, invoking maternal authority to cement her social and political authority during the federal period.[13] While Anna Foncha was John Foncha's "backbone," supporting "him in all political endeavors" and his number-one political advisor from the moment they married, she was also a political force in her own right.[14]

Anna Foncha directly advocated for women's advancements, economically and socially. She founded all-girl schools in Njinikom and Mankon, and with the West Cameroon Council of Women's Institutes (CWI) helped found a preschool in Buea.[15] In a lengthy guest editorial, "My Life as the P.M.'s Wife," that appeared in journalist Ruff Wanzie's column in February 1964, Foncha gives copious details about her home and garden before outlining her activities in women's associations and her influence on her husband and other political men, thereby softening the political nature of her statements. She outlines her activities with the West Cameroon Federation of Women Social Clubs and Associations (WSCA), such as touring throughout West Cameroon to meet numerous women. She says she can bring to her husband the concerns of women she meets when she tours West Cameroon. "Although I am not a Minister, these complaints occupy my thoughts . . . and something should be done to ameliorate them. I often find time to speak to the Prime

Minister and other secretaries of state about these complaints and requests." But in the same editorial she offers particulars of her home to soften the subversive political tone. Her new home was a *Schloss*—using a German term for a building similar to a palace or manor house—that German colonial officials had once owned. She notes that her husband's rise to prime minister gave her "a comparatively bigger house to look after although my duties as a mother of seven [at the time] have not changed much."[16] In such statements, Foncha relates to her readers by highlighting her domestic duties and paints herself as a motherly figure with political authority who calls on her counterparts to join women's organizations. She suggests that they, too, can prioritize nationalist duties in their lives, even if they are busy mothers. But Foncha's overtly political concerns for women's welfare in the country suggest her political power. Her editorial is ultimately a serious political piece that addresses concerns about women's social and political roles in West Cameroon, although it is partially disguised as a domestic piece. Her statements about the role of women's organizations and her direct appeals to her husband to address these concerns suggest a sincere interest in improving the lot of women.

At the same time, Anna Foncha drew from her international experiences and connections to learn more about developing and structuring women's organizations in West Cameroon. She had extensive experience traveling abroad during her tenure as a political wife; for example, in 1964 she went on a whirlwind tour to Egypt, the United Kingdom, France, Italy, the Netherlands, and the United States. In the United States she met with delegates of the International Council of Women in New York, representatives of the National Catholic Welfare Conference, with female senators, and with women members of the African-American Institute in Washington, DC, to discuss women's civic activities, training women for leadership, and organizing women's groups.[17] In Egypt she met with eight female parliamentarians, a female minister of social welfare, and members of women's organizations with whom she discussed "women's positions in political life, social and cultural life and what help Egyptian women could give" to women in Cameroon. At the end of her tour in Egypt, President Gamal Abdel Nasser Hussein, the second president of Egypt, awarded her "a first class honour of the Egyptian Women. This honour is called Al Maral." As Melinda Adams argues, such international interfaces resulted in the development and the emergence of newer women's organizations in Cameroon.[18] In an interview with Cameroonian historian Walter Gam Nkwi, Foncha explained that she made contacts extensively when establishing Cameroon's Catholic Women's Association (CWA), learning more, for example, about the development and structure of women's organizations in Nigeria.[19]

Plans for the CWA began in early 1964 when Anna Foncha, on the six-country tour with her husband, visited Catholic women's organizations in the United States with an eye toward creating the CWA.[20] On returning to Cameroon, she launched the association with the help of Josepha Namen Mua, a KNDP parliamentarian in the British Southern Cameroons and the wife of a parliamentarian in the West Cameroon Legislative Assembly;[21] Prudencia Chilla, the second West Cameroonian female parliamentarian in the CNU state's Federal National Assembly and the first Anglophone woman to publish an autobiographical novel (*Promise*, under the pen name Jedida Asheri); and Dorothy Atabong, an education officer for the West Cameroon government who would go on to serve as one of CWA's regional presidents and vice president of the World Union of Catholic Women's Organizations (WUCWO).[22] The latter two had had contact with the Catholic Women's League and Catholic Mothers in England in the early 1960s. Bishop Jules Peeters of Buea gave them his ecclesial approval; CWA officially started in Buea in April 1964. Anna Foncha would likewise incorporate her CWA activities with her maternal role, and the organization, similar to the WSCA and the CWI, had maternalist undertones. The original founders of the CWA, including Anna Foncha, were known as "Mothers of the Church," and the terms "aunt" and "mother" were often used for leaders of the CWA.

Gladys Endeley, like Anna Foncha, exerted great political energy during the federal period, although she supported the opposition Cameroon People's National Convention (CPNC) party. She was a West Cameroonian civil servant, the section president of the Women's Cameroon National Union (WCNU) of Fako, and the first vice national president of the WCNU.[23] She had six children with Samuel Endeley who was the brother of CPNC leader E. M. L. Endeley. She was born on July 5, 1928, in Victoria, in the modern-day Southwest Region. Gladys was of mixed ethnicity—Bakweri (Christian) on her father's side and Fulani (Muslim) on her mother's side. Her father, Carl Makangai Steane, was a professional educator who had studied in Germany in the early 1900s and fervently believed in formally educating all his children, six daughters.[24] The youngest of their six daughters and a lifelong practicing Christian herself, Gladys had connections to northern Muslim Cameroon through her mother and the southern Christian Bakweri people through her father. President Ahidjo was a Muslim Fulani from the north, a commonality that allowed her to establish a connection with him. She was also useful to northern Muslim politicians who used her to show that they, like Christians, could empower women.[25] At the same time, her southern Christian connection would make her an asset to southern politicians; her sons described her as a valuable resource who could be trusted by all sides. While Endeley used her mixed identity to negotiate for male politicians, she focused on fostering a collective identity and encouraging women to dismiss ethnic loyalties when leading women's organizations. In doing so, women like Gladys Endeley, who themselves had mixed ethnicities, could imagine an Anglophone panethnic identity, demonstrating how female political elites may have navigated ethnic politics differently than their male counterparts.

Gladys Endeley also had the formal education that politically powerful women of the period required; she attended Aggrey Memorial College in Arochukwu, Nigeria (1943–48), then University of Leeds in the UK (1955–58) to study the social sciences.[26] At Aggrey "her leadership qualities were . . . obvious and captivating. She beat the boys and broke the tradition when she became school prefect" in her last year, a rare thing for a young woman at the coed school. The principle of Aggrey described Endeley as being "exemplary in scholarship, character and conduct" during her studies in Aggrey. At Leeds she was an active member of the student union—her biographer writes that she joined because she did not want "to be left behind"—reflecting a propensity for active membership in organizations that would continue after she married.[27]

Upon returning home from Nigeria, she worked for the Cameroon Development Coporation (CDC) as an accounts clerk, where she met her husband, Samuel, a pharmacist at the time. The young suitor "soon discovered that the young lady working in the accounts department was not just a pretty face and became bent on making her his life partner."[28] A member of a wealthy Bakweri family who had served in many influential positions in West Cameroon and the United Republic of Cameroon, including E. M. L. Endeley's position as leader of the CPNC, Samuel was admitted into Middle Temple in London in 1959 and eventually earned his law degree. He would later serve as the paramount chief, or highest-ranking political leader, of the Bakweri people in Buea, from 1990 until his death in 2015. Gladys and Samuel Endeley married in a Christian wedding in 1953 soon after meeting.[29] While their marriage would eventually produce six children, they also found the time to further their education early in their marriage.

On returning home from the UK, Gladys later worked in the West Cameroon Ministry of Local Government and the West Cameroon Ministry of

Natural Resources.[30] Endeley's biographer writes that Gladys spoke in favor of "women's rights and basic human rights," calling on women to use their education for the good of the country asserting that "if women are not educated then, the country was at a detriment."[31] The biographer further mentions that Anna Foncha and Delphine Tsanga, a Francophone Cameroonian woman who was a key leader in the National Council of Cameroonian Women (NCCW) and later the WCNU in East Cameroon and who penned a novel under her name titled *Vies de Femmes* (Lives of Women) in 1983, were two of the politically powerful women Gladys "spent time fraternizing, discussing [and] debating with." One of her sons, Ngomba, remembered in an interview with his mother's biographer that she also "worked well with many other civil servants from Nigeria, Sierra Leone, and other countries." From these encounters she learned "what was happening in their home countries especially about what the women were doing to better themselves and the society as a whole."[32] But despite her busy schedule, Gladys' biographer describes her as traveling frequently "[w]ithout shirking her responsibilities"; she would bypass her servants—"cooks, stewards, drivers, [and] gardeners" as her biographer reports—"to clean, and to prepare food" for the family of six herself when she was home.[33]

Both biographical and oral sources suggest that Samuel was highly supportive of Gladys's social and political success. As her biographer concludes, early in their marriage, "[h]er husband, the young pharmacist . . . knew that he was married to a progressive woman and supported her considerably."[34] Mariana, their only daughter and the youngest of their six children, explained to me in an interview that her mother engaged in weekly church activities and cooked dinner for her household in addition to working outside the home; her activities included working for the WCNU, opening up a local maternity clinic, and consorting with other female political elites that her mother's biographer does not mention, such as Germaine Ahidjo, the president's wife; her niece Gwendoline Burnley; and Elizabeth Muna, the wife of the third prime minister of West Cameroon. Like Anna Foncha, she traveled extensively, such as attending the meetings of the Associated Country Women of the World in the UK, Germany, and Switzerland. Her daughter disclosed that every time her mother traveled she "looked around and said 'what can I bring back? How can I come back and make things different?' I mean, we always laughed because every time she came back there was some new change that had to happen in the house. She went to Ghana one time and came back with something called black soap." Gladys's daughter credits her father's patient and progressive nature, which "allowed" her mother's political activity;[35] even as a child she knew her father could require her mother to give up her professional and political activities. Her daughter further shared, "my mom was one of the first, I call it 'feminists'—I didn't see that back at that time but . . . . Her biggest motivation was motivating women from all levels." While Gladys Endeley may have never called herself a feminist, at her 2010 funeral, even the mayor of Buea declared that she "proved that a woman can do what a man can do."[36]

Historicizing the lives of Foncha and Endeley deepens our understanding of how such women advance political authority while adhering to dominant ideas about gender roles for women. Both women emphasized hybrid ideas of womanhood that drew from both local and international norms of gender that intersected with their social and political positions. Both women were Christians who emphasized maternal power both at home and when openly advocating for women's social and economic advancements. Additionally, they formed alliances with Francophone political elite women, exchanging thoughts and feelings beyond the national borders even though tensions were prevalent among West and East Cameroonian women's groups.[37] They also made connections outside of Cameroon. Both women travelled extensively on the continent, Europe and the United States—a luxury few women of their time could afford—fostering transnational links that bolstered their women's organizations. According to Melinda Adams, it was via such associations and connections that the organizations from Cameroon gained access to international conferences and support to travel to such occasions; they also obtained new information and an opening to invite women leaders of other countries to Cameroon. As individuals travelling across the globe and experiencing the world, women such as Foncha, with her international connections, permitted women's groups from Cameroon to feel like they were in fact "part of a larger, global movement."[38]

Analyzing the lives of Foncha and Endeley likewise complicates narratives of female political elites who engaged in feminist activities, albeit explicitly proclaiming or implying that they were not feminists. As scholarship shows, one consequence of the long history of suspicion of overt feminists and conflation of feminism with sexual promiscuity and unfitness for marriage is that many African women have openly rejected feminist ideology.[39] Though Anna Foncha and Gladys Endeley were not self-identified feminists, they engaged in a wide range of what some feminist scholars have identified as "feminist actions,"[40] which included creating and supporting the initiatives of women's organizations. But while women such as Foncha and Endeley perceived the limits of their power, they were not completely what Amina Mama calls "femocrats"—women who had few ideas of their own and drew most of their power from being married to politically powerful men.[41] Women like Foncha and Endeley exercised significant personal agency in enacting change in women's social, economic, and political lives. The actual changes women's organizations and clubs made in advancing women's social, economic, and political rights belies the argument that they mostly focused on garnering political power and wealth for the first ladies and other political wives in their leadership. As the next section will show, their participation in key women's organizations at the time, along with other educated women, deepen our understanding of how they carried out a conservative yet progressive nationalist politics that advanced women's social, political, and economic participation.

"GET TO WORK IN YOUR CLUBS": "APOLITICAL" POLITICS IN WEST CAMEROON'S TWO KEY WOMEN'S ASSOCIATIONS

Gwendoline Burnley, the first woman parliamentarian to be elected to the West Cameroon Legislative Assembly, and Josepha Mua, who was a KNDP parliamentarian during the period of British rule, founded the organization, the WSCA, that would eventually become the CWI in 1962, and Anna Foncha served as its president until its dissolution in the late 1960s.[42] The WSCA, which appears to have started going by the name CWI around March 1964, was itself an umbrella organization that brought together "over 60 registered women's social clubs" from throughout West Cameroon.[43] Although the KNDP seemed to have a women's wing with branches in Buea, Mayuka, and Tiko, with Anna Foncha as the leader, the CWI was more visible and appeared to have more public support and financial backing by the KNDP government.[44]

CWI leaders from around West Cameroon met once a year. During these meetings there were exhibitions, lectures, and exchanges of ideas. They discussed projects of social reform, such as opening maternity wards and opening the first preschool school (in Buea, in September 1964) at these meetings. Many of the plans they discussed in CWI meetings came to fruition. They created leadership training courses for local women's social clubs and provided scholarships to women to study in the UK with financial backing from the West Cameroon government.[45] They also fostered international links, by, for example, associating with the National Federation of Women's Institutes in London and securing formal affiliation with the Associated Country Women of the World, an international organization emphasizing membership for both rural and urban women, headquartered in London, and in 1963, with the International Council of Women, founded by American social reformers and women's rights activists Susan B. Anthony and Elizabeth Cady Stanton, in 1888.[46]

The WCNU had its roots in East Cameroon, but it had branches in the West and East Cameroon States after 1966 and became increasingly important in West Cameroon over the course of the late 1960s. Like the CWI, it secured association with the International Council of Women.[47] It was created as the NCCW in 1960 with the explicit purpose of increasing the political and economic participation of Francophone Cameroonian women. The NCCW was originally an independent, apolitical organization; Ahidjo co-opted the organization and it became an appendage of his CNU party in 1965 and was renamed the WCNU.[48] Thus, it had much the same relationship to the CNU as the CWI did to the KNDP. The KNDP and CNU financially supported these organizations. Both the CWI and the WCNU groups were multiethnic in composition and membership, with educated women with moderate or high socioeconomic positions taking most leadership roles.[49] Both organizations' official mission was social and educational. It is also evident that the cultural emphasis on women's commitments to family was a central part of their activities.[50] Though the exact membership numbers are hard to ascertain, both organizations had branches established in most urban towns in the West Cameroon State. While leaders and members of women's organizations in West and East Cameroon rarely collaborated, as Melinda Adams shows in her work on Cameroonian women's organizations, they did communicate and attend one another's conferences.[51]

The mandate to be apolitical manifested in such circumstances as the CWI's constitution requiring all affiliated clubs to be nonpolitical. This was necessary because an overtly political women's association would threaten the male-led state and because President Ahidjo, like his counterparts in the Democratic Republic of the Congo, Ghana, and Tanzania, considered all opposition parties to be illegal from the start or early on in their rule. The CWI existed for a period under this logic, but Ahidjo required it to merge with the WCNU in the late 1960s under the same logic he used to support the one-party state in 1966—consolidating political power would bring about political and social unity in the Federal Republic. While there was debate in the KNDP and the CPNC on how to preserve Anglophone political power within the hegemonic francophone republic, the apolitical nature of the women's organizations safeguarded them from political rivalries among opposing Anglophone parties, a point stressed by John Foncha in a speech given to Mamfe women in 1965. In this speech he urged KNDP members to form smaller social clubs and eschew conversations on politics, cautioning women "not to be dragged by some men folk or some selfish women into unnecessary political quarrels which only help to retard the progress of the country. Some of these political movements are quite subversive as they tend to raise the people against the government's plans."[52] Determined to not incite "unnecessary political quarrels," the apolitical status of women's organizations encouraged their leaders to focus on the rhetoric of ethnic, social, and, seemingly incongruously, political unity.

Focusing on women's collective unity likewise offered strength in numbers and thus a degree of autonomy for women's organizations in male-dominated political sites. With respect to the Ugandan context, Aili Mari Tripp asserts that women's associations must strive to safeguard their autonomy in the landscape of neopatrimonial politics, "which has sought to restrict women's mobilization to nonpolitical concerns." Tripp contends that neopatrimonial politics, which include clientelistic practices combined with patronage politics—in other words, the transfer of goods or jobs in return for political support and loyalty—hinder the autonomy of women's organizations. As Tripp argues, "To mount pressure on the state, Ugandan women's organizations have worked to include a broad cross-section of women irrespective of their ethnic, clan, religious and other backgrounds. They have found that they need the breadth to build their movement."[53] This statement is applicable to women's organizations in West Cameroon, where, comparable to their Ugandan counterparts, women strove to preserve a degree of autonomy by harnessing the power of numbers and proclaiming their political neutrality when trying to draw in members. Thus, Anglophone women strove to fuse a unified Anglophone national identity by urging their counterparts to forget ethnic affiliations and foster collective identities through women's organizations.

Ruff Wanzie's statements about Anna Foncha in an October 1964 *Cameroon Times* column affirms that leaders of women's organizations emphasized their apolitical status as a way to avoid male interference and preserve autonomy. In October 1964 she wrote that male politicians who suggested that Anna Foncha's tour of West Cameroon was political "must not interfere with women's affairs or encourage political discriminations among them." She clarifies:

> Madam Foncha is not a politician. There are women's clubs, societies, and councils in this country. There is also a council known as the West Cameroon Council of Women's Institutes. In this council there are women KNDP and CPNC members. . . . It is in this council that Madam Foncha was elected President General of Women's Groups. As President General of all women's clubs, it is her duty to take interest in all women's affairs. That is why she tours all over West Cameroon. . . . Some politicians' suggestions that Mrs. Foncha's tour is political are not true.[54]

In subsequent columns, Wanzie, as well as fellow journalist Clara Manga, frequently assured their female readers that women's organizations only advanced members' status socially and that they had no political side. Indeed, in February 1965, Foncha convened a meeting with executives of three KNDP's women's wings in Buea, Muyuka, and Tiko and urged them to accept freely any of their friends who wished to join, even if they had once supported the opposition party, the CPNC. Urging the women "to identify themselves as people belonging to the same group," she strove to eschew political divisions among women and foster unity.[55]

Efforts to avoid male interference did not fully work; male state officials sometimes attended the meetings of women's organizations. For example, R. N. Namme, the parliamentary secretary to the Ministry of Primary Education and Social Welfare in the West Cameroon Legislative Assembly, attended a November 1965 meeting of the Victoria Divisional Executive of the CWI and urged members to solve their marital problems according to "the African's point of view," meaning by deferring to their husbands and avoiding conflicts with their husbands.[56] At the September 30, 1967, meeting of the WCNU chapter in Bamenda, Benedict Nchine Mukong, a state official in the new CNU-ruled government, warned members that their organization was "not a political organ." Rather, he claimed, it was a means to care for women's social welfare. He suggested that women with political ambitions should seek office at the CNU branch level because that is where "politics . . . could be practised."[57] But few women made it to the CNU branch where they might engage in "real" political activities.

The attendance of men like Namme and Mukong at the meetings of women's organizations did at least give the appearance that the government of which they were a part of took women's concerns seriously.[58] It also allowed them to ensure that these organizations were not becoming political in the sense of discussing legislation or organizing political protests. At the same time, in the eyes of the West Cameroon government and the leaders of the women's organizations, the presence of male politicians at the meetings of women's organizations legitimized these organizations and their nation-building projects.[59] Subsequently, the organizations secured financial support from the state, a key advantage of maintaining affiliation with the KNDP, and later, the CNU government.

Without openly disagreeing with the understanding that women's clubs were nonpolitical, leaders and members of the WSCA/CWI and the WCNU argued that joining the organizations would grant them social authority and allow them to contribute to the development of the nation.[60] The fact that politically elite women such as Foncha, Burnley, and Gladys Tombise Difo, the women's special representative in the West Cameroon Legislative Assembly, played key roles in encouraging women to join these ventures suggests their political intent. In 1964, Foncha was particularly active in urging women to participate in women's organizations, which she tied to nationalist endeavors specifically.[61] Her fall 1964 speaking schedule alone, for example, includes speeches in Modeka and Missellele, both villages in the modern-day Southwest Region; in Kumba; and in her hometown of Bamenda, urging women to join the WSCA.[62] In mid-October in Modeka, she emphasized that the West Cameroon government financially supported various WSCA projects, thus indicating the state's approval of its sociopolitical activities. In early November in Kumba, Foncha urged women to "wake up from their slumber" and "fight for nation-building" by developing local branches of the WSCA. In late November in Bamenda, she explained that the CWI, by this point no longer referencing the WSCA, "aimed at getting women together in order to be better able to help themselves."[63] She cited the rapid increase in women's access to education as assurance that the government recognized the significant roles they played in society. Contending "that the hand that rocks the cradle ruled the world," Foncha concluded that women must form social clubs because the welfare of Cameroon depended on them. It is mothers, Foncha implies, who "mother" the nation, literally and symbolically.

Anna Foncha's 1964 mobilization efforts went beyond giving speeches. She participated in varied "native" dances with women during events with other female political elites. The general importance of knowing West Cameroonian local dances was expressed by a guest writer of Wanzie's column

Anna Foncha surrounded by women dancing a local West Cameroon dance. 1960s. Image courtesy of National Archives of Cameroon in Buea.

in February 1964. The writer lamented that women "for one reason or the other, find it something degrading to dance our traditional dances, today. . . . If Europeans take delight in dancing their own music, I see no reason why we should not feel proud of dancing our own native dances."[64] By dancing with women in local dances, Anna Foncha displayed her commitment to preserving cultural values. Journalist Ruff Wanzie included a photo of Foncha dancing the "Njang," a Bamenda dance, with prominent female political elites at a women's party in Buea in an early August 1964 entry in her women's column. "It is a pride to know one's own native dances," captions the photo. A couple of months later another photo that ran with Wanzie's column showed Foncha surrounded by women dancing the "Banso" dance during her visit to Ekona, a town located slightly north of Buea.[65] By dancing "native" dances with women in diverse towns in West Cameroon, Foncha and her supporters fostered aspects of affective nationalism as defined by Elisabeth Militz and Carolin Schurr. Militz and Schurr reference celebrated contemporary Azerbaijani dances as one way

> the nation also takes shape through bodily encounters and joyful as well as painful affections. In what we call "affective nationalism", the nation emerges in moments of encounter between different bodies and objects through embodying, sharing, enjoying or disliking what feels national. . . . [Such local dances] has the potential to affect, to unify differently marked bodies, and thus to create something new, such as a feeling of national belonging.[66]

By dancing together, Foncha and her supporters fostered a sense of national belonging. At the same time, many of the dances came from Foncha's home region of the Bamenda Grassfields, including the Banso, or Nso, dance and the Njang. In this way the dancers bridged ethnic differences to forge an affective sentiment of national unity in supporting Anna Foncha and in supporting one another.

Beyond dancing together, the creation of Women's Day was another way that leaders of women's organizations mobilized women during the 1960s. CWI leaders developed Women's Day during a CWI meeting in November 1964 when members agreed that a special day, March 31, should be set aside each year to focus on women's importance in West Cameroon. During the meeting, members outlined the four essential purposes of the day: to celebrate the founding of the CWI, to reaffirm the unity and similarity that existed among all women, to advance the dignity of women, and finally, to demonstrate "that given the opportunity, women can contribute in a big way to the economic, social and political advancement" of the country.[67] Following the November meeting, Gwendolyn Burnley, secretary of the CWI, shared details of activities that would take place on Women's Day in the *West Cameroon Press Release*, the official press release of the West Cameroon government. "On that day," Burnley divulged, "all women's activities will be given prominence. The activities will comprise of display of women's work, radio talks, rallies, native dances and others which will be held throughout the [West Cameroon] State."[68] She further shared that "prominent women in the society" would give speeches during rallies throughout the day. Women's Day rallies subsequently took place in all parts of West Cameroon, with thousands of attendees assembling together in all the divisions and subdistricts to, in the words of Ruff Wanzie of the *Cameroon Times* on March 12, 1966, "rededicate themselves to the course of humanity and to help their less fortunate colleagues to keep abreast with the changing times."[69]

On March 31, 1965, Foncha addressed a crowd of thousands of resplendently attired West Cameroonian women and men to launch the first annual

Women's Day celebration, which the CWI had convened. Foncha addressed the crowd in the Buea government stadium: "We inaugurate today Women's Day in West Cameroon . . . in the presence of all women of this division and representatives from all the divisions of West Cameroon. . . . A day like this makes *all* Cameroonian women one," she told them. Her audience is clear: "all the March Thirty Firsts to come, Cameroonian women will be looked upon to speak of, and find themselves as the women of one single country. . . . here I am talking to women of West Cameroon." She continues: "It is the dearest hope of all our hearts that we make true the saying that 'united we stand, divided we fall'. . . . We are here being asked to acknowledge our identity not by what tribe we come from, but as of West Cameroon by birth or adoption." Foncha's speech concluded:

> Get to work in your clubs and see how we can bring to the notice of the world the activities of women in Cameroon. . . . Borrowing the words of the late [US] President Kennedy I will say to you country women to ask not what the Council of Women's Institutes or the country can do for you, but what you can do to make this institution and country a brilliant success.[70]

Women, she suggested, were responsible for their own social and political improvement. They must "fight" to prove to themselves and to men that they have the right to help lead the nation. Uniting and imagining themselves as being connected by birth to West Cameroon, not to potentially divisive ethnic groups, was crucial.

KNDP male politicians and other political wives likewise used Women's Day rallies and celebrations as a forum for emphasizing women's importance to the state and reaffirming their political support. L. M. Ndamukong, secretary of state for education and social welfare, observed during the first Women's Day that the "rally is a striking demonstration of the solidarity of women. . . . Women have a great part to play in the progress of the nation, and their clubs are the means whereby they can meet and express their views and ideas."[71] Natalia Jua, the wife of the second prime minister of the federated state of West Cameroon (Augustine Ngom Jua) and Elizabeth Muna, the wife of the third prime minister (Salomon Tandeng Muna), echoed Anna Foncha's sentiments about women's collective unity during subsequent anniversaries of Women's Day. Jua reminded women about "the great task of nation-building," and that "[a]ll women are by nature, mothers" and that this "disposition makes [women] better. . . . suited to be the builders of [the] state in particular." Addressing a crowd of more than 6,000, Muna urged women to unite "for a better understanding, goodwill and true friendship."[72] Although Women's Day was only celebrated from 1965 to 1968, it allowed female and male members of the political elites to use the long history of women's collective mobilization for social and political reasons. Tweaking the purpose of the mobilization to fit their realities, women borrowed from the long history of women's (maternal) collective mobilization to shape gendered nationalist ideals.

"GET TO WORK IN YOUR CLUBS": WOMEN'S COLUMNS AS "NONPOLITICAL" STAGES

Female journalists used their columns as another forum from which to rally women's political participation. Journalists Ruff Wanzie and Clara Manga frequently gave in-depth summaries of the meetings of women's organizations and clubs that they attended or made short announcements about the location and times of upcoming meetings.[73] Writing as "Auntie Clara" for the *Cameroon Champion*, Clara Manga,[74] for example, wrote in a February 1962 column that she had "talked about the importance of women's clubs and organizations in a community. . . . I am also very happy that some women are rising to the call."[75] She lamented that she knew of "existing women clubs, but [that] they seem to be asleep." But economic stratification and political divisions threatened women's social unity and their ability to be active. She urged women to abandon their political differences, complaining that "the few women's clubs that exist seem to be divided. . . . politics seems to have spoilt everything." She called on educated women who had traveled abroad to teach their less schooled counterparts about how to behave, asserting, "We are supposed to be civilized. Most of our women have been abroad, why can't we be broad minded and put politics aside when it comes to social life[?]"[76] She urged educated women to remember their leadership duties in women's organizations, but reminded them to include less-schooled women and those of lower socioeconomic positions.

Balancing, in some respects, the suggestion that in seeking "liberation" African women broke with their past, journalists invoked a long African tradition of female power. In an October 1966 column Ruff Wanzie invoked her role as what I term a "print griot," using print media to exercise the key roles of traditional griots as professional storytellers who "narrate history, and

A women's organization meeting, ca. late 1960s–1970s. Image courtesy of National Archives of Cameroon in Buea.

serve as spokespersons," recalling that in the past "women who were given chieftaincy honors as queens, [with the names] '*Manfor*,' '*Yar*,' '*Nafoin*,' '*Viyu*,' participated in the political affairs of traditional governments at the time," suggesting that female power is a longstanding African tradition.[77] In September 1964, Wanzie inserted a photo of White House Secretary Geraldine Whittington, a black American women, shaking hands with President Lyndon Johnson with the comment in the caption: "On the White House secretarial staff since 1961 she is the first negro to be named a private secretary to a President of [the] United States."[78] Wanzie carried on in this way, including records in the form of newspaper clippings and photos of what she considered to be achievements by women in the fields of politics, sports, and higher education in both Europe and the United States. This copy-and-paste method is not new in the postcolonial period. As Derek Peterson and Emma Hunter contend about the colonial period, African newspapers were not "always framed within the geographic space of the nation. . . . newspapers were composed of materials that were authored elsewhere and subsequently clipped, translated, and reprinted."[79] Such methods only added to West Cameroonian women journalists' efforts to shape political identity and nation-building by offering visual representations of foreign women's efforts to advance politically. They used this approach while claiming to be penning "nonpolitical" content in their columns. But like the commentary of black men who wrote for *Bantu World*—"the first newspaper targeting black South Africans"—Wanzie's inserted photo of Whittington also suggested transatlantic connections between people of African descent throughout the world. She (visually) connects black (African) women's endeavors to make political advances, fostering female camaraderie and support across the Atlantic. It is quite possible that the photo was added to nurture the belief that Cameroonian women had the same capacity, like black American women, to persistently fight for their own social and political rights.

It is anachronistic to call West Cameroon's female journalists feminists, although they highlighted women's social, economic, and political marginalization. Wanzie, for instance, underscored women's marginalization in various professional fields in her October 1966 column. She lamented the little presence of women in "the press and radio" as well as a lack of female "pathologists, dietitians, lawyers, librarians, accountants, architects, [and] taxi drivers," saying that equality in these arenas would "contribute to the total advancement of the Cameroon nation." She urged educated housewives to join women's organizations in service to this end, saying that their Western counterparts did. She bemoaned men who "forbid their wives from attending club meetings" and called on educated women to "set an example and [offer] encouragement" likely to shift such dynamics.[80] Clara Manga also urged women to "fight" for their rights and attend the meetings of women's organizations regardless of male opposition at home in her February 1962 column.[81] These deviations from Cameroonian societal beliefs that women should submit to male authority at home held women responsible for their social, economic, and political progress. These women leaders saw participation in women's organizations and "fighting" for social and political equality as a way to be taken seriously.

At the same time, Manga cautioned women that they must not threaten male authority in domestic spaces if they want to improve their social and political status and, in some cases, avoid divorce. Like Wanzie, Manga summons her role as a "print griot" to give lessons about suitable marital relations by sharing a hypothetical conversation between a husband and wife:

> A woman once asked her husband, "Darling how much of your political life would you want me to share?" "Well" said the husband "[I]t all depends.

> Much as I'd like you to share every part of my life, I would not like you to take any active part in politics, though you have to know a little of what goes on in the political world so that you are not left out of [the] discussion. I would rather wish you remained your sweet smiling self, join one or two women's club[s]. . . . I do not say it is wrong for women to be in politics . . . but I'd rather [my wife], you stayed out it. . . . Men want to relax after the heated debates in the House.

Similar to griots who draw from anecdotes and folkloric tales to illustrate larger lessons, Manga draws from the above anecdote to conclude about women's political activities: "Wives of the party in government or opposition must forget their husbands differences and write [*sic*] to make life light for their husbands in the evenings. It is very foolish and immature for women to allow the social life of a country to flop because of political differences."[82] She implores women to instead focus their energy on forming clubs and thus "catch up with other women in other lands": "Form clubs not only for senior service women but clubs to include all the ranks. . . . In doing this you will be doing a lot to help the ordinary woman and their husbands and the entire community will appreciate the usefulness of your learning." She posited this as a way to show the value of educating women. Manga's language here is careful: women simply "helped" men in their nation-building endeavors and did not meddle with "real" political affairs, which were only for men. Educated women needed to "fight" for their rights without threatening male authority, working with men and emphasizing women's and men's complementary roles in national development. Accordingly, women such as Anna Foncha often termed their speech tours as "family visit[s]."[83] By such means, elite women might garner sociopolitical authority without threatening male political authority—or other women who espoused patriarchy.

Journalists such as Wanzie and Manga lauded the accomplishments of male-led political parties to emphasize the nonthreatening nature of women's political activities and to openly defer to the prevalent idea that men should own the political sphere. In a December 1964 article, "Women Can Now Be Proud," Wanzie applauds the KNDP for recognizing women's nationalist activities and efforts to "fight" to be recognized as leaders of the nation by improving their social and political status. She begins by detailing the high-society dance of the year, then provides a short, exultant blurb announcing that the KNDP government has proven that "women have equal rights, amenities and facilities as the men" by unanimously voting for a woman to be the woman secretary in the Central Working Committee of the KNDP-led West Cameroon government. The details of the society dance blunt the subversive nature of Wanzie's announcement. After describing the dance, she shares that the KNDP convention in Kumba "wholeheartedly accepted" "women's suggestions" and thanks the government for giving women a "big honor."[84] Wanzie implies that the government rewards women when they strive to participate in nationalist activities. By proving that they are useful and respectable citizens, they "earn" equality with men.

Journalists such as Ruff Wanzie and Clara Manga at times pushed female politicians' agendas by featuring their guest editorials. In this manner they were like the Mexican female journalists, studied by Cristina Devereaux Ramírez, who shaped Mexican national identity by frequently serving "as philosophers, poets, historians, and mouthpieces for politicians."[85] They frequently devoted their columns to outlining the varied social and political activities of these women, often encouraging their readers to support their endeavors, but careful not to emphasize the political nature of their support.[86] In July 1962, Manga's column featured a lengthy letter from Gwendoline Burnley calling on her readers to "hurry up and register members of the" WSCA. She stresses,

> Sisters, you may disagree with the way things are running but your criticisms outside the Federation will be very ineffective. Come in and effect change for the better. . . . you can only do this as a member. . . . Women in other countries are suddenly ahead in all fields. We must not lag behind. . . . everyone is asking "why are the women so silent?"[87]

The idea that women's associations were the main way for women to be heard is evident here, even from a woman who found more direct means of affecting politics. By calling her readers "sisters," Burnley uses emotional expressivity to call for women's unity and stoke feelings of sisterhood. Wanzie would also guest-feature Gladys Tombise Difo, the women's special representative in the West Cameroon Legislative Assembly, in subsequent columns in 1964. For instance, in a March 1964 column, after expressing happiness that the *Cameroon Times* has reintroduced the women's column, Difo encourages women to vote for KNDP politicians in the upcoming elections: "I wish to take this chance to call on all women of West Cameroon; to vote solidly for the KNDP candidates." She further says, "We now know that it is only the KNDP that can work in conjunction with [Ahidjo's] *Union Camerounaise* for real unity. . . .

Remember that any vote for any another party is a wasted vote because [the] KNDP must win to continue the good work they have started."[88] Lilian Lem Atanga and Alexandre Djimeli show in their work on contemporary Cameroon that female journalists and female politicians continue to join forces to deploy women's political prospects.[89] By appearing in the media, such as in women's columns, female politicians and political activists in 1960s and early 1970s West Cameroon, worked together to "propagate . . . discourse[s] of change and female inclusion in politics and decision making positions."[90] Giving space to women like Burnley and Difo was one way to do that. As the next section will show, female journalists such as Ruff Wanzie and political elites such as Anna Foncha would continue to collaborate when advocating for the West Cameroon national costume.

"WOMEN SHOULD ACCEPT AND USE OUR NATIONAL DRESS": THE WSCA AND NATIONAL CLOTHING

The fashioning of a women's national costume is a prime example of women's associations' efforts to produce collective identities in West Cameroon. The national attire did more than visibly represent women's collective unity. Because dress has long played a central role in many African societies, it naturally became a vehicle to drive representative Anglophone national identity, nationally and internationally. West Cameroon's endeavors to fashion a national costume were part of a larger nationalist trend sweeping Africa in the early postcolonial period as various nations contested, challenged, and forged new national identities.[91] Thus, Cameroon was not the only African country to link clothing to nationalism in the early postcolonial years; individuals in Ghana, Nigeria, and Sudan, for example, appropriated traditional dresses into national costumes during the 1950s and 1960s.[92] In fact, West Cameroon women elites looked to the national costumes of Ghana and Nigeria, as well as to traditional (male) Cameroonian attire, to inform the development of their own national costumes. Within this context, they continually used their acute awareness of sociopolitical conditions in Cameroon and other African countries to shape West Cameroonian nationalism.

Members of the WSCA took the lead in choosing a national garment for West Cameroonian women, announcing the conditions of a competition for the best-designed national costume in the *Cameroon Champion* in August 1962.[93] The competition took place in February 1964 at the Buea Mountain

Hotel, where the showroom "was filled up with good looking women in different African and Western attires." Ruff Wanzie diligently reported the outcome of the competition in her column: "at long last a costume matching the Bamenda's men's dress was selected. . . . it matches the men's attire and is greatly appreciated by some men."[94] The selected women's design, the Bamenda cloth (also known as the Toghu cloth), was a heavy black cloth with bold, colorful embroidery. But the selected costume had no official name at the end of the competition. On August 15, 1964, Wanzie told readers, "In other countries women's costumes have names. In Ghana there is the Kente, the Accra, etc. In Nigeria—the Akwete, Ekotieboh." She asked, "What is the name of the West Cameroon Women's National Costume?" The paper published feedback from readers a week later. A resident of Buea suggested "Bamenda," saying, "After all, 'Accra' is a town in Ghana and 'Tshekiri' is a tribe in Nigeria. Our costume has the Bamenda design and therefore should be called 'Bamenda' because the originators of the design are people of Bamenda."[95] From then on, the new national costume would be called the Bamenda costume.

The traditional nature of the dress superseded concerns about gender boundaries. Bamenda men, especially individuals of royal lineage, originally wore the Bamenda traditional costume during the era of European administrative rule, and John Foncha had frequently worn it at official state events and in news photos during his political career.[96] The Bali ethnic group from northeast Nigeria and the Grassfields of western Cameroon had introduced the Bamenda costume in the Bamenda Grassfields area around the middle of the nineteenth century. Men widely used the costume in Bamenda, Wum, and Nkambe, in parts of Mamfe Division (Widekum and Bangwa) in West Cameroon, as well as Bamiléké regions in East Cameroon. However, women rarely wore the cloth until the WSCA selected it for the national costume. J. A. Kisob commented on this in a 1963 Cameroonian magazine, *Abbia: Revue Culturelle Camerounaise* (Cameroon Cultural Review), praising the choice.[97] The fact that Kisob applauded the WSCA for adopting a traditionally male attire demonstrates how fashioning a national costume might cross various forms of gender boundaries to achieve larger goals of national and cultural unity. Although the fabric for the national costume was originally from Bamenda, the hometown of Anna and John Foncha, it was just one piece in a vast colorful jigsaw puzzle that formed an Anglophone panethnic identity.

While WSCA leaders may have striven to turn the Bamenda (national) costume into one that all genders and ethnicities might embrace, financial disparities among women raised issues of affordability, threatening the template of national unity. Ruff Wanzie argued that the costume was too expen-

WOMEN'S SPECIAL

Our Women Should Accept And Use Our National Costume — Madam Foncha

Before I further comment on the Cameroon Women's National Costume which was criticised and condemned by some women in the women's column of 29th February, 1964, I would like to refer first of all to the different African Costumes.

Ghana has two kinds of costumes; the kente and the over lapping shirt-pleated blouse on wrapper. The kente is for occasions and a set of it costs approximately 15 pds. The Ibo occasional costume, known as George. A set of which costs not less than 12 pds. The Yoruba women's costume which is loom woven, a set costs at times 30 pds. The Sierra-Leone woman's costume costs not less than 15. pds.

Our proposed national costume is even cheaper, judging from the prices of the national costumes of other countries. I still encourage our women to accept and use this costume for occasions.

Girls traveling abroad should be in position of one each so as to make known to people of the world what our own costume looks like. It is not the style of dress which really matters but the type of cloth and designs. You can produce different styles from this same material.

There is a plan of sending samples of this material abroad so that imitations of it could be printed and sent to Cameroon in order that all women regardless of rank can afford for one.

There is a plan of organising and distributing groups of local designers of this material to Mamfe, Kumba and Victoria — East Cameroon so that women in these areas arrange for theirs without having to travel for distances.

We have already decided to select a second national costume for daily use, and the competition for this comes on soon.

I still appeal and encourage our women to use this costume for it is greatly appreciated by the majority of people in this country and abroad.

Protectors Of Culture

Domestic Science

Anna Foncha wearing the West Cameroon women's national costume. From *Cameroon Times* no. 40, vol. 4 (March 14, 1964): 3. Image courtesy of National Archives of Cameroon in Buea.

sive to be a national costume that everyone could afford, pointing out, "A national costume should be a dress which is common at any place and which everybody can afford to buy easily. The Bamenda cloth does not fall within this range. The costume . . . is too costly to be a national costume." Kisob also recognized the cost issue, saying it was surmountable if "[m]odern domestic science teachers" were to "lend a helping hand" by training more young women to make the costume.[98]

Reflecting her authority in the paper of her husband's party, Anna Foncha disagreed with Wanzie in a guest editorial in Wanzie's column in March 1964. She responded to Wanzie's objection by claiming that the national costumes of other West African countries, including Ghana, Nigeria, and Sierra Leone, were more expensive than the new West Cameroonian costume. Nevertheless, she states that the costume would be manufactured abroad so that "all women regardless of rank can afford for one." Regardless of the costs, she "still appeal[ed] and encourage[d]" women to use the costume, saying the costume was "greatly appreciated by the majority of people in [the] country and abroad." She argued that young women who traveled overseas should don the Bamenda costume "so as to make known to people of the world what our own costume looks like."[99] Thus, Foncha beseeched her counterparts to use the costume to represent West Cameroonian national culture internationally.[100] By donning the costume, women not only displayed their unity visually, but specifically advertised their membership in a West Cameroonian women's organization—Anglophone political unity thus resonating globally.[101]

"THE CNU HAS COME TO STAY": THE DISSOLUTION OF THE CWI

The autonomy of West Cameroonian women's organizations ended by the late 1960s. President Ahidjo dissolved the multiparty system in Cameroon in 1966, two years after the WSCA created the Anglophone national costume. He established the CNU on September 1, 1966, through a merger of his own party, the Union Camerounaise (UC), with the KNDP and two other smaller political parties.[102] The WCNU became CNU's ancillary organ at this time. The CWI persisted for a full year after the merger of the parties, but by 1967, there were political tensions between the CWI and WCNU. The president of the WCNU subsection in Buea declared that a single-party state was important at a celebration of the CNU's first anniversary in September 1967.[103] She described a multiparty system as a barrier to national progress. In October, the Bamenda WCNU passed a resolution calling for a merger with the CWI, and in November the regional president of the Victoria WCNU, made a radio announcement threatening women who joined any political organization other than the CNU with political retribution.[104]

The WCNU's rhetoric of women's political importance, however, was continuous with that of the CWI. Ahidjo's wife, Germaine Ahidjo, who became the symbolic mother of both federal states in 1966, similarly espoused the rhetoric that by joining the WCNU, women might obtain social advancement. West Cameroonian newspapers began publishing translated speeches she made from East Cameroon, such as a 1968 speech that appeared in the *Cameroon Times* calling on all women "to unite and get all hands on deck for the emancipation of the Cameroon women and for national construction."[105] The speech stated that the popular perception that a woman's only place was in the kitchen was now obsolete. Germaine Ahidjo pressed readers to join forces with their "men folk in the task of nation building" by being "united under the banner of [Ahidjo's] Cameroon National Union."

Anna Foncha tried to protect CWI from the hegemonic machinations of the agents of the Francophone government by emphasizing the apolitical status of the organization. She issued a statement in early November 1967 from Yaoundé, the capital of East Cameroon, explaining, as the *Cameroon Times* reported, that "the CWI is purely an economic and social organization." Her statement was reported thus:

> [T]he CWI is the common meeting ground of many clubs composed of women from all quarters of the towns and villages who want to practice one particular handicraft, etc. for the benefit of advancing their personal incomes and the improvement of the women folk. While doing this they are at the same time fulfilling the government's call for national reconstruction.[106]

The implication was that the CWI was no threat to political unity and that women who occupied their time with economic activities improved Cameroon's economic development. She explained that the organization did not allow political discussions during meetings and that CWI membership was compatible with loyalty to the CNU. But she emphasized that CWI members have a duty to preserve allegiance to the CNU: "[A member's] duty is to report and to discontinue their membership of the CWI at any moment they find that the CWI is influenced by or subject to the authority of another political party or is working against our Party [CNU].[107] Clearly, Foncha recognized that to permit political conversation in the CWI would lead to its demise. Her location in Yaoundé instead of Buea seemingly reflected her acceptance of the end of the KNDP and deference to Ahidjo and his CNU-dominated government. In much the same way that she would later defend her husband's political actions in a statement in 2014 to the Francophone paper the *Cameroun Tribune* (see my conclusion in this vol.), Foncha's physical presence in Yaoundé demonstrated who was really in power and illustrates how Anglophone female political elites navigated public space, figuratively and literally, to negotiate their political autonomy and identity. In 1967, from the East Cameroonian capital of Yaoundé, Foncha pressed women to be loyal to the new CNU, even cautioning them to avoid women who might be loyal to other political parties such as her husband's now defunct KNDP.

Foncha had no need to speak in favor of the CWA, where she remained active. As a religious organization with strong international presence and support, it was not seen as a threat, and Francophone Cameroonian women joined it. Yet outlawing Anglophone Cameroonian political parties made CWA, and Anna Foncha's role in it, all the more significant. CWA thrived after 1966, crossing linguistic and geographic boundaries and working alongside Francophone women by using religion as a connecting force, underscoring religious devotion and activities as a point of unity. Moreover, like many women's organizations in both Anglophone and Francophone regions of Cameroon, CWA members leaned on their international affiliations to survive post-1966, including establishing branches in the UK and in the United States, including in Georgia, Maryland, Minnesota, Texas, and Virginia. As Melinda Adams argues, transnational connections better ensured the survival of domestic organizations during the time of federalism because the "state found it far more difficult to eliminate groups that had transnational linkages," thus allowing women's group to "challenge more effectively the government's constraints on their activities." While the hegemonic Francophone government ultimately collapsed the CWI into the WCNU, the CWA had, in the words of Adams, "staying power" and still exists today.[108]

But the CWI had no such protection. Though WCNU members in Kumba thanked Foncha for the statements she made in early November 1967 from Yaoundé, they continued to suggest that the two organizations could not coexist.[109] For instance, the regional president of WCNU Kumba argued in mid-November that it would be financially and socially impossible for women to meet their church, family, CNU, and financial obligations while maintaining CWI membership.[110] Gladys Tombise Difo attempted to diffuse tensions between CWI and WCNU members while addressing a crowd of women at the Victoria community field on November 13. She explained that the CNU was "a new hegemony for all the defunct political parties." She stressed that the WCNU was "a social and nonpolitical organization for women who remain[ed] loyal to the CNU at the cell branches [or] subsection" levels. As Anna Foncha had, Difo warned women against discussing political issues during meetings. Rather, they should focus on their achievements and their country's welfare and "aim higher until they attain international reputation in their activities." She assured women that the new CNU-backed government would reward them with scholarships for secondary and university education. Though Difo implied that the CNU was the dominant political power throughout Cameroon, she sought to ease ongoing tensions by declaring in the same speech that the CWI was also a social organization with the right to operate like the WCNU.[111] It was never technically illegal to be a member of the CWI post 1966, but concerns about political retribution effectively destroyed the organization by the late 1960s, as Ahidjo had decreed that the WCNU should absorb all women's organizations in both Anglophone and Francophone regions of Cameroon.

THE ROAD TO A UNITED REPUBLIC: POLITICAL PARTICIPATION AND IDEAL WOMANHOOD AFTER 1966

The circumstances that led to the events of 1966 make better sense when viewed from the perspective of a family model for the organization of the state. For instance, "political fatherhood" within the African context can demonstrate the theme of impotence or virility as an embodiment of the African leader's sociopolitical condition.[112] Michael Schatzberg argues that political legitimacy in many parts of Africa "rests on the tacit normative idea that government stands in the same relationship to its citizens that a father does to his children." Thus, the president is regarded as the father figure of the entire nation, which comprises all the citizens of the nation; all are brothers and sisters involved in the process of national development.[113] In other words, Ahidjo became the firm, strong "father of the nation" when he dissolved the federal structure and launched a unitary state.[114] Thus, from his perspective, Cameroon was no longer a country of two distinct "nations." Instead, it was one nation in which citizens were part of one political party that united them, a point that he repeatedly made in the late 1960s.[115]

Ahidjo's actions illustrate a symbolic age hierarchy, in which West Cameroonian male politicians were infantilized by their Francophone "brothers," who stripped them of their political power, becoming the patriarch while the Anglophone "siblings" had to submit, as "children," as "sons." As Schatzberg's work demonstrates, if African presidents are framed as "the 'fathers' of their respective national 'family,'" then political opposition or political disunity is portrayed as "petty sibling rivalries of those lacking in maturity." Consequently, the "'father' must occasionally 'discipline' naughty and immature children for their own good." Ultimately, as Schatzberg contends, "[t]he political consequences of framing the political discussion in this manner are important as the metaphors contribute to an implicit 'infantilization' of the population." Ahidjo's symbolic paternalism was reflected beyond policy and administrative changes.[116] Achille Mbembe argues that paternal images of Ahidjo were reflected verbally and visually: "It was during Ahidjo's presidency that the practice began of placing portraits of the head of state in public places. . . . the largest stadium in the capital and certain main boulevards and public spaces were named after him while he was alive." He explained that the respect Ahidjo garnered in political circles simply enhanced the cult of personality which led to titles such as "Father of the Nation, Great Comrade, Apostle of Peace, Providential Guide, Indefatigable Builder of the Nation, The Man of February 1958, The Great Sportsman, Far-Sighted Guide, The Great Helmsman."[117] Salomon Muna, the third and last West Cameroon prime minister, between 1968 and 1972, invoked the image and language of Ahidjo as father of the Cameroon nation. Addressing the West Cameroon Legislative Assembly in late June 1969, he implored parliamentarians to build a "a real Fatherland and a new civilization" by uniting behind the CNU, remarking that the CNU "aspire[d] to build and create a national community which is conscious of its solidarity and collective destiny."[118] By using paternal language to describe the CNU party—and the party's potential to unify all Cameroonians— he posits Ahidjo as the "father" of the Cameroonian nation, the patriarchal figure of a large national family to which all Cameroonians belonged, regardless of ethic, linguistic, and geographical boundaries.

But after 1966, female political elites found new ways to preserve women's social and political power by taking a more accommodating path. Female journalists refocused on women's domestic roles, love, and emotional problems in their columns. Those who had used their own names, such as Wanzie, retreated behind pen names to avoid persecution or losing their jobs as civil servants.[119] Wanzie started writing as "Cousin Lizzy" after 1966. Just as many Anglophone men found roles in the Francophone-dominated CNU state, many leaders of the CWI continued to try to drive advances in women's lives. Anna Foncha and other Anglophones worked with Francophone women in the WCNU to develop initiatives, seminars, informational pamphlets, and other reform projects to push for women's social, economic, and political advances throughout the country.[120] Pragmatically speaking, the CNU gave women's organizations economic support just as the KNDP had, presenting itself as a progressive government in charge of a socially advancing country.

For instance, the WCNU obtained dedicated buildings, such as "Women's Houses," that it could use to organize and provide services such as domestic science classes, thereby increasing women's access to some form of formal education throughout the country.[121] Gladys Endeley's only daughter and the youngest of her six children shared with me during an interview that under the WCNU, her mother helped at a home economic center where pregnant young women could pursue continued education; their schooling included learning how to type, sew, cooking, nutrition, and childcare.[122]

Perhaps many Anglophone women ultimately joined the Francophone-dominated WCNU after 1966 because many members shared similar notions of womanhood. Surveys, interviews, and reports from women's-only seminar training sessions carried out in urban Francophone Cameroon in the 1970s suggest that French-speaking women held similar views about family structure, formal education, and marital relations as their Anglophone counterparts, one in which women should be progressive but adhere to traditional gender norms within domestic spaces; radio transcripts seemingly from around the same period buttress this assertion.[123] A 1982 WCNU book, *Integration of the Cameroonian Woman into the Economic Development Process*, includes interviews with various Anglophone and Francophone women in the professional workforce, such as civil servants, lawyers, doctors, pharmacists, and managers of companies, who express almost identical ideas about suitable gender norms and roles. For instance, while all the women highlight their academic and professional accomplishments, they stress that a woman should emphasize motherhood, wifehood, and domestic duties. Geneviève Fouda, a manager at Saint Marthe clinic in Yaoundé, asserts that despite all of her academic and professional accomplishments, she "remains firmly attached to the traditional notion of the family. In this way, she becomes flattered and comforted once she hears people talk of her as being: the daughter of . . . , the friend of . . . , the fiancée of . . . , the mother of . . ."[124] Undeniably, Fouda's emphasis on simultaneously progressive and conservative ideals of womanhood is indistinguishable from that of her Anglophone formally educated counterparts. Responses such as Fouda's illuminates how ideas about gender norms are more similar than dissimilar throughout Cameroon, crossing the Anglo-Franco border, then and probably still today.

Moreover, just like past leaders of the CWI, women in WCNU branches in Anglophone regions continued to espouse an ideal womanhood that was both traditional and progressive.[125] For example, the WCNU branch in Victoria (Limbe) held a two-day conference of the WCNU in 1970 based on the theme of "the ideal Cameroon womanhood." Prudencia Chilla, the second female parliamentarian in the West Cameroon Legislative Assembly, was present at the conference. "[T]rue Cameroonian womanhood," she told the attendees, "must take its roots in the traditional background of the country," contending that "women should carefully blend this background with the new needs and opportunities, which are being occasioned by inevitable changes." Chilla maintains that "true Cameroonian womanhood should reflect a God-fearing nature, God's plan for the marriage of man and woman," which would allow women to overcome challenges, participate in making Cameroon great, and establish the stable homes and healthy families that form the cornerstone of any great nation.[126] Chilla's envisioning of this ideal womanhood reflects a continual pattern of associating perspectives of suitable hybrid womanhood with nationalist duties throughout Cameroon regardless of different cultural backgrounds.

Chilla's autobiographical novel, *Promise*, published in 1969 by a Nigerian press under a pen name, further illuminates the hybrid notions of womanhood Chilla herself embraced as she was coming of age in Bamenda under British rule during the 1930s and 1940s. Through the eyes of the protagonist Asheri, readers see how Chilla grapples with issues of Christianity, patriarchy, and adherence to gender norms such as marriage, forming her own vision of a distinct hybrid womanhood as she matured and obtained a formal education, eventually traveling to Nigeria to earn a teaching degree.[127] As Joyce Ashuntantang concludes about the protagonist, "Asheri confronts the marginal position inhabited by women in her community who are already forced to endure the margins as colonized entities. Her search for self-determination becomes a search for an autonomous identity and voice; an identity and voice heavily suppressed by the triple bind of Christianity, colonialism and patriarchy." Ashuntantang powerfully concludes about the work, "[v]iewed within the frame work of postcolonial feminist discourse, *Promise* takes its place as one of the early pieces of literary resistance to female oppression by an African woman."[128] Yet despite the feminist undertones in *Promise*, Chilla never openly identifies as a feminist—perhaps reflecting the suspicion of feminism that was common in Africa then and today—choosing to publish under a penname. Instead, she advocates a slightly less progressive notion of womanhood in her public role as a politician. Lilian Lem Atanga writes that Cameroonian female parliamentarians must negotiate "different identities in a society that constructs them both as traditional women with expectations to fulfill their traditional gender roles, and modern women who should perform their roles as educated female parliamentarians within a modern Cameroonian context."[129] While Atanga's conclusions refer to modern-day female parliamentarians in Cameroon, I temporally extend her conclusion to the political activities of 1960s and early 1970s female politicians in the West Cameroon State. The feminist undertones in Chilla's work as compared to her public political stance illuminates how African women political elites occupy a space of great ambiguity and contradiction as they must straddle conflicting societal expectations of their behavior and identity.

The space of ambiguity female political elites such as Chilla faced occurred in a time period when few women, and likewise few men, were formally elected to office after 1966. Ahidjo co-opted women's advancement, in a sense; he appointed some women he considered loyal. This included Delphine Tsanga, who he co-opted into his political party in East Cameroon in 1964 and Gwendoline Burnley into the West Cameroon Legislative Assembly in 1968, where she served until 1972.[130] Delphine Tsanga's novel, *Vies de Femmes*, which she published under her own name, like Chilla's work, reflects the varied struggles women confront and the diverse ways in which they claim agency in Cameroonian society. Although Tsanga never openly identifies as feminist, much like Chilla, Juliana Makuchi Nfah-Abbenyi observes that "[o]ne of the main issues that I see in this novel concerns women's bodies, women's sexuality, and the way sexuality is related to polygamy and exploited by economically well-off men. . . . Although many of the stories about the lives of these women sound familiar, each woman seems to live out her sexuality on her own terms." Nfah-Abbenyi concludes that Tsanga's "fictional analyses of sex, marriage, and patriarchy will be read as an open protest against discriminatory practices towards women and their sexuality."[131] While Tsanga's novel was published well after Chilla's work, Tsanga, like Chilla, occupied political positions in women's auxiliary wings of the Francophone Cameroonian government that emphasized "women's affairs." Tsanga found a literary space in which to explore and voice Cameroonian women's struggles as well as agency and empowerment, thus illustrating how Cameroonian female political elites, regardless of their Anglophone or Francophone backgrounds, found avenues to continually voice women's gender struggles and gender equality tinged with feminist undertones post-1966.

Women's decisions to support Ahidjo's CNU party even allowed them to further their careers in the still-intact West Cameroon government in the late 1960s and after 1972, in the United Republic. Additional women that Ahidjo appointed that he considered loyal included Prudencia Chilla and Gwendoline Burnley, who had helped found the CWI.[132] Women like Chilla and Burnley continued to access political power in Ahidjo's single-party state, where anyone seriously aspiring to attain a significant level of prominence in the country had to join the CNU.[133] Chilla obtained a position as federal deputy in Ahidjo's CNU government and in October 1970 she "urged women-folk to sink their differences and work in line with the ideology of the CNU Party" at a CNU conference in Kumbo. She asserted that "separatism and divergent groups could only lead to the weakening of women's position." "Those who worked against a united front," she maintained, "were not doing women a service." Burnley used her political experiences in the West Cameroon State and in the CNU party to become a member of the first National Assembly of the United Republic of Cameroon in 1973. Her designation as a parliamentarian created the route to her being appointed to the Second Committee of the World Conference of the International Women's Year held in Mexico in summer 1975, and later that year, to an assigned position in the Cameroon delegation to the United Nations General Assembly.[134] It is very possible that women like Burnley and Chilla, like their CWI counterparts, genuinely believed that a single-party state, and a unified women's organization, would provide the political tranquility Cameroon needed, as well as financial support for their activities. Indeed, larger numbers could produce greater social, political, and economic improvements; most of the women who were active in politics between 1966 and 1972 were in the WCNU.

Ahidjo also continued to increasingly appoint women to government positions throughout the 1970s. In 1963, four women occupied cabinet positions in the federated state of West Cameroon (nine in the larger East Cameroon), and a decade later, in 1972, the number increased to seven in English-speaking regions (twenty-one in French-speaking Cameroon).[135] In 1975, Ahidjo supported the United Nations' proclamation of the International Women's Year and sent female delegates to the world conference in Mexico City, where over 125 nations adopted recommendations that women participate equally in all parts of society.[136] In addition, Ahidjo ratified the 1979 United Nations Convention on the Elimination of all Forms of Discrimination against Women.[137] In doing so, he could claim to be supporting women's emancipation and the social progressiveness of the United Republic, in much the same way that the West Cameroon State had looked to women as markers of societal progression. In using this approach, Ahidjo's United Republic practiced many of the same strategies as his male counterparts throughout Africa. Idi Amin in Uganda, for instance, "tap[ped] into global discourses about women's liberation" in the 1970s, by promoting women to high-level positions in his government in response to the International Women's Year in 1975. Through such actions, Amin, like Ahidjo, attempted to "demonstrate that he was a progressive—not repressive—political leader." Alicia Decker contends that in Amin's Uganda, "[th]e rhetoric of women's empowerment was also useful because it gave representatives of the state a platform upon which to discuss women's citizenship duties," a similar strategy that applied to Ahidjo's Cameroonian state.[138] During a speech in celebration for the 1975 International Women's Year, Ahidjo strove to convince women of their social and political importance to the nation. In the speech, he encouraged women to take a positive approach and to acknowledge their duties as mothers, wives, and citizens, and also to work harmoniously with their male partners to achieve national development.[139] The president connected suitable Cameroonian womanhood to citizen duties; he made it clear that women might stoke national progress by subscribing to dominant gender roles and conduct. Like his Ugandan counterpart, he used such opportunities to "perform on a global stage" and showcase his progressiveness of Cameroon.[140]

Mabel Smythe, an African American diplomat who served as the US ambassador to Cameroon from May 1977 to February 1980, verified President Ahidjo's appointments of women to government in a 1981 interview for a government-sponsored oral history project on US foreign affairs. She recollected that Ahidjo told her that Cameroon had "a great many able women" and that the government was encouraging women "to take positions of importance." She elaborates on her tenure as the US ambassador to Cameroon: "I had a reception for a group of women who were attending an international conference in Cameroon. And the Cameroonians I invited included the first woman, an MD, to teach at the medical school; a woman magistrate; the senior woman member of Parliament." In 1978, Ahidjo's regime had determined that at least 10 percent of the members of the National Legislature should be women. Smythe pointed out, however, that in Cameroonian society "there were still a good many reservations about full equality for women."[141] Though Smythe's statements describe the period after 1972, they reflect political ambitions that both the Anglophone and Francophone governments harbored during the 1960s and 1970s, to show that Cameroon was advanced.

Women's associations, then, gave women ways to access social and political power. They did this by emphasizing power in numbers and urging women to unite to improve women's social and political status broadly within the nation. Leadership asserted that they were nonpolitical even though they were founded as ancillary organizations of major male-dominated political parties. Nevertheless, they made the case for participation by claiming that women could only gain rights through the organization themselves. The CWI's efforts to fashion the national costume was one project in which women performed "nonpolitical" political work while staying in step with their counterparts in Nigeria and Ghana. Yet female political elites emphasized an ideal womanhood that was accessible only to formally educated women who were civil servants, housewives, or worked in the professional workforce. Although they had limited time, and the financial means to hire servants, such women strove to accomplish household duties and be deferential to men. Profiles of women such as Gladys Silo Endeley emphasized that they tried to prepare food for their families themselves despite their busy work schedules. The next chapter examines how female political elites sought to promote an aroma of a distinct Anglophone cultural and political identity in the kitchens of busy, educated Cameroonian women.

CHAPTER 3

"God Will Be Eating Grass"

Cooking Anglophone Nationalism

"Your course now will dismiss all the fears of husbands," Natalia Noh Jua reassured teachers when visiting a class at the Government Domestic Science Center in Buea in December 1965.[1] Natalia Jua was the wife of Augustine Ngom Jua, who succeeded John Foncha as prime minister of the West Cameroon State from 1965 to 1968.[2] Jua was a powerful political mother from the start of her husband's term. In formal speeches, she encouraged nationalism and collective unity among West Cameroonian women, urging them to engage in various nationalist activities.[3] Her December 1965 visit to the domestic science center in Buea served her larger objective of persuading women to focus on West Cameroonian nationalist projects. This particular domestic science class focused on the use of local West Cameroonian products and cuisine. From December 11 to December 22, Kate Ebenye Idowu, the senior education officer for the West Cameroon government during the 1960s, supervised the group of domestic science teachers who experimented with the diverse local cuisine comprised of corn, rice, beans, taro, and plantains to produce a West Cameroonian cookbook. Jua applauded these efforts during her visit, describing cooking as important and necessary to married women's lives. As a press release outlining Jua's speech by the West Cameroon government explained,

> Many husbands had hitherto condemned domestic science as being confined only to the region of European foodstuffs. A domestic science mistress was supposed to learn in the cookery section mostly how to prepare foreign foods. . . . [But now] [t]he husband would not need to buy food articles outside his home. . . . A cookery book specially treating the methods of cooking

> local Cameroon food articles is the obvious outcome of this enterprising experiment.[4]

Expressing delight "that all the dishes were of local foodstuffs," Jua said they were attractive and delicious enough to prevent husbands from buying imported food.[5] She shares her delight in that the teachers applied "knowledge acquired from other lands to suit his environment [local conditions]," noting that the mark "of a true teacher is adaptability to [her] environment." Pleased with the course goal of adapting global knowledge of cookery to the local West Cameroonian context, she offered the domestic science teachers financial support so they could continue in the great endeavor "to raise the standard of cookery . . . throughout the [West Cameroon] territory."

This chapter explores ideas about cookery as another tool to carve a distinct West Cameroonian cultural identity and to advance Anglophone separatism in the Francophone-dominated Federal Republic. By emphasizing the importance of women's cookery in domestic science (also termed "home economics"), publishing recipes in advice columns, and producing the first (Anglophone) Cameroonian cookbook, female political elites and journalists maintained that women's everyday household tasks were central to the development of the nascent state. They emphasized issues of cookery as a way to highlight traits of a conservative and hybrid womanhood. By cooking for their families, women, who were generally the main cooks in Cameroonian societies, might assemble cultural elements to form the Anglophone identity. Women might also adhere to prevailing ideas about gender relations by preparing cuisines that appealed to their husbands; female journalists at times informed wives in their columns that if their husbands were unfaithful, it must be because of their poor cooking skills.

But the *type* of food women cooked mattered. Educated Anglophone urban women drew from and reworked Cameroonian, West African, and international culinary tastes to shape everyday cookery practices. Domestic science courses and published recipes urged women to cook local cuisine from the geographic areas of West Cameroon's many ethnicities. However, cuisine that traversed the Anglo-Franco border, as well as international borders, also made an appearance. Thus, the everyday practices and symbolism of West Cameroonian cultural identity and nationalism, such as cooking, came to figure into a larger Anglophone national identity expressed though women's domestic labor.

Women "flagged" and embodied a hybrid Anglophone national identity by selectively drawing from local and international culinary tastes while also deferring to male authority and respect at home, as defined by ideals of suitable womanhood. James McCann argues that "the role of food and cooking [can] both [be] the symbol and the substance of a national identity."[6] Asserting that food can function as an identifier of everyday nationalism, Igor Cusack argues that "[t]he development of a national cuisine will involve the summoning of a variety of dishes into the ambit of the discourse of the nation, and the very mention then of some national dish will quietly flag the nation."[7] Jua's December 1965 statements about the domestic science cookbook project makes it clear that being an "authentic" African woman means cooking for one's husband. While her statements do not entirely clarify whether "foreign foods" entice women away from preparing traditional Cameroonian cuisine or whether their husbands come to prefer Western cuisine, the promise is clear that cooking local African cuisine dishes can maintain dominant ideas about gender relations in which husbands rely on their wives to feed them. By connecting with happy marriages the cooking of local African dishes and the avoidance of "foreign foods," Jua refashions ideas about cookery along local patriarchal lines. Yet she also lauds the teachers for adapting their knowledge about culinary elements from "foreign foods" to a local West Cameroonian context. By applauding the use of various cultural elements as if they were spices that would create an identity of fused cultural flavors, female political elites invited a distinct Anglophone national identity into women's kitchens.

Who were the women who might have read published recipes in newspapers or cookbooks or attended classes in domestic science centers such as the one Jua visited? With whom did the discourse about a hybrid, conservative womanhood as articulated through food most resonate? Domestic science classes frequently focused on young girls and young adult urban women, who might attend such classes in primary and secondary school. In fact, two women in Bamenda, one who owned a dressmaking business and the other who was a retired civil servant who opened her own bakery, shared with me that during the 1960s, obtaining a domestic science education was perceived as a key identifier of a cosmopolitan identity for young adult women.[8] Thus, domestic science centers were sometimes an attractive alternative to other formal schooling options. Adult women who had graduated from secondary school might attend domestic science centers or colleges in Cameroon, Nigeria, or abroad to achieve advanced degrees; such women were future teachers of domestic science classes in secondary schools or in domestic science centers. Domestic science courses focused on formally educated women because female political elites saw such women as leaders in preserving Anglophone national identity, and also because they considered formal education to be a threat to African identity. Domestic science classes, which would reinforce women's proper roles as the cooks in households, were the remedy. While funding study-abroad scholarships and applauding formal education and formal workforce participation, female supporters of domestic science sought to address the danger this advancement posed to their counterpart's ability to please their husbands and protect traditional gender relations. By learning to cook varied dishes after they studied abroad, women might claim a hybrid conservative African identity, assuaging anxiety about the breakdown of their traditional roles.

In spite of the curriculum's limitations, the skills women learned provided opportunities to become economically self-sufficient because they could become small business owners.[9] Domestic science courses also allowed many women to become primary or secondary teachers, or, in a few cases, to enter the formal political structure as civil servants. Having framed themselves as "good" women who focused on suitable roles such as cooking, civil servants were nonthreatening, facilitating access to government careers. Kate Idowu, for example, was in charge of the December 1965 domestic science course in Buea, part of her role as senior education officer in the West Cameroonian government. She attended a short course at the University of London on developing questions about home economics for the General Certificate of Education (GCE) exam during the late 1960s, the better to train West Cameroon's home economics teachers.[10] In this manner, women like Idowu used conservative gender norms to socially and politically advance in a male-dominated political landscape.

The minority situation of Anglophone Cameroonians also turned issues of cookery into matters of cultural survival. Political elite West Cameroonian women called upon an embodied nationalism that implied that women's everyday actions, such as the foods they cooked, might project a suitable Anglophone Cameroonian image within varied spaces. Thus, educated political elites considered it important to assemble local recipes into a cookbook and to stress indigenous Anglophone cuisine in domestic science programs and political rallies, to maintain Anglophone separatism and cultural autonomy domestically, nationally, and globally. As this chapter shows, culinary tastes from the West and food choices that traversed West Africa and Cameroon generally, informed the definition of Anglophone cuisine and thus of a hybrid Anglophone womanhood that women might embody and perform in their kitchens. Nevertheless, they subtly juxtaposed Anglophone womanhood with its Francophone counterpart, suggesting that cooking and keeping house were inferior in East Cameroon because Francophone women were not as good housekeepers. One male interviewee, a former civil servant, told me apologetically (conscious of my Francophone Cameroonian background), "I'm very sorry about it but the worst housekeepers I have ever met are French Cameroonian women. . . . the French Cameroonian women likes to be gorgeously dressed, you know, but doesn't, generally know how to take care of things . . . they're expensive. Whereas our women and our men were brought up in thrift."[11] Even as he suggested French Cameroonian women are not authentically African, he tied the superiority of Anglophone women to having been "brought up the Anglo-Saxon way." He described domestic cleanliness as an inherent Anglophonic trait, one that embeds Anglophone Cameroonian characteristics in a broader, global Anglophonic culture.

Although many Anglophones I interviewed suggested that Francophone Cameroonian women lack domestic skills, my experiences reveal that cooking is commonly considered a vital feminine skill throughout Cameroon. As a native ethnographer (see Appendix: Methods and Sources), I observed during my field research in 2011 that family members, colleagues, and even interviewees often asked me what cuisines I like to cook. Whether I like to cook was not a question, because I self-identify as a woman. Others assumed that because I had lived so long in the United States, I would not know Cameroonian cookery. For example, as a guest in the home of close family friends in Buea, I cooked *le poulet DG*, a dish of roasted chicken with vegetables and fried plantains that was once popular only in Francophone Cameroon; the dish now has regional variations throughout modern-day Cameroon. The two men in the family, whom I consider cousins because of the closeness of our families, were quite surprised to know that I could cook Cameroonian cuisine. *Le poulet DG* is of particular significance; "DG" means "director-general" because, according to research, it used to be that only economically and politically important individuals could afford the dish, such as managing directors and other chief executives of large organizations.[12] After expressing their shock and tasting the dish, one of my "cousins" jubilantly proclaimed me to be a true Cameroonian woman and loudly announced that my bride price, also called "bridewealth"—the payment paid by the male suitor to his wife-to-be's family—had now dramatically increased because of my cooking skills. He jested that my family should now increase the number of cows, goats, and sheep (he particularly identified mutton, the meat of adult sheep that are older than one year) they demanded from a suitor.[13] I was delighted, of course, at the compliments, but it was also evidence of how, regardless of linguistic or cultural boundaries, most Cameroonians see the ability to cook as a key aspect of defining ideal Cameroonian womanhood. As my "cousin" continued to tick off the list of demands my family should request for a bridewealth while happily eating *le poulet DG*, it was clear to me that a woman's culinary skills exhibit her adherence to dominant gender norms that facilitate gender relations throughout mostly patriarchal Cameroonian societies.

The efforts of female political elites to promote hybrid West Cameroonian cuisine and culinary tastes not only occurred within patriarchal domestic settings, but also within the context of a policy of "Cameroonization" across the Federal Republic in the 1960s. This policy was part of a larger pattern of "Africanization" that occurred throughout the era of nationalism and decolonization on the continent from the 1950s to 1970s. Leaders of various African states Africanized their countries; in the Democratic Republic of Congo, for instance, the president, Mobutu Sese Seko, placed Africans in public service, the military, and private enterprise and replaced the European names of towns with African names in the 1970s.[14] In Cameroon, both the West and East states reorganized public administration, banks, and enterprises and replaced with Cameroonian citizens foreign nationals who had taken their jobs in the civil service during European rule.[15] Jua's statements that women might "return" to their African roots by cooking local African food for men were likely part of this continent-wide Africanization. But they were also related to feelings of disadvantage and marginalization, not unlike the embrace of French-inflected food customs French Canadians adapted from early to mid-1900s in a mostly Anglophone country.[16] To encourage Anglophone women to embrace ideal gender roles and relations, female political elites implied that their husbands' and children's success at work or school, good humor, and happiness all depended on their cooking.

The blending of local, Western, and Nigerian culinary tastes also speaks to the hybridity of Anglophone Cameroonian subcommunities. As John Mbaku contends, "local [Cameroonian] cuisine has been affected significantly by external influences, which were brought about by colonialism, Christian missionary activities, the spread of Islam, and, in recent years, globalization."[17] Although the British mostly ruled Southern Cameroons separately from Nigeria, Anglophone Cameroonian culture was hybridized; it was partially British-Nigerian, influenced by local cultural values as well as British ones. Even after the administration of the British Southern Cameroons was split off in 1954, ambitious individuals in the territory found many of their educational and work opportunities in Nigeria, including in government and Christian missions.[18] The long-standing connection between Nigeria and Anglophone Cameroon influenced culinary preferences. To stress their British heritage and separateness from Francophone Cameroon, the West Cameroon government offered domestic science scholarships for study in Nigeria and the UK, and female journalists suggested British cuisine for particular circumstances, such as when hosting British guests in their homes.

ASSEMBLING DOMESTIC SCIENCE PROGRAMS

The British administering period, 1922 to 1961, set the tone for domestic science classes in post-independent Cameroon. Christian missionaries, like their counterparts in settler-colonial Zimbabwe, the Belgian Congo, and Kenya, used such classes to transfer European ideas about domesticity to African women during the early twentieth century, striving to create "good" Christian wives and mothers who were "prepared to remain in the home and instill Christian values in their children."[19] Missionaries taught women "how to live" by encouraging them to attend domestic science education courses, mixing religion in with cookery, housekeeping, sewing, dressmaking, health, hygiene, and maternal education.[20] The records of the Women's Corona Society in the British Cameroons, an organization formed from British women administrative employees, shed light on how European-themed culinary style was taught to Cameroonian women. Although there were restrictions in the subjects taught, Melinda Adams argues that a certain population of the women were able to make use of domestic science education, allowing them to be in leadership roles, which in most cases assisted women to be more active in public life. Moreover, as she finds, domestic science education permitted women to have a source of income, because women used gained knowledge about sewing and baking to open small businesses. For certain women, domestic science education also offered opportunities to travel abroad and to obtain professional employment.[21] West Cameroonian women who embraced this opportunity prospered economically, gaining chances to travel to other countries and serve in professional roles in numerous economic fields.

The West Cameroonian elites' efforts to emphasize domestic science education as a means to create "good" wives and mothers was a continuation of European practices during British rule; similarly, they strove to shape women's appropriate domestic tasks and gender norms. Home economics (or domestic science) was only taught in primary schools in the West Cameroon State until the mid-1960s, when secondary schools began to offer courses in the subject. It was at this time that the GCE, the standardized exam students took at the conclusion of their secondary and postsecondary education, began to include lessons on home economics. Although the exam was developed and scored in London before and after British rule,[22] female political elites nevertheless heavily endorsed the field of home economics and domestic science centers by attending their openings, extolling their benefits, and encouraging teachers to teach students how to cook West Cameroonian cuisine. It was Anna Foncha who formally opened the Government Domestic Science Center in Buea, in early August 1964. On this occasion, she gave a speech in which she stated that although most women worked in offices and factories, a woman's place was still in the home and "there [is] nothing like a good home."[23]

Other political elite women also praised domestic science lessons. Advice columnist Ruff Wanzie, instructing parents to force their daughters to cook at home, pointed to the domestic science lessons they took at school.[24] Gladys Tombise Difo, the women's special representative in the West Cameroon Legislative Assembly, also exalted the importance of domestic science courses when addressing female students at a secondary school in Mamfe in November 1964. They should become "good housewives for future husbands," concentrating on domestic science classes, proving the usefulness of their education. "You are staff bearers of the nation and you must always remember that you belong to the state," she told them, calling on them to "continue the struggle of nation building" that her generation had begun. She concluded her speech with a fierce reminder "that the wind of change blowing across Africa had developed into a hurricane in Cameroon and [that] the women had been caught in that storm."[25] Such statements suggest that adult women garnered sociopolitical authority by instructing their younger counterparts. Through such speeches, they intended to inculcate prevailing gender norms in younger generations. Women like Difo warned young female students that the nation's future was at risk if they did not remember the political importance of preserving gender norms within their homes and future marriages, simultaneously reminding them that they were part of larger continental shifts and that they needed to keep up with their counterparts throughout Africa.

Domestic science centers were not the only spaces that taught young women about cooking and feeding families in ways that bolstered West Cameroonian national and cultural identity. The discourse and emphasis on women's cookery were also part of West Cameroonian government–sponsored celebrations that took place yearly on Women's Day, March 31, beginning in 1965.[26] Among the celebrations of women's domestic activities were cooking demonstrations and public talks on nutrition and the presentation of "native dishes [local West Cameroonian cuisine]."[27] These celebrations highlighted women's contributions to their families, communities, and nation. Women's associations such as the CWI were intimately involved in these activities, and politically influential women played a significant role by extoling the benefits of domestic science in speeches.

Further suggesting the depth of their commitment to domestic science, the West Cameroonian government sponsored female teachers who wanted to attend domestic science centers and schools in Nigeria and in the UK.[28] The West Cameroon government also considered it worthwhile to disseminate a press release about West Cameroonian students taking three-year classes at Bath College of Domestic Science at the University of Bristol in the UK.[29] In October 1964, the *Cameroon Times* reported that three West Cameroonian women would participate in a nine-month course focused on child-rearing, hygiene, nutrition, sports, and cookery to earn housekeeping diplomas in London.[30] Although the number of women sent abroad to study in domestic science schools in 1964 was minimal, returning students often taught domestic science classes in secondary schools or in domestic science centers, influencing a larger audience of female students who either accessed independent sources of income or went on to become domestic science teachers themselves. Thus, like elite Chinese women who trained as homemakers to manage homes as wives and mothers, from early- to mid-twentieth century China, elite West Cameroonian women helped build a modern and progressive Anglophone nation by exposing themselves to a wider world and using their knowledge to create new ideas about a hybrid West Cameroonian cultural identity.[31] As Helen Schneider describes with respect to Chinese women who trained as homemakers from the 1920s to 1950s, middle- and upper-class West Cameroonian women such as Kate Idowu who studied home economics abroad used the "new knowledge and skills associated with improving their abilities as managers of domestic space." Women such as Idowu translated their newfound abilities "into professional careers outside the home."[32]

The West Cameroonian government showed its political influence when it urged women to study abroad. Study-abroad students boosted the nation's global presence, and the number of West Cameroonian women studying in the UK grew over the federal period, strengthening West Cameroon's connection with the UK. Research suggests that foreign students enhance a nation's competitiveness and global presence by fostering sociopolitical relations with various countries. The students thus become valuable resources due to their specialized education and knowledge of foreign cultures, all skills that might help improve the social, political, and economic spheres of their own countries.[33] By emphasizing young women's study in the United Kingdom and Nigeria, the West Cameroon government facilitated a process by which it associated predominant gender norms with progressive ideals to form a new national identity.

Domestic science education also allowed some women to enter the world of politics or at least remain politically relevant. Josepha Mua, a Kamerun National Democratic Party (KNDP) parliamentarian in the Southern Cameroons House of Assembly (1959–61) and the wife of a parliamentarian in the West Cameroon Legislative Assembly, for example, earned her home economics degree from Seaford College in West Sussex, UK, in the mid-1960s. According to her biographer, her position as divisional inspector of primary education (1968–75) "helped to bring home economics as a subject into the national curriculum."[34] Susan Eyong, an Anglophone Cameroonian appointed to the Cameroon National Union (CNU) parliament in 1970 and who founded the Manyu Women's Palm Oil Cooperative between 1973 and 1975, shared with her biographer that being educated in home economics in the Teacher Training Center Shagamu in Lagos, Nigeria, opened her eyes to the social and political advances women were making elsewhere. The biographer describes Eyong as telling family and friends stories of women's advances in the medical and legal fields and of Nigerian women who drove cars, bolstering her case with photographs because she did not expect to be believed.[35] On her return from Nigeria, she taught domestic science courses in various schools including in Mamfe. But because Eyong was a formally educated woman, and taught domestic science in various schools, she shocked family and friends when she decided to marry a polygamous man, becoming his third wife.[36]

Nevertheless, Eyong parlayed her marital experience to gain social and political power in her community and beyond. She became involved in women's associations in Mamfe and also became a noted advisor to polygamous couples due to what her biographer calls "her sense of fairness [and] high moral standing." Because "her successful marriage to a polygamist boosted her standing," men in her community particularly admired her and "approached her for [marital] advice." As her biographer further writes, "her reputation as a woman who loved justice and one who was always fair and forthright" facilitated her interactions with "strong men" such as, to name two, Nerius Namaso Mbile, a key leader in Endeley's Cameroon People's National Convention (CPNC) and Emmanuel Tabi Egbe, the cofounder of the Cameroon United Congress (CUC), a party split from the KNDP, who also served as speaker of the West Cameroon Legislative Assembly and became vice minister of justice in the Federal Republic of Cameroon. As her biographer emphasizes, "she was close to politicians and leaders of all political shades and colors and her decisions were taken based on principles and not political demagogy."[37] Eyong parlayed these diverse political connections into her career in parliament.[38] Her experiences show the many ways that Anglophone women managed their social and political landscapes and expressed diverse notions of ideal Anglophone womanhood. While Eyong diverged from most formally educated women of her time by entering a polygamous marriage, she nevertheless used this experience to garner social and political authority and respect while also advocating for domestic science.

"A WIZARD IN HOUSEWIFERY:" COOKING WITH AUNTIE KATE

While Josepha Mua and Susan Eyong would be known for their domestic science knowledge, it would be Kate Ebenye Idowu, who had earned domestic science degrees abroad as a younger woman during the period of British rule, who would become one of West Cameroon's best-known domestic science teachers in the 1960s. Kate Idowu was a West Cameroonian civil servant who was also a well-known domestic science teacher. An article about Idowu in the online magazine *Success Story*, written when she was eighty-eight in July 2008, titled, "Aunty Kate: The Book, the Cook, the Educator and Homemaker," described her background.[39] Born in September 1919 in Victoria (renamed Limbe in 1982), she was the aunt of Gwendoline Burnley, the first woman parliamentarian to be elected to the West Cameroon Legislative Assembly. Idowu completed her primary schooling in Victoria and Kumba and attended a teaching school at the Kudeti Training Center in Ibadan, Nigeria. She later earned diplomas in home economics at the University of Durham, England, and the University of Oregon in the United States.

As part of her role as senior education officer in the West Cameroon government, Idowu taught domestic science classes in educational centers for schoolgirls and women in numerous West Cameroonian cities, including Victoria, Buea, and Bamenda. She also supplied food for private parties, made cakes for business purposes, and catered food for special-interest sociopolitical groups during national and provincial governmental celebrations in West Cameroon.[40] A former civil servant for the West Cameroonian government I interviewed, the same gentleman referenced earlier in this chapter, said she was "a wizard in housewifery and cookery."[41] *Success Story* describes her as one of many examples of "Cameroonians at home and abroad who aspire towards great positive achievements." The writer opined that Idowu believed that domestic science courses shaped students into moral and proper Cameroonians, describing Idowu's history of training teachers, caterers, housewives, and both girls and boys who lived with her learned how to cook and bake.[42] She clearly played a substantial role in legitimatizing the importance of the field of domestic science in homes, academia, and society generally.

Idowu published a cookbook in the 1970s, *Auntie Kate's Cookery Book*, a culmination of her teaching experiences when heading domestic science courses in Buea.[43] As Igor Cusack observes, such publications were far more commonly published in Anglophone Africa than Francophone Africa.[44] French Cameroonian recipe books emerged at a later date; one of the earliest was published in 1985, with French aid, *Le Grand Livre de la Cuisine Camerounaise* (The Big Book of Cameroonian Cuisine).[45] Idowu's cookbook, published the decade before, contains sections on nutrition, names for various foods, recipes, menu-planning, availability of food over different seasons, examples of traditional utensils, prayers, rules, and relevant Christian sayings. Idowu writes in the introduction that she aimed to create "a full, reliable textbook of cookery and nutrition" "[f]or the teachers and students of Home Economics" and for "the housewife and carter, who may or may not have had the advantage of specialist training."[46] The front cover of the cookbook highlights Idowu's achievement as a wife by referring to her authorship name as "Mrs. K. E. Idowu" and underlines her prestigious educational background by citing the sources of her degrees. The acknowledgment and foreword by Idowu's sister, Gladys Silo Endeley, who was the first vice president of the Women's Cameroon National Union (WCNU), as well as E. M. L. Endeley's sister-in-law, call attention to what Pamela Feldman-Savelsberg describes as "emotion-laden social networks."[47] Acting collectively, politically powerful women—in this case socially and politically prominent sisters—sought to advance women's social, political, and economic rights by working together and supporting each other's nationalist endeavors, thus creating a sense of

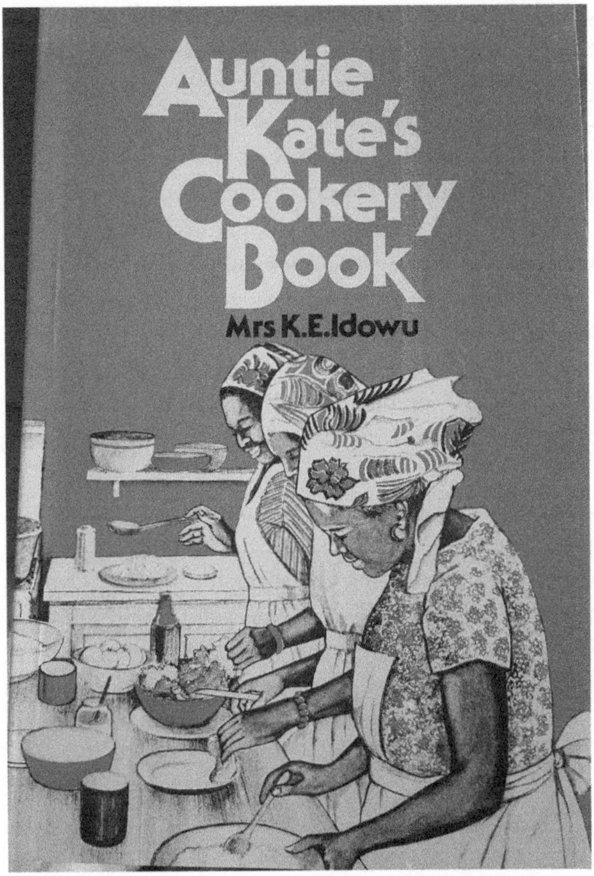

Kate Idowu published the first (Anglophone) Cameroonian cookbook in 1976. But she compiled the recipes in December 1965, when she supervised a special domestic science course in Buea. Image courtesy of Macmillan Education.

emotional belonging among a select group of politically elite women. In the foreword, Endeley, who also signs herself "Mrs.," assures readers of Idowu's credentials as a caterer and says that the recipes come from all regions of Cameroon. Claiming that "[i]n African cookery quantities of ingredients are difficult to standardize," she says it is Idowu's expertise and the influence of Western cookery that allow her to list "useful measurements and quantities."[48]

Idowu's cookbook is rich in cultural relics. As texts, cookbooks can, as Karin Barber contends, allow us to understand "social relations, ideas and values in the cultures that produce them."[49] In the introduction, Idowu emphasizes the importance of domestic science centers. "Many girls in schools all over the country today," she writes, "express the great desire to go to a Domestic Science Centre. Parents, too, are anxious for more Domestic

Science Centres to be established in all the areas where there are schools, to give girls the opportunity of this essential training." She describes the need for cookery books like her own as "very pressing" given the importance of domestic science. She communicates that "[t]he housewife who can provide good and nourishing meals for her family protects their health and wins their heart," thus emphasizing women's roles in fostering love through cooking by stoking family happiness and bodily health.[50] By keeping the family well fed and nourished, women nourish the well-being of the nation and its citizens.

Idowu's recipes traverse West African and Cameroonian/Nigerian cultures. They include *egusi* soup, a dish made from pounded squash, melon, or gourd seeds; palm nut soup; corn *foofoo* (or *fufu*), made from pounded starchy crops such as cassava, yams, or plantains; fried plantains; *chin-chin* and *garri* biscuits, dried cookies made from cassava; *jollof* rice; *akara* balls, a popular Nigerian snack of spicy fried beans; and *moi-moi*, a Nigerian steamed black-eyed peas pudding. The cookbook touts Idowu's ties to the West, including Western dishes such as pineapple fritters, coconut cake, apple meringue, and jelly corn muffins. Reflecting the diversity of West Cameroon culture, the recipes originated across the southern regions of Cameroon, including the Western Highlands where Anglo and French identities are both present. Recipes also crossed the Cameroonian/Nigerian border.

Beyond recipes, Idowu includes drawings of "native" produce such as plantains, local cooking utensils such as pepper stone, local spices such as *jowe* (the word for hot pepper in *Mokpwe*, a language that Bakwerians speak), and photos of traditional and modern kitchen equipment, such as the mud oven, charcoal basket cooker, and metal oven. She shows the diversity of kitchen equipment that women might access in rural and urban regions. In doing so, she seeks to reach a diverse socioeconomic and geographical audience, without assuming that their cooking appliances will all be the same.

Including dishes from throughout Cameroon was part of a larger trend women political elites used to forge ethnic unity through cookery, an approach similar to the one they used when leading women's organizations. To conceptualize the cuisine of a region with diverse ethnicities, *Auntie Kate's Cookery Book* focused on cuisines from throughout Cameroon, reflecting the attempt to forge a unified hybrid Anglophone ethno-nationalist identity. The recipes invited women to exhibit their sophisticated cooking skills and show their cosmopolitanism through their ability to please both European and African guests with their varied culinary skills. But who read Idowu's cookbook? How large was the reading market? While Cameroonian women increasingly accessed formal education in the 1960s, probably only a small population of West Cameroonian teenage and adult women read Idowu's cookbook. In 1964 in West Cameroon, for example, approximately 7 percent of teenage girls over the age of fifteen had primary education and only 2.3 percent had technical, secondary, or higher education.[51] While only a small minority of women most likely read Idowu's cookbook, reading it facilitated formally educated women's participation in larger discourses about Anglophone Cameroonian cultural practices. As Sarah Walden asserts, the very act of "*reading* about cooking engages public discourse on . . . values and requires women to place themselves at the center of this conversation."[52] In other words, reading Idowu's cookbook and cooking the proposed recipes possibly fostered a sense of cultural identity (and knowledge) among literate women who had obtained some level of formal education.

Beyond offering information on nutrition, "generic and local names" for different foods, recipes, weekly menus, and "seasonal variations in food availability," the book includes prayers, kitchen rules, and biblical proverbs. The proverbs, Christian sayings, and other "wise sayings" in her book reflect Christian influence on Idowu's worldview of women's proper use of time, particularly as it pertained to domestic affairs and how women might continue to honor God and their faith when completing household tasks. Her "Ten Golden Rules for the Kitchen" include what seem to be mostly Western-originated aphorisms, such as "Things done in a haste are never done well," "Leave nothing dirty, clean as you go," "Waste nothing, want nothing," and "A watched pot never boils."[53] She also offers the principles, "A fool and his money are soon parted" and "Do not live to eat. But eat to live," and, for teenagers, "Don't let your parents down; they brought you up," "Stand for something; or you'll fall for nothing," and "Give your all to Christ; He gave His all for you."[54] By offering guidance to her younger counterparts, Idowu, like Anna Foncha and the women journalists who penned advice columns, emphasized her maternal role while shaping larger ideas about the suitable comportment of young women, who were part of the target audience of the cookbook. Thus, the cookbook illustrates the underlying assumption that her readers are Christian and formally educated, which reflects how, in general, cookbooks, as texts, can provide ethnography of communities and a national vision.[55] But to be clear, Idowu's book provides an ethnography of a specific community, formally educated Christian women and their daughters; her aim is that the book "will serve the need of students and teachers

[and] housewives."[56] It is these "modern girls" she aims to hybridize—to both Africanize and Westernize—by endeavoring to instruct them on indigenous, local cuisine.

Other overtones of a hybrid African identity are evident in the cookbook. Idowu inserts Christian quotes (e.g., "if your God is dead, try mine. He is alive") and provides kitchen prayers: "Bless my little kitchen, Lord, I love its every nook, and bless me as I do my work, wash pots and pans and cook."[57] These quotes invoke the many locales from which Idowu derives her varied knowledge about gender ideals. She rounds them out with local Cameroonian proverbs: "A hungry man should look for food from a house that is sending out smoke"; "Hunger cannot kill a hard-working man"; "A plantain on the hill must always bend its head to look at those below"; "A cow does not know the use of its tail until it's cut off"; "Take your time or else you will meet the buffalo's horns"; "If every cocoyam is good, what will the pigs eat?"; and "Four walls and a roof cover all the troubles in the house."[58] Idowu also highlights traditional Cameroonian riddles such as:

> *I am a hunter. I killed a deer but carried home only the blood, leaving the animal behind. Who am I?*
> *Answer: a palm-wine tapper.*[59]

> *There is one pot of eru [a Cameroonian vegetable cooked in palm oil with seafood or meat] that the whole world eats once a month. What is it?*
> *Answer: the moon.*[60]

> *Which is the mountain that you climb from the top?*
> *Answer: fufu.*[61]

As a rich textual ethnographic source, Idowu's cookbook exemplifies Barber's argument that texts are interpretations and commentaries on social facts; they reflect attitudes about the prevailing social reality at the time of production.[62] Much like the riddles, jokes, proverbs, and folktales in the Onitsha Market Pamphlets that were consumed in Nigeria from the 1950s to the 1970s, Idowu's cookbook is a combination of oral traditions, traditional proverbs, and Biblical allusions that evidences the "triumph of Christian missionary education."[63] By intermingling Cameroonian and Western proverbs and Western and Nigerian recipes, Idowu creates a cookbook typical of what Shameem Black's study of the meaning of South Asian diasporic cookery describes: "an advice manual on being at home in the world during an age of globalization."[64] Idowu reimagines a hybrid Anglophone cultural identity embedded in a wider globalized world.

Exceptional culinary skills loomed large in Idowu's understanding of suitable womanhood. Yet her emphasis on Cameroonian riddles and proverbs afforded her the role of a "print griot" similar to that of her journalist counterparts. By invoking Cameroonian riddles and proverbs, she imparts indigenous, or local, knowledge about a worldview embedded in an African Christian context. The stylistic approach to her didactic prose that she uses to impart moral lessons is similar to what Marie-Soleil Frère observes about journalists in French-speaking Africa in the early 1990s; their writings "very close to the oral style of the griots. The stylistic characteristics, the use of metaphors and images, the way the story is built are common to both 'story-tellers.'"[65] Idowu presents riddles and proverbs to her readers, engaging her audience as a story-teller much like a traditional griot.[66] While her readers may gain knowledge about a wider role through the recipes she chooses, they are also reminded, through the proverbs and riddles, to prioritize local African perspectives on life and cultural values. Ultimately, from her maternalist position, Idowu is everyone's wise and warm aunt, shepherding women through instructions on cooking. By providing Christian quotes, Idowu reinforced her devotion as a Christian and her endeavor to continue to foster an affinity for Christianity in her life and the lives of others.

Idowu's peers describe her as the ideal Anglophone woman, illustrating her social and political influence as well as her domestic skills. The *Success Story* profile describes her as a crafter as well as a good cook, saying she "made different types of household decorations by knitting, crochet, tie-dye, macramé [decorative fabric made through the use of knotting techniques] . . . 'you name it, she could make it.'"[67] Further, as a middle-aged woman:

> She was never idle—if not cooking or baking, her hands were always busy making something useful from cloth, wool, thread, ropes. . . . She was an ardent farmer, growing vegetables, yam and fruits in her back garden and flowers around her house. . . . She has always made her faith in God a priority and organized daily night prayers in her home. . . . As a member of the Ebenezer Baptist Church [at] Great Soppo [in Buea], she was active in the women's group.[68]

The profile concludes, "Mrs. Kate Idowu, Aunty Kate, is a great Cameroonian woman who has trained many young girls and boys, women, to be house proud [and] economically viable and take good care of their families."[69] Most West Cameroonians were Christian due to the activities of British missionaries, and the Christian work ethic and negative orientation toward poorly spent leisure permeate her book and apparently even her lifestyle.[70] Idowu's constant busyness made her a proper Christian woman; she used her time in a "right" way by adhering to prevalent gender norms and endeavoring to be a good example to her counterparts and younger generations. She led by example. Further, by striving to teach young boys, and by being an "ardent farmer," she reflected a hybrid womanhood that was progressive and still adhered to dominant gender ideals.

"HE WHO COOKS RICE AND STEW IS A RICH PERSON": HYBRID CULINARY PREFERENCES

The appearance of hybrid culinary tastes in Idowu's cookbook took place in a changing social and political landscape in Cameroon. Growing trade between West and East Cameroon shaped new understandings of "authentic" and cosmopolitan foods. Between 1922 and 1972, a complex, hybrid culinary culture developed in urban West Cameroon, similar to the one found in the colonial Gabon Estuary where African individuals "incorporate[d] foreign consumption patterns into their own lives."[71] Though Western imports sometimes completely replaced local culinary styles, it was common for many African communities to *integrate* European elements in their eating and cooking. Jeremy Rich, for instance, argues that instead of wholly marginalizing local African "consumption practices, a messy process of appropriation and borrowing took place among African communities."[72] In a continuation of trends that started during British rule, West Cameroonian dishes were a hybrid of traditional and European foodstuffs. As in the colonial Gabon Estuary, urbanites incorporated influences from diverse locales; East Cameroonian, Nigerian, French, and British food preferences shaped urbanite ideas about the food women should prepare, shaping new, cosmopolitan Anglophone Cameroonian identities. Various cuisines emerged as a result of negotiations between the local and the foreign, such as chin-chin and French beignets, popular snack foods at the time.[73] Moreover, while female journalists urged women to "go back" to preparing mostly African cuisine, they also recommended that they prepare British dishes for British guests. Ultimately, culinary taste and cookery became aspects of performative domestic labor in which women played out countless ideas about the old and the new.

Clara Manga, writing as "Auntie Clara," focused on cookery as a means for women to create a hybrid West Cameroonian cultural identity. In the first of a series of articles in 1961, she inquired, "Can we the modern Cameroon girls boast of being able to prepare the delicious dishes our grandmothers used to prepare in their days?" She laments, "It's such a shame that we have learned so much of other people's ways of eating [and] we have lost ours completely." Though she never unambiguously defines who these "other people" are, it can be inferred that she's referring to British or French individuals. She claims that Cameroonians "take delight in imitating other people" but argues that such "delight" should not precipitate the loss of African cookery. At the same time, she admits that she herself lacks knowledge of some traditional dishes. She presents a set of Bakwerian recipes, including *ngonya veembe*, a green soup made from cocoyam leaves that is frequently consumed with fufu, a dough like substance made from starchy food crops such as cassava, while promising to publish at least two recipes from every division of West Cameroon, which she ultimately provided in later columns.[74] Manga counseled women on suitable African dishes to prepare when hosting parties in a September 1962 column:

> The luncheon is usually a heavier meal than dinner, and the housewife should pick dishes to suit her local conditions [and] the tastes of her guests and the money at her disposal. Care should be taken that heavy food like Yam Foofoo [fufu] are not served at dinner parties, as many people cannot digest this at night. The average African has [a] large . . . course meal or two if for a special occasion. A three-course meal would be definitely as much as would be needed at an African luncheon party, as most of the foods are starchy and filling.[75]

Manga called for British dishes if British guests are in attendance, reflecting how the legacy of British rule continually shaped West Cameroonian cultural identity. In such cases she recommended that readers adhere to the Western custom to serve appetizers before the main meal, proposing salads, tomato soup, roast meat, and banana pudding.

Manga's use of food to support conceptions of West Cameroonian cultural identity participated in a larger tradition of nationalist food movements, which scholars have documented in many postcolonial African countries.[76] In these movements, the consumption and preparation of "authentic" or local cuisines becomes central to postcolonial nation-building projects. Unlike Kate Idowu in her cookbook, Manga never once publishes dishes from East Cameroon.[77] The published recipes gesture toward something distinctly West Cameroonian that Anglophone Cameroonians could easily identify and consume. In other words, in the spirit of Benedict Anderson, they invoke notions of an imagined palatable Anglophone community.[78] Through published recipes, Manga guards West Cameroonian cultural identity against Francophone domination in the republic. Yet she also encouraged women to selectively adapt Western culinary tastes, such as serving British dishes to British guests, because participating in global culinary trends was central to adding the flavors of a new cosmopolitanism to West Cameroonian identity.[79]

Although she was formally educated and broke new ground as the first female journalist in the British Southern Cameroons, Manga's admission that she cannot prepare African cuisine suggests a personal challenge to normative gender roles. As Audrey Gadzekpo describes, it may not be unusual for women journalists to defy gender norms—the Ghanaian journalist whose life she examines, Mercy Kwarley Ffoulkes-Crabbe, had a baby out of wedlock when she was forty and remained single for nine years, but her "Gloria" columns espoused dominant ideas about gender behavior and influence, such as criticizing women who remained unmarried in colonial urban Ghana.[80] Like Ffoulkes-Crabbe, Manga occupied a space of great ambiguity and contradiction. Although she exhibited Western culinary tastes that bolstered and justified her social authority, the access to social power they imply allowed her to craft new cultural identities and shape new ideas about the "traditional" while condemning behavior that she at times practiced. Like her familial title "Auntie," her confession that she does not know how to prepare indigenous recipes made her relatable; she was self-deprecating as well as authoritative. Manga's influential position facilitated her role as a "print griot," allowing her to invoke the role of a teacher, symbolically placing herself in her readers' kitchens where she educates them about cooking local cuisine.

Manga's intense attention to food suggests an awareness that food and drink choices reflect cultural identity. From her viewpoint, women can show that they are "good" women, unharmed by formal education, by adhering to prevalent norms, such as preparing "heavy food," starchy dishes, for guests. At the same time, a wife can use a particular type of food to represent her family's prestigious social status. As Jeremy Rich shows in his examination of changing food patterns in the colonial Gabon Estuary, food consumption is closely related to social status.[81] Therefore, from Manga's standpoint, a "good" woman not only adhered to dominant gender ideals by cooking for her family, she used her education and social status to stress her cosmopolitan demeanor in proper situations. She impressed her husband by cooking traditional cuisine but preserved the family's cosmopolitan status by preparing Western cuisine in appropriate settings.

Oral interviews and surveys conducted in 2011 in Buea and Bamenda confirmed that women in 1960s urban West Cameroon connected nonnative food to prestige, respect, and cosmopolitanism. Women from Bamenda described salads, stew, sardines, rice, pastries, fruit juice, popcorn, fruit jam, and omelets as new and appealing food items during the 1960s. At the same time, they described local Cameroonian dishes from various part of Cameroon and previously not known to them as shaping new cosmopolitan identities. These dishes included *ndolé*, *koki*, egusi pudding, fried plantains, and *achu*.[82] Fidelia Ngum, an energetic woman who lived in Buea and, in retirement, was a seamstress and also sold food products in a makeshift shop by the roadside to support her family, said that some of these foods denoted broad-mindedness and respect in West Cameroonian society. Reflecting on the popularity of French bread and sardines in the 1960s, she commented, "Our food is that pounded foo-foo [fufu] now. It was different, so [when] someone will present you bread and sardines that was a big thing! We see bread and sardines as a French style of food. . . . because for us we like heavy food. . . . Anglophones like heavy food. . . . in the morning you eat your fufu and eru."[83] Ngum also identified tomato stew, and jollof rice, a West African version of pilaf or paella, as the local food people preferred. But she recalled preparing salads as a young bride:

> At first, people don't know even this salad. Lots of things people did not know. But today you eat all those things. We prepared them ourselves. But at first, and that's why some of those people, even our . . . grandmothers or our elderly ones, that's why when they come to your place [and] you prepare those things they say . . . "mmm . . . it's raw" . . . "God will be eating grass" . . . "we don't eat carrots." At times you prepare carrots like that and they say "no, I will not eat." Because they never knew. . . . Francophone people know much about salad. . . . It has not been long since I started eating salad. . . . When I got married that's [when] I started eating salad. Because I've come closer to others, to people, and seeing them doing it.[84]

The reception of certain foods such as salads among older Cameroonians highlighted generational schisms. Most Cameroonian cultures are Christian and hierarchical, and people show respect to their elders.[85] As Ngum found out, serving salad to elderly family members could violate this code of respect for elders, who saw it akin to serving paltry food to God.

But salad's role as an indicator of a progressive womanhood rang true even to the highest echelons of political power. Even Gladys Endeley, who was said to be well-versed in cooking local Cameroonian cuisine—one of her sons even claiming to her biographer that his mother's exceptional cooking skills loomed so large in Cameroon that it facilitated his access to government officials in 2010[86]—became well-known for her elaborate salads. Their only daughter Mariana, the youngest of their six children, shared in an interview that although she was well-versed in Cameroonian cuisine, her mother was celebrated for her salad making skills: "my mom's specialty—everybody knew my mom for her salad . . . you know how it is when Africans with their—always—occasions—looking for people to make stuff. My mom's was salad . . . she made it in a special way . . . it was a big thing . . . we knew that."[87] Albeit generational pushback to the increased preparation of salad, women from varied social, political, and geographic backgrounds increasingly prepared salad as part of their everyday diets, thus shaping hybrid Cameroonian cultural identities.

Fidelia Ngum further revealed that specific food products also shaped courtship between young women and men during the 1960s and 1970s. Providing French bread and sardines was a way of courting a woman, showing that the suitor was willing to spend money on her. She explained, in a conspiratorial tone, that a man would "sacrifice" his money to buy sardines, about 100 francs a can during the 1960s. In a whisper, Fidelia disclosed that many women became pregnant because of French bread and sardines.[88] Though she was probably exaggerating when she implied that these foods were a way to talk a woman into bed, they suggest that "French style" food was enticing in that it showed a certain level of prestige and social status.

Foreign foods, both from out of the country and from *within* different areas of Cameroon, thus had complex connotations, reflecting new understandings of progressive identities emerging in the 1960s and early 1970s. These new considerations reflected the changing sociopolitical and economic realities of West Cameroon. During the federal period, the Yaoundé government undertook various projects to unite West and East Cameroon economically and politically. First, work on the Tiko-Douala Road, known as the

Reunification Road, began in October 1965. This facilitated "the transfer of West Cameroon export products through Douala" and initiated the extension of the Douala-Mbanga railway to Kumba, which opened in 1969.[89] Second, between 1969 and 1973, the state diverted "imports and exports to and from West Cameroon" to "the port of Douala in East Cameroon." This left the two West Cameroonian ports of Victoria and Tiko as "virtual ghost towns."[90] These changes marginalized Anglophone Cameroonians economically; some scholars and activists point to them as evidence of unjust economic occupation by Ahidjo's government.[91] However, migration and trade between East and West Cameroon increased because of the changes, which boosted cross-influence of the two regions' cuisines, just as long-standing contact with Nigeria influenced Anglophone Cameroonian's culinary preferences. The *New Standard*, a West Cameroonian newspaper, observed in 1969 that Anglophone Cameroonians had become used to French bread—"the boulangerie bread"—which had been unknown in the British South Cameroons but ubiquitous in French-ruled Cameroun.[92] According to oral interviews, Anglophone Cameroons today typically eat French bread in the morning, and Francophones typically eat Anglophone Cameroonian dishes such as fufu and eru, and achu (yellow soup made with grinded limestone and oil and served with pounded yams).[93]

Thus, changing tastes in food products was not happenstance in West Cameroon; it mirrored the economic and agricultural realities of citizens at the time. Because of increasing rice cultivation in 1960s Cameroon,[94] interviewees frequently mentioned that rice denoted wealth, prestige, and respect in that decade. Vanessa Yonkeu, a woman in her early fifties at the time, who had owned a small clothing shop for over thirty years and lived in a predominately Anglophone Cameroonian section of the Francophone capital, Yaoundé, told me:

> In those days, we cook . . . plantains, fufu and eru . . . and koki. . . . we were not cooking groundnut soup [peanut soup], but now we cook groundnut soup. In those days, rice and stew, is once a year. But now we cook rice and stew nearly everyday. . . . But we did not cook it frequently, once a year, one time. . . . because at that time, they say "he who cooks rice and stew is a rich person.". . . At that time, you don't have money . . . you no cook rice and stew. But now, at any time, you cook rice and stew. . . . and at that time when you want to cook rice and stew, you hide [the rice], so that a neighbor should not see, so that witchcraft would not come in.[95]

In a group interview, Nesah Tabot and Juliana Muhnjuh, both married women, also remember rice as a wealthy person's food. I met both women on a warm November day in 2011 as they made *chin-chin* together to sell in their respective food shops in Buea. Both women were originally from Bamenda; Tabot, a housewife and mother of four, had lived much of her life in Kumba and had recently moved to Buea upon "retirement." Muhnjuh, mother of two, lived much of her life in Tiko and had worked in the Tiko council. On retirement, she too moved to Buea. As Tabot recalled, "If you cooked rice that means you are rich. It was the best food at that time. . . . people thought it was nice . . . because rice was scarce, and people thought it was dear." Muhnjuh added, "At Christmas day [when] you go to somebody's house, [if] they give you rice they respect[ed] you." Bekene Eyambe similarly shared that on Christmas day they cooked rice to commemorate the special day.[96]

Tabot's and Muhnjuh's statements suggest that cooking rice brought both beneficial and detrimental outcomes. While rice became a principal marker of wealth in the 1960s, it also had the potential to bring bad luck to a person and his or her family. Thus, those who had rice hid it from neighbors who could not afford it, to avoid inciting jealousy or, superstitiously speaking, bad luck. In doing so, they aimed to avoid inviting misfortune. These examples showed that food provides an opportunity to shape identity not just by consumption, but also through everyday food preparation. Tabot's and Muhnjuh's statements about rice show that the "appreciation of foreign tastes signifies wealth."[97] Through cooking and by concealing new commodities from specific community members, people like Tabot espoused the belief that rice symbolized wealth and defined the types of food that the progressive or cosmopolitan woman should aspire to prepare.

"MEN ARE VERY PARTICULAR ABOUT THEIR MEALS": FOOD AND GENDER RELATIONS

Numerous sources indicate that food and cookery significantly shaped relations between women and men in urban West Cameroon, and also ideas of womanhood as expressed in gender relations. A woman was a "good" wife if she prepared new delicious dishes every day for her husband, which might possibly stop him from engaging in extramarital relationships. A wife's good cooking skills might entice her husband to stay committed to the marriage and strengthen ties to his home.[98] Oral interviews revealed that a woman's cooking substantially shaped the atmosphere of her marriage. A woman named Bekene Eyambe, a stay-at-home mother of eleven, described the importance of a husband eating well, using the Cameroonian Pidgin English (Cameroonian Creole) word for eating, "chop." Originally from Kumba, she explained that as a young bride in the 1960s she understood, "when you want [to] cook, you go cook heavy food." She explained that if a man visited your house and did not *chop*, he would ask, "Who are you?" But, as she further disclosed, "If a man visited your house and ate, he would leave the house and tell people, 'This woman is a good woman, if you go [to] her house, you must chop.'"[99] Cookery supported a conservative conception of ideal West Cameroonian womanhood among urbanites. "Heavy food" here refers to local dishes with starchy ingredients such as yams, koki (similar to moi-moi), and plantains. Eyambe and others told me these dishes staved off hunger for longer periods than lighter food, inciting happiness, good spirits, health, and perhaps even happier marriages.

Female journalists also claimed that a wife's cooking skills influenced her marital standing.[100] In addition to emphasizing the nation-building aspect of cooking local cuisine, Manga repeatedly referred to its marriage-protecting qualities in her columns. For example, she introduced a recipe to her readers in August 1962 thus: "Ladies O, [*sic*] this is something you must try. I recommend it when you want something special from him. Ask for it when he is at [the] table. I bet you won't be refused your request." Later, in November 1962 she wrote, "Cookery is something every woman must learn and know if she wants to hold her man because men are very particular about their meals." "[O]f course every housewife who can afford a cook should have one," she told them. "But I admire the housewife who prepares her husband's food herself with the help of her cook, if she has one."[101] It was common for middle- to upper-class women to have servants at home to help with cooking and other domestic chores, but they were expected to personally cook food for their husbands as a sign of deference to male authority and adherence to dominant gender relations in the marriage. Thus, while the cosmopolitan woman might show her social position by working and having servants, ideal womanhood continued to be fashioned along patriarchal lines. In the same November 1962 column, Manga stated that if her brother's wife did not know how to cook, she would tell him to divorce her, noting, however, that women with poor cooking skills do not make it to marriage anyways: "Such girls hardly get married in life for during courtship, the meals they prepare tell so much about them."

Ruff Wanzie agreed in an August 1964 column that a women's cooking skills said much about her willingness to adhere to gender ideals and to keep her husband content. She called on women to vary the meals they served, asserting, "It is an unimaginative housewife who serves the same thing every day. . . . [D]on't be afraid to experiment."[102] In a follow-up August article titled, "Which is your Perfect Wife?" Wanzie further informed her readers that "The house wife must be a good cook for man naturally values his meals very much. . . . Wives should remember to welcome home husbands with smiling cheeks always. . . . A tasteful delicious dish served to them after that makes them feel on top of the world."[103] In August 1972, Manga's column ran a guest editorial by Beckley Sammy and Signals Victoria echoing her and Wanzie's sentiments about cookery and gender relations; the authors identities remain ambiguous. They claimed: "[I]f your husband goes out despite all your efforts to keep him at home, then: (1) Study the type of dishes he likes best; (2) Prepare the dish yourself, and not the housemaid or boy. It may be the other woman knows how to cook better than you do." Noting that "men like decent dishes, which will give good health and the strength you desire," they instruct wives to feed husbands in the morning to promote good health and good spirits and so that "the day's work will be done with happiness."[104]

While the authors all acknowledge that proper women must know how to cook well, they emphasize that wives can garner special favors from husbands by using their cooking skills and diversifying the dishes they cook at home, thus associating urban women's domestic labor with deference to male authority in the home. Wanzie even goes so far as to imply that a wife's cooking skill might help advance her husband's career by helping him "clinch an important deal" with a client.[105] A man's colleagues might regard him in a better light if his wife cooks exceptionally well, and a wife who fed her husband well contributed to his good spirits throughout his workday. This drove him to be a good, hard worker, which in turn helped maintain the family's good socioeconomic status. Thus, a woman's ability to serve good meals was considered essential to ensuring peaceful coexistence with her husband as well as his professional success.

Manga's opinion that even women who employ cooks should personally prepare meals for their husbands reflects a cultural norm that continues today. Many ethnic groups in Cameroon consider it honorable for a woman to cook for her husband.[106] Gladys Endeley's daughter even professed in her interview that although her mother was frequently busy and had servants at hand, she always found time to personally prepare her father's food, explaining that conceivably it was because "her husband wanted to eat her food."[107]

Performing a small amount of cooking while servants did the heavy lifting allowed women to work while adhering to gender norms that borrowed from both Western and local ideas about gender relations.[108] Though they may be elite middle- to upper-class women, their actions show that they are not above fulfilling domestic duties themselves; they ascribe importance to prevailing gender roles and to respect for male authority by personally preparing their husbands' food.[109]

But, as the next chapter demonstrates, women's efforts to underpin larger Anglophone cultural values were not limited to kitchens and domestic science classes or to cookbooks. Another arena was beauty contests, which were national and global stages on which West Cameroon might present the ideal woman citizen, one whose aesthetic labor visually presented the physical manifestation of the ideal Anglophone woman. Through events such as "British Week" that stressed a type of embodied nationalism in which a contestant's bodily comportment and conduct mattered just as much as her educational background, political elites endeavored to visualize a hybridized ideal Anglophone identity beyond the kitchen.

CHAPTER 4

"Beauty Contest Not Only for Free Girls"

Modeling Anglophone Identity

"Girls have a wrong notion about beauty competitions. It rumours that in order to win, a girl has to make love to all male judges. What are your own impressions, and what advice can you extend to future interested girls?"[1] "Cousin Lizzy," writing as Ruff Wanzie, eagerly posed this question in March 1972 as part of an interview with Elsie Ikome for her column in the *Cameroon Times*. Twenty-year-old Ikome, who worked as a bank clerk for Cameroon Bank Ltd., had swept major West Cameroonian beauty pageants, including Miss Fako Beauty Queen. As Wanzie wrote, she had most recently "stole[n] the hearts of hundreds of spectators" as she took the crown for the West Miss Africa Football Cup in Buea. She would soon advance to the highly anticipated nationals in Yaoundé to compete against Francophone contestants. In response, Ikome confidently told Wanzie,

> False rumours are like wild fire. . . . No men have come to me for love deals before or after the competitions. . . . Beauty competitions are not meant for wayward girls. . . . A girl has to be well mannered in order to represent her country in such competitions. I, therefore, call on school leavers [British English: a pupil who has not graduated from high school] and young female workers to answer competition calls.[2]

While Ikome was a school-leaver herself, the fact that she had taken some credits at Saker Baptist College, an all-girl secondary school in Victoria, is a marker of middle-class status. "I am ambitious," she told Wanzie in a confessional tone, "but ambition should be made of sterner stuff. I may keep my present job, [and] accept any other regard that awaits me as a beauty queen or get married if I find a suitor. My beauty does not distract me from being a useful citizen."[3] Ikome's statements indicate how beauty contests in West Cameroon facilitated dominant ideas about gendered citizenship duties through the performative power of pageants. By "sterner stuff," Ikome suggests that it is important for her to use her time usefully, fulfilling her duties as a beauty queen and contributing to the economic sector as a bank worker. But she also implies that she prioritizes eventually achieving essential qualities of ideal womanhood, such as marriage.

Wanzie seemed to likewise believe that marriage should be Ikome's ultimate goal. The journalist emphasized Ikome's domesticity in her account, saying that the winner of multiple pageants was in the kitchen before the start of the interview, which took place in Ikome's home in Bota, a section of the seaside city of Victoria. She effused, "[Ikome] came out of the kitchen smiling sweetly at me and I was impressed that a 'queen' could be so busy over domestic affairs [w]hen she could have been painting her lips and fingers or relaxing on a cosy [*sic*] bed reading novels." Ending the interview to let "the beauty queen finish up her cookery," Wanzie muses that beauty queens could indeed "make excellent housewives."[4] As Wanzie's interview with Ikome suggests, beauty contestants dismissed fears that they might reject prevailing gender norms, highlighting their domestic skills and envisioning marriage as an intrinsic part of their future. Thus, they outlined the suitable conservative womanhood that contestants could display.

This chapter considers how beauty pageants became yet another space for West Cameroonian urban and political elites to represent their national pride, distinct Anglophone cultural identity, and economic strength in an especially potent way—through representations of the female form. Throughout much of Africa at the time, the rise of beauty pageants was seen as a national and cultural signifier of a progressive postcolonial African state. But because women often represent the values of their cultures, nationalist movements throughout postcolonial Africa have frequently placed women's moral qualities and chastity at their center. Journalists such as Ruff Wanzie as well as political elites used the bodies of contestants as symbolic platforms on which to debate emerging views of West Cameroonian nationalism and to simultaneously create and preserve selected cultural values, thus informing a blended West Cameroonian identity. While these standards were hybrid feminine ideals, they were a necessary part of consolidating Anglophone Cameroonian national identity. Standards of physical and moral feminine perfection became central to the West Cameroonian nationalist project because the stakes were high. Thus, anxieties about women's bodies (class, sexuality, gender) shaped multiple feminine ideals that were both conservative and cosmopolitan and that navigated multiple spaces: local, national, regional, and international.[5]

The age and educational status of "beauty queens" became a critical factor in shaping discussions of beauty contests; as potential biological and cultural reproducers of the Anglophone nation, they functioned as a barometer of the preservation of suitable gender norms, moral qualities, and cultural values. Like their counterparts elsewhere in colonial and early postcolonial Africa, educated urbanites in West Cameroon believed that education and the attendant social positioning should confer morality and social responsibility.[6] Similar to Emily Callaci's conclusions about "[t]he salaried working girl" in 1970s urban Tanzania, she "held out the promise of making Africans collectively modern. . . . [and] was a diligent and professional worker and a product of the nation's growing educational system." Callaci further argues that such a professional working woman was "[a] fashionable dresser, [who] signified the growth of consumer markets and urban leisure pleasures." Similarly, formally educated women in West Cameroon, many of who were professional workers, participated in beauty pageants were, like working girls in urban Tanzania, seen by many formally educated elites "[a]s emblems of a modern consumer economy, a productive and educated workforce," and thus (visually) represented West Cameroon's "rising place in a global order."[7] Thus, beauty contestants framed upholding cultural values and maintaining sociopolitical identity as their duty to spur progress. Beauty pageants became the sites of such preservation.

Pageants were spaces in which to construct a particular feminine beauty and define Anglophone Cameroonian bodily comportment. Oluwakemi Balogun argues that through beauty pageants, women's bodies can function as "symbolic sites where debates about the development of a nation take place."[8] By invoking embodied nationalism, elites scrutinized the visual signals of proper Anglophone bodily comportment—the way a contestant walked, smiled, and talked—as a way to present the physical manifestation of ideal Anglophone womanhood on the community, national, and international stages. Just as they did in developing the national costume, West Cameroonian political elite women looked to their West African counterparts, specifically Nigeria, concerning ideas about beauty and suitable bodily practices. Europe and the United States also provided models. These transnational counterparts presented a basis for reinterpreting African women's bodily practices and comportment.

Closely associated with ideal feminine beauty and suitable bodily comportment was the question of morality and authentic Africanness. In the interview with Ikome, Wanzie emphasizes that the beauty queen was not "painting her lips and fingers." The reference to cosmetics invoked stereotypes about "free women" in 1960s and 1970s urban West Cameroon, sexually loose women who wore too much makeup and, worse, short skirts and wigs. Ikome, Wanzie implied, is not a "free woman" because of her limited cosmetic use. Ikome in turn emphasizes that she was a shy competitor who "couldn't stand the eyes of the public"—a claim her record of frequent competition belies—and she calls herself "minor" in relation to more beautiful competitors. At the same time, she says she endeavors to "steal the show in Yaoundé" by striving to "keep a good shape, [to] be natural and [to be] smart." By embracing modest comportment and emphasizing internal qualities, Ikome advances larger ideas about how "natural," or "authentic," bodily performance might define physiological practice and suitable bodily movement.

But contestation about the nature of ideal womanhood, as modeled on stage, revealed economic stratification and the hybrid nature of Anglophone womanhood, which was both conservative and cosmopolitan. Local administrative officials, female journalists, and other educated urbanites sought to protect class boundaries by suggesting that pageants would not welcome sexually lax women because they were unqualified to model the nation's progress on the global stage. The allegations of loose sexual behavior that Ruff Wanzie acknowledged in her interview with Elsie Ikome, if only to dismiss them, reflected this dynamic. While most urbanites believed that the behavior of ideal contestants, who were mostly formally educated, should not suggest sexual impropriety, urbanites drew from varied local and international ideas about gender norms, bodily rituals, and comportment to differently refashion beauty ideals. Although contestants frequently donned Western attire and newspapers ran pictures of them in swimsuits, mostly bikinis, they were nevertheless expected to exhibit traits of local African modern womanhood through their comportment and conduct. Subsequently, beauty contestants and educated urbanites drew from local and international ideas about sartorial practices and aesthetic rituals to shape new local standards of African feminine beauty.

The interview with Ikome in March 1972 preceded President Ahidjo's abolition of the Federal Republic by only a few months. While the article suggests that energy was still devoted to propping up West Cameroonian claims to nationhood through pageant winners such as Ikome—a male journalist would express blithe national pride after Ikome's eventual win in Yaoundé—Wanzie's use of a pseudonym, "Cousin Lizzy," anticipates the collapse of such projects. She switched to using a pseudonym when President Ahidjo eliminated the multiparty system in 1966; Wanzie feared political retribution because of her KNDP affiliation. The pseudonym facilitated her continued involvement in West Cameroonian nationalist activities, including promoting beauty contests. Like Wanzie, other political elites continuously found ways to unambiguously emphasize their political and economic autonomy through pageants after 1966. For example, they celebrated their British heritage in events such as British Week in 1968, which climaxed in a Miss British beauty contest. As the following sections will show, by holding beauty contests and sending winners to the UK, Anglophone political elites expressed Anglophone separatist intentions and political authority in a time of increasing encroachment by the East Cameroonian government and France. Ultimately, beauty contests show how issues concerning economic stratification, morality, and the hybridity of Anglophone gender norms and cultural values fed larger concerns about a representative Anglophone national identity.

In historicizing beauty contests, this chapter uses the spatial configuration of pageants to visualize and walk through issues of ideal Anglophone womanhood, cultural values, political identity, and economic mobility as they emerged on stages. While I use the figure of Elsie Ikome to examine the lived experiences of contestants, I also examine how outlines of the ideal contestant, the "good" woman, reversed stereotypes about the "bad" woman or "free woman," and how they further complicate perceptions of suitable Anglophone womanhood. I also turn to the side stage to look at key advocates of beauty competitions—female journalists, women and men government officials, and political wives such as Anna Foncha. In turning to these supporters, I investigate how they used pageants to safeguard the boundaries of who could represent West Cameroon on stage and how this discourse and their participation in pageants bolstered Anglophone nationalist sentiments. Also, I look at the audience. While journalists condemned them for sometimes acting unruly during competitions, audiences used pageants as a space for debating larger ideas about suitable political participation and suitable comportment and attitudes, by, for instance, accusing judges of rigging beauty competitions. I draw the curtain on the chapter by looking at how pageants reflected the changing political landscape of Cameroon.

STAGING BEAUTY PAGEANTS IN WEST CAMEROON

Pageants during European Rule and Toward Independence

Ruff Wanzie's interview with Elsie Ikome in March 1972 reflected both a history of disdain for beauty contests that went back to the era of European rule and the fact that they had taken hold in independent West Cameroon. The connection between beauty contests and cultural identity has its roots in colonial-era Africa generally.[9] Prizes substantial enough to offer a significant route out of poverty attracted black African women to compete in beauty contests,[10] and glamourous photos of black American women published in various magazines encouraged the practice.[11] The "New Negro," a black American movement for racial equality that started in 1917, and the works of African American intellectual leaders, such as Marcus Garvey, W. E. B. Du Bois, and Booker T. Washington, inspired the black male editors of the South African newspaper *Bantu World* to hold beauty contests to "combat racist denigrations."[12] The official pageant documents for Miss Africa, which the newspaper ran as a photo beauty contest, described it as "a project of racial uplift." As Lynn Thomas describes, organizers saw the contest as a way to connect pride in Africa's precolonial past to "a politically progressive and commercially vibrant future."[13] In Central Africa, women in the Belgian Congo formed elegant ladies' societies and members purchased matching outfits and entered "dance, beauty, and 'elegance' contests."[14]

At the same time, many black Africans saw beauty pageants as fringe events and depraved Western imports. White European settlers were more likely to enthusiastically participate, supporting, for example, no less than three beauty contests in 1960 among the white European population in South West Africa (modern-day Namibia): S. A. Mannequin of the Year, Miss South West Africa, and Miss Railways for South West Africa.[15] But initial attempts to organize beauty competitions in British Southern Cameroons met considerable resistance.[16] For example, British members of the Women's Corona Society chapter in Bota proposed a beauty contest as part of the Victoria Centenary Celebration in 1958, but Cameroonian members did not approve.[17] The Bota chapter regularly coordinated baby shows (where they disseminated information on hygiene, nutrition, and health care to mothers), children's parties, and needlework competitions for the celebration, but Cameroonian women refused to help, perhaps because they perceived it to be an immoral Western import.[18]

By the end of British administration, Anglophone Cameroonians were more receptive to beauty contests. The Southern Cameroons held a Miss Victoria beauty pageant in February 1960 in the town of Victoria, and the Miss Southern Cameroons beauty contest took place in September 1961.[19] The Miss Independence contest occurred in West Cameroon in October 1961 as part of the reunification celebrations and to commemorate the country's independence from the United Kingdom.[20] The successful enshrinement of beauty pageants in West Cameroon probably reflects the influence of their West African counterparts. Just as they looked to other parts of Anglophone Africa in developing women's organizations, female political elites looked to pageants in Nigeria and elsewhere—via newspapers and personal travel experiences—as signals that these events indicated social progress and a local cosmopolitan tradition. Hence, similar to the contemporary Belizean competitions Richard Wilk studies, feminine beauty ideals in urban West Cameroon were "appropriated, recycled, reintegrated and reinterpreted, worked into existing cultural patterns and localized."[21] The inclusion of the Southern Cameroons in the 1959 Miss Nigeria contest, and the resulting crowning of Nene Etule, an eighteen-year-old from Southern Cameroons as Miss Nigeria in 1959, may also have influenced the development of pageantry in Cameroon.[22] Unquestionably, by the late 1960s, pageants were so popular that some male letter writers to newspapers begged for the development of a male counterpart, a "Handsome Contest" or "Master Cameroon" to complement "Miss Cameroon," prompting a male letter writer in Victoria to inquire, "Do the people who stage these beauty contests forget about men? Does it mean that women are more regarded on earth than men?"[23] Despite some men airing grievances that there were no beauty pageants for men, women continued to be the main figures on pageant stages.

Throughout the 1960s and early 1970s in West Cameroon, beauty contests were held several times a year in different towns with the sponsorship of state officials, local companies, newspapers, and local tourism offices and programs. As Colleen Ballerino Cohen, Richard Wilk, and Beverly Stoeltje argue, pageants mold individual contestants into representatives of sponsoring institutions and hold them accountable to these institutions. In this manner, they claim, pageants identify young women "as signs of social and civic institutions, including the family and the business, the community and the nation."[24] In 1969, for example, the African Tourism Programme focused on creating and developing numerous "fields of competition," including beauty, cooking, and sports competitions. Such initiatives by local tourism boards in towns throughout West Cameroon encouraged young women to advocate for and represent local companies and the newly independent nation.[25]

Miss West Cameroon dance at Victoria Community Hall, 1962. Monica Manga was 1962 Miss West Cameroon. Image © MINCOM Cameroon, courtesy of African Photography Initiatives.

West Cameroonian National Identity in Pageantry

Young women participated in pageants for upward social and economic mobility, as their counterparts throughout the world did and still do. By stating that she is eager to "accept any other regard that awaits [her] as a beauty queen," Ikome positions herself as upwardly mobile. Most were high-school- and university-aged women, usually midteens to early twenties. Many were also teachers at the primary or secondary level or bank clerks, two of the most common professions for women at the time. Newspaper reports scrupulously detailed the education background of each contestant, going as far as to reveal names of schools and diplomas obtained. Contests were restricted to unmarried women with no children. For instance, in 1967 the ministry of tourism sponsored the Miss Victoria beauty contest and advertised that the "competition is open to all childless single females who are between the ages of 18 and 23."[26] Further, by offering winners material goods associated with domesticity and beauty maintenance, and opportunities to travel abroad, pageants reflected both cosmopolitanism and conservative values. Prizes included money, watches, clocks, electric hair coilers, cosmetics, sewing machines, dresses, bedsheets, handbags, and cloth. Winners experienced a wider world when they won trips to the UK or France. Winners also gained access to the prominent social and political elites who attended the contests. Political and economic elites such as directors of banks; leaders of the West Cameroon Federation of Women's Social Clubs and Associations (WSCA), Women's Cameroon National Union (WCNU), and Cameroon National Union (CNU); administrative officials; and even clergymen often made appearances and used the pageants as spaces to visibly reaffirm their political and economic prominence, sometimes personally donating money as prizes and even participating as judges. Clergymen no doubt served a key role in signaling that pageants were moral events.

Pageants also served as spaces to advance nationalist goals and to affirm women's suitable gender roles, as household caretakers and as the "daughters" and "mothers" of the nation. The Miss Social Club 1964 contest in Buea serves as a prime example. In February 1964, the WSCA, which Anna Foncha led, organized a dance to raise funds to build a kindergarten; a beauty contest was the climax of the event. Anna Foncha, who was outfitted in brightly colored traditional attire dotted with stars, gave a speech before the beauty contest in which she thanked attendees for their financial support and "urged the people to wear the Cameroon native [national] costumes, the latest design of which was recently chosen for them by the [WSCA]."[27] Professional female dancers with diverse ethnic backgrounds "displayed traditional airs" (showing local dance moves). The *Cameroon Times* published a photo of the clothing of the three contestants for Miss Social Club, the winners of the Miss Bamenda, Miss Buea, and Miss Kumba contests— an off-the-shoulder Western-style dress, an ankle-length Western-style long skirt set, and a knee-length Western-style skirt set, respectively. Beauty contests reinforced ideas about young women's suitable gender roles by offering domestic prizes such as sewing machines. The winner, Miss Bamenda, proclaimed her joy to a *Cameroon Times* interviewer thus: "Being so happy and grateful to the organisers of the social club, I carried my big prize of sewing machine away which I never dreamt of getting one like it." As Anna Foncha's presence at the Miss Social Club contest illustrates, political elites used pageants to support nationalist projects and to legitimize women's roles as "daughters" and "mothers" of the nation. In this case, the contest raised money and brought attention to the WSCA's kindergarten-building project, supporting the organization's goals of making social advancements in women's lives while focusing on children as markers of domesticity and motherhood.

The example of the Miss Social Club contest also shows that pageants were spaces of cultural production in which political elites could highlight facets of West Cameroonian cultural identity. Foncha used the contest as another outlet to encourage the audience to don the West Cameroonian national costume, and the pageant showcased local dances and "native" cuisine. Professional dancers from West Cameroon often performed in conjunction with pageants. For instance, the Miss Victoria 1967 contest occurred in late June in conjunction with competitions in which restaurant owners in Victoria competed to cook local cuisine and dancers from ethnic groups from throughout West Cameroon showcased local dances.[28] Yet the pageant contestants also reference the progressive side of West Cameroon through their Western attire. Through such combinations, West Cameroonian pageants incarnated multiple notions of aesthetic and cultural values to shape distinct ideas.

The Miss Social Club contest also illustrates how pageants were safe spaces for political elites to *visually* emphasize Anglophone ethnonationalism. As Richard Wilk's work on beauty pageants in Belize suggests, because ethnic divisions might threaten unity and camaraderie in a country, pageants "make ethnicity, a potentially dangerous and divisive issue, into something ornamental and safe. . . . As long as it remains focused on artistic performance, the government sponsors ethnic expression."[29] Thus they serve the needs of the political elite if done for nationalistic reasons and artistic expression. Pageants supported ethnic expression as art; local dances and "native dishes" expressed ethnicity without any threat. Therefore, beauty pageants supported the forging of a unified national identity within a culturally diverse state, forming an agglomerate and hybrid panethnicity that various ethnic groups might embrace. For instance, the Banso, Kom, Meta, Bali, and Bayangi ethnic groups—the background of the professional female dancers in the Miss Social Club 1964 competition—are, like the Fonchas, from the western Grassfields of Cameroon, in the contemporary Northwest Region of Cameroon, while the Banyang are originally from the Mamfe region, in the modern-day Southwest Region of Cameroon. Showcasing local dances from throughout West Cameroon was one more way Foncha sought to forge a unified Anglophone ethnonationalism that all Anglophone Cameroonians might embrace, ideologically and visually. This could change attitudes about ethnic loyalty that might have threatened unity. At the same time, the preponderance of western Grassfields ethnicities' local dances suggests that they dominated this new ethnonationalism, not least because they shared the Fonchas' region of origin. Panethnic unity only went so far—the fabric of the national costume came from the same region, as did many of the strategies of fostering women's collective mobilization that Foncha invoked to spur women's political rallies.

Foncha was not alone in attaching other events to beauty pageants as a way to fuse a united Anglophone identity. O. S. Ebanja, president of the Fako Divisional Tourism Board, issued a press release in August 1969 describing dancing, singing, "gastronomy competitions," wrestling and soccer matches that would coincide with the forthcoming beauty competition, to fulfill the mandate that "Cameroon culture must be portrayed." The same press release provides the rules for the singing competitions, including the requirement that they have "[o]riginality with Cameroonian background." It also notes, "production of native dishes in hotels is included in these programs in order to encourage hotels to serve tourists with native dishes whenever necessary. Members of the public are invited to . . . taste of the good dishes prepared by women up the [Mount Cameroon] mountain."[30] Those who attended beauty competitions might also "consume" palatable ideas about a panethnic West Cameroonian identity. These expressions of ethnicity and cultural identity presented West Cameroon as a unified nation in which diverse cultural identities coexisted in harmony. In this manner, political elites continued to co-opt women's domestic labor to perform labor on behalf of the state. Like their counterparts in the modern-day US Virgin Islands, pageant culture legitimized cultural productions, such as highlighting "native" dances, while creating "an ambassadorial, albeit fictional, place within the political machinery for the young female participants."[31] By competing in pageants, and thus engaging in performative labor, Anglophone Cameroonian beauty contestants represented and "performed" traits of ideal womanhood and West Cameroonian cultural identity that would resonate on and off the pageant stage.

"A BEAUTY COMPETITION IS A NATIONAL UNDERTAKING": AUDIENCE PARTICIPATION

A month after lamenting the postponement of the April 1962 Miss West Cameroon beauty contest due to lack of interest, Clara Manga was explicit in an article for the *Cameroon Champion*: "I would also like the entire public to remember that a beauty competition is a national undertaking." Reflecting the cultural affinity West Cameroonians felt for Nigeria, with shared British administrative legacies, she pointed to Nigerian participation as a reason for West Cameroonian women to enter: "If you read the *Daily Times* [a Nigerian newspaper] these days, the same thing is taking place all over Nigeria now. So why not in the Cameroons, especially now [that] we are independent?"[32] Clara Manga was not the only journalist to make this case.

Beauty pageants in West Cameroon were community undertakings, underpinning collective efforts to shape nationalist projects. Judges, contestants, their parents, audience members, and elite economic and political members of society all had vested political and cultural interest in the contests. Often, hundreds of people attended pageants. Audience members included market women, bankers, and government officials. Diverse government organizations, such as the WCNU, social clubs, corporations, and even newspapers sponsored beauty contests. For instance, the *Cameroon Champion* organized the Miss Independence contest in 1961, and the Cameroon Commercial Corporation (CCC) organized the Miss CCC contest. The CCC was a retail distributor for rural and urban areas in the West Cameroon State. The West Cameroon government established the CCC in hopes of improving the nation's economy and counteracting the shrinkage of retail trade that had occurred since independence.[33] The WCNU organized a contest in 1970, the Miss WCNU.[34] Breweries such as Guinness and Brasseries du Cameroun organized special competitions on New Year's Eve and New Year's Day in Victoria and Kumba, illustrating the political and economic links of beauty pageants.[35]

Festivities such as Christmas dances and fundraising events for humanitarian causes such as raising money for the Red Cross Society were also frequently the backdrops for beauty contests. Newspapers reported the names of state officials and economic elites who attended the contests and interviewed them about their enjoyment of the events, making them sites of sociopolitical importance and authority. The list often included the prime ministers of West and East Cameroon as well as other public officials and presidents of leading women's organizations. These political elites often served as judges or personally sponsored contestants by purchasing clothing and hiring makeup and hair stylists. As in beauty pageants in the US Virgin Islands in the colonial and postcolonial period, politically elite women and men used their influence to become involved in pageants.[36] For example, O. S. Ebanja, president of the Fako Divisional Tourism Board and Gladys Difo, the women's special representative in the West Cameroon Legislative Assembly, both served as judges more than once. The judges for the Miss Brasseries du Cameroun and Guinness 1972 contests in Victoria and Kumba were all editors of leading newspapers of the time—*Cameroon Times*, *Cameroon Outlook*, and *Hero*.[37]

State officials often emphasized the nationalist element of these pageants. In 1967, for example, G. C. Kisob, the senior district officer of Kumba, gave a speech at the end of the Miss Kumba Beauty Queen contest explaining that the "contest was one of many organized by the Federal Government in the year of national tourism." Kisob underscored the West Cameroonian government's expectations of increased tourism in the West Cameroon State, noting that beauty contests would entertain visitors likely to "swell" the economy. He urged other "beauties now hiding" to come forward for future beauty contests.[38] Young women, he suggested, could fulfill their national and civic duty by supporting the business of tourism and galvanizing local communities.

Beauty contests were as much about audience members as about the competitors. Some members of the political elite argued that lack of community support for beauty contests hindered nationalism. In September 1962, Clara Manga expressed disappointment that West Cameroonians "showed very little interested in the [Miss West Cameroon] Beauty Queen of the year." She laments,

> It is a pity that our country still has not got enough public spirited or open-minded people. They claim to be highly educated, but socially, I am sorry to say, most of them fall below average. A beauty competition in other civilized countries is a national affair. . . . The social life in our country is still very low.[39]

Manga understood the Miss West Cameroon 1962 contest as a nationalistic duty. All citizens, she implied, should be interested in the person who would represent West Cameroonian cultural identity on a national and international level. At the same time, she criticized the behavior of some individuals among the 400 hundred attendees, writing several months before, in June 1962,

> I was surprised to see some high-ranking men [that] you would think should know what it is to respect the decision of the judges, hooting like hooligans. . . . And I cannot understand why they hooted and shamed [one of the contestants]. . . . I appeal to our men and women to learn how to put their emotions, however strong, under control in public.[40]

Thus, pageants also served as a safe space in which to censure actions that seemed disruptive to the social life and activities of local communities and therefore as hindering national unity. Such censure is similar to criticisms of women who refused to participate in women's organizations and were therefore considered to be hindering national unity. Just as women were told to behave in suitable ways when engaging in women's organizations, attendees at beauty pageants were condemned for not behaving in an acceptable manner and publicly harming Anglophone integrity and pride.

Pageants served as more secure areas to criticize social and political behaviors that audiences perceived as destructive to the perceived decorum of Anglophone identity. While women journalist accused beauty pageant attendees of unruly behavior, attendees used pageants as spaces in which to condemn the unsuitable comportment and conduct of contestants and judges. As Colleen Ballerino Cohen, Richard Wilk, and Beverly Stoeltje argue, beauty contests "evoke passionate interest and engagement with political issues central to the lives of beauty contestants, sponsors, organizers, and audiences—issues that frequently have nothing obvious to do with the competition itself."[41] They conclude that "[b]y choosing an individual whose deportment, appearance, and style embodies the values and goals of a nation, locality, or group, beauty contests expose these same values and goals to interpretation and challenge." In November 1969, citizens in Victoria drafted a letter to the minister of information and tourism protesting the crowning of Kate Matute of Buea, asserting that the contest was rigged, challenging who they believed to be the embodiment of ideal beauty. People of varying socioeconomic status, from market women to directors of companies, signed the letter, which included complaints that the judges awarded high marks to one of the contestants and swayed the results of the contest:

> The protest holds that a female member of the panel of judges groomed the contestant while another judge was responsible for her robe, thereby demonstrating their interest in one of the contestants. . . . Miss Matute, who finally won . . . was not a popular choice. . . . To select a girl who was obviously, at least to the majority of the public, not a BEAUTY in comparison to the others, and considering that her progress throughout the contest has had a dubious surrounding, it would amount to [a] high-handed disregard of the opinion of the public.[42]

The letter went on to explain that protestors were appealing in the interest not only of that year's contest but of future contests. They warned that if the minister of information and tourism for the Federal Republic of Cameroon, Paul Fokam Kamga, did not review Matute's victory, the "public confidence in the process of selecting beauty queens may be shaken."[43] Richard Wilk contends that judging beauty contests can be "an exercise that simultaneously divides people and brings them together. While they will never agree completely in their judgments, [people] can often agree on the terms of disagreement. Beauty contests engage diverse cultures and communities in exactly this kind of shared discourse and contention."[44] Complaints about rigging pageants reflected the tension between the ideal of respectable public contests of open democracy and the influence of covert processes through which power and privilege provided an advantage, mirroring more general concerns about proper Anglophone conduct.[45]

By criticizing the electoral process, audience members, such as those in Victoria in 1969, invoked collective understandings about an Anglophone identity tied to propriety and a moral perspective. Audience members were interactive and vocal from the stands. Their perspectives and reactions to beauty contests illustrate the nuances of how local community members used pageants as vehicles to express differing ideas about West Cameroonian political participation and perceived decorum of Anglophone identity.

"D-DAY FOR BEAUTY QUEENS": TENSIONS OVER IDEAL WOMANHOOD

While beauty contests increased over the course of the 1960s and 1970s, Wanzie's reference to rumors of trading sex for judging points reflected the persistent aura of impropriety around them. Likewise, Elsie Ikome's conflation of ideal womanhood with being "proper" and heeding gender norms was in part a response to slander. Yet Wanzie gave Ikome a forum because, like various members of the educated urban elite, she had an interest in framing beauty pageants as a rightful place for upstanding, moral young women who engaged with cosmopolitan ideals of beauty while adhering to suitable traits of conservative womanhood.

The question of whether "free women" participated in pageants reflected larger anxieties about the sexual morals of young unmarried women. As per the suggestions of other scholars, urban residents throughout Africa expressed a similar concern.[46] Newspapers and oral evidence suggest that, even though "free women" specifically meant sexually loose young adult women, the line was frequently blurred, and any single woman might be accused of being a "free woman," her unmarried status alone implying that she might threaten dominant gender norms. A missive to the *Cameroon Times* by a Joseph Bimi from Kumba counseled readers to identify "free women" by their possession of "durable and costly things like radiograms [combined radio and record players], foot machines, [and] first class furniture," saying that it would require multiple boyfriends to fund such purchases. "Such a girl is a civilized harlot who uses her education in luring more men," he warned.[47] Such assertions defined "free women" as those frequenting bars, smoking cigarettes, drinking beer, wearing "short skirts and wigs," using "too much makeup," and engaging "in illicit sexual activities, often with married men," perhaps for pay.[48] Anxiety about "free women" was really about waning male authority over young unmarried women in a period of changing gender roles and women's increasing move into the formal workforce. Beauty contests and their supporters endeavored to redress the problems by stressing a womanhood that adhered to traditional norms, regardless of the contestants' formal educational background.

Beauty pageants became one more way for the elite to impose ideal gender norms on women, retaining power by disciplining the "dangerous class" of women who did not adhere to these norms and who may have threatened West Cameroonian cultural values. Most urban West Cameroonians were poor; as Thomas observes concerning South Africa under similar economic conditions in the 1930s, "appearances were especially important in defining class differences and claiming respectability."[49] Some of the anxiety surrounding beauty pageants, then, had to do with the threat that young women of lower socioeconomic status would begin to pass as the educated elite and acquire social privileges that urban educated elites preferred to keep for themselves. If permitted, "free women" might use pageants to make class boundaries more permeable, hindering elite efforts to exhibit beauty queens as socially progressive, sexually moral, and adhering to local values of gender norms. Accordingly, female journalists and other urban elites sought to protect class boundaries by suggesting that sexually lax women were unwelcome as pageant contestants and unqualified to signal the nation's progress toward modernity. Wanzie's reporting of Elsie Ikome's opinion that beauty contests are not for "wayward girls" exemplifies this. State officials and female journalists who promoted beauty pageant contestants thus fought a double battle: to attract young middle-class women to compete and to police class and social boundaries. Columns such as Wanzie's encouraged young women to compete and all of Anglophone Cameroon to look on beauty contests with reverence. Thus, journalists and public officials in postcolonial Africa played a vital role in the organization of beauty pageants.

Contestants and pageant advocates sought to bring an air of respectability to pageants by emphasizing the potential upward mobility and progressiveness that beauty competitions offered. As Oluwakemi Balogun and Kimberly Hoang argue, it is common for women's bodies to bear a particular burden of "represent[ing] their nation's rising status in the global economy" by being groomed and coached, wearing expensive clothing, and winning material and financial prizes that provide upward mobility.[50] In August 1969 the *Cameroon Outlook* editor promoted the Miss Lunar Beauty Contest that was to take place in Victoria, thus:

> Beauty is the gift of nature. You might even commit to memory this passionate line penned by an English poet: "A thing of beauty is joy forever." A stronger reason exists if you know that the mere display of YOURSELF at the selection dance might end up with prizes in cash and kind, going places and having your gorgeous pictures spangling the pages of newspapers and magazines.[51]

While the call for contestants suggests that young women should cultivate an appreciation for the gift nature has given them, it also promises economic compensation for displaying this "gift." Even Elsie Ikome, who portrayed herself as shy and meek, compared her recent victory as West Miss Africa Football Cup to winning a "lottery ticket."[52] In exchange for such economic compensation, contestants exercised a type of performative labor for the state, much as women did in women's organizations and domestic science centers, as Ikome's reference to being a "useful citizen" in Wanzie's interview insinuates.

Beyond receiving prizes and attention, female contestants of beauty pageants expressed interest in proving their social and political importance as daughters of the state. Ikome's local win as Miss West Africa Cup in 1972 meant that she would compete at the national level in Yaoundé and thus represent Anglophone regions of the country at the federal level. In urging formally educated middle-class women to compete in beauty contests, Ikome fulfills her nationalist obligation. She embraces modest comportment, implying that her physical beauty, although probably a deciding factor in her string of wins, is not as important as fulfilling traits of ideal womanhood such as eventually getting married. These qualities, she implies, are linked to her nationalist obligations to be a good citizen, thus framing herself as a "good" woman not concerned with frivolous concerns such as physical beauty. Instead, she uses her time to contribute to the state's economy as a bank worker and, as Wanzie observed, by remaining busy with "domestic affairs." In this manner, Wanzie and Ikome linked suitable attributes of womanhood, such as cooking and plans for future marriage, to an ideal gendered citizenry that was performed on pageant stages.

Some public officials did not play this role as carefully as Wanzie and Ikome. During a meeting of the Meme Divisional Tourism Board in June 1969, the government's tourism officer, D. E. Ebong, announced that West Cameroon would participate in the Miss Africa contest for the first time that year. Ebong conceded that "street girls" (prostitutes) were known to compete in Cameroon's beauty contests, which was "unlike other countries where only sophisticated women do take part," but he hoped it would be otherwise.[53] He attempted to soothe anxieties about the sexual mores of beauty contests by explaining that Miss World 1968 was earning a doctorate when she postponed her exams to participate in the contest. The reference to a global contest suggests how West Cameroonian urban elites turned to other nations to inform their nationalist projects. He advised the Tourism Board in Meme to organize a Miss Meme contest—implicitly to find possible representatives for Miss Africa—and specifically asked them to invite high school students as a way to crowd out the potential participation of "free women." He emphasized the economic advantages of entering beauty competitions by pointing out that former Miss Kumba found employment in Douala, a Francophone economic hub about an hour west from Buea, while Miss Mezam found employment at the Buea Tourism Office, suggesting that the Miss Africa contests offered an advantage in the job market. While acknowledging the presence of countervailing forces, Ebong frames beauty pageants as stages of respectability where young, formally educated women could access respectable careers in an assortment of economic sectors. Formally educated women, according to Ebong, were ideal contestants because they embodied everyday ideas among the urban elite about modern citizenship—their education and domesticity were made visible, and this display was critical not only to their futures but to that of the nation.

Ebong was not the only pageant-booster to invoke the Miss World competition in promoting West Cameroonian pageants. Female journalists recommending that their readers compete inserted pictures of Miss World participants and winners. In July 1966, the *Cameroon Observer*'s women's column ran two images and a description of Lesley Langley, a white British woman who was Miss World 1965, describing her as an admiralty clerk and giving details of her bodily measurements: 37-24-37.[54] In November 1967, the *Cameroon Times* published images of four African women who participated in the Miss World 1967, from Uganda, Tanzania, Nigeria, and Ghana.[55] Such references suggested that West Cameroon's progressiveness was on par with their British *and* their African counterparts who participated in beauty pageants, thus identifying pageants as suitable African activities.

Nonetheless, the stereotype that prostitutes or women of questionable sexual virtue competed in beauty competitions persisted, and Ebanja, the president of the Fako Divisional Tourism Board, acknowledged as much in a letter that ran in the *Cameroon Outlook* in August 1969, just as Ebong had. Yet he argued that most of the contestants kept their morality and sense of cultural identity intact, asserting that the idea that beauty contests is a matter for "free women" should be dismissed. He argued,

> In the first place, I am inclined to believe that some of the most beautiful girls do not belong to the "free class" group. In fact, I have reasons to believe that the majority of the most beautiful girls belong to the reserved and controlled class who are either developing into womanhood or are planning their future in a noble manner. One of the purposes of selecting these girls is to show nature's excellent creation.[56]

In other words, "street girls" might participate, but they were unlikely to win. In using words such as "reserved," "controlled," and "noble," Ebanja references the suitable comportment and behavior of contestants that will distinguish respectable women from "free women." Such women, Ebanja is convinced, reflect "nature's excellent creation," defining ideas about "authentic" beauty by associating it with what he deems suitable comportment and conduct.

Accusations of lax morals may be one reason that Miss Faso Agricultural 1973, eighteen-year-old Rose Bitioe, emphasized her Christian faith in discussing her victory. Acknowledging that her parents were initially reluctant to let her compete, Bitioe explained in an interview with the *Cameroon Outlook* that she entered the contest because she wanted to "display her beauty, 'a gift from God'. . . . and want[ed] to encourage young beautiful girls for future competitions." In doing so, she underlined her belief in God, suggesting that pageants were a moral activity and emphasizing their compatibility with respectable behavior. She further shared that two social welfare officers, acquaintances of her parents, had trained her to move and smile in a way that they thought would increase her chances.[57] Bitioe described the coaching as "moderniz[ing]" her movements, suggesting a departure from a more local African style. In their introduction to *Global Beauty, Local Bodies*, Afshan Jafar and Erynn Masi de Casanova write that it is common for nations to seek to elevate themselves and claim modernity by establishing body disciplining and modifying regimes for women who supposedly embody progress.[58] As Oluwakemi Balogun asserts in her work on contemporary Nigerian beauty pageants, "nations must appear to embody both traditional and modern models of femininity in order to shore up national boundaries. . . . specific framings of the body shape how the nation is managed and configured." Balogun argues that this is part of the machinery of beauty pageants that highlights upward mobility and progressiveness: "'Grooming' contestants focused on changes in both demeanor and physical embodiment, which was directly linked to the class mobility of contestants."[59] The same logic can be applied to neighboring Anglophone regions of Cameroon.

But while Bitioe won money and a radio, measures of upward mobility, her reference to her faith underlines a humility that trumped physical beauty and monetary gains. Christian contestants such as Bitioe framed pageant participation as the duty of young Christian women, whose God-given physical beauty they should share as a signifier of their gratitude to God. In this manner, Bitioe goes beyond virtue to define ideal Anglophone womanhood as embodying Christian morality. Karen Tice identifies a similar dynamic in contemporary US beauty pageants. She explains that describing pageants as glorifying God's gift to them—their beauty—is common for many born-again Christian contestants, who seem to use this claim "to justify their pageant participation and purify its corporeal aspects, including following God's design and promoting Christianity."[60] Thus, Christian contestants like Rose Bitioe and her contemporary American counterparts position competing as doing a service to themselves, the nation, and God, debunking prevailing ideas about the immorality of beauty pageants.

BODILY IDEALS AND URBAN IDENTITIES

This section highlights the experiences of Elsie Ikome to look at how pageants informed larger ideas about ideal bodily movement, comportment, and physical beauty and how these attributes were associated with an urban identity. In the same way that I examined the lives of Anna Foncha, Gwendoline Burnley, Gladys Endeley, and Kate Idowu in chapters 1, 2, and 3 to highlight larger ideas about Anglophone Cameroonian women's social and political roles, here I examine the experiences of their younger counterparts, specifically Elsie Ikome as a pageant contestant. Her story encapsulates women's individual agency in the context of social constraints and limited definitions of ideal Anglophone womanhood, even for contestants who supposedly had all the requirements. Ikome's experiences suggest how dominant gender norms shaped young Anglophone Cameroonian women and how these women reshaped and challenged these ideas amid the politicized environment of beauty pageants. Examining these experiences reveals the ambiguities regarding female beauty contestants, who both affirmed and challenged dominant gender norms related to suitable comportment and feminine beauty ideals.

"How Elsie Came to the Forefront": Bodily Comportment and Conduct

When Wanzie wrote about her in March 1972, Ikome had swept major West Cameroonian beauty pageants, including Miss Fako Beauty Queen and West Miss Africa Football Cup, and she would soon represent Anglophone regions of the country at the federal level. While Wanzie was convinced that Ikome epitomized suitable womanhood and was thus a good representative of West Cameroonian cultural values, a famed journalist for the *Cameroon Outlook*, Adolf Mongo Dipoko, was at first not convinced. While Wanzie focused on Elsie's recent wins as evidence of her suitable comportment and adherence to gender norms, Dipoko's article, published eight days after Wanzie's interview, highlights her early beauty competitions. He suggested that she was over-confident and had too much pride, and that for this reason she had placed second in a beauty contest in the Bay Saloon in Victoria. Dipoko observed, "When Elsie Ikome told a panel of judges at the Bay Saloon early last month that she came into the beauty show only as an emblem of encouragement to other shy girls, she seemed to be toying with those trail potentials of women mostly to combat emotions" [meaning to show off her competitive advantage in front of the losing competitors].[61] He elaborated, "And when the judges found it convenient to announce their result, Elsie came second place, next to Miss Efeti." He added, "But this development came closer to the temptation of personal value in the eyes of other people." While the judges may have found Ikome's response haughty, Dipoko attested that she had the support of the "Victoria population," who believed she was merely her confident self: "To the Victoria population, she was the Elsie they know. . . . And whether her flounces offended anyone [or not], it still took her the usual time [to travel] from her mile one residence to the office. At least this is what those who know Elsie think of her."

Dipoko further argues that Elsie's overconfidence attracted positive media attention: "When Elsie caught the eyes of our camera man Eddy John last year, and she was the first West Cameroon girl to pose so emotionally before a press camera man, the *Fako Magazine* picked her up for their Cover girl." Dipoko recounts an interview with Elsie:

> in an unusual ecstasy mixed with the flamboyance of a city girl, she told me in an interview that she will have an edge over all other contestants who will trail behind her. To me, it seemed a little of a hyperbole and when she finally did win at the regional in Buea, I found myself defeated for failing to assess how much she was beautiful. Yet she was not lacking. From a springboard, she moved to Yaoundé . . . [and] Elsie brought home what for a decade, since reunification, [what] West Cameroon has never won. That alone is consoling. Elsie, an employee of the Cameroon Bank Limited, has round her little world [and] expanded in dimension [her world has expanded].

Dipoko's March 1972 extensive accounts of Elsie's beauty pageant experience highlight conflicting issues of suitable bodily comportment and demeanor. Perhaps, he speculates, Elsie's overconfidence displeased the judges. Yet pageant advocates engaged in a discourse in which they encouraged young women to be less shy and more confident and to participate in beauty competitions; the survival of the competitions depended on it. In 1972 pageant boosters were still conscious that contestants could be scarce; in April the Miss West Cameroon 1962 beauty contest in the Community Hall in Victoria was postponed for several months because, as Clara Manga (writing as "Auntie Clara") of the *Cameroon Champion* observed, in spite of the success of the accompanying [ballroom] dance, "Hundreds of people attended, waiting anxiously [for] the time of the competition, but unfortunately after midnight only four of the [seven registered] beauties had arrived. Those from Bamenda, Mamfe and Kumba did not turn up."[62] The *Cameroon Times* similarly observed the presence of timid contestants in the Miss West Cameroon 1967 beauty contest reporting that contestants "moved around casting faint smiles to the anxious audience. There were marks of blush in the faces of some of the girls when at the second stage they appeared individually in swimsuits." Two contestants failed to participate in the second stages of the competition, presumably because they were too modest to appear on stage in a swimsuit. The Miss Radio Buea 1967 contest was canceled because no contestants came. An article in the *Cameroon Times* about the event described it as a signal that the young women of Cameroon were a disappointment, concluding that they "displayed the highest humour of timidity."[63]

While pageant advocates expressed disappointment that young women were too shy to enter pageants—probably reflecting widespread perceptions among urbanites that pageants were immoral—larger ideas about how specific comportment and demeanor for women hinged on the locale and circumstance. Ruff Wanzie, for example, encouraged women to be timid in matters of the heart: "Girls now chase men instead of men chasing them. Our girls say it's civilization to chase a man. It is not our tradition nor culture for a woman to chase a man." Although women in West Cameroon do not have to wait for suitors, "sit[ting] like a duck in a shooting gallery," she counsels that "[i]t's the pride of a woman to be shy to a certain extent, to show the feminine qualities in her manners, laugher, speech, posture, etc."[64] Subsequently, Wanzie encourages them to be more forthright when socializing in public. Women who are too shy, she argues, cause embarrassment in social gatherings.[65]

Not surprisingly, expectations of timid comportment and a somewhat measure of a confident attitude in pageants in which contestants appeared on stages in swimsuits came to define performative womanhood. Proper bodily comportment and movement were ways for contestants to demonstrate West Cameroon's progressiveness. While Wanzie attributes positive qualities to Ikome, noting her cheerful disposition and that she was "smiling sweetly,"

Dipoko thought her walk, "her flounces," betrayed a haughty attitude. Onlookers at other beauty competitions described the suitable comportment of contestants by using such terms as "quiet," "unsophisticated," "intelligent," and "lovely smile." Patience Nganda, the winner of the Miss West Cameroon 1967 pageant was certainly not a shy contestant, sharing with a *Cameroon Times* reporter: "I had confidence in myself before I entered the hall," and that she retained that confidence because, "[i]t is not only beauty which matters; gait too counts."[66] She shared that a Mrs. Crawford, a Jamaican woman who helped her choose her wardrobe for the contest, spent three hours teaching her how to walk and pose. Nganda asserts that a woman's bodily movement and proper gait exude a type of beauty and self-confidence that ensures success in beauty pageants. These descriptions recall Dorothea Schulz's description of modern-day Malian beauty pageants, in which she observed that spectators commonly attribute positive personal qualities to women who show the right posture and emotional expressions.[67] Further, as Marie Grace Brown contends in her work on fashion and body politics in the first half of the twentieth century in Sudan, "there is nothing universal or unbiased in the ways our bodies move. . . . our physical habits are not natural or automatic, but the result of carefully taught social processes. Thus, techniques and movements are not much different than other marks of identity found on our bodies."[68] With this perspective in mind, a contestant's outwardly comportment in 1960s beauty pageants in West Cameroon determined her attractiveness and skillfully crafted and learned bodily (physical) representation of progressiveness. The fact that Nganda was formally educated (at a secondary-education government school in Kumba) further highlights how a woman's emotional confidence and bodily practices might trump the use of cosmetics and other aesthetic and bodily rituals conflated with "free women." Nganda's statements suggest that learning "proper" bodily stance helped her gain confidence and consequently be a more attractive contestant. She maintained a respectable exterior look by relying on her confidence and bodily comportment, with her formal education as a foundation. Her acknowledgment that a Jamaican woman taught her how to walk and pose for the contest not only suggests the diversity of the Cameroonian population in Anglophone Cameroon, but how varied cultural practices informed vernacular ideas about "carefully taught social processes" of sophisticated bodily disposition in the 1960s.

As Elsie Ikome's March 1972 interview with Wanzie reveals, the physical appearance of pageant contestants in West Cameroon harnessed attitudes about young women's embodied practices. While Ikome would inform Wanzie she was a shy competitor, Dipoko's account suggests otherwise. Her confidence challenged ideals about suitable comportment for women and pageant contestants, redefining what it meant to be a "good" woman. Her "flounces" launched her to prominence and offered her upward social mobility. She would be the first Anglophone woman to win a national beauty competition in Francophone Cameroon, even as she challenged prevailing gender norms and shaped new ideas about acceptable comportment. Even Dipoko, despite his original hesitations about Ikome because of her supposed haughty attitude, had to reluctantly admit that Elsie's win in Yaoundé was "consoling."

Elsie Strives to "Keep a Good Shape": The Commodification of Beauty and Bodily Ideals

Cameroonian cultures have always "considered a robust shape a measure of health and wealth," and the fetishization of women's thinness of the 1960s and 1970s in Western cultures had considerably less traction in Cameroon. Yet some urbanites started to prize slimness, at least for women.[69] Ikome's 1972 interview with Wanzie reflects these conflicting body ideals. Belying the claim to shyness, she proclaims that she endeavors to "steal the show" in Yaoundé by striving to "keep a good shape, [to] be natural and smart."[70] The meaning of "a good shape," was a source of tension that reflected varied issues about Westernization, Africanness, and the blending of global and local ideas about feminine beauty standards and bodily ideals. Because many new beauty products came from the West, this blending became imbricated with the commodification of beauty.

Thin, as the Western women's magazines would say, was in. Advertisements in West Cameroonian newspapers called on women to keep a good shape. In August 1968, the Venus de Milo, a Victoria-based hairdressing salon, advertised their new "slimming machine"—an exercise machine. The *Cameroon Times* journalist sent to investigate the new "slimming machine" reported "a long queue of fashion and beauty conscious women who lined the salon wanting to take [the] slimming course."[71] Anne Fosah, a frequent guest columnist in the women's column of the *Cameroon Workman*, was among the beauticians who described the response to the *Cameroon Times* reporter.[72] Fosah and her colleague Najat K'kongsen told the reporter that the salon's newly arrived beauty equipment included, in addition to the slimming machine, a super flavita, a body machine that could cure "acne pimples, black and white heads, eczema. . . . and any other skin diseases."

A year after the Venus de Milo debuted its slimming machine and attending course, the male editor of the *Cameroon Outlook* proposed that such courses were a way to prepare for beauty competitions. In an open letter to the female readers of the paper, he wrote of an upcoming beauty pageant:

> You just cannot afford to miss this big opportunity if you are a cute girl with a good figure. Are you over weight, then start a "slim course" today so that you might cut down some kilograms. Have black heads and ugly scars which embarrass you? Then you do not need to undergo a plastic surgery before the contest. Just call at your local chemist, and he will show you a boxful of creams which will get those ugly marking away before the competition starts in Victoria, on August 9th.[73]

While the appeal began by asserting "Beauty is the gift of nature," this passage makes clear that beauty was more a function of economics than nature. In recommending that women change their bodies to fit the ideal, he tied the Western ideal to what he deemed to be suitable African aesthetic rituals.

But beauty contests could also be a space for female nonparticipants to exhibit their beauty off stage. Many women journalists endorsed the use of beauty products such as cosmetics for nonparticipants as a key part of attending beauty pageants and performing varied ideas of suitable bodily practices. Although they cautioned that excessive cosmetic use would be perceived as sexually lax, they nevertheless included extensive instructions on how to use cosmetics, such as how to wear lipstick. A guest column that beautician and entrepreneur Anne Fosah contributed to in the *Cameroon Workman*'s women's advice column, "Women's Bay," which was hosted by Atuk Maformusong, for example, provided detailed instructions on cosmetics for women planning to attend beauty pageants in early August 1969. The instructions were alongside two pictures of beauty pageant winners captioned "Nene Etule" (Miss Nigeria 1959) and "Monica Manga" (1962 Miss West Cameroon). The suggestion was that by following Fosah's instructions, women might look like Etule and Manga. The opening paragraphs of the lengthy column, is penned by the regular columnist Atuk Maformusong who began with the following colorful statements, which culminate by revealing an upcoming mysterious event: "[T]here is something striking in the news. . . . What could it be?— Planting season for the late maize? No! Not that! Take another guess. . . . The International Year of tourism [?] Yes, that is right! It is the talk [of] the news! Yes! It is our own trip to the moon." Maformusong proceeds to explain that the announcement that the International Year for African Tourism for the

Fako Division will begin in early August 1969, when the preliminary rounds for Miss Fako will take place in Muyuka, Victoria, Tiko, and Buea. Finalists would compete on September 30 in the famed Buea Mountain Hotel where the competition for the West Cameroon national costume had taken place several years prior. Other activities in the program included a soccer match, local dances, wrestling, a canoe and bicycle race, and a choir competition. Maformusong further writes, "Well! Ladies, and for all women who care, this is a grand opportunity to shake up the cold and keep the limbs warm again. Certainly, I will be there. . . . You certainly need some preparation before the trip—good hair dressing and make-ups?" Maformusong thus introduced Fosah's forthcoming advice, writing, "It's another tip from Mrs. Fosah on make-ups and on our healthy surrounding." Stressing that her instructions are for "appropriate make-up for a fashion-conscious girl or woman," Fosah counsels such women to "[a]lways make sure when buying your cosmetics that you do not buy cheap cosmetics for cheap things sometimes cost more in the long run." She advises, "[a] smooth, clean skin, a good shade of powder well applied to match your complexion; a good choice of lipstick, nail polish and a good application of these cosmetics gives you an attractive and enticing appearance in the public and, in our particular case, at all activities of the 'Intra-Fako Tourism.' Again, this is a step forward."[74] In her instructions, Fosah links cosmetic use with cosmopolitanism, social mobility, and ideal womanhood. Women might "step forward" by spending money on quality cosmetic products (read: not "cheap things"). By following her advice on cosmetic use, women might exhibit their fashion-consciousness in a sort of grand public performance—taking their own trip to the moon—much like beauty pageant winners Etule and Manga, or like Elsie Ikome, who expanded the dimension of her "little world."

A modeling school that opened in June 1979 in Kumba was the logical extension of the preceding decade's commodification of beauty. The founder, Esther Hensen Gwanmesia from Bali Nyongo, a town in the Northwest Region of Cameroon, described herself as "the first Cameroonian to qualify in modelling." Gwanmesia had completed her early education in Bamenda and a nursing and midwifery degree at Banso Baptist Hospital before leaving for East Africa with her Dutch husband in 1972. They moved to Holland in 1977 where, according to the *Cameroon Outlook*, "she embarked on an intensive course in modelling." In an interview with the *Cameroon Outlook* in December 1979, she explained that "modeling is now a career for girls involving designing, beautifying, figure control and ensuring that they accomplish pleasing personalities. It also involves all wares, as dresses, earrings . . . watches, bangles, shirts, jumpers, etc." The paper reports that Gwanmesia saw her school as a way of "improv[ing] . . . African women's beauty."

> She has always seen that the African women, in spite of her natural beauty, is copying Western-style which tend to disturb her figure. "The whole carriage of a woman must be controlled," she declared explaining that sometimes sluggishness in women come[s] from artificial habits. Asked about the courses she would run, [she said] she would concentrate on urbanized girls. She would convince them to know themselves, their background, health, [and] eating habits, so that they could get all fat deposits in bodies properly assimilated [meaning, presumably, proper amount of fat throughout the body].[75]

Gwanmesia's modeling school did not open until late 1979, after the period this book discusses, but it represented a culmination of the larger issues about aesthetic rituals, bodily movements, and "authentic" beauty in Anglophone Cameroon that were present during the federal period. Like other urban, formally educated women in this period, Esther drew from her international worldview, personal experiences, and local ideas about beauty to visually and ideologically shape a hybridized African feminine ideal and suitable comportment. She condemns both African adoptions of Western styles and "sluggishness" as artificial, illustrating how a global worldview and local ideas about suitable conduct produce notions of authenticity. Her focus on urban young women suggests how ideas about cosmopolitanism shaped ideals of womanhood embedded in an urban setting.

Various scholars have examined the appeal of slimming down and beauty products to middle-class and professional working women in sub-Saharan Africa as a means to achieve upward social mobility and to fulfill new ideas about physical attractiveness and cosmopolitanism.[76] But women journalists also challenged Westernized bodily ideals, and therefore beauty contests. Elizabeth Nkuku Nwigwe, a writer for *Africa Woman*, *Cameroon Outlook*, and the *Cameroon Post* as well as a contributor to a weekly radio program on Radio Buea that addressed civic and women's issues, wrote a 1969 letter to the *Cameroon Times* under the headline "Grumbling Aloud." Nkuku Nwigwe objected to judges' implementation of Western beauty ideals:

> I have witnessed beauty competitions in Nigeria and Cameroon. One fact remains unchanged, and that is the judges all look forward to slim girls win-

> ning the show rather than plumpy girls. . . . It is true that we Africans have adopted many good things from the Whiteman. . . . [B]ut I do not agree with the adoption of their standard of judgment when it comes to selecting beauty queens. . . . We are a continent of robust people, both males and females. Why then can we not accept a plumpy stature as a beautiful one?. . . . The Whiteman has had his taste for slim girls all along. Should I take for granted that Africans too have adopted this same taste?

Nkuku Nwigwe attributed a preference for "straight pointed noses" to the same Western influence that prized attributes uncommon in Africa, calling "bony hips and a dry chest" "not truly African." Nkuku Nwigwe elaborates by sharing the history of a particular bodily practice, the fattening of young women as a ritual that signals entry to womanhood that takes place in some areas of Nigeria, as a way to contend that a robust figure is more beautiful than a slim one: "take for example an old custom in old Calabar in Nigeria. A girl is fully matured for marriage only after 'being in what they called [a] fattening room.' When she comes out one could still find plumpy [*sic*] women among them." She surmises, "If Africa adopts the plumpy stature as a beautiful one, I'm sure those African countries with more slim young women will produce plumpy ones for [beauty] competitions." She concluded, "The African should not lean too much on the Whiteman's error of judgement. . . . We have our tastes; they have theirs." Nkuku Nwigwe argued that judges should "maintain an all-African standard in what to look for in a beauty and not become slaves to the Whiteman's standards and tastes. . . . I would here humbly contribute some points to help judges of beauty competitions."[77]

Nkuku Nwigwe's standards put self-confidence front and center: "(1) How smartly she steps before a crowd. (2) How upright she carries up her figure. (3) How neatly she's dressed. (4) How sweetly she smiles. (5) How intelligently she reasons and speaks. (6) How polite and well behaved she is. (7) How confident she is of herself." Physical attributes take a back seat in Nkuku Nwigwe's proposed judging system. Her emphasis on intelligence suggests the importance of displaying educational level. In asking judges to maintain an African standard of beauty, Nkuku Nwigwe seems to refer to Pan-Africanist discourses of the time that implore black women to adhere to recognizably authentic physical and aesthetic attributes. Further, she invokes her role of what I term "print griot" to drive home her point about what she perceives as an ideal authentic African beauty that is rooted in African history and long-standing local bodily practices. By referencing the long history of the fattening practices that occurs in some areas of Nigeria, Nkuku Nwigwe fulfills the traditional role of a griot as a historian, teacher, and, having been educated in Nigeria herself, the role of a witness—a key role that griots play as "one who sees and then announces the news," thus playing the role of an "oral document" (as she asserts, she had "witnessed beauty competitions in Nigeria").[78] Thus, by invoking the role of a "print griot" while stimulatingly appealing to Pan-Africanist discourses of the time, Nkuku Nwigwe sought to shape Cameroonian cultural (black) consciousness by challenging the persistent global imagery of beauty as synonymous with whiteness and its converging set of attitudes and bodily disposition.

Even Wanzie, who had described Ikome in such glowing terms in March 1972, mused in a column a few weeks prior, "We have oftentimes talked about this thing called beauty. But true to myself, I have not yet found the answer. Everyone has a different way of appreciating beauty. . . . I, therefore, wonder how judges of beauty competitions define the word beauty." She further writes, "It is amazing that those who have been turned away as not being beautiful enough are jewels of beauty to other people. Which makes me wonder what beauty actually is."[79] However, the journalist conceded that she was not the right person to judge a woman's beauty. Though both men and women served as judges, Ruff Wanzie concluded that in everyday life, it is generally "men [who] are better judges of women's beauty than women themselves, [and] I leave them to give the answer."[80] This concession to male authority reflected larger systems of power and gender norms, in that both women and men believed that women beautified themselves for men. While she does not explicitly tie her discomfort to a conflict between African and Western ideals as Nkuku Nwigwe did, it seems possible that Wanzie reflects ambivalence and anxiety about what it means to simultaneously integrate the global and the local, the national and the transnational into a modern, sophisticated, African feminine beauty ideal. Moreover, the fashioning of beauty ideals along patriarchal lines reflected concerns of the patriarchal Pan-Africanist discourse at the time; black men and women on the continent and in the diaspora saw black women's bodily and aesthetic rituals as a way to preserve racial pride.[81] Similarly, ideal Anglophone womanhood was entwined in this larger discourse where some urbanite elites believed that women's "natural" beauty and black (African) body shape would preserve authentic African aesthetic and bodily ideals, as referenced by Nkuku Nwigwe. Within this context, beauty contestants simultaneously reflected the nation's progress and a hybrid black African modernity and culture.

Elsie's "Flamboyance [as] a City Girl": Beauty Ideals and Urban Identity

Urban and rural sensibilities also clashed in beauty pageants. Adolf Mongo Dipoko of the *Cameroon Outlook* excuses Elsie's flamboyant behavior in part by associating it with urban identity, which called on women to be self-confident, a marker of progressive comportment. Beauty pageants shaped vernacular (or local) understandings of cosmopolitanisms across urban Africa.[82] Thus while urbanites identified the ideal contestant, who was both cosmopolitan and progressive in her attire and movement, they also held her to local ideas about gender norms and suitable compartment. She should be somewhat timid and demure when discussing her pageant experiences and avoid being too flamboyant.

While West Cameroon's urban elites tied much of their identity to urban settings, rural women challenged their perspectives by also competing in beauty contests. In 1969, for example, eighteen-year-old Martha Ayuk, "a village girl," as the *Cameroon Outlook* described her, won the Miss Meme Division contest. The news report asserted that Ayuk's win had broken the "myth of the township girls," sharing that, "No one ever believed a village girl could be crowned Miss Meme despite the odds. Not even the villagers themselves."[83] Coverage in the *Cameroon Workman* indicated that the judges' decision was unanimous, adding that Ayuk did not use "oil paints in the names of 'make-up' to catch the eye" but let her natural beauty show that she "deserved the crown."[84] Martha Ayuk's win raised questions about cultural identity in urban settings. The claim that villagers themselves were shocked at Ayuk's victory suggests the propensity for beauty contests to be associated with an urban identity. This may have been true; research from across Africa in the period shows that both rural and urban Africans understood urban women seemed to exude an aura of chicness contrary to their rural counterparts.[85] At the same time, the "free women" stereotype was urban. While it was also associated with wearing too much makeup and thus failing to value their God-given natural beauty, it also suggests that beauty queens who do not wear too much makeup and value their God-given natural beauty possessed a hybrid urban-rural identity.

REPRESENTING THE COUNTRY: FRANCOPHONE-ANGLOPHONE RELATIONS AT HOME AND ABROAD

Beauty pageants reflected the changing political, social, and economic landscapes of the Federal Republic of Cameroon. While pageants offered West Cameroonian political elites a way to make themselves visible on the global periphery, internal influences and the hegemonic nature of Francophone Cameroon shaped their precarious political and economic standing. Throughout the 1960s, East Cameroon companies increasingly took over those of West Cameroon, and these companies, along with Francophone politicians and women's organizations such as the WCNU often sponsored pageants, especially after 1966.[86] Subsequently, the Francophone state essentially dominated pageants in Anglophone Cameroon after 1966. For example, Banque International pour le Commerce et L'Industrie du Cameroun (BICIC) sponsored Miss B.I.C.I.C. 1968, which took place in Kumba, one of the most populous towns in West Cameroon, after BICIC took over Barclays Bank D.C.O., a British multinational bank that had a branch in West Cameroon.[87] Pageant stages had always reflected the prevalence of migration across the East/West Cameroon border, and Francophone women who lived in West Cameroon sometimes won West Cameroonian beauty pageants and vice versa.[88] The connection between West Cameroonian national identity and pageants was thus not based on the exclusion of Francophone contestants.

Although Francophone women participated in West Cameroonian beauty pageants, British and Nigerian ties provided much of the basis for constructing Anglophone identity through pageants. For instance, the proceeds from the Miss Mamfe Red Cross 1968 contest went to "aiding the Nigerian-Biafra refugees in Mamfe."[89] These actions most likely invoked West Cameroon's cultural affinity with Nigeria due to their shared British administrative legacy. Pageant winners frequently traveled to London as part of their victory tours, highlighting the nation's economic and political ties with Britain. By sending winners abroad, political and economic elites strove to maintain their presence in the global economy. Sending winners abroad strongly signaled West Cameroon politicians' intentions to maintain economic and sociopolitical links with their former European administrators, demonstrating the state's independence within a Francophone Cameroonian hegemonic republic.

By planning events such as British Week, a weeklong celebration that the city of Victoria and the British Consul in Buea cosponsored, West Cameroonians articulated their status as a minority in the hegemonic Francophone republic and claimed a way of interpreting European values through an African lens. In one example, Elders and Fyffes, a UK banana importer, funded a trip for Miss West Cameroon 1962, sixteen-year-old Monica Manga, to the UK.[90] The banana industry was important to West Cameroon, and the trip took place before the UK revoked West Cameroon's preferential status in the banana trade, which would cripple banana producers in the country.[91] Clara Manga signaled the importance of the visit in the *Cameroon Champion*, saying that the winner had been chosen expressly because she would "represent the country well [in] the U.K."[92] She observed that Gladys Endeley, who was serving as a West Cameroonian civil servant at the time, would be coaching Manga on how to comport herself on her visit to England. Like many other postcolonial African pageant winners, Monica Manga used her position to "gain attention" for her country and build "ties to other countries around the world." Representatives such as Manga obtained access to political leaders and performed the role of mediator "between the general public and the state."[93] They bore a specific obligation to speak for their people and advance the country's economic interests. By training Manga in British culture, political elites sought to make her an exemplar of West Cameroon's progress and respectability to promote congeniality.

Details from Monica Manga's departure from Cameroon and her visit in the UK illustrate larger worldviews about a distinct Anglophone identity. Clara Manga went with the teenager to Tiko, a port town in the modern-day Southwest Region of Cameroon. The journalist reported afterward that "the two terrible men from the East [Cameroon State] in the Security Office" had delayed Manga's departure to England.[94] Highlighting such incidents amplified Anglophones' claim that the federal states could never be culturally united because of differing comportment and conduct. A government press release reporting on Manga's trip declared that she exuded positivity and graceful social etiquette, complimenting the clothing styles of British women by sharing with a London-based journalist that British women "are much smarter than our girls and this is hardly surprising considering the impressive variety of clothes on sale in your big stores."[95] But Manga's admiration for the British was not one-sided; the report shares that "[t]he British public has had plenty of opportunity to admire her." She gave a radio interview for the BBC, local papers published photos their photographers took of her, and she even made a television appearance that was reported to be "seen by millions of viewers all over Britain." Manga was an international emblem to convince the world that West Cameroon was a modern country with sociopolitical autonomy and a strong sense of cultural identity and polite decorum.[96] Her visit visibly illustrated West Cameroon's continuing political and cultural affinity with Britain.

Miss British Week 1968, the pageant at the climax of British Week, had the same message. British Week included exhibit stands by businesses, such as the Cameroon Development Corporation (CDC) and the United Cameroon Trading Company. Social activities included golf, soccer, drama, and singing by local Victoria students.[97] As the first permanent British settlement in Cameroon, Victoria was very conscious of its ties to British culture.[98] Esther Ebong, a "charming Cameroon bank clerk" from Kumba, won the Miss British Week crown on November 16, 1968.[99] A British Consul representative made closing remarks after the beauty contest ended, citing the "goodwill" and cooperation that existed between the two nations. The representative lamented that he and the participants would "no longer be joining in the fun of the coconut sky, the shooting gallery, the golf, etc.!" He highlighted the connection between West Cameroon and Britain as a reason for the success of the celebrations: "This can be due to nothing less than the enormous amount of latent goodwill which exists between our two countries and which needs only a spark to fire it."[100] He concluded by predicting British-Cameroonian ties would only strengthen in the future.

In reality, the British Consul was probably more convinced of West Cameroonian national pride than of the country's political autonomy and independence. The loss of Commonwealth Preference in 1963 had been devastating, including to the company that sponsored Monica Manga's trip to the United Kingdom.[101] An April 3, 1963, confidential report from a member of the Foreign and Commonwealth Office underlines the British government's fears that cutting trade relations with West Cameroon would leave the former British territory vulnerable to additional economic and political domination by East Cameroon:

> The reasons for wanting to continue Commonwealth preference for West Cameroon are mainly political. Although it is true that in 1961 the West Cameroonians voted to join the ex-French Republic of Cameroon . . . they still retain a measure of regional autonomy in the present Federation. . . . [I]f we do not help West Cameroon to hold its own economically, it will be swallowed by the larger East Cameroon, and its separate institution will disappear.[102]

These words would prove prophetic, but British leadership decided to revoke the status anyway, perhaps feeling that Francophone hegemony was inevitable. Banana producers were among the most vulnerable to the loss of preference; Manga's voyage to the United Kingdom on an Elders and Fyffes banana boat signified the strong economic and political ties between Great Britain and the West Cameroon nation at the time. Nonetheless, British Week in late 1968 celebrated a connection more cultural than practical.[103] For West Cameroonians, British imperial links marked their individuality within the federation. Thus, even in the absence of formal preference, British diplomats desired a continuation of the British/West Cameroon connection that British Week celebrated, and the complex task the Miss British Week set for young women reflected their preferences as well. Through events such as British Week, Anglophone Cameroonians crafted a distinct cultural and national identity that was physically conspicuous on pageant stages.

But as the next chapter illustrates, another way to create a distinct Anglophone Cameroonian identity was to regulate women's verbal behavior off pageant stages. While undertaking field research in Buea in 2011, I quickly learned that condemning gossip was another means of invoking an embodied nationalism. Censure of gossip framed perspectives on how women's everyday conduct, in this case, their verbal patterns, might reflect proper Anglophone Cameroonian comportment and social values within homes, markets, and varied community spaces.

CHAPTER 5

The Plague of "Gossips and Vindictiveness"

Mediating Social Behaviors and Delineating Public and Private Spheres

One cloudy August afternoon in 2015 in Buea, my research assistant and I were walking back from the National Archives of Cameroon, which is nestled at the base of Mount Cameroon, an active volcano fondly known by many locals as the "chariot of the gods." We had just spent a few hours combing through archival materials and were discussing our titillating findings about women gossiping during the 1960s in urban West Cameroon. My assistant, an older and close family friend I call "aunt," has lived in Buea since young adulthood, and she brings an eyewitness's perspective to the work. Reflecting on the archival materials, she recalled that in her own experience, gossip frequently crossed private and public boundaries and threatened the gossiper's respectability in her community. For over an hour we discussed this, striding past makeshift produce shops, restaurants, and small businesses on our way to our residence near the University of Buea, greeting friends, neighbors, and community members. As each approached, my "aunt" turned to me and counseled me in a hushed, conspiratorial tone about what personal information about myself to divulge and what to "protect." She told me that little has changed about the impact of gossip in contemporary Cameroon, explaining, "When you pass, and no one knows about anything, they leave you alone. Even if they don't leave you alone, they are conscious that [any gossip they spread about you] to other people is a lie . . . but when they know your secrets, they start to look at you in a way."[1] She feared that gossipers would instigate community tension and disunity by attacking others' integrity publicly and exposing people's private problems. As if affirming her ominous statement, the clouds burst into showers halfway to our destination, the rain driving the "chariot of the gods" behind thick heavy mist. We quickly hailed a taxi for the rest of our journey home.

This chapter synthesizes the research of that day and several others, as well as the insight of my "aunt" and other interviewees, exploring the political, social, and personal dangers that exposing secrets presented in urban West Cameroon amid social and political change in the 1960s and early 1970s. Anxiety about the exposure of intimate secrets illustrates how degrees of knowing and degrees of belonging facilitated suitable comportment for women, specifically the embodied practices of women's verbal behavior and how it was thought to facilitate national and community dis(unity). As my "aunt" assistant observed, a woman might "protect" her respectability in public by carefully guarding her intimate secrets. In doing so, she facilitated her sense of belonging in the community, avoiding judgmental looks and condemnation of her character and virtue. During the 1960s and early 1970s, educated urbanites and female political elites considered gossiping an inherently feminine activity,[2] as they do in contemporary Cameroon. They nevertheless sought to redefine gender norms by beseeching formally educated women to avoid gossip and to use their time usefully whether working, at leisure, or attending women's organizations. Women might be rebuked for sharing information about people's private lives with neighbors, friends, or coworkers, in markets, playgrounds, shops, bars, schools, or workplaces. At the same time, as this chapter will show, gossip became a way for political elites to criticize "bad" women citizens. Thus, such individuals appealed to an embodied nationalism to bring visual representations and verbal practices of ideal Anglophone womanhood within nationalist endeavors. Denouncing gossip facilitated the political elites' invention of women's role and behaviors in the political process, especially in women's organizations.

This chapter continues to explore how Anglophone political and urban elites alike strove to shape imaginings of a West Cameroonian nation and respective cultural values, doing so because Anglophone identity was so precarious in the Francophone-dominated republic. I make a multilayered argument. First, I contend that gossip condemnation, as well as *sharing* gossip, informed imaginings of community and national belonging. Female political elites' condemnation of gossip was a way to criticize women who did not suitably participate in national development, politically, socially, or economically. While local community members condemned gossip, they also relied on it to stay abreast of the welfare of neighbors and others. As this chapter shows, gossip can foster intimacy and community belonging by binding "gossipers together in an imagined community of shared values," even as it subjects them to community censure and sanctions.[3] Second, I assert that the censure of gossip was one way to mediate women's social conduct and to delineate public and private spheres. As Kathleen Feeley and Jennifer Frost argue in their work on gossip, "[g]ossip makes private matters public, and, for many, gossip's most transgressive quality is precisely how it blurs the imaginary yet influential boundary between public and private."[4] Criticism of gossip by female journalists and letter writers became means for educated individuals to express fears about women's public reputations, their declining religious morals, and how women should properly use their leisure time in an urban setting. Female journalists, for example, advised married individuals to "protect" information about their marriages. Leaking marital woes in public spaces weakened marital relations and impaired a couple's public respectability. By criticizing women who publicly exposed their marriage problems to community members, elites strengthened the boundaries between public and private spaces within local communities. Although the two arguments at the core of this chapter may seem to be at odds, both arguments illuminate how urban elites strove to create an ideal womanhood associated with preserving West Cameroonian cultural values and respectable comportment, verbally and behaviorally.

While elites censured all women for gossiping, their condemnation mostly resonated with formally educated individuals. Urban and political elites believed that formal education conferred a higher social position and a type of public respectability. Luise White argues that gossip "is not just any kind of talk: it reports behavior; it rests on evaluating reputations."[5] If gossip "reports" behavior that departs from community or cultural norms,[6] then in urban Anglophone Cameroon it became a way to censure formally educated female elites when they displayed behavior not deemed respectable. Moreover, they set a poor example for their counterparts in lower social and economic positions. For instance, a 1964 missive to the editor of the *Cameroon Times* read, "The future of this country lies mostly on the shoulders of the educated people." The writer, who identifies him- or herself only as Eyong, located in Victoria, concludes: "The earlier [the] bad habit [of gossip] is stamped out, the better for our growing generation."[7] If formally educated women gossiped, such opinions suggested, it was because they were following the poor example of other formally educated women. Only by curbing their own bad behavior could they hope to be role models for the rest of the nation.

Like the previous chapters, this chapter examines a facet of monitoring and regulating Anglophone Cameroonian women's behavior by a small subset of elite women who garnered social and political authority in national and domestic spheres. The wives of political heavyweights, for example, saw gossip as hindering women's social and political autonomy in nationalist spaces and undermining their political power in the West Cameroonian government. Political wives argued that gossip might undermine their own authority by obstructing women's participation in women's organizations. In cautioning their peers about gossip, these female elites also looked to the conduct of their West African counterparts. They selectively borrowed from the conduct of female members of women's organizations in other parts of Africa to reinvent how "good" and "authentic" African women might conduct themselves in women's organizations and when participating in nationalist activities.

Discourse and the censure of gossip were fashioned along religious and patriarchal lines. A Christianized worldview shaped perspectives on how women should properly use their time. Female journalists and other urban elites associated gossip with laziness and considered it a barrier to "good" and useful "productivity and utility," and therefore to proper Christian behavior.[8] As Max Weber points out in his work on Protestant perspectives about the suitable use of time, "Waste of time is thus the first and in principle the deadliest of sins. . . . Loss of time through sociability, idle talk, luxury . . . is worthy of absolute moral condemnation."[9] Hard work, according to this line of thinking, decreases opportunities for illicit entertainment and pleases God. Conversely, idleness was a vice, the devil's playground, and gossip was evidence of idleness. Ultimately, gossip was an illegitimate activity. Ruff Wanzie, a columnist for the *Cameroon Times*, framed gossip as a symptom of leisure, saying morally lax women gossiped when they had too much free time. As Wanzie warned, "Satan always finds work for idle hands."

Moreover, women were suspected of gossiping and being idle in the absence of a patriarchal authority at home and in the professional workplace, specifically white-collar jobs. Female journalists condemned housewives for being idle while their husbands worked and said that professional women were prone to gossip in the absence of male managers. In this line of thinking, men's use of time was legitimized—the "daily active man" did "beneficial work"—while women's use of time needed to be regulated because they were less likely to use their time in a "profitable way."[10] One woman relayed to me her thoughts about men's perceptions of wives who worked outside the home during the 1950s and 1960s. Living in a largely Anglophone section of the Francophone capital Yaoundé, Vanessa Yonkeu was in her early 50s at the time and had owned a small clothing shop for over thirty years. She revealed that many husbands did not allow their wives to work outside the home because "they [men] had their blocked ideas, that women can go and misbehave outside."[11] In many ways, the accusations that formally educated women who worked outside the home supposedly devoted their "leisurely hours" to gossipping and "misbehav[ing]," was, like the stigmatization of the "free woman," a way to express anxiety over women's increased autonomy, and their changing economic roles at home and in the public arena.

The discourse on gossip that this chapter examines serves as a natural transition to a discussion of the boundaries between public and private spaces in West Cameroon, spatially and verbally. While the first four chapters of this book primarily focused on creating embodied ideal womanhood in public nationalist arenas, this chapter begins to focus on embodied constructions in local community locations and more private domestic areas. Using gossip as a lens of analysis allows us to see how it moves through circuits that flow between the public and private spaces. I begin by examining how censure of gossip reflects concerns about women's participation in nationalist projects, for example, the West Cameroon Council of Women's Institutes (CWI), and in the economic infrastructure, in marketplaces and the professional workplace. My discussion ends by examining concerns about gossip in the more intimate spaces of the local community. By doing so, I demonstrate how gossip travels and infiltrates locations that are otherwise unreachable, and how the importance of "knowing secrets" shaped verbal practices and behavior in everyday life. I specifically address anxiety about husbands and wives sharing private information about their lives and gossiping about the private lives of neighbors, all of which were seen as crossing private and public boundaries and threatening a person's respectability in public spaces.

"PETIT GOSSIPS AND BACK-BITING": FORGING UNITY IN WOMEN'S ORGANIZATIONS

Political wives and female journalists created new areas of cultural and political power for themselves by censuring gossip and demarcating the boundaries of women's acceptable behavior in nationalist spaces. In this process, condemnation of gossip fostered sentiments of national belonging and forged unity among women who collectively sought to preserve suitable cultural values, further legitimatizing their social and political importance to national development. Key figures such as Anna Foncha and journalist Ruff Wanzie used their positions to seek a public forum for their belief that gossip threatened national unity in West Cameroon.

In an extensive column that ran in the *Cameroon Times* in May 1964, Ruff Wanzie blamed gossip for the disintegration of women's organizations. She maintained that gossip reduced members to frivolity and flippancy; they lacked proper morals and regard for nationalist duties: "Women have tried from time to time to form groups. Such groups have always ended up in quarrels and fighting as a result of one woman gossiping. . . . Call the next meeting after that and only the president and secretary will attend." She detailed the collapse of women's organizations because of gossip: "[The] '[m]eeting [is] postponed' and it will continue to be postponed indefinitely. Meanwhile new groups spring up electing their own officers, blaming the former officers for the split and failures of meetings. These various groups at last fail to live up to and to fulfill the purposes for which their society was formed." Wanzie connects the disintegration of women's organizations to the loss of women's political power: "Now our women are facing problems. They find it difficult to put their problems to the government because their societies are not strong enough."[12] In this environment, Wanzie's statement that women's gossip weakened her countrywomen's sociopolitical organizations constitutes more than moralistic censure. Gossips, Wanzie implied, hindered women's collective unity and efforts to gain political emancipation.

Wanzie wrote approvingly of the women in a women's society in Sierra Leone who refrained from gossip:

> The women of Sierra Leone 15 years ago formed a society known as "The Bondo Society." It . . . will never fail because the women hold fast that people should concern themselves with only what concerns them. They have actually run this society up to date without any aid from men. . . . It is through this society that they put their petitions to the government and govern themselves. The secrets of this society are never let out to non-members.[13]

Wanzie emphasizes here that the women of the Sande/Bondo secret society are tight-lipped, unlike many of their counterparts in West Cameroon. She noted exceptions, however: "Congratulations go to the [West Cameroon] Federation of Women's Social Clubs [and Associations], to the section of the Women's International League for Peace and Freedom, to the Triangle Club and other societies whose members are taking a big step to stamp out gossiping and its evils. Long live these leading clubs run by [Anglophone Cameroonian] women."[14] As chapter 2 described, women's organizations conferred sociopolitical authority on women at the time; they were an important way for women to address issues such as women's access to formal education that the patriarchal state might otherwise ignore. As both a moral and a demographic force, women's organizations were crucial to the project of preserving national autonomy. Consequently, gossip threatened the West Cameroon State itself as well as the advancement of women.

Wanzie's censure of gossip illustrates how female political elites drew from continental ideas about women's organizations. While female political elites like Wanzie—both a journalist and a West Cameroonian civil servant—drew ideas about women's political engagement from their Western (European and North American) counterparts, as chapter 2 showed, they equally drew ideas about women's political participation from their West African counterparts. They created new philosophies about women's political engagement in West Cameroon by drawing on ideas about women's political engagement in traditional women's associations in West Africa, such as the Bondo Society in Sierra Leone. The Bondo Society, also known as Sande, is a secret women's society that exists in Sierra Leone, Liberia, Guinea, and some regions of Côte d'Ivoire.[15] The society has existed since the precolonial period, although Wanzie thought it had been founded recently.

Filomina Chioma Steady describes the Bondo Society as an organization that provided "socialization and education" for young women, holding initiation rituals that marked their transition "from childhood to adulthood."[16] Steady argues that Bondo Societies, which have a religious component, also function as "regulatory mechanisms of social control and judicial mediation" that "promot[e] the socioeconomic development of their communities." She points to their secret nature as "enhanc[ing]" their mission of "maintaining law and order [and] meting out punishment." Similar to the Anlu society of the western Grassfields of the Northwest Region of Cameroon, Bondo Societies protected women when social norms were breached, and also censured men who disrespected and mistreated women.[17] While women's associations were a de facto prerequisite to political engagement in Cameroon, women in Sierra Leone used Bondo to strengthen their political position and authority by connecting elite Bondo members to politically powerful chiefs.[18]

Wanzie selectively draws from various aspects of Bondo Societies to shape discourse on gossip and the conduct of members of women's organizations in West Cameroon. She attributes the successful unity of these societies to secrecy and calls on her countrywomen to implement a similar strategy. She cites secrecy as fostering a sense of community and national belonging in Bondo members and urges her countrywomen to adopt a similar model. Thus, she distinguishes "good" secrecy, which unites women as they strive to advance politically without men's help, from gossip, which she sees as divisive. Good secrecy provides strength in numbers; "bad" secrecy, filtered through gossip, causes disunity and mistrust.

Political wives such as Anna Foncha and Elizabeth Muna likewise saw gossip as a threat to the unity of women's organizations. Speaking to crowds of women in Tiko, Mamfe, Bamenda, and other English-speaking urban towns in the mid-1960s, Foncha chastised women for gossiping. In May 1965, she lectured to more than 200 women at the fourth annual meeting of the CWI on the subject of "threats" to the advancement of the council. Her speech begins, "We must guard against those traits which tend to keep back progress in our groups, those tendencies which are likely to destroy or disintegrate our groups." Loose-lipped women were among the worst factors that inhibited unity in women's groups: "There are certain women who, out of sheer mischief . . . invest [into] malicious stories and unhealthy gossips about others. Such women should be disciplined when they are discovered. They should be removed from our clubs before they can do any great harm."[19] Women like Foncha encouraged organizations to monitor the behavior of their members, weeding out those who were prone to gossip. Thus, Foncha held women responsible for social unity and political loyalty generally, and for the progress of women's organizations charged with encouraging nationalism.

While her husband was politically opposed to Foncha's, Elizabeth Muna concurred with Foncha's position against gossip, and she spoke against it publicly.[20] Muna was the wife of Salomon Tandeng Muna, who served as the third prime minister of West Cameroon, from 1968 to 1972 and vice president of the Federal Republic of Cameroon from 1970 to 1972.[21] When her husband took office, she embarked on speaking tours in which she reminded women that "unity and hard work are the basis of a successful and happy nation" and that joining "organized women's groups demonstrate unity and peace."[22] She gave her first known speech that focused on gossip on February 3, 1968 at a reception the Women's Cameroon National Union (WCNU) branch in Buea held in her honor. As Anna Foncha had, she emphasized the importance of refraining from "petit gossips and back-biting" to achieve a united front in nation-building campaigns.[23] She urged the women to join the Cameroon

National Union (CNU) "and help her husband carry out the task which has been confided in him by the recent appointment as Prime Minister," describing his new post as "not [an] easy task." One week later on February 10, at a reception at the WCNU branch in Tiko, a member read a letter of address enthusiastically welcoming Muna to the town on behalf of the "devoted wives and loving mothers" "[who] command great respect in homes and society" and made up the WCNU. The statement called on Muna "to use the good qualities of a housewife and loving mother" to help Tiko women "crush the plague of gossips" in a society "plagued with gossips and vindictiveness." A report of their statement said that the women emphasized that "they are looking up to her to stimulate this sisterly love, kinship and unity among them, as well as service for their fellow women and neighbors."[24]

The women of the WCNU branch in Tiko used the trope of motherhood and wifehood to buttress their social and political importance in domestic and nationalist spaces. Like the women who participated in the Federation of South African Women during the period of apartheid that Meghan Healy-Clancy studies, Anglophone women's condemnation of gossip illustrates how "the extended family and the broader society [were] spaces where mothering happens," extending beyond the responsibility for one's own child and the child's biological father.[25] In this role, WCNU members among Tiko women strove to preserve cultural values and guard against unsuitable traits such as "gossips and vindictiveness," in other words, "mothering" and caring for the welfare of their society beyond their private homes.[26] By doing so, they used their societal roles as wives and mothers to legitimize national belonging.

Further, Tiko women fostered sisterly camaraderie with Muna by urging her to "use the good qualities of a housewife and loving mother" to help them in their endeavors to forge unity in the WCNU and in their community. By associating terms such as "good qualities" with "housewife" and "loving mother," the women of the WCNU branch in Tiko shared their beliefs about the ideal traits of womanhood. "Good" women, married women and mothers, eschewed gossip in their communities and within nationalist spaces. Moreover, if gossip created community disunity, then condemnation of gossip forged social and political unity. Widespread condemnation probably did not stamp out the practice, but the denunciation itself cemented unity among the Tiko members of the WCNU. In this, the women illustrated their unity and adherence to dominant gender norms, which further legitimized their important roles in homes, communities, and the nation.

While Foncha designed her speeches on gossip to unite women under the

Kamerun National Democratic Party (KNDP)-ruled state and Muna designed hers to create unity under CNU rule, they used similar rhetoric. Gossip condemnation consolidated their sociopolitical authority over other West Cameroonian women; disunity within women's organizations might pose a threat to this power. By urging women to unite by desisting from gossiping, while simultaneously encouraging these women to support their husbands, both Foncha and Muna strove to create and delineate boundaries of an ideal womanhood within nationalist spaces. Denunciations of gossip by political wives such as Muna helped to define and shape educated women's ideal citizenship duties.

As "mothers" of the nation, it was only natural that female political elites focused on the behavior of their younger counterparts, school-aged girls and formally educated young adult women. Ruff Wanzie, herself a political wife, informed her readers in a 1964 *Cameroon Times* column, "Throw away the bad habit of gossiping and face realities coupled with your education. . . . 'If you educate women you educate families of the nation.'" She advised, "Lead the illiterate girls and women towards the formation of successful societies, and the building up of a well-to-do nation; for the future generation depends on the efforts of the educated women of Cameroon today."[27] Like their adult counterparts in women's organizations, female political elites feared that the formally educated youth, the future cultural bearers of the nation, might gossip and thus "waste" time by disregarding their nationalistic obligations.

Gossip led to idleness, Wanzie, Muna, and Foncha warned, and indolence would lead the nation's daughters to corrupt actions. In her address to the local divisional branch of the CWI in Kumba in October 1964, Anna Foncha advised mothers to work hard, care for their homes, and make sure that their daughters were not idle.[28] Likewise, Wanzie advised parents that their daughters should spend school vacations with them, the "guardians," and not with relatives or friends. She counseled, "Let them help you with all your work both in the home, market and farm. Do not give them room to be idle else this will lead them into loitering about or roaming the streets."[29] Wanzie also cautioned school-aged girls not to gossip, directly tying the issue to their participation in all-girls organizations. In a 1964 column, she recommended student organizations as an antidote to idleness: "Authorities and mothers should know that it is idleness which brings about practices of immorality among girls today. If these girls are always occupied in the organizations, they will also think less of evil." "Beware girls," she warned, "of gossiping, envy and suspicion."[30] Like their adult counterparts, young girls were to police the decorum of their peers by avoiding those who gossiped and engaged in other immoral activities. Idleness fostered "social evils" that tarnished women's morality and turned them into depraved citizens. Indeed, gossiping was perceived as a gateway activity that made young girls susceptible to other illicit behaviors. It was the "mothers" of the nation, those who solidified their social and political importance by caring for the welfare of their society, who were important in facilitating the process of teaching the nation's children about suitable behavior.

But condemnation of gossip also reflected larger political changes in West Cameroon, as Francophone East Cameroon's hegemony over West Cameroon expanded and grew in strength in the late 1960s. As the CNU merged with various Anglophone and Francophone political parties, rumors and gossip about the political circumstances threatened not only women's political unity, but the position of the KNDP and Cameroon People's National Convention (CPNC) politicians, who either genuinely endorsed Ahidjo's creation of a single-party state or did so out of fear or greed for political favor. For instance, in 1968 Nerius Namaso Mbile, a key leader in Endeley's CPNC, encouraged West Cameroonians to remain united and to support Ahidjo's move. Mbile had been elected from the Southern Cameroons to the Eastern House of Assembly in Nigeria in 1951, and he became a key CPNC leader in the 1960s who held political posts in the West Cameroon government. In 1968, he sought to forge West Cameroonian unity against a rapidly changing political landscape by calling on West Cameroonians to stay united. Mbile, the minister of lands and survey at the time, visited Ndian on the southern border between Cameroon and Nigeria to encourage them to support the "launching" of the Ndian CNU subsection in the area. He urged those in attendance "to desist from sectionalism, gossiping and enmity" based on political differences. A transcription of his talk reports, "After recounting to the people of the inconvenience caused during the days of party politics [the period of a multi-party system], he called on all, in the name of our able and God fearing Leader, His Excellency Ahmadou Ahidjo to desist from sectionalism, gossiping and enmity as these vices he emphasized, only help to keep us aloof from one another."[31] Gossip, Mbile recognized, had the power to undermine Ahidjo's CNU government and possibly Mbile's political authority in a Francophone-dominated government, just as it could undermine female leaders.[32]

INDUSTRIOUSNESS AND IDLE CHAT

Condemnation of gossip illustrates how journalists and letter writers moralized women's everyday use of time. Such urbanites reviled women's idleness, saying that it contributed to the demise of a Christian work ethic. When they wrote about gossip they often discussed how women should use their time at home and at work more broadly, urging them to conform to ideal Christian behavior and to fashion their behavior along patriarchal lines. Christians could show their dedication to God by working hard at worldly endeavors.[33] Gossiping women failed to meet religious expectations. In 1964, Ruff Wanzie described gossip as "pleas[ing] the devil."[34] Two years later, in a similar vein, she asserted that "temptation finds its way into our minds during leisure hours," describing housewives as idle until they had to cook their husbands' lunch at two o'clock. She tied gossip to housewives' misuse of their time:

> When we have nothing to do, the friend steps in to occupy our minds with horrible imaginations. . . . The occupation which Satan finds very easy to drive with good results into the minds of women of this category is gossiping. They assemble in the house of one of the women who is very liberal. If you ever had the chance to listen to them as I have done on two occasions when my presence in a neighboring room was a big "secret," you will be excited to laughter because of the strange gossips you hear from some of these housewives. Topics for discussions range from talks on the behavior of other women they dislike, to calling of names and painting pictures of the evils of other women from discussing about their husbands, to jealousy of some progressive neighbors, and a lot of foolish talk which you cannot associate a decent society with.

By lamenting that a "corrupt" friend might "occupy" a women's mind with "horrible imaginations," Wanzie condemns wives who waste their time at home, implying that they are failing to fulfill their domestic obligations. Moreover, she identifies the "bad" woman, the "very liberal" friend, who, in her divergence from proper gender norms, tempts other women to waste their time also. Accusations of idleness and gossip really reflected concern that stay-at-home wives might not engage in normative gender tasks, such as child-rearing, cooking, and fulfilling other domestic obligations.

But women who kept themselves busy working outside of the home did not escape condemnation for gossiping. Wanzie implies that women were likely to waste time while engaging in economic activity. Such condemnations of gossip distinguished shops, offices, and markets as sites of gossip, notably all vibrant spaces of socioeconomic activity. In her 1964 column, Ruff Wanzie maintained that for "working class women [women in the professional workforce], leisure is any moment which warrants the absence of the boss from the office." She summarized the dangers that "free" time posed to professional women:

> No matter the length of time, these women are sure to pick up a topic for discussion which will please the devil. Perhaps they may prefer to talk about the ones they have in [their] heart—the very angels they adore. Or do you think they would be interested in discussing the names of co-workers which usually stems from jealousy and envy? Perhaps they may discuss all three in a flash; but one thing is sure; that the absence of a "senior" in the office is time when normal duty is replaced with idle talk.[35]

From Wanzie's perspective, with the patriarchal figure absent, women might misbehave at work. Respite was a temptation to Christian women to engage in sinful behavior by being idle.

Wanzie's suggestions about how women should use their spare time illustrates how economic positioning and Christianity influenced educated women's suitable use of time in lieu of gossip. Emmanuel Akyeampong and Charles Ambler contend in their work on leisure in Africa that during colonial rule, "[c]olonial officials, European capitalists, and missionaries. . . . believed that structured 'play' with rules and in a time framework inculcated time consciousness, discipline, courage, and endurance in Africans." This perspective "fit into capitalist and Protestant notions of 'purposeful leisure,' and redirected Africans from 'corrupting' leisure activities such as dancing and idle gossip."[36] Christianized formally educated Cameroonian women might, as Wanzie counsels in the April 1964 column in the *Cameroon Times*, avoid "day-dreaming in the gardens or houses" by going on picnics, drinking (but not too much so as to avoid "behav[ing] like a lunatic"), debating, swimming, reading, visiting the sick in hospitals, and attending the meetings of women's associations.[37] From Wanzie's perspectives about "purposeful leisure" activities, it is evident that the meaning of "leisure" "is a social and cultural construct" that reflects class and is undeniably fluid.[38] While she urges women not to day-dream in gardens, she suggests activities that she believes are befitting for women who were no doubt in a middle to higher income bracket. It is these educated Christian women, many of them housewives and women who worked in professional sectors, that had the education, finances, and the *time* to engage in Wanzie's suggested leisurely activities. By being active in women's associations and visiting the sick in hospitals, and by engaging in activities such as reading and debating, formally educated women proved that they did not waste their free time but instead used it in purposeful and meaningful ways—by contributing to nationalist and development efforts.

The *Cameroon Express* ran a letter in 1968 that echoed Wanzie's description of gossip as a waste of time. Chifor Aloys from Victoria wrote that gossiping had always been "the happy past-time of women. . . . women's daily programmes are tinged with the melancholy of a group that appreciate idle talk or groundless rumour to doing beneficial work." Women gossipers, he wrote, masked their idleness through gossip: "Though unsubstantial, women have justified themselves to this characterization with the motive that the gap of idleness on their part that exist[s] between them and the daily active man, just has to be bridged—by gossiping." He warned women "to beware of and completely obliterate gossiping, whose harmful effects can hardly be recalled or mentioned without pain. . . . Let women abate this nuisance of a social evil."[39] Molara Ogundipe-Leslie's arguments about African men's view of women's work apply here. She explains that "men tend to take lightly the labor of their female counterparts in the business and educational professions, considering women's jobs hobbies and wondering what women do which makes them so tired at the end of the day."[40] But in fact African women had never been idle. Urban and rural women in Cameroon had long served as the economic backbone of the nation, working as farmers, traders, and sellers in markets while also managing domestic tasks such as cooking and motherhood.[41] Given Anglophone Cameroonian women's increasing access to the formal economy in the 1960s and the 1970s, many urban elites commended women's formal education but feared that educated women might threaten cultural mores regarding gender behavior.

Working women like Elizabeth Nkuku Nwigwe responded that they were too busy contributing to the economy to misbehave and were indeed ideal role models and good citizens. Nkuku Nwigwe wrote women's advice columns under pseudonyms, but in a West Cameroon government press release in 1970, she wrote under her own name, "Let us remember that business keeps us busy and leaves no room for idleness, gossiping, jealousy, hatred, suspicious and superstitious beliefs. [Women working] promotes love, co-operation, understanding and unity among women of different tribes in the same country." She called attention to women who worked in open food markets, contending that "[b]usiness is also for the ordinary house-wife with little or no education at all."[42] Thus, she explicitly tied businesswomen's eschewing of gossip with their real value to the nation as a source of West Cameroonian unity and economic advancement.

EXPOSING "SECRET LIVES" IN PUBLIC

What also irked the urban elite was that gossip tarnished a person's dignity and respectability by crossing the boundary between public and private arenas. Their diatribes figured women gossipers as spreading unconstrained private reports about friends, neighbors, and other community members, thereby instigating chaos and anxiety within communities. Bell Laurent Baratier from Victoria avowed in a missive to the *Cameroon Times* in 1968 that gossip and rumor in communities stain people's "integrity and justice as God commanded."[43] Eyong testified in a letter to the *Cameroon Times* that because of jealousy, gossipers aimlessly roamed the streets looking for stories about scandal and mischief. Eyong connected this to a wider Christian worldview, just as Baratier did:

> Remember the proverb which says, "Every man for himself and God for us all." Try to stop the habit of discussing matters that do not concern you. Most people had involved themselves into trouble because of gossiping. . . . Individuals and societies [should] look into possible remedies to stamp out gossiping and its evils.[44]

Eyong perceived gossip as a threat to community unity that could only be stamped out through collective community efforts. By placing condemnation of gossip in a Christian worldview, letter writers such as Eyong and Baratier actively defined a respectable urban identity.

Women journalists likewise perceived gossip as fracturing community peace and individual integrity. As "Auntie Clara," in a 1963 post, Clara Manga wrote in her *Cameroon Champion* women's advice column: "In this little town of ours, people like to poke their noses into things that do not concern them. . . . There is so much gossip in this place, all because people cannot find a better way of spending their leisurely hours." She connected gossip to deeper evils: "The women especially take great delight in gossip, and you always find if you probe into their most secret lives that those who gossip more are those who do [the] worst things."[45] Wanzie echoed Manga's standpoint that gossip marred community unity and tranquility: "Happiness in society and homes nowadays is always ruined by gossip. The talkative woman comes telling you stories under the pretense of gossiping, and they are out to ruin the happiness in your house and the society to which you belong." She claimed that "educated women who are supposed to lead others ride high on these attitudes and talk so much about nothing instead of getting agendas that could help solve the problems of our women."[46] Besides asserting that educated women should model better behavior and solve social problems, Wanzie described gossip as an intrinsically feminine activity tinged with immorality, distracting from worthy pursuits and publicly disrupting community cohesion and tranquility. Moreover, she associated gossip with the power to travel into the privacy of people's homes, possibly disturbing domestic tranquility.

While acknowledging the association between gossip and the feminine, two letter writers denied that it was a female-only pastime. Eyong's letter to the editor of the *Cameroon Times* in December 21, 1968, charged:

> In the past, people thought the women were the only people who indulged in these expensive jokes, but now it is for both sexes. Ruff [Wanzie] should therefore, not blame the women alone. Certain men gossip more than women. Some men use it as a SURE and SHORT cut [way] to win a woman's love. They do this by gossiping with a relative of the one concerned, on unfounded stories about her, if their frequent visits are ignored.[47]

Chifor Aloys fervently agreed: "Today's social evils manifest themselves in many ways. . . . gossiping which had been long referred [to] as the happy past-time of women only is fast becoming a masculine monopoly. . . . some of these male gossipers seem to be outpacing their traditional counterparts real fast." Yet gossip was still understood to be inherently feminine and in that it exposed a man's weak masculinity if he engaged in the practice. Aloys laments that all men's masculine pride is in jeopardy when men gossip: "[T]hat men too have taken to gossip mongering, and that men too have to be warned against such a social evil, is very painful." He tied men's gossip to idleness, saying, in "offices, in public, at home, just anywhere, when there is nothing doing, men occupy themselves with talk about others' affairs."[48] He concluded, "It goes without much stress [meaning emphasis] that cowardice is the implication of gossiping." What perturbed Aloys the most was *how* men were using their idle time—to engage in *feminine* activities such as gossiping. Thus, gossip emasculated men when they adopted this inherently feminine practice. Yet both writers still found women to be the source of gossip. Thus, deeper analysis of their diatribes reveals that men's gossip still began with women. Gossip remained feminized.

Anthony Zumafor, who served as a former civil servant for the West Cameroon government in the 1960s, had a different view of gossip and its association with gender. He told me "even that advice [columns] in the papers [were] part of the process of gossiping. It did not concern [worry] our men."[49] He saw women's advice columns such as Manga's and Wanzie's as gossip. I found this confusing at first: strictly speaking, the columns did not contain gossip. But I believe he was referring to advice on love and romance, and letters these columns ran that often shared identifiable details about the people involved in their inquiries. For example, a "tormented housewife" penned a long letter to the *New Cameroon* in 1971 detailing her husband's extramarital affairs and gave identifying information about the life and address of his mistress. She explained that the individual in question was a Bakweri woman, twice divorced, who lived on Street One Tiko and kept an earthen pot by her bed—"could it be she has charmed my husband?" the female letter writer facetiously inquires.[50] She further discloses that she clandestinely followed her husband one night to the woman's house and knocked on the door and that the mistress shouted, "[G]o, is it now you can come to my house, why did you not arrange with me during the day?" The female letter writer laments that "neither my husband nor this woman will come out." These details did constitute gossip.

Yet contrary to Zumafor's memory, gossip was never exclusively the preserve of women journalists. Male journalists gossiped and policed gendered boundaries just as women did. In fact, Patrick Tataw Obenson's popular satirical column in the *Cameroon Outlook* in the late 1960s and 1970s, which he wrote under the penname "Ako-Aya" (he claimed that the name meant "let them take and cook"), frequently provided gossip he gathered on his travels in urban Anglophone Cameroon. He shared what he deemed report-worthy adventures and encounters in diverse spaces, from inside taxicabs, hotel bars, *Makossa* concerts to funerals.[51] Although he was better known for social and political commentaries, his biographer Ephraim Ngwafor dedicates a whole chapter to the gossip that Ako-Aya uncovered and shared, saying "[i]t was said of Ako-Aya that he was omnipresent. Hence the belief that he could uncover any story, be the events that happened in the darkness of the night. All these were subsequently exposed the following week in his column. The result was that, one had to do a U-turn, before indulging in any mischievous activity, for fear that Ako-Aya was watching. Indeed, he genuinely played the role of BIG BROTHER in George Orwell's 1984."[52] Anthony Ndi pointed out in his work on the history of West Cameroon that Ako-Aya's "sharp pen spared no one, not even close friends and relatives."[53] Ako-Aya himself took great pride in his superb skill of being able to find gossip-worthy events in any corner of urban West Cameroon; in an August 1971 column, for instance, he promised to uncover more salacious gossip for his readers, assuring that "whatever is happening down the coast—in Buea, Tiko, Victoria and Kumba, that is me coming. . . . I am coming to write about all of them 'one by one.'"[54]

Ako-Aya posted a story in 1973 about a widowed woman who seemed to have miraculously recovered a week after her husband's death, for example. "'I go die today,'" the woman supposedly shouted in tears when her husband died. "At the grave-yard," Ako-Aya explained, "she fell inside the grave desiring to be buried with the man she loved." He elaborated:

> But my dear reader, before a week was out, I found her in long black flowing robes, dancing to the tunes of Ekambi Brilliant [a popular Cameroonian Makossa singer]. You should have really knocked me down with a feather. As soon as she saw me, she started raining abuses on me, "Go and write," she shouted. I hear she smokes "banga" [marijuana] and is a drug addict. Do I blame her[?][55]

The anecdote clearly shows that Ako-Aya was willing to share gossip, extending not only to the woman's public conduct but to rumors that she smoked marijuana. For a male journalist, being "omnipresent" and "Big Brother" was socially powerful. Conversely, a female journalist was merely a "gossip columnist." Regardless, it is likely that such social news from various towns created a sense of community belonging through print. Similarly, the women's advice columns that offered advice on love and romance to people in need created a sense of community belonging. Gossip about individuals in one's town, or in other towns, created a space to stay updated on the welfare of neighbors and other community members and to facilitate "the possibility of a new form of imagined community" and national belonging through print space.[56]

Although Ephraim's reference to Orwell is humorous, it has a dark undertone. Community members could easily fear having their own intimate secrets aired in public. Clara Manga of the *Cameroon Champion* declared her commitment not to become involved in such activities when she informed readers that gossipers "hear little things about other people's homes and go out [to] make long sweet stories with them especially if they have an interested audience. Anything that happens between husband and wife should be entirely their own business." She warned, "If they are foolish enough to expose their home affairs, the public should still try to mind their own business. . . . I do hope husbands and wives will learn to guard each other's secrets and send the 'busybodies' away to mind their own business."[57] Ruff Wanzie similarly claimed in a March 1964 column that gossip transgressed private and public boundaries and brought trouble to marriages. She cited gossip as one of the key causes of the increasing divorce rate in urban West Cameroon. While acknowledging the role of a generational shift away from arranged marriages and the greater education, financial independence and resulting assertiveness of women, she claimed that gossip played a pivotal role in fertilizing "the seed of resentment" in marriages. In a column headlined "Causes of Divorce," she named phrases such as "I heard your hussy say that," "I saw your wife with Mr. X," and "Miss B. went out with your husband." "If such gossips are not remedied from the start," she warned her readers, "they would bring about divorce."[58] It is difficult to ascertain exact data on the divorce rate in urban West Cameroon in the 1960s and 1970s, but the social and personal dangers of the exposure of intimate marital woes, or secrets, were great. Both Wanzie and Manga contended that marital woes needed to stay in the home space. When gossip entered public spaces, it could impinge on the couple's reputation for integrity and respectability, encouraging people to "look at [them] in a way," as my "aunt" assistant put it.

Several months later on May 2, 1964, Wanzie specifically condemned women who exposed their marital woes in public spaces: "Men always wonder why women stay so long in the market and in the shops. In fact, some women spend such time gossiping about their husbands, boyfriends and other women, comparing what they have bought, culling up stories and planting unnecessary grudges at home against the husband. Wives only return home after that to nag their husbands, and in doing so they drive them from home all day long only to sit back and complain: 'Our husbands never stay at home.'"[59] From Wanzie's perspective, wives who exposed their marital woes diverged from gender norms and made homes inhospitable for husbands, who then decided to "never stay at home." By nagging husbands and causing grudges, women lost domestic bliss. They stepped out of line and challenged male authority at home and in public by complaining about their husbands, thus harming both of their public reputations. Spilling marital woes and "secrets" to the public might bring public condemnation of the behavior of both the husband and wife. But scrutiny focused on wives.

As the next chapter demonstrates, urbanites believed that married women should exhibit calm demeanors and suitable public conduct when confronting marital woes. By doing so, they preserved their respectability and paid deference to male authority regardless of the calamities. The "tormented housewife" who wrote the letter detailing her husband's affair with a woman who kept an earthen pot by her bed was certainly not concerned with how exposing her marital woes might shape her public dignity. She inquired if she should physically fight the woman—the "men-huntress" as she calls the mistress—sue her "for causing disharmony," or divorce her husband "and leave the children with him." She shared her intent to report her woes to the two Bakweri associations that both she and the mistress attend, and to the young woman's aunt (who lives on Street 7 as she disclosed), although, as she states, "friends have advised me to be calm." The editor responded by discouraging her from

> doing any of the unwise, ignoble measures contemplated. Rather seek more interviews [conversations] of a friendly persuasion with your husband over this matter, bringing home to him the stark realities of the consequences of his misguided action. If this step fails, report to his aunt, [the Bakweri group] meeting and finally, seek the help of [the] Social Welfare Department or legal advice.[60]

The editor encouraged her to seek counsel outside the marriage, but only as a last resort. Instead, the editor urged her to confront the marital problems from within the marriage, possibly guarding her marital privacy and public respectability. As the next chapter shows, if women preserved dominant gender norms in their marriage and home, their homes reflected the nation's respectability and integrity writ small. Screeds against the behavior of married women, such as nagging and complaining about absent husbands having extramarital affairs, became another arena for shaping ideal womanhood and defining married women's suitable conduct and embodied comportment.

CHAPTER 6

"My Husband Stopped Maintaining Me So I Beat Up His Girl"

Jealous Housewives, "Women Extremists," and Public Conduct

Enraged housewife Alice Nguti attracted a crowd of neighbors to her Victoria home located at Half Mile on Sunday, April 21, 1968, when she attempted to lock her husband's mistress in her home. It is unclear whether her husband, who worked for Plantations Pamol Du Cameroun, an agricultural industry business, knew his wife was present when he foolishly invited his mistress to their home. Alice later told a reporter that she had "smilingly welcomed" into her home the young woman, a former student of the Queen of the Holy Rosary Secondary School in Mamfe, a southwestern town near the Cameroon-Nigeria border. The young woman countered that she was Alice's husband's fiancée and that Alice, unsurprisingly, had not been in the least friendly. Independent reports agreed, however, that Alice taunted the young woman, whose name does not appear in the newspaper account, saying she should stay in the house and marry her husband "instead of flirting around with him." Her fury growing, and the crowd of nosy neighbors expanding outside her home, Alice locked the door and told the young woman "to stay and share the household duties." A violent struggle ensued, and Alice later complained to the police that "her blouse was torn in the exercise." The younger woman managed to escape from the home and run past clamorous neighbors at the scene. The Victoria police investigated the incident. Journalists at the *Cameroon Times* got wind of it from a secret source in the police station, a common investigative practice for prominent English-language papers of the time in 1960s urban West Cameroon.[1] Subsequently, on April 27, 1968, a week after the incident, the newspaper splashed details of the event under a large, salacious headline: "Housewife Won't Let Husband's Girl-Friend Out."[2]

As comical as the story might seem, in exposing her marital woes, Alice Nguti was threatening her own public respectability, just as her neighbors' gossip about her after the incident might do. At the same time, the community might concur with the older woman's view that her husband's girlfriend was attempting to avoid the responsibilities that came with marriage and therefore posed a threat to her own respectability by not adhering to prevalent gender norms and codes of conduct. As this chapter shows, while admitting that women like Alice Nguti acted with some justification, urban elites nonetheless condemned such married women for openly challenging male authority and gender norms and damaging the public respectability of marriage itself.

This penultimate chapter examines the shared perspectives of educated urbanites on how formally educated married women and men should act, and what a modern urban marriage and family should have looked like during the 1960s and early 1970s. The chapter also conveys the notion that a respectable home functions as the Anglophone nation writ small. Educated urbanites specifically condemned as "women extremists" formally educated married women who behaved unsuitably, to shame them for openly challenging respectable public behavior, diverging from ideal womanhood and normative gendered behavior. This chapter is inspired by the works of Dorothy Hodgson and Sheryl McCurdy, who contend that many postcolonial African married women were labelled "wicked" because they "disrupt[ed] the web of social relationships that defin[ed] and depend[ed] on them as daughters, sisters, wives, mothers, and lovers."[3] These women "directly or indirectly challenged" cultural expectations of gender roles and relations within marriages. As Hodgson and McCurdy assert, such women "continue to live their lives outside the boundaries of 'acceptable' rules and behaviors, thereby shifting their community's expectations about gender roles and relations in new directions."[4]

Yet as Jane Parpart observes about the reconfigurations of gender on the Zambian Copperbelt from the 1930s to the 1960s, ideas about "wickedness" and "respectability" were fluid, with "[m]any supposedly 'respectable' women adopt[ing] some of the strategies of their 'wicked' sisters when seeking to challenge or at least redefine male (and even female) authority and control. Rejecting the norm that personal problems should be handled privately. . . . [e]ven 'respectable ladies' discovered that a public scene could achieve the desired results." As Parpart asserts, these "unacceptable behavior could garner sympathy if a woman was seen as a victim, especially of male abuse."[5] I apply a similar logic to analyze 1960s urban West Cameroonian married women, who female journalists and male authors of letters to newspapers also implied were "wicked" or "extreme" because they seemingly refused to adhere to the standards of ideal wifehood, to become "good" women, and who, like Alice Nguti, challenged ideas about public respectability by airing marital woes in public, hoping to foster sympathy from newspaper readers and community members.[6]

But why did it matter that married women followed proper gender relations in the home? Preservation of male authority and other cultural values within the home reflected the nation's cultural values. Many political elites believed that a marriage-centered family strengthened both society and the West Cameroonian nation. Subsequently, such individuals beseeched notions of embodied nationalism that filtered into women's everyday domestic spaces. Women who adhered to proper marital behavior, many individuals implied, projected a suitable Anglophone Cameroonian persona and esteem domestically and in community spaces. Thus, female journalists, for instance, implored women to preserve patriarchal ideas about gender relations within marriages. For instance, in 1964, Ruff Wanzie wrote that if "the wife is the undisputed boss," the marriage and family "is never happy and children from such a family never grow up properly to be good citizens in every way." Though she admits that the "man must assist his wife in many of her tasks," assisting too much might make children "feel that they have no father—merely a mother and assistant mother who is their father. . . . it leaves the children confused as to the roles of men and women in the world with resultant failure on their part to develop normally and live successfully as adults."[7] Hence, failing to exhibit proper gender relations threatened women's role as "mothers" of the nation who biologically and symbolically reproduced the nation's cultural values. Women who challenged perceptions of suitable marital relations threatened the family's strength and stability and ultimately threatened the nation's principles.

Like gossip, the behavior of women in their marriages became a source of anxiety because of social changes. The fact that wives could have access to their own money through their formal employment seemed like a significant threat to dominant ideas about domestic and sexual roles.[8] While the shifts were actually small in real terms, the specter of female financial empowerment seemed a significant threat to marital stability. Yet as with other aspects of women's behavior, individuals regularly proposed that educated women should model higher behavioral standards and attitudes for others by preserving the norm of female submission to their husbands. Thus, condemnation of married women's unsuitable behaviors focused on those who were formally educated and either stay-at-home wives or working wives. According to Wanzie and others, some of these elite women used their educated status and their un-African interpretations of gender to publicly thwart gender hierarchies and gender norms on the streets of Anglophone Cameroon. For instance, journalists castigated women who, especially in public, criticized their husbands or husbands' mistresses, saying they violated gender-specific cultural mores. Yet female journalists and women and men alike also blamed single women, often identified as "spinsters" or "spare tyres," for threatening the sanctity of marriage by either engaging in sexual dalliances with married men or by choosing to remain unmarried. Although dominant Christian morals held that men and women alike should be monogamous in their marriages, patriarchal attitudes gave men, but never women, some latitude for dalliances. Thus, Cameroonians judged women more harshly for sexual misconduct than they judged their male counterparts. Openly subverting men's liberty to have extramarital sex, according to female journalists, threatened respect for Anglophone Cameroon's patriarchal authority. Instead, female journalists strove to affirm marital monogamy as the ideal by encouraging women to keep a calm demeanor when facing marital woes, and thereby possibly preserving a married couple's respectability in the community.

Elites hailed women's educational and professional achievements but feared that educated wives considered themselves exempt from dominant notions of appropriate gendered conduct. For instance, both sexes condemned educated wives for undermining male authority if they publicly confronted husbands about their extramarital liaisons. Men more frequently blamed women's formal education for their own perceived loss of status; they alleged that educated women had a superiority complex and became too domineering in marriages. However, female journalists asserted that if women carefully adhered to cultural mores about gender, formal education could define the modern African woman. In doing so, they sought to define a society in which married couples and their families were progressive yet adhered to prevalent gender norms. Further, instead of calling on husbands not to engage in extramarital affairs—or even to not participate in such flagrant public humiliation as inviting their girlfriends to their wives' homes—male and female letter writers as well as some journalists shifted the blame to women. Married women, "women extremists," and single women, identified as "spinsters," were to blame for posing a threat to the stability of marriages.

Discussions of gender and marital relations were part of a larger political project. Again, the general belief that Francophone women had lower standards of respectability fed the sense that the boundaries of Anglophone Cameroonian women's acceptable conduct needed to be marked in a hegemonic Francophone republic.[9] The behavior of married women in relation to infidelity became another way to call for women's adherence to gender norms to maintain a distinct Anglophone Cameroonian culture that unified the Anglophone community countrywide. While journalist Patrick Tataw Obenson (Ako-Aya) expressed his relish of East Cameroonian women's "easy" ways, his 1971 columns about them support the West Cameroon perspective. In one such column he enthused,

> I like these Douala [a Francophone city] beauties. . . . provided you are anxious to spend the money, the goods [sex] are delivered to you. Contrast these with our West Cameroon beauties, with their lack of husbands where you must bribe [them] with Especial and Beck [beers] and *suya* [spicy shish kebab] before the green lights are shown [to] you, and the setting must be at the Atlantic beach and you must go home around three [instead of spending the night].[10]

Ako-Aya implied that West Cameroonian women withheld sexual favors more fastidiously than their Eastern counterparts. Hence, women's "proper" behavior and actions had symbolic implications for a strong West Cameroonian cultural identity. In other words, enforcing gender roles, particularly regarding educated married women, helped maintain masculine authority while supporting a directly threatened regional autonomy.

Here I highlight cultural practices regarding marriage that have been prevalent through much of urban and rural West Africa since the late nineteenth century. Most women in precolonial and colonial regions of Anglophone and Francophone Cameroon deferred to their fathers, husbands, or some form of male jurisdiction. Most precolonial West African societies recognized polygynous marriage, though colonial administrators and Christian missionaries challenged the practice among converts and those they wanted to convert.[11] Colonial men wielded broad, unilateral authority in their households over wives and children; married women might try to control the behavior of cowives or their children, but not of their husbands.[12] Unlike men, women who wanted to adhere to a conservative womanhood during and after British rule in urban West Cameroon were not considered to be adhering to traditional norms if they drink and speak their minds openly—the preserve of men.[13] Bridet Teboh, for instance, asserts in her research on the social and economic history of women in British-ruled Moghamoland, located in the western Grassfields, that "married women were advised to be more modest and chaste in dress and demeanor than unmarried females. For example, women during the colonial era avoided wearing very short skirts, bright colors or clothes 'that might attract attention' to their physical qualities."[14] Fidelia Ngum, a formally educated mother of four who was a seamstress and also sold produce and homemade food in a small shop by the roadside and a long-time resident of Buea, said that proper married women avoided entering bars alone in the 1960s and 1970s. She had this to say about the consequences of a married woman entering an "off license" (a bar) alone: "if you go there even where you're married, they'll give you a name, [they think] either you're looking for men . . . so they will say 'look at that one. She wants to become a prostitute.' That's when they will start, [and] talk about your dressing, 'look at the way she's dressing.'"[15] She explained dance halls, especially for single young adult women, were respectable places where women might go and socialize instead of bars.

Men's freedom came with responsibilities, however; men were obligated to house and financially support their wives and children, and men who failed to do so might be shamed by their wives and family members. But, unlike women, men rarely faced public condemnation for straying from the marital bed if they supported their wives financially. Conversely, community members might label married women like Alice Nguti as "women extremists" who publicly challenged male authority. In many ways, these women were much like their "free women" counterparts. Although married, if they acted outside the control of their husbands, they were "free" and therefore dangerous. Elizabeth Nkuku Nwigwe, writing as Sister Dolly in the *Cameroon Outlook*, even asserted in July 1970 that women might enter a life of crime if free from male control:

> They condemn, leakout [meaning expose] their husband's confidential matters and even set up a barricade which in simple understanding lay the trace [foundation] for more serious happening to follow in the name of crimes. . . . there stand[s] only one thing which can easily be identified as the prime attraction to women into the crime world. This is the free life. Where a woman

> feels herself free from the immediate control of a husband, or so, and looks at the whole human world as a wide and limitless sphere [which] she is tempted to many things in life. . . . she can easily be wooed into the elusive glory of alcohol, and then she begins to lose her womanly considerations to many things in life and thus measure herself up with the men folk.[16]

Given such worries, it was reasonable to call on women to accept their husbands' infidelity rather than exposing it in public. Hence, women were more likely to evade vice if they married and preserved men's authority within the marriage and domestic space.

MARRIAGE, HOUSEHOLD ECONOMY, AND "PROPER" CONDUCT

A series of missives throughout the 1960s suggests the level of concern about the social and economic advancement of women in urban Anglophone Cameroon. Many of the letters conflated women's formal education to their demeanor toward a suitor or husband. Further, the letters highlighted issues that cropped up if "literate" [or formally educated] wives worked, often pointing to the control of financial resources in the marriage as a significant source of concern.[17] Three letters that ran in the *Cameroon Observer* in October 1963 concerned whether an illiterate or a literate wife is more useful to her husband. One of the two who resoundingly praised illiterate wives, Macnus Mbonya of Tiko, commended his sister-in-law, "an illiterate woman who cannot pronounce John correctly," as the best wife he had ever seen in action:

> Through thick and thin has she stood with my brother. . . . To contrast, I know of a gentleman who married a literate girl but when he was involved in a case [i.e., suffering financial difficulties], it became impossible for the girl to continue as a wife, and [she] once had the guts to address the gentleman as a thief. Added to that, she occasionally came to dances in the company of other boyfriends while the husband was at home mourning his sorrows.

The other pro-illiterate wives letter, by E. Njoh from Victoria, declared that "the literate wife is only proud of the husband when he is in the high income earning group and that when the tide is low, love diminishes considerably." He claims, "Many a literate wives have deserted their husbands because they were involved in cases."[18]

The third reader defended educated married women. A woman signing herself Elli Ngolle from Tombel wrote that, "[m]ost men who object [to] having educated wives do so in fear that an educated wife will be able to check his weaknesses. In these days of excessive drinking which too many a man [uses to] portrays his wealth, only the sound advice of an educated wife will count better."[19] Ngolle contends that educated wives helped keep men respectable by discerning their faults and weaknesses and actively tried to amend them. She attributes moral supremacy to women, claiming that educated women confer an air of morality on their men. Thus, an educated wife checking her husband's bad behavior posed no problem but rather encouraged good conduct.

Drawing from a then-common stereotype, the two letters by Mbonya and Njoh describe literacy as an engine for violations of cultural mores on gender relations. Wanzie, herself literate and formally employed as a civil servant, nonetheless attributed such violations to overly Westernized women who had travelled abroad.[20] In a lengthy March 1966 column, she accuses such women of violating West Cameroonian "indigenous culture." She asserts that men who travel abroad return with "just the bare knowledge that took them away from their motherland and should they bring back any strange cultural practices, they are usually those that fit squarely or almost into our own cultural practices" whereas women endeavor to "revolutionize our customs overnight." She censures their haughtiness, saying a woman of this type

> shuns the company of certain people on whom lies the foundation of her life in society; talks the grammar [foreign lingo] even to those who find it difficult to understand pidgin [Cameroonian Creole]; snubs certain classes of people especially those who wish to interview her for friendship, [stating] "He or she is not suitable". . . . adding ironically, "This is not what we do over there." Over there[,] where?. . . . Some of these girls believe too that any girl or woman who has not been abroad cannot speak or write sense, be a good social mixer or dancer. . . . Simply because these girls spent six months in Europe, perhaps for a typing course or so, they claim to know all that pertains to education, politics, journalism, nursing, in short, all fields of mental and social endeavor. . . . Let us, when we return from our study tours show our people that we are still the same daughters, free mixers, nation builders etc. as we were when we left home.[21]

From Wanzie's viewpoint, some educated women use their experiences studying abroad to promote unsuitable Western cultural values that challenge

African cultural standards and expectations. Her criticisms betray gendered assumptions about educated persons' behavior, overtly alleging that men are not susceptible to such behavior, while some educated women challenged standards of behavior too much. Within this framework, some educated men, such as Mbonya and Njoh, similarly agreed that education gave women too much independence and too great a sense of entitlement.

"The Working Housewife—For Better or For Worse"

For Patrick Obenson, writing as Ako-Aya, formal employment was the problem. In an April 1971 Ako-Aya column in the *Cameroon Outlook*, he shares that he visited an out-of-work friend whose wife had a job. He reveals that the wife did not cook dinner after he arrived and then, "in the morning she slept on, and on, not caring to wake up and prepare breakfast for us. She left for work, taking the keys of the cupboard which contained breakfast things. '*Buy una own*' [Cameroonian pidgin English: buy your own] she shouted back when we asked for the key. This was a wife who was 'jelosing [*sic*]' her husband when he was working and earning a good salary. This is a woman who fought other women because of her husband, now, however, the scales are turned, and life is like that."[22] In addition to the working wife who locked up the food before she left for her job, Ako-Aya described a woman who had an affair with her husband's friend while her husband was in Britain, then had an abortion on learning that he was about to return. He noted wives who shed "crocodile tears" when their husbands died, and women who took over the marriage when husbands were having financial difficulties.[23] Ako-Aya even complained in a September 1970 column that working married women became haughty and stingy, refusing to share their earnings with their husbands. He claimed that educated women who grew accustomed to modern amenities such as cars, gas cookers and refrigerators were greedy: he cites a friend's working wife who "refused to pay the cook [with her own money] even though she knows the cook is doing what rightly, she ought to do if she were not working." His diatribe ended by declaring that he would never marry an educated woman who worked.[24]

In the same month that Ako-Aya vowed never to marry an educated working woman, the *Cameroon Outlook* published a cartoon titled "The working housewife—for better or for worse." The image shows a married couple leaving a bank. The woman holds a large bag of money. The caption above her encapsulates her thoughts and reads, "Thank heavens I have banked my own pay."[25] Readers would understand the cartoon as accusing working

"The Working Housewife—For Better or For Worse." From *Cameroon Outlook* 2, no. 69 (Sept. 11, 1970), 6, courtesy of National Archives of Cameroon in Buea.

wives of selfishness. By treating their pay as their own, instead of a wage for the family, and seeking economic independence, women fractured expectations of shared property with the husband, presmably the chief household budget manager. Both female journalists and readers who wrote to newspapers cautioned that wives might use their earnings on cosmetics to attract immoral sexual attention and diverge from normative expectations of gender roles.[26] Thus they disparaged women's claims to absolute financial autonomy, although evidence suggests that women nonetheless continued to bank their pay separately. If husbands no longer controlled financial resources, women might exert inappropriate authority in domestic and community spaces. The cartoon reflected Ako-Aya's opinion that educated married women deviated from what he deemed proper comportment.

In fact, contrary to views of female journalists, in some Cameroonian rural societies women had more financial power than urban women. Scholars have documented the traditional division of households in the Bamenda Grassfields in the Northwest Region of Cameroon. Miriam Goheen's work, *Men Own the Fields, Women Own the Crops*, describes women's labor as the linchpin of male status and power. Examining the Nso chiefdom, a people of the Bamenda Grassfields, from the nineteenth century to the 1990s, she shows the importance of women producing both crops and children. Goheen examines power struggles between the chiefdom and the state and between men and women, as women increasingly rejected long-practiced Grassfields marriage customs. Although Nso men dominate their society, women have their own power. As Goheen's title suggests, men own the land, but women's labor controls the crops. Historically, women kept the profits of the crops they sold after feeding their families.[27]

In contrary, as Stella Nana-Fabu contends, uneducated urban wives of highly educated men—the illiterate wives who readers of the *Cameroon Observer* had praised—were highly vulnerable. They lacked the power that subsistence farming gave their counterparts in rural regions. And allowing them to engage in small trading of domestically produced goods or services shamed their husbands as it revealed that they could not earn enough to feed their families. The urban uneducated wives of highly educated men thus often depended completely on their husbands for social status and economic security.[28] In this manner, educated men and women constructed new idealized definitions of urban masculinity and femininity that diverged from long-standing practices in which women played a crucial role in their families' economic survival.

"Who Should Keep the Family Purse, the Woman or the Man?"

At the same time, female journalists acknowledged that some men should let their wives control the finances. In a 1964 article, for example, Ruff Wanzie writes, "Some husbands have written asking my view on why wives always quarrel with their husbands when husbands refuse giving them extra allowance apart from food money. . . . Husbands fail to know that wives, whether they work or not, have to be given . . . a little amount every month as pocket allowance for them to use it as they like." She recommends that "in homes where the husbands are squanderers, and think not of their financial stand in the next day, ill health emergencies and education of their children, it will be justified if the wives take charge of the family's savings."[29] Two years later, she reiterates the same advice in her women's column. Wanzie advises separate bank accounts in such situations to prevent marital discord. Averring that times have changed, she remarks:

> In Africa in days gone by, our grandmothers after selling their farm produce, gave the money to their husbands who kept it together with theirs. This meant

> that husband and wife had one common purse from which the husband spent money for the up-keep of his wives, children and relatives. Whenever the wife demanded money . . . the husband readily gave her such money without complaining or furrowing.

Wanzie compared West Cameroonian practices with those of Europeans:

> In Europe it is generally the custom for husband and wife to have a common family bank account with both husband and wife having a right over it. . . . Today, Africans even though married by Western standards have not dropped the custom of extended family system. Now that monogamy is slowly but surely taking over polygamy, the wife does not enjoy the right of inheritance. . . . because the husband's relatives claim his money and property [after death] leaving both wife and children stranded.

Wanzie suggests that the system of a common family purse only works if women have access—whether, as in "Africa in days gone by," because her husband would never say no to her, or as in Europe, because she had equal access. This contrasted with the system current in West Cameroon at the time, in which even widows had no assurance of access to the family purse. Consequently, she ultimately embraces greater equality in wives' control of finances.[30]

Notably, Wanzie's argument here invokes what I term the "print griot." Similar to the traditional griot Thomas Hale describes, a journalist like Wanzie was a "historian [who] emerge[d] as a 'time bender,' [by] link[ing] past to present and serv[ing] as a witness to events in the present, which he or she may convey to persons living in the future."[31] As Hale describes about traditional griots in West Africa: "[t]heir view of history cannot be dismissed just because it does not contain dates and because it is oral rather than written."[32] Likewise, Wanzie's claims here lack scholarly support, but her narrative about women's gender roles in the past, like those other griots in Africa from around the same time, provides insight into, as Hale notes, "notions of what constitutes the past."[33] Hale describes griots' role as "far more than simply the retelling of the events. It is a reading of the past for audiences in the present, an interpretation that reflects the complex blend of both past and present values." Wanzie, as a "print griot," traces past marriage relations to interpret, at the time, how changing marital and family relations in West Cameroon have disadvantaged women. While modern marriages are monogamous, she asserts that the family system has not adjusted to changing marriage norms to continue the financial protection of widows, and husbands have diverged from long-practiced gender norms by refusing to share their joint income with their wives. Through her retelling of the past, Wanzie condemns husbands for departing from past traditional norms in marriages.

Writing as Sister Dolly in July 1970, Nkuku Nwigwe view is bleaker than Wanzie's. She accused her readers of both sexes of improperly managing family finances. She censures both husbands and wives, claiming:

> We are now faced with one of the most intriguing affairs which pollutes sometimes, the orderliness of our married homes. Who should keep the family purse, the woman or the man?. . . . There is the belief that women are lovers of luxury and are extravagant. . . . most women, even housewives, have tended to use money intended for food and other house requirements for cosmetics and other trivialities. . . . The man who should be the head of the family is so engaged in other affairs that one often wonders if a man can be responsible for the family finances. Most men spend long hours in pops [bars] with girlfriends, calling for exorbitant drinks. . . . forgetting their suffering wives and children at home, who depend wholly on them. . . . you hear men accusing their wives of extravagance while the women, in return, lay the blame on husbands. But one wonders who should be relied on. Since all are extravagant, who should then keep the purse?[34]

The journalist still conveys prevailing expectations about attributes and behavior appropriate to women, though she condemns both sexes for mishandling household finances. She concludes that despite a woman's education and changing attitudes about marriage, men were still the natural leaders of households and should thus manage the finances. However, from Sister Dolly's perspective, such men comport themselves improperly if they fail to curb their wives' spending or provide for the women and children who "depend wholly on them."

The above discussions show that newspaper columnists' prescriptions for women's roles betray a selective embrace of African authenticity. As Marc Epprecht argues in his work on sexual identities, specifically homosexuality in Africa, colonial rule and postcolonial nationalist sentiments shaped discourses about African authenticity and norms regarding sexuality.[35] Perceptions about African authenticity, as Epprecht contends, often regurgitate colonial stereotypes about Africans. Yet these perspectives were neither stagnant nor uncontested. Male letter writers in West Cameroon suggested that formally educated and empowered women were un-African even when they accepted changes in household financial control. For example, they asserted that men should completely control household finances, even though this was contrary to precolonial and colonial practices in which women had a say, and often an independent income.

Even while raising the alarm about societal changes, female journalists lauded modern women who worked for pay, arguing they could do so without endangering either their marriages or their respectability. Thus, unlike many male letter writers to newspapers, or like Patrick Obenson, female journalists generally rejected absolute patriarchy. They also questioned male privilege by suggesting that women might subvert gender hierarchies if their husbands failed as heads of households. Citing European marriage customs to exemplify how modern African marriages should operate, as Wanzie did, was common. However, female journalists stopped short of disrupting gender hierarchies completely, even in extreme circumstances. They implied that motherhood held primacy in situations where a woman was married to a profligate husband, encouraging such women to prioritize their roles as mothers to ensure the well-being of their children. Similarly, an educated wife should bow to male authority by letting her husband control household finances, though only if he provided for her and the children. Although both female journalists and male letter writers endeavored to reorder gender hierarchies along patriarchal lines, contrasting their views suggests contradictory viewpoints of appropriate gender hierarchies and differing embraces of local and international concepts of gender normalizations.

Oral interviews and surveys suggest that formally educated women felt they could work while maintaining traditional gender relations. Mary Ghanghi, a long-time resident of Batibo, a town situated in the modern-day Northwest Region, shared her thoughts in a survey about progressive married women during the period of study. A retired civil servant who owned a bakery, she says a progressive woman was one

> who could dress well, cares about her family affairs, struggles to be a bread winner for the family. Does not drink alcohol to the extent of being drunk. She is an example for her children and the community she comes from. She does not point to [look to] attract men. She should be concerned about her children's education. Does not take decisions alone without the consent of the husband. Listens more and speaks less. . . . They refuse to remain only in the kitchen. They stood high and did not allow the world to swallow them. They stood high in society.[36]

While Ghanghi had some level of formal education, and had long worked in the formal economy, she nevertheless saw her duties of wifehood and motherhood as primary in her life. Ghanghi contends that while wives might work and undertake "struggles to be a bread winner for the family," they could preserve gender norms by taking care of their children and deferring to male authority by always seeking male "consent." Ghanghi suggested that education might define an ideal progressive wifehood that preserved dominant gender norms and maintained respect for male authority within the home.

"NEVER ATTACK OR FIGHT YOUR HUSBAND PUBLICLY": EDUCATED WIVES AND PHYSICAL VIOLENCE

Discussions of physical violence and criticisms of the overbearing attitudes of educated wives within marriage also reflected anxiety over changing gender expectations. Many letter writers suggested that a man's physical prowess expressed both his manhood and status within his marriage and community. In an August 1964 editorial entitled "Which Is Your Perfect Wife?" Wanzie encouraged educated wives to be "quiet or murmur some words of apology" to angry, harshly speaking husbands.[37] She counsels women to wait until their husbands are happy and then "put forth your problem, if you were to blame him, blame him then." But, as she asserts, "Never attack or fight your husband publicly." Wanzie connects her defense of reverence for male authority to the emerging roles and authoritarian tendencies of some educated wives in a December 1965 column. She warns, "Nowadays, men are remarking that it's useless educating girls. . . . Some [women] even show a domineering attitude if they are more educated and earn more than their husbands. These men will dare not say so if they live in sweet and peaceful homes." She proclaims that the home "should be a woman's first attention" and advises wives to prepare good meals. Educated women with office jobs who fail at "making the homes well disciplined, well organized and very sweet" face consequences: "When we become disrespectful to our husbands, and also neglect our home duties, our husbands have the right to stop us from working. Educated wives of Cameroon must prove to the men the worth of education."[38] An educated woman must still bow to her husband's desire that she stop working if she failed in her duties or stopped being submissive. Women's education must pose no threat—socially, culturally, economically, or physically—to men.

John Mbabit's October 1964 letter from Bamenda to Wanzie suggests the source of her concern about physical threats. He asks, "Is it right for a woman to slap her husband first?" saying he congratulated himself for remaining unmarried after he saw his sister-in-law slap his brother. He condemns the display as a public challenge to his brother's authority within his marriage. Mbabit's letter asks, "Does it mean African literate wives are being taught to slap their husbands first, Ruff?" Wanzie responds, "African literate wives are never taught to slap husbands first," maintaining that African husbands see that as "disrespect and provocation."[39] Although asserting that educated women are taught to be nonviolent, Wanzie recognizes the threat women's violence poses. "House-wives have, in down-right cold blood, inflicted inhuman tortures to their husbands. Have a look [a]round our hospitals and the stories would tell themselves," she alleges in a December 1965 post. For evidence, she cites the death of a man bitten by a snake while sleeping at a neighbor's after his angry wife barred him from the house. "These cases become a sort of show-case," she claims, saying people flocked to the hospital bed of suffering men "to see and know how wicked wives could be to their husbands." She argues that such violence by women against their husbands generally drew crowds, suggesting

> that the men become curious to see their counterparts who have fallen victim to the woman folk. [While] women might be wanting to know who it is that has fallen prey to their counterpart and henceforth to jubilate that the woman too can be stronger than the man or to blame the woman for doing so. . . . the men may think that the women are becoming wild or are power drunk and want to be free or wear the trousers.[40]

For Wanzie, some wives' violent conduct tarnished the image of all women as protectors of West Cameroonian cultural values, especially if women applauded each other's transgressions. Women supportive of other women's unruly behavior exacerbated anxieties that women cannot follow "proper" normative behavior within their homes and communities. From Wanzie's perspective, successful marriages required strong patriarchal authority; a wife's "resounding victory over a man" deepened fears of disarrayed male authority.

Mbabit was not the first to express concern about women striking men first. The phenomenon of some female boxers boxing men in the ring in the 1960s and 1970s prompted Ako-Aya to write, in an August 1971 column—with the apt title, "Man Fit Die O" (Cameroonian pidgin English: man can die)—"I want to lead the search for this female boxer who is said to be at large. I cannot understand why girls have taken the upper hand in striking the men first when they know that they will eventually be the first to get a belly ful [*sic*] of the beating." He gives additional examples of women he deemed too physically abrasive toward men in the same column: "Take this one at this local-joint who slapped a gentleman three times on the jaws for asking to dance with her. . . . this girl thinking herself a Joe Frazier [an African American professional boxer] called another boy and slapped him for making comments about her conduct."[41] Ako-Aya's condemnation, like Mbabit's, suggests a real fear that women increasingly physically challenged gender norms, even when participating in sporting activities.

In April 1970, Sister Dolly informs wives that "married men have suffered humiliations at the hands of over vigilant married women and their cries have come to me." She argues wives should accept extramarital affairs:

> The madam in the house is secured. . . . she is married and therefore she enjoys protection. Birds have their quiet nests; foxes their holes but, poor surplus women have nowhere to lay their heads! The mere fact that a man has chosen one woman to be mistress in the home should give that woman an over-all victory over the numerous girlfriends her man may have outside. This alone is sufficient to make a married woman relax her vigilance over her man. . . . It is when you in the house are bossy and forcy [meaning forceful] about the woman outside and you will not give your man a breathing space by nagging and swearing that your man gets fed up with the home and drifts farther from you and enjoys a relaxed state of mind in the home of the other woman. . . . Stop bothering your man!

She contends that "[e]ven highly educated women who should know better behave mean at times to both their husbands and the woman outside." A man, she proposes, is entitled to "manly freedom." Women should "be blind to the petty things he does outside" the marriage. That Sister Dolly would condone a married man's extramarital affairs when his wife is nagging him too much highlights how understandings about "natural" gender norms for the sexes shifted to fit larger patriarchal cultural values. Being "the mistress of the house," she maintains, is "a crown of conquest."[42] Excessive nagging only encourages men to seek comfort elsewhere. Vigilant wives violate their duty and imperil expected norms facilitating that behavior. They should enjoy the social and economic protections of marriage without seeking more equality.

A month later, Sister Dolly further denounces "women extremists"—

disruptive wives whose actions bring "shame to all women folks." She accuses women of becoming "'traffic police' on the country's highways just to track down their husbands." She reminds married women,

> [N]o matter how good they are to their husbands, their husbands may still have a roving eye on that other woman somewhere. . . . Fighting men in public spaces with cudgels or bottles all for the sake of the other woman has become very rampant these days. . . . Why fight your man in public? Why stand wildly and shamelessly in corners of the road to waylay your husband in order to disgrace him? Who bears the disgrace at the end? The woman of course because the man has the license by right to love a second or a third woman if he so desires.[43]

Sister Dolly suggests that a wife instead confront her husband with "tears of disappointment" in the privacy of their "bedroom and appeal to him for better behavior." She calls public conflicts with a husband's mistress "exposing your nakedness" and "invit[ing] a crowd through your deeds to witness your shaken position in the home." The "seal of public disgrace," she warns, will "seal your marriage failures." Many West Cameroonians believed that domestic problems should stay between couples or within the family. Equating physical violence with nakedness was no accident: confrontation stripped a woman of her dignity. Neither Wanzie nor Nkuku Nwigwe, writing as Sister Dolly, were self-declared feminists in any usual sense of the word, but their statements illustrate that they perceived the limits of patriarchy and perhaps were strategizing about how to protect the position of educated women in the new conditions by warning them against being too haughty. Stephanie Newell observes that many female writers of this era shied away from association with feminism because of suspicion toward "women libbers" and their conflation with promiscuous unmarried women.[44] Nonetheless, these West Cameroonian writers instructed women to become autonomous even while adhering to predominant gender roles and reacting unemotionally to men's extramarital conduct. They implicitly recognized a woman's right to object to infidelity in appropriate ways, suggesting that patriarchy could encompass a woman's critical response to her husband's extramarital liaisons.

Although female journalists' descriptions of wives becoming "traffic police" had intended humorous undertones, the same journalists highlighted the seriousness of intimate partner violence on the part of women, and called attention to it.[45] While Cameroonians had long considered violence in marriages a private affair, humor created a space for publicly addressing violence, helping readers access critical issues in educated married women's lives. Although the journalists and newspaper readers' decrials of violence by women may have reflected real incidents, the suggestion that women's violence outstripped men's was probably not grounded in evidence. Rhetoric about "violent women" in columns such as Wanzie's reflected, rather, a greater cultural tolerance of men's violence against women, which evidence suggests was more common than women's abuse of men.[46] A 2003 Committee against Torture Report shares that some Cameroonian men have long used physical violence to force their female partners to submit to the patriarchal society's norms and that "domestic violence continues to be seen as a private matter by the law enforcement officials."[47] Women's changing economic power in the 1960s and early 1970s may have increased violence against women. The idea that financially independent African women sought frivolous pursuits betrays an abusive postcolonial misogyny. Educated working women may have faced backlash from husbands trying to reassert dominance, which helps explain the prominence of the debates I have uncovered in newspaper columns and letters. Commentary on domestic violence may have reflected anxiety over women entering the workforce and other changes West Cameroon faced in the Federal Republic.

ACCEPTABLE PUBLIC SHAMING AND VIOLENCE

In 1960s urban West Cameroon, despite the critique of unruly wives as "un-African," scenes of housewives publicly humiliating their husbands continued a long-standing West African practice of publicly shaming men who broke social norms. In precolonial Anglophone Cameroonian societies, women joined together to condemn and prevent men's abuses, physically and verbally. The Anlu practice that Kom, Laimbwe, and other women used to fight dominance over agriculture in the waning days of British rule (chapters 1 and 7) was more commonly turned on individuals who broke community morals. These included extremes of physical abuse by men, such as when a man physically abused his pregnant wife.[48] Similarly, a movement known as *titi ikoli*—literally, "a thousand vulvas" in the Mokpwe language—had provided a certain level of discipline among men who directed sexual insults at women of the Bakweri, an ethnic group found in the Southwest Region of Cameroon. But similar practices were seen in other parts of Cameroon in the precolonial period as well in the period of British rule.[49] However as Shirley Ardener argues, in the latter part of British rule, women mostly abandoned these measures to resort to the more formal court rulings; their postcolonial counterparts also resorted to such matters to seek answers to their marital problems.[50] For instance, Emily Burrill demonstrates in her work on colonial Mali that although colonial men wielded broad, unilateral authority in their households over wives and children, as "patriarchal heads, family providers, and payers of bridewealth[,]" "African women's abilities to leave unsatisfactory marriages, choose their own marriage partners, or determine the conditions of marriage were upheld" by the colonial legal system at times.[51]

Other West African countries have similar practices of publicly shaming men to call attention to serious grievances. Judith Van Allen writes that Igbo women publicly shamed men to resolve individual and collective grievances during British rule in Nigeria. Tactics included boycotts, strikes, and "sitting on" individuals. To "sit on" a man, also called "making war" on him, "involved gathering at his compound, sometimes late at night, dancing, singing scurrilous songs which detailed the women's grievances against him and often called his manhood into question, banging on his hut with the pestles women used for pounding yams, and perhaps demolishing his hut or plastering it with mud and roughing him up a bit." Women might sanction a man thus "for mistreating his wife" or "violating the women's market rules."[52]

By opposing public humiliation of men who ducked their responsibilities, journalists such as Nkuku Nwigwe and some male readers actually broke with predominant West African traditions that allowed women to publicly condemn men who broke from social norms, thus demonstrating that their ease with long-sanctioned protest modes had its limitations. They redrew the boundaries of acceptable forms of protest against men within domestic and community spaces to actively reinterpret the power of women's long-standing access to modes of authority. Reinterpreting these social mechanisms allowed women to define African authenticities that reflected vernacular, continental, and global ideologies about gender norms. In 1960s West Cameroon, scorned wives might seek recourse in formal court procedures, as they started to do in the waning days of British rule, and they might be pardoned for their violent behavior if their husbands were failing to support their dependents. For instance, in late July 1967, observers at the Victoria Magistrate's Court eagerly listened to the testimony of a scorned wife—Mary Tarh testified before a crowded courtroom that shortly after the birth of their third child, her husband "stopped giving her food money, and was having an love affair with another girl," and that she had no choice but to assault the other woman physically. Adjourning the case to permit Tarh's absent accusers to be present (they may have been absent because they feared public humiliation), the magistrate proclaimed nonetheless that "[a] housewife has every right to defend her marital right," meaning not her husband's marital faith but his financial support.[53] The magistrate ultimately treated her leniently because he felt that Tarh was entitled to food money; her assault of the alleged mistress was excusable because her husband had failed to support her and the children. If her violent behavior subverted dominant gender norms, he had outright ignored them.

Tarh might not have been treated leniently if she had attacked her husband rather than his girlfriend. It was common to propose publicly humiliating single women as an alternative to humiliating husbands. Robert Alah's April 1967 letter to the *Cameroon Times* editor, for example, proposes that "married women should form unions to deal with single girls who prefer married men to bachelors."[54] He suggests that "[o]ur women should resolve to make it impossible for any married man to befriend unmarried girls; and also forbid unmarried girls from befriending married men." In a June 1970 *Cameroon Outlook* column, Sister Dolly provides a letter from a group of wives in Buea who did as Alah proposed. The letter suggests that publicly chastising a group of women offered an alternative to directly confronting and reproaching men. The missive reads in part:

> Until you will learn to go to a bachelor you will hardly find a husband. . . . You are being used to satisfy the animalistic instinct in men—spare motor tyres or bicycle wheels. . . . The title "Mrs." supersedes any doctorate degree a woman can achieve in her life history. . . . be grateful for married women for allowing their husbands to uplift you from your strait of depression caused by your failure to achieve a husband.[55]

Single women, in turn, collectively responded to Buea housewives two years later in Wanzie's advice column. Writing as Cousin Lizzy in February 1972, Wanzie provides an overview of the letter: "These young unmarried women have asked me to convey to housewives this message: That they spinsters do not vie for relief positions [temporary relationships]. If they love a man and wish to live with him, they'll do so as wives and not as reliefs, be the man married or single. . . . When it is their turn for marriage, they'll be properly wedded and not disguise their intentions."[56] Married women censured their single counterparts for flouting sexual morals and evading gender expectations by remaining unmarried. From the single women's perspective, fostering marriage-like relationships served as an alternative method of maintaining gender role expectations. The letter makes apparent their hope to marry eventually, thereby further upholding standards of desirable gender-role behavior. Like the letter from housewives Sister Dolly quotes, it does not question the behavior of married men who have extramarital relationships; instead, they uphold the authority of men and discuss how women might preserve or defy behavioral expectations for women.

Clearly, if married women were to preserve respectability during marital troubles, they should limit how far they pushed gender boundaries. Yet comments such as Wanzie's in a December 1965 column that some married women were "power drunk" and wanted to "wear the trousers" were more than censure about married women's behavior: they reflected concerns that through dress choice, married women might challenge male authority in domestic and public spaces. As the last chapter shows, by literally wearing trousers, urbanite elites expressed anxiety that married women and their single counterparts might visually challenge the expected social and physical boundaries separating gender norms for women and men.

CHAPTER 7

"When Women Wear Slacks"

"Single-Trouser Nationalism" and Public Space

"I would not for anything['s] sake dance with a woman wearing on slacks. There would be no grace in the whole show—it looks as [if] (bone to bone) two men [were] dancing together," exclaimed a flabbergasted male letter writer from Victoria in his February 1962 letter to "Auntie Clara"—Clara Manga's women's column for the *Cameroon Champion*. Manga had censured women who wear slacks to public spaces of good repute one week before, and the writer, identified only as Dogo, was full of praise: "You have scored 100% on your column. . . . The truth is bitter but it must be spoken." He lamented,

> How I wished I was the priest in a Presbyterian church one Sunday when a certain lady entered the church in slacks. I would have had no alternative than to ask her to walk out. If women don't know when and at what time certain dresses should be put on, let them ask from those who have gone abroad to more civilized countries.[1]

Women in slacks, such writers implied, did not respect male authority and showed themselves as ignorant, uncivilized, and mindless followers of fashion trends. They endangered predominant Christian expectations about the marked distinctions between the sexes, which many Cameroonian Christians believed were God's commandment. Pants signaled disrespect for patriarchal authoritative figures, including priests. Some letters called on educated women to model better fashion choices and to visibly embody suitable gendered behavior for women. By condemning women who wore unsuitable clothing in spaces of good repute, individuals such as Dogo and Clara Manga sought to define class boundaries, public respectability, and cultural values.

This chapter examines how debates about women's sartorial practices, specifically the wearing of slacks, came to be another area for negotiations about ideal womanhood and public behavior regulation within urban settings in 1960s and early 1970s West Cameroon. Concerns such as Dogo's reflected larger beliefs that women's sartorial practices mirrored cultural values; this perspective shaped nationalist and culturalist discourses. As Nira Yuval-Davis asserts, women become the symbolic bearers of "the collectivity's identity" because of societal beliefs that they possess the authentic voice of their culture.[2] By this line of thinking, anxiety over women wearing slacks disclosed an underlying concern about formally educated women supplanting male authority and usurping dominant cultural and religious values within West Cameroonian societies that were male-dominated and Christian. By condemning the practice of women wearing trousers, critics employed what Tanya Lyons calls "single-trouser nationalism," which I believe is a form of a visual embodied nationalism. Lyons asserts that through this form of nationalism, "in a patriarchal state . . . women are expected to be the symbols of the nation in long skirts, and men are supposed to wear the pants."[3] In accord with this visual paradigm, many urbanite elites thought that Anglophone women should wear dresses, a visual symbol of their deference to male authority, and Anglophone men should "wear the pants," visibly marking them as leaders of their homes, communities, and nations.

Through public dress regulation, urban elites envisioned public spaces in their communities as theaters in which to perform and reaffirm their social positioning and uphold the prevailing cultural values of an urban identity. Churches were emphasized as places of good repute that women in pants might besmirch. Women who wore slacks in hotel bars, a space where Westerners might see them, were accused of being un-African and thus inviting criticism about the nation's cultural values from the Western world. The elite frequented both types of spaces, and thus they became sites of interclass regulation through the supervision of educated women's clothing choices, as Dogo's urging illustrates when he refers to women who have "gone abroad to more civilized countries." But endeavors to place constraints on the public behavior of individuals not seen as fit to circulate in "respectable" places were not confined to urban West Cameroon. In her research examining the reconfigurations of gender in the Zambian Copperbelt from the 1930s to the 1960s, Jane Parpart contends that "[t]he emerging Copperbelt elite often defined themselves in opposition to the 'disreputable' classes, even seeking physical distance from them."[4] Consequently, they "supported efforts to constrain 'disreputable' behavior in town" by "set[ting] up their own institutions, such as dance clubs, debating societies, and elite drinking establishments, where they could socialize with their own kind."[5] Like their Zambian counterparts, "aspiring urbanites" in West Cameroon attempted to demarcate physical boundaries that reinforced socio-economic stratification in urban spatial settings, striving "to establish their position as 'respectable' members of the urban community."[6] Further, these "aspiring urbanites" physically regulated the mobility of women who donned unsuitable clothing in public; women were forcibly pushed out of prestigious members-only private venues, for example.

Records demonstrate that many residents went far beyond forcing women out of specific venues. Local officials and community members—the gendarmerie, landlords, and hotel owners to name a few—started regulating women's mobility in urban spaces at an alarming rate by late 1972, the transitory period in which President Ahidjo replaced the Federal Republic with the United Republic, tightening the power of the central (Francophone) government. The gendarmerie and community members identified women they believed to be prostitutes when they wore trousers, wigs, and miniskirts in spaces of good standing, and forcibly pushed them out of towns and into rural areas or "villages" as many newspaper reports phrased it. In doing so, urbanite elites positioned rural zones as the locus of African authenticity, "good" and "traditional" places where "hard-working" women resided and where "bad" women could go "home" to be rehabilitated.[7] But the respectable urban identity that urbanites sought to define was contradictory and hybridized. Urban women sought to frame themselves as being "traditional" like their rural counterparts and comported themselves suitably. In many ways, expelling "bad" women into rural places stoked ideas of a respectable African "authenticity" within the urban setting, putting suitable Anglophone cultural values on public display, nationally and internationally.

Perspectives about slacks-wearing women were not monolithic and revealed the selective embrace of "authentic" African values. Urban Anglophone Cameroonian women and men (re)interpreted international and local fashion trends, such as slacks, differently. Many Anglophone Cameroonian women construed the wearing of slacks not as a threat to male authority, as presented by many male letter writers to newspapers, but as a practice in which women could still adhere to ideal womanhood as long as they were conscious of when and where they wore them. Female journalists mostly approved of slacks as new symbolism of a cosmopolitan identity. That these women would incorporate slacks into larger definitions of a cosmopolitan feminine ideal illustrates, as Hildi Hendrickson contends, that "clothing and other treatments of the body surface are primary symbols in the performances through which modernity—and therefore history—have been conceived, constructed and challenged in Africa."[8] But while women such as journalist Clara Manga might have approved of slacks and classified them as symbols of modern womanhood, they identified specific places to which they might be donned, thus interpreting the usage of such attire by connecting to ideas about preserving dominant cultural values and suitable behavior. For example, Manga and other female journalists felt women might wear slacks to offices, outdoor picnics, and boxing tournaments and look progressive and cosmopolitan rather than disreputable and unfeminine, while drawing the line at slacks in church or a formal dance hall. But others felt that educated women who donned slacks might encourage women of loose sexual morals, or from a lower socioeconomic position, to mirror their styles and thus pass as belonging to the urban educated elite, similar to their fears about sexually loose women competing in beauty contests (see chapter 4).

Men's letters to newspapers, by contrast, were more likely to argue that women should *never* wear trousers, implying that women who wore slacks confronted male power and exercised authoritative social control not permitted to their gender. That some men would be concerned that women might garner social authority though their everyday sartorial practices demonstrates, as Jean Allman argues, that "power is represented, constituted, articulated, and contested through dress."[9] Although Cameroonian men had long worn Western-style slacks since British rule, some perceived women's slacks as a new Western import and accused slacks-wearing women of meddling in "men's affairs." But as Kathleen Sheldon argues about anxiety toward women's sartorial practices throughout early postcolonial Africa, "men were readily adopting western slacks and shirts, or other non-African clothing . . . without facing legal censure, making it clear that the issue was not 'western' versus 'African,' but cultural ideas about women's sexuality."[10] Case in point, as chapter 2 showed, Anglophone Cameroonian men seemed to have no problem with women appropriating the Bamenda male outfit as the West Cameroon national costume; perhaps because it was a local attire and possibly because it supported nationalist endeavors. But because many men associated slacks with participation in illicit sexual activities, some male (and even some female) critics implied that women *visibly* transgressed gender boundaries and cultural values. Further, men inferred that economically independent slacks-wearing women feminized men, striving to obtain men's social and economic authority as heads of households, churches, and communities.

The discourse on women's sartorial practices that this chapter examines serves as a final transition to a discussion of the spatial and visual boundaries between public and private spaces in urban West Cameroon. Chapters 5 and 6 primarily focused on embodied constructions in local community spaces and more private domestic spaces by examining commentary on gossip and married women's public behavior. This final chapter examines the construction of the *visual* representation of embodied nationalism in the urban terrain by inviting the reader into local community venues, hotels, members-only clubs, and describing the efforts to keep women out of local spaces that were perceived as being respectable. The geographic focus of this book thus has been the largest and most influential Anglophone towns in Cameroon. By navigating outside of them by the end of this final chapter, I will present the larger map of women's sartorial practices and how they reflected larger issues about Anglophone identity and cultural values. Against the backdrop of rapidly changing social, political, and economic conditions throughout West Cameroon, sartorial practices became, as well as an intimate space of politicization, a key site for fabricating and challenging larger cultural identities and social norms.

Regulating Cultural Values through Clothing

In linking women's dress practices to morals and cultural and national identity, urban elites in West Cameroon participated in a discourse that became common in colonial and postcolonial sub-Saharan Africa and in many other countries in the Global South.[11] Miniskirts spurred heated discussions that linked women's clothing to sexual immorality, women's changing economic mobility, and the disintegration of dominant cultural values in 1960s and 1970s Tanzania, Zambia, and Uganda.[12] Andrew Ivaska shows in his work on youth culture in 1960s Tanzania that officials of the youth league of the dominant political party in the country, the Tanganyika African National Union (TANU), organized public demonstrations in Dar es Salaam in the 1960s in which protestors condemned miniskirts and wigs and objected to tight bell-bottom pants for men or women.[13] These protests underlined a variety of concerns, including: "the morality of new urban youth cultures, authenticity in national cultural policy, the perceived sexual escapades of the capital's new elite, the aims and content of university education, and gendered battles over issues of marriage and women's work and movement in town."[14] Young women's behavior and clothing practices were often the focus of such politics.

Letters to newspapers and newspaper reports show that educated urban West Cameroonians similarly equated specific clothing such as miniskirts and trousers with the decay of feminine virtues, anxiety about women's changing economic positions, and prevailing Cameroonian cultural values. Residents suspected women who donned these inappropriate clothes of being sexually immoral or being prostitutes, and thus stifling the "masculine economy" by slyly convincing naïve and unsuspecting men to spend money on them.[15] A September 1968 missive to the editor of the *Cameroon Express* avowed, "I've often seen the wearers of mini-skirts stoop down to pick up fallen articles and the shortness of their dresses make them look immodest. . . . I look on wearers of mini-skirts as indecently dressed persons."[16] An August 1971 column in the *Cameroon Outlook* states unequivocally that miniskirts are "weapons capable of destroying morals." The columnist, a man signing himself Decimal Charles, asserted that miniskirts posed a danger no less than enslavement: "For centuries women have fought for certain basic rights for their sex, particularly the right to be respected . . . and not the pawns and slaves of men's passions," he lamented. "Yet today, they stand to lose these rights and once again become slaves—not only to men's passions, but to the DEVIL himself, because they seem no longer willing to 'fight' for their right to be respected."[17] Just as joining women's organizations might provide access to greater rights, as chapter 2 showed, women had to fight for their emancipation while adhering to gender norms in their dress. Charles proceeded to provide an overview of negative reactions around the world to miniskirts—or "PAGAN FASHION" as he writes—from Cairo, Egypt, Tokyo, Japan, to Toronto, Canada, concluding that "mini-skirts, see-through clothes and other female innovations that emphasize nudity, provoke the male to the point where he is unable to control his libidinal impulses." Numerous missives expressed similar opinions.[18] Although letter writers sporadically condemned men's clothing choices as well, it was largely women's clothing choices that generated the threat.[19]

Though both slacks and miniskirts caused anxiety about gender norms, they generally did so in different ways. Letter-writers implied that women in trousers publicly demonstrated a social authority that belonged to men by showcasing their independent source of earned income as women who worked in offices or earned income through illicit activities such as prostitution, thus disintegrating larger cultural values about suitable gender norms. While both miniskirt and trouser wearers challenged cultural values about sexuality, women in slacks also threatened cultural values about the proper physical attributes (and associated social privileges and power) distinguishing male and female bodies. Ultimately, slacks-wearing women seemed to be pushing the boundaries in "'fight[ing]' for their right to be respected." In her study of women who participated in the Zimbabwean liberation struggle, Tanya Lyons found female fighters wore trousers as a signal of resistance—a visual representation of fighting for Zimbabwean emancipation—but after independence they reverted to skirts "as a sign of respect for their families," and to avoid being considered "too rough," equated to prostitutes, or accused of being exceedingly liberated.[20] Women, Lyons concludes, "are still expected to carry the burden of being the 'visible markers of national homogeneity'" and cannot apparently "achieve this in mini-skirts or trousers because men cannot conceivably control them."[21] Similarly, in 1960s and early 1970s urban West Cameroon, women's emancipation was limited to adhering to expectations embedded in the patriarchal society. While applauding women's increased access to formal education, urbanite elites blamed some women's clothing choices for slowing the advancement of women's rights. Thus, West Cameroonian women's "emancipation," like that of their Zimbabwean counterparts, had limits and dress choice reflected this. As the next section will show, like their Zimbabwean counterparts, Anglophone Cameroonian women also donned slacks when fighting against European rule.

TRACING THE "SLACKS CRAZE"

Abandoning Gowns for Trousers in the Anlu Rebellion, 1958–61

Anxiety about slacks-wearing women in postindependence West Cameroon possibly stemmed, in part, from a women's rebellion that occurred in the British Southern Cameroons. Kom women in the Bamenda (western) Grassfields participated in an uprising against British administrative rule and local African rule from 1958 to 1961. Women protested "against British administrative interference in agriculture—normally their domain—and the alleged plan by the ruling political party, the Kamerun National Congress (KNC), to sell Kom land to Nigerian Igbos." In the late 1950s, the two prominent political parties in British-ruled Cameroon struggled for power: E. M. L. Endeley's KNC and John Ngu Foncha's Kamerun National Democratic Party (KNDP). Believing that the KNC would sell their land to the Igbos of Nigeria, Kom women turned their support to the KNDP. The women invoked "*anlu*, a centuries-old women's organization generally deployed against people who violated the Kom moral code." They "interfered with burial rituals; hurled insults at men in public; demanded the closing of schools, courts, and markets; set up roadblocks; destroyed and burned property; and defied both traditional and British authorities."[22]

Women participants of the Anlu Rebellion stressed an embodied nationalism in which—via bodily gestures, comportment, aesthetic and bodily rituals, and dress choice—they strove to protect women's long-standing agricultural authority and bolster the political power of the KNDP in the Southern Cameroons. As Henry Kah argues, women in the western Grassfields renegotiated the parameters of gender norms and relations, and some men felt that they had been rendered powerless during the revolt. Although the women's strategies also included stripping naked in order to emphasize the seriousness of their grievances, many women temporarily donned slacks to symbolize claiming local men's power. In addition to Kom women, the Laimbwe of the Northwest Region of Cameroon challenged male authority by wearing men's pants as a way to figuratively claim men's power.[23] Kah explains that Laimbwe women used "the power of dress" "as a potent weapon against the colonial system and the restriction of women's political space." As he points out, wearing trousers "symbolized power, control and influence."[24] Anlu participants' association of trousers with the movement was so powerful that men who women targeted as being KNC supporters, or for supporting the British administrative system, were "considered to be gown-wearers and not trouser-and-shirt wearers. These were men who before the revolt exercised authority epitomized by the trouser and shirt." Wearing trousers, Kah argues, symbolized women's demand for political power.

By symbolically "claiming" men's attire, such as trousers, participants of the Anlu Rebellion signaled their "disapproval of the actions of men and their support of the colonial administration."[25] For instance, Laimbwe "[w]omen wore trousers and shirts and imitated members of male masquerade societies [ceremonies or dances by masked performers], deliberately invading male public space and demanding a share in governance in Laimbwe land."[26] Women also stripped men of their power by "creat[ing] a parallel administrative structure" that was led by women.[27] As Kah concluded, by challenging local political structures, women "symbolically wanted to exchange their gowns for the trousers and shirts of men. . . . they believed themselves ready to step into the shoes of the male leaders of their communities, and exercise or share in the decision-making process of their communities."[28] In striving to protect their agricultural authority, women in the Bamenda Grassfields facilitated the 1961 political victory of the KNDP in the British Southern Cameroons.[29]

The association between wearing trousers and symbolic male power had history in other parts of colonial Africa. When a nationalist leader was arrested in 1922 and put in a police station in Nairobi, Kenya, female political activist Mary Nyanjiru lifted her dress over her head and "challenged the timid men" nearby "to take action to free" the leader by yelling, "You take my dress and give me your trousers. You men are cowards. What are you waiting for? Our leader is in there. Let's get him."[30] Like the Anlu women who donned slacks *and* stripped naked to show authority, she showed her nakedness as a symbol of bad portent. Similarly, in South Africa in the 1950s, the wife of a Pan Africanist Congress (PAC) leader in the Western Cape told a conservative male audience that they should give women their trousers and take women's dresses to attract men's support for the PAC, which at the time was a black South African nationalist party.[31] This strong visual association between trousers and (male) power possibly made anxiety about women wearing slacks pervasive in the post-independence period in urban West Cameroon.

"THE TROUSER IS SYMBOLIC OF THE MALE'S AUTHORITY": GENDER RELATIONS

Men and women seemed to have slightly divergent perspectives about women wearing slacks in urban West Cameroon during the 1960s and early 1970s. Newspaper records suggest that male letter writers were concerned that women would win social rights through cross-dressing. Unlike their male counterparts, urban women in Cameroon found ways to integrate the use of slacks into interpretations of a progressive womanhood that was still deferential to male authority. Clara Manga's February 1962 commentary on the "slacks craze" began, "Ladies I am not criticizing you, but only want to help if you'd allow me to. . . . I am not saying slacks must not be worn. They are alright if worn at the proper time and to the proper place. Why hide your beautiful legs in them all the time?" Yet women must not wear slacks to go out in the evenings. She framed this as a duty to their partners:

> If I were man I'd be very disappointed if I came to pick my girlfriend up for a dance or party and found her dressed in slacks. It's just like going out with another man. It is the duty of every girl to make herself look lovely for her

> young man to take [her] out in the evenings. This applies also to housewives please. Make your husbands proud of you in parties. Do you ladies not like to see the look of admiration that lights up your boyfriend's or husband's face if you have to go out with him and you are well-dressed? I'm sure you do because you like to be admired, and told how beautiful you look.

Manga acknowledged, "I'm not saying you cannot be admired in slacks. . . . Only the other day I saw two girls going to a boxing tournament in their slacks and they were just smashing." Yet women should limit slacks to "sports, picnic drives, [and] walks." She concluded, "[w]ear slacks my good ladies . . . [but] most important of all don't wear them to church."[32] Manga's assertion that women might appropriately wear slacks when engaging in various activities constructed a new measure of suitable African womanhood. Wearing dresses and skirts on romantic liaisons make a woman "well-dressed" and "beautiful," according to Manga. A man's approving gaze might be the reward of any woman who wore a dress and adhered to the ideal feminine bodily aesthetic. By contrast to Manga's suggestion that all of her readers had "beautiful legs," Dogo noted with some pity in his earlier referenced February 1962 letter that some women wear slacks to hide "abnormal legs which in most cases is no fault of theirs but nature; but nevertheless, this should not be an excuse for wearing slacks in dancing halls or church houses. Those with average or normal legs do so blindly and stupidly." But slacks were not feminine enough to beautify women's figures, particularly when donned in spaces of good repute. Thus, wearing them represented a failure to adhere to a feminine beauty ideal.

Manga urged deference to men's expectations that women wear clothing that would emphasize the physical difference between women and men, particularly on romantic liaisons. Just as journalist Ruff Wanzie assured women that "men are better judges of women's beauty" in beauty pageants, as shown in chapter 4, the male gaze should determine women's clothing choices.[33] Men, from Wanzie's standpoint, are the most important evaluators of their beauty. At the same time, Manga recognized the limits to unbounded male authority when she replied to Dogo's February 1962 letter stating, "I must however disagree with your method of dealing with a church goer in slacks if you were a priest. If I were the priest I would either summon her before me or call at the lady's house after service and advise her."[34] By urging women to wear dresses and skirts at other times, especially on romantic dates, Manga outlined the boundaries of modern womanhood within a larger West Cameroon patriarchal society.

Manga and Ruff Wanzie's advice about when to wear slacks also reveals how specific public spaces and activities were associated with women of particular social positions. Wanzie begins an extensive commentary for the *Cameroon Times* in 1966 by explaining that women should only wear slacks for morning shopping, picnics, while boating, during evening strolls, when at home, and on the beach. They should not be worn at parties or balls, "places of repute where those in attendance are supposed to be modestly dressed so as to be pleasant to every other person in attendance."[35] Journalists' references to the specific activities in which women might don slacks shows that their advice resonates with only a specific group of women—women of the upper and middle classes who had the time and finances to play sports, go to boxing tournaments, and go on picnics and walks. The endorsement of slack-wearing in some contexts by female journalists, such as Manga and Wanzie, reflected a hybrid feminine beauty ideal that was contingent on class and understood places of good repute in an urban setting.

Dogo attested that women did not always defer to men's opinion of their clothing choices however. A more detailed excerpt of his February 1962 letter to Clara Manga's column implies that men's pride are hurt when women fail to heed their fashion advice: "Sometimes we men try to advise women politely on certain irregularities but wanting amendments [changes in fashion] they get offended and challenge us back in rough terms." Seeking changing dress practices, or "amendments," he implied, had made women too "rough" for men to manage. Given this, he saw preventing women from wearing slacks as a crucial function for women like Manga. While praising Manga's antitrouser advice, he lamented, "If you [had] devoted your column long ago [to] such advices it would have been more useful than too [much advice about] love affair[s]." He also saw women's organizations as playing this role, telling women, "There is no harm or shame in asking how something worth doing should be correctly done. This is why a woman['s] society is very necessary."[36] Educated women were accountable for regulating the behavior of other women; women's organizations and dedicated women's advice columns became key spaces in which to regulate women's attire.

Fears that women who wore trousers went too far in challenging gender boundaries were at times expressed very blatantly. Martha Njoka, a columnist for the *Cameroon Outlook* in the late 1960s, asserted directly that women in trousers were a threat to masculine power:

> One only needs to listen to the hisses and catcalls of the males as a female in trousers walks past them to know that there is still something out of the

> ordinary [to see a] woman in trousers. But I said earlier that the trouser is symbolic of the male's authority. Say what you will there's every ample proof to show that men are made a shade higher than we women.[37]

Worse than challenging men's power on the street was defying men's authority in their marriages:

> A pair of trousers in those days, and even up to now, has been predominately for men. . . . there are those of us they call educated who want to dominate our husbands. You want to attend a dance, for instance, and [you] ask him, and he says "NO.". . . . But do we accept the "NO"[?] [Instead] we nag, and nag, and drive the poor man mad.

Njoka's use of the plural term "we" summons an air of camaraderie when criticizing her fellow educated women's behaviors. In doing so, she constructs herself as a sisterly confidant who is offering much-needed advice on how to manage marital relations. Njoka further explains that educated wives do not have to completely submit to their husbands. Yet they must respect the authority of men as heads of households:

> There is always a middle course, that of mutual respect for each other and seeing the other man's point of view[.] [A]nd please, if your man has always given you a long rope to pull, don't think he's a fool and please don't show him you're the boss—you [are] not, he is.[38]

Njoka asserts that women should not don slacks at all. She is thus more extreme than Clara Manga or Ruff Wanzie, and more in line with men who wrote letters to the editor about the evils of slacks. Ultimately, Njoka contends, slacks posed significant danger to gender relations. Women who donned trousers fractured the visual representative of an ideal patriarchal marriage that preserved West Cameroonian cultural values: the husband wore the pants, and the wife showed deference to male authority by donning conservative female attire such as a dress or a long skirt.

A February 1970 missive penned by a Charles Ngwa in Victoria to *Daily Life* reveals deeper fears about trouser-wearing women. Ngwa had been writing letters to West Cameroon newspapers on the topic of women's clothing frequently for several years.[39] It was clear that by 1970, Ngwa considered himself a great connoisseur of fashion for women. His 1970 letter explained that some women's fashion are "worth looking at" "but [that] some can scare one to hell." He accused women of "stealing" trousers from men and male attire in general: "They took over from men the wearing of trousers and shirts and now there is a form of dress that when a woman wears it, she looks like a 'flying bat.' This is a conversion of the '[a]gbada' men wear." He added,

> [W]omen tend to be interested in men's affairs more but the men are simply not interested in their own. How will the men look like when they too wear blouses and skirts, frocks and gowns? We the men, as I feel, are simply being cheated and as such, something must be done about this fashion business. Men, what do you say? Speak out for I do not like the way women are delving into our affairs.[40]

From Ngwa's perspective, slacks are only for men because it visibly reflects the differences between the sexes; he implies that slacks visually reaffirm men's authority within the nation. Thus, although he believes that women should never wear trousers, Ngwa also calls upon aspects of embodied nationalism like his female counterparts. Women who wore trousers visibly threatened men's authority and marred *visual* representation of ideal Anglophone womanhood. Further, women in trousers diverged from authentic gender codes of behavior because they supposedly embodied masculinized traits and obtained social authority when they wore slacks. Research shows that urbanites in countries across Africa expressed concerns similar to Ngwa's about women's masculinization through much of the twentieth century. In the 1930s in South Africa, for example, black urbanites accused the black "modern girl" of turning into a "she-man" due to her disregard for prevailing feminine responsibilities and indulging in smoking and alcohol, speaking "township languages," wearing trousers, and spending time on "romance."[41] From Ngwa's perspective, nothing less was at stake than the crumbling of manhood in West Cameroonian society. Like Dogo and Njoka, he accused women who wore pants of obtaining men's rights—in other words, of delving into "[men's] affairs." Though the female journalists and male letter writers disagreed on the context in which the wearing of slacks was acceptable, both groups shared the belief that the clothing item reflected dominant patriarchal norms and boundaries.

"DON'T LET THE WORLD, PARTICULARLY THE WESTERN WORLD, LAUGH AT US": PUBLICLY PERFORMING RESPECTABILITY

Beyond endangering relations between women and men during romantic liaisons and within marriages, West Cameroonian urbanites were likewise concerned that women who wore slacks publicly exhibited loose sexual and religious morals. It is no surprise that much of the criticism about women donned in slacks focused on particular spaces, such as churches, hotels, and member's-only social clubs. Even those who might accept women wearing pants in other settings objected to it at church. Sister Kamara, for example, saved her greatest clothing-related revulsion for women who wore trousers to church. In an August 1968 column for the *Cameroon Voice*, she condemned women in trousers at "respectable dances, hotels, [and] bars" but called slacks in church "most disgraceful." Sister Kamara was clearly concerned that slacks-wearing women marred the ideal image of a respectable and pious woman. But her criticism about women's clothing practices in church was not confined to Africa. For example, research shows that in the nineteenth century, clergy and communities condemned women who wore pants to black American churches.[42] Anthea Butler found that black American Christian women who wore modest clothing to church believed that they exhibited "ideal[s] of the sanctified woman" and "differentiate[d] themselves from other urban groups . . . free from temptations, in the midst of urban vice."[43] As Butler concludes, rigid dress codes were a way to project "inward holiness" and freedom from temptation.[44] Similarly, in urban West Cameroon, women who donned slacks to church threatened the image of "the sanctified woman" who preserved her sexual morality and avoided "urban vice."

Like Clara Manga, Sister Kamara negotiated the spaces in which slacks should be worn. She felt that slacks were appropriate in some contexts: "[M]y pen-ultimate advice to our women and girls is to use these slacks at the real occasions and not at random. . . . Wear your slacks to films, picnics, excursions, strolls and nobody would mind." She questioned the respectability of girls in slacks at a membership-only social venue and connected slacks to poor comportment, saying that "[g]irls in slacks could be seen in the above places moving about wriggling and writhing like snakes in pain [due to the tightness of the pants]. . . . This is seemed to be a mark of sophistication mostly among our low classed girls." She added, "Girls who would so disgrace the Cameroon women like those at the Ombe Rock Club would not be true Cameroonians at all. . . . Don't let the world, particularly the Western World, laugh at us for the African women has got beauty and grace which she is proud of and will ever retain."[45] From the journalist's perspective, women who wore slacks to suitable spaces threatened ideals of true and authentic Anglophone womanhood that emphasized conservative attire and sexual reservation in places of good repute. But the journalist also ties dress choice to a modernized African womanhood that stresses "beauty and grace"—suitable bodily comportment. While selectively embracing Western attire, she placed boundaries on *where* this attire could be worn. These limits reflect an endeavor to protect class boundaries by guarding which *type* of Anglophone woman can properly represent West Cameroonian values in spaces that possibly included both a local and foreign audience.

Letters to newspapers likewise suggest that various members of the urban educated elite were gravely concerned with how women's clothing practices represented respectability in front of foreigners, suggesting that the impact of women's suitable sartorial practices expanded beyond local community spaces. For instance, guest columnist Cyprian Agbor shared in his 1970 *Cameroon Outlook* opinion column that

> In a few African cities such as Lagos [Nigeria] and Cairo [Egypt] some women, even though they appear in Westernized circles, they set the example [in] their African costumes. Instead of a short transparent mini, they prefer flowing, decorated native costumes which command even greater beauty and prestige in society. Some people would talk to a girl they found in one of those wild minis anyhow, but would not dare to address the same girl in such a rough manner if they met her well-groomed in the African attire.[46]

Similar to many female journalists of the time, Agbor looks to other African countries to compare and contrast diverse African cultural values and uses his knowledge of international cultural affairs to shape expectations of West Cameroonian cultural values. From his standpoint, it was important that women visually embody the nation's advancement, respectability, and sense of cultural pride in front of foreigners, similar to their counterparts in Nigeria and Egypt. From his perspective then, reputable women donned African attire, showing respect for African cultural values even when part of predominantly "Westernized circles."

Like Sister Kamara and Agbor, journalist Ruff Wanzie's criticism of women's dress practices had strong nationalist undertones. She too believed that women's clothing practices reflected cultural values nationally and globally.

In her 1966 column, under the ominous headline "When Women Wear Slacks," Wanzie praised the actions of men who protected the nation's morals by policing women's clothing choices. Community members also had an obligation to censure women's clothing choices in spaces of perceived respectability. She shared a story about men who exhibited their disapproval of women wearing trousers in Victoria Club, a prestigious members-only private club:

> During club nights in this club, certain fancy women [euphemism for prostitute] in their undersized transparent slacks and short knickers, exposing almost every inch of them were mercilessly and disgracefully turned out. . . . I began to notice thereafter that keener and stricter measures were being adopted to see to it that all who attended the club were not only well dressed, but that they were well behaved. This indeed is a bold move to check indecent behaviors in our women folk especially the free type [supposedly sexually loose women], who, in their bid to be fashionable and modern, have lost every gram of shame and tended to the charm and respect that a woman should normally command and possess. . . . I should like to say "BRAVO" to the Victoria Club members for their judicious sense of decency aimed at correcting useless or indecent practice.

Wanzie pleaded with "decent women folk, all [women] members of all clubs in West Cameroon to join forces with these fore-sighted men, intending reformers, to combat all that is evil in our society, especially that which pertains to the women folk." She went on to connect feminine clothing to nationalism:

> This is very necessary, following the proverbial saying that "what the womanhood of a nation is, so are its citizens." If we women really want to build a decent and healthy nation worthy of its name, we must have to work hard enough to achieve that goal. Once we fail to [do so], this becomes more painful and disgraceful, not only to ourselves but to the outside world at large, where we tend to lose every inch of international respect and recognition. . . . because the outside world would cease to reckon on us when the question of morals are concerned. . . . [Women] wake up and join forces with our men to stamp out completely what is bad in our women folk and replace it with what is generally accepting and befitting of [our] womanhood.[47]

Wanzie invokes embodied nationalism through her reproof of women's sartorial practices, behavior and comportment. Women who misbehave and don slacks do not project a suitable persona and esteem locally, nationally, and internationally. Thus, the indiscipline of sartorial practices was an urgent nationalist endeavor, and she encourages women to work together with men to protect what she believed were authentic West Cameroonian national and cultural values. In many ways, Wanzie's censure reflects rhetoric by female political elites who also encouraged women to "join forces" with men; in a 1968 speech, Gwendoline Burnley, the first woman parliamentarian in the West Cameroon Legislative Assembly in the 1960s, encouraged men to "[h]old the hands of their wives in the race" to socially and economically advance the nation and powerfully stated, "[s]how [me the] women of the country and I know what the men are."[48] Women validated their social importance by preserving respectable cultural norms on the community and international level when they worked together with men to police women's behavior and dress choices.

Ruff Wanzie and Sister Kamara's criticism of women who wore slacks around a local and foreign audience reflected deeper concerns about class blurring and ideal womanhood. Both proclaimed that women who wore slacks signified that they were sexually loose, not that they were sophisticated. In advising their readers, they sought to reestablish a class line between upper and middle class women and women from lower socioeconomic positioning with supposedly dangerous sexual liberty. They also proposed that educated women should model better behavior, rather than acknowledging others' point of view that slacks were *not* fashionable and sophisticated. Through this regulation, some female journalists endeavored to visually shape and define physical representations of the feminine ideal that would be reflected to a local and international audience.

But oral sources present a complex picture about the regulation of women's dress practices in West Cameroon in the 1960s and early 1970s. Asong Martha Ebey, a retired grocer who was born in Kumba but resided in Buea, explained in an interview, "In those days . . . it was okay for women to wear trousers because nobody can tell you [not to] wear trousers. And you know the name of the trousers in those days? *Bongo*. Those big big ones."[49] Tita Agnes of Bamenda agreed, associating slacks with trendiness specifically.[50] Ngum Magdalene Beghang of Bamenda associated cosmopolitanism with a variety of fashion choices in the 1960s, including trousers, the indigenous male *agbada* (a loose-fitting and wide-sleeved garment worn by West African men) as well as *salamanda* footwear, or high-platform boots.[51] Not one interviewed individual accused women who wore slacks of publicly exhibiting loose sexual and religious morals, nor did they recall slacks as a sign of immorality or indecent behavior. Yet, in other parts of their interviews, some of the same women half-heartedly admitted that they had once worn miniskirts and hot pants but stopped due to family and community pressure; such pressure was sometimes successful. Martha Ebey, for instance, reluctantly admitted that pressure from neighbors forced her to stop wearing "mini [and] trousers" so that she would look respectable in public.[52] While it is certainly possible that present-day views of pants-wearing affect the memories of women such as Ebey,[53] the newspaper evidence, along with oral evidence, demonstrates that women, more than men, embraced women's wearing of trousers and were more likely than men to suggest that pants were compatible.

"MASS SWOOP ON FREE WOMEN BEGINS": PROTECTING "MASCULINE ECONOMY" AND "CLEANING" PUBLIC SPACES

While community pressure regulated women's dress, as with individuals who actively patrolled women's dress choice in the Ombe Rock Club and the Victoria Club, there were never any federal laws against specific attire in West Cameroon. It was common, however, for postcolonial states across Africa to codify dress norms to legitimize their authority as the arbiters of morality and cultural expression. Countries such as Tanzania, Malawi, and Uganda banned miniskirts, hot pants, and other attire deemed to be sexually provocative Western imports during the 1960s and 1970s. In East Africa in the 1970s, the Ugandan military ruler Idi Amin endeavored to establish political legitimacy by enacting policies about women's dress.[54] In the same decade, the Western and Central African governments of Nigeria and the Democratic Republic of the Congo "banned citizens from importing, buying, or wearing Western styles of dress. The ban was intended to instill national pride."[55] West Cameroonians did propose similar laws. In his 1968 letter to the *Cameroon Express*, Charles Ngwa, always quick to share fashion advice for women, pointed out that "mini-skirts have been banned in Zambia already."[56] While the missive shows that some people called for the West Cameroonian government to officially outlaw miniskirts, it implies that the West Cameroonian government had not done so by 1968.

Evidence suggests there were some local community officials who took it into their own hands to regulate women's dress in the late 1960s. In a November 2011 interview, Asong Martha Ebey recollected that a magistrate helped alleviate prostitution by instituting clothing policies. She remembers,

> A woman's common dressing was this wrapper that we tie, and this kabba that we wear. But there came a time that . . . when young girls loved wearing this mini. . . . Which finally the person who stopped this dress was late Magistrate [Ngonje], he's now of late [died]. He stopped it, because you cannot bend down!. . . . by then, prostitution was just too rampant. . . . More women have engaged themselves in business instead of prostitut[ion]. . . . He stopped miniskirts because women were selling themselves outside. . . . girls came to realize it wasn't good, so they changed.[57]

While Ebey could not remember if this policy was enforced in Buea or another Anglophone town, or in the courts of other magistrates, newspaper reports about local officials taking matters into their own hands support her claims. For instance, in his 1968 letter to the *Cameroon Express*, Charles Ngwa, shared that he had "heard of a magistrate [in West Cameroon] who disciplined indecently dressed persons in court," asking, "Why can this not be tried again?"[58] In May 1969, the sub-prefect of Victoria Central Subdivision signed an order requiring those "wearing miniskirts and dresses and those taking part in 'show' activities [attending a nightclub or going to the beach] to obtain weekly permits obtainable from the Sous Prefecture."[59] Individuals were charged 5,000 Central African francs for the permits. In December 1970, a prefectural order issued by the senior Fako divisional officer announced that women not accompanied by men were not allowed in hotels in the cities of Victoria and Buea. The ban was designed to "curb the excess display of indecency with foreign visitors [because] the women constitute a nuisance to visitors."[60]

By late 1972, local officials and community members started to interpret revisions to a new federal law to regulate women's dress choice and mobility within urban spaces at an alarming rate. Specific women were rounded up in raids in different towns and forced to return "home" to rural spaces. "Free women," single and independent women of a certain age who were suspected of prostitution or of having loose sexual morals, were caught up in these raids to "sweep" cities "clean"—in both West and East Cameroon—after President Ahidjo amended the Cameroonian Penal Code on October 5, 1972.[61] The amendments with regard to the Law on Prostitution and Loitering "prescribed severe penalties for prostitution."[62] Though the law did not codify dress norms, "free women" were sometimes identified by their clothing and aesthetic choices—trousers, hot pants, wigs. The gendarmerie identified women not only by their clothing, but by their having an independent source of income without evidence of legal employment, and by their employment in brothels (prostitution was and is illegal).[63] Women between the ages of fifteen and forty with independent sources of income seem to have been the target. In October 1972, a male gendarme in Victoria shared with a *Cameroon Times* reporter in Cameroonian pidgin English, or Cameroonian Creole, that the gendarmerie had recently carried out "a serious raid on free women" in order to "hasten their exit" from their homes: "Dam wan be de na for make dem sabi say trouble de for back. . . . You go see am dam week weh I de come so [This was to make them aware that trouble is still to come next week]." While there are no records of the exact number of women swept up in the raids, one source noted that in Victoria, over 3000 "free women . . . have been hit by the condition of the decree."[64] The same report said that that many of these women were "thinking of returning to their respective villages."

The forced exodus of "free women" marked them as enemies of the state because of their supposed immorality and refusal to follow local Cameroonian gender norms. A journalist for the *Cameroon Outlook* known simply as Fesse signaled her approval for the ejection by underlining the danger that "free women" posed to Cameroonian society in October 1972, addressing them directly:

> You are an enemy to the Nation because the husbands, fathers, politicians, civil servants, [and] law-enforcement officers you deal with will end up in debt, involved in fraud, make inefficient fathers and husbands and will not command necessary respect among those over whom they are supposed to rule, or work, especially if their promiscuity is known.[65]

Fesse espoused a sexual double standard in which the only way to regulate men's behavior was to regulate women's. She framed it as a way to preserve patriarchal cultural values by maintaining men's roles as leaders of homes, communities and the nation. By focusing on women, individuals such as Fesse were similar to the Buea housewives who published a letter to single women in the *Cameroon Outlook* in June 1970, urging them to leave their husbands alone (chapter 6); they charged women with the responsibility for adhering to gender norms that paid deference to male authority, economically and socially.

Beyond being classified as sexually loose and being an "enemy to the [n]ation," "free women" were defined as having additional marked characteristics. They were described as living "a nomadic life" and refusing to marry and have children; frequenting bars; smoking cigarettes; using drugs—one male letter writer attested that they "sterilized themselves by taking dangerous drugs"—drinking beer; wearing short, transparent slacks and skirts; wearing wigs; using "too much makeup"; and engaging in "illicit sexual activities, often with married men."[66] One man candidly defined "free women" in his letter to the *Hero* as "working class girls and women who have by their attitude scared away men who might have married them and have embarked in full [on] the business of prostitution, their jobs notwithstanding." He elaborated,

> They are to be seen . . . strolling up and down the streets in the attempt to catch a man for a deal, or for a free drink in a hotel or a bar. They dress in a deplorable manner. They expose their pants when they sit down. They smoke like hell and the advanced ones smoke the marijuana, what we call Indian hemp. They drink only few brands of beer such as Gold Harp, big Guinness, Becks, and gin. Their language is always immodest especially when they are tipsy. All statements made by these architects of crime are immoral. . . . I wish their trade were licensed so that [the] government could make money from it. These girls are agents of embezzlement.[67]

As the statement suggests, one way that sexually free and economically independent women embodied and performed their own ideas about cosmopolitan womanhood was by following global fashion trends of the time, such as donning slacks. While applauding women's formal education as an asset to the nation, many urbanite elites decried Western clothing as the embodiment of foreign or international identities. Anxiety about "free women" was really about waning male authority over women who increasingly used their education, or their sexuality, to improve their socioeconomic positions. Moreover, because women who donned slacks were associated with hotels and bars, as well as specific illicit activities, community members strove to regulate their presence in such spaces.

As a native ethnographer (see Appendix: Methods and Sources), I was surprised at some of the continuing stereotypes about economically independent women that persist in Cameroon today. I learned the gendered significance of the preceding letter's reference to big Guinness, a bottle containing one pint of beer, on a 2015 visit to Cameroon. While undertaking research in Buea I often purchased beverages to share with friends and family members on outings and frequently purchased big Guinness. I did so out of economy, but a family friend teased me about it, observing that he had never in his life seen a Cameroonian woman buy or drink big Guinness herself. He explained that it was mostly men who purchased bottles this big. He said that women might spend extra money to purchase two small bottles of Guinness if she wanted to drink one pint, rather than posing the threat to masculinity inherent in buying the larger bottle. I took this to mean that the fear persists that a man may be seen as unable to provide for a woman if she buys her own big Guinness. The situation brought to light that regardless of an Anglophone or Francophone background, women with independent sources of income continued to challenge prevailing ideas about suitable womanhood.

Perhaps anxiety over economically independent Anglophone and Francophone Cameroonian women being able to buy their own big Guinness prompted "free women" raids in both Anglophone and Francophone regions of Cameroon where residents justified the raids by implying that it protected "masculine economy". There is no evidence of violence, but rather military and police actions where identified "free women" were forcibly rounded up in raids. In October 1972, the *Cameroon Times* reported,

> The forces of law and order have plunged into action to weed out women of easy virtue from townships and send them to their homes [read: village]. . . . free women without evidence of livelihood [are] being rounded up in Yaoundé for prosecution. . . . free women who jumped the police drag-net in Douala [a French-speaking economic hub] and arrive in Yaoundé were picked up. In Tiko . . . members of the forces of law and order have continued with dawn to dusk raids during which free girls and women with no tangible means of livelihood are being picked. . . . the Tiko streets . . . are void of the "huge trousers" wearing and mini girls. Some of the girls and women . . . have escaped to the fishing ports in Tiko.[68]

The paper further conveyed,

> The usual queue under street lights in Tiko . . . [is] no longer there . . . Meanwhile in Victoria, the popular Church Street and half mile where the sun

> never sets has lost its popularity. . . . because it is no longer the place where women with painted lips [euphemism for sexually loose women who wear too much cosmetics] entice husbands into their hideouts. The usual centres of attraction where prostitution is at its highest point have been abandoned. . . . The raids are continuing and the women are still on the run.[69]

Despite the women being "on the run," the paper shared that on the roads of Isokolo, Ngeme, and Karata "[s]everal cars are also understood to have been frequenting [these] road[s] as it is believed some of the free girls are taking [business] over there."[70] A resident of Victoria attested to the *Cameroon Times* that the ban on prostitution had many advantages; it increased the stability of marriages, renewed conjugal fidelity, regularized marriages, protected youth from public immorality, and forced "prostitutes to take up useful employment." He emphasized that the new law "brought protection to masculine economy"; in other words, men did not feel tempted to drain their finances by fraternizing with women of ill repute.[71] But as the October 1972 *Cameroon Times* report showed, some men did not seem interested in protecting their "masculine economy" from "painted lips" women, continuing to actively seek them out.

Additional reports document the "exodus" of "free women" from towns to villages. With a hyperbolic title, "5,000 Free Girls Start Journey Back Home: End of an Era," a reporter for the *Cameroon Outlook* observed in an October 1972 column that "Free girls in Kumba have begun their journey back to their respective homes [read: villages]. . . . bar proprietors and landlords have been badly affected by this exodus. Drinking houses are almost empty every night. . . . In Yaoundé . . . the journey back to villages has been forced on the women."[72] Landlords in Victoria also issued ejection notices to women tenants who had no visible means of income. A journalist for the *Cameroon Outlook* observed that "[t]he move is seen as one intended to put the ban on prostitution into execution in a quiet way. . . . landlords are pursuing this policy only on point of decency." Additionally, because of the ban, the journalist believed that many women contemplated returning to their respective villages, while many others quickly turned to other respectable forms of earning income, such as trading, selling fruit, and becoming seamstresses. It was emphasized that many women were "looking more towards attracting themselves to honest boyfriends."[73] But reports suggested that places of entertainment, and the economy, were suffering in Victoria, Tiko, and other Anglophone towns. In Tiko, bars, "especially those that had kept private rooms for illicit affairs," had reported drastic decrease in sales.[74] In Victoria, according to one newspaper article,

> Banks say most of the women had already closed their accounts . . . . Beer houses are virtually empty each night and cinema houses have recorded the biggest drop in the clientele as more than half [of] the population in Victoria with tremendous buying power is going underground. It is not known whether this loss of buying power will affect the industries which employ several Cameroonians but it is known that several landlords have been badly hit and that house rentage [*sic*] is bound to drop.

The same reporter stated that "[i]n Mamfe, most of the women are reported to travel straight to their villages while others are spending a few days in Mamfe Town and the bars there are [open and] doing brisk business."[75]

In the end, the forced "exodus" of free women did not hold up, and discourse—as evidenced in print media— about the event seems to have faded by 1973. It seems that that the drastic decline in economic activities in large towns was a fundamental reason why the ban did not hold up. Even journalists who applauded the ban had to admit that bankers, bars, hotels, and landlords suffered economically because of the ban. It appeared that it was economically independent women, the ones with "tremendous buying power," that played significant roles in cultivating economically healthy towns. Thus, while urban residents strived to regulate the behavior of financially independent women because they ostensibly challenged gender norms, in the end, it was their economic aspirations and activities that helped keep towns economically stable and robust. Soon, by 1973, the long queues in banks were to return, and men would quickly forget about protecting their "masculine economy" from "painted lips" women as they returned to frequenting bars in Kumba, Victoria and other large towns where the sun would, once again, never set.

It is interesting that the West Cameroon State was not like many African countries that officially banned hot pants or miniskirts, despite strong opposition among many urbanites and political elites. The structure of the federal government may have been determinative. While the West Cameroon State was semi-autonomous, lawmakers could not create many laws, especially in the later 1960s, when miniskirt bans were increasingly common in other countries. But West Cameroonians' efforts to exert control of their geographic spaces was part of a larger occurrence in many African states, such as

Julius Nyerere's Tanzania, where he employed the socialist idea of *Ujamaa* in an effort to promote national development by emphasizing "communal agriculture and economic self-reliance," thus striving to develop wealth in rural spaces.[76] In West Cameroon, individuals sought to "sweep" the cities clean by regulating the movement of women they understood to be challenging gender norms, identifying them partially in the manner in which they diverged from physical representations of the feminine ideal.

Ultimately, urban elites in West Cameroon, seemingly like their Francophone counterparts, reinterpreted Ahidjo's constitutional changes regarding prostitution and loitering to regulate women's dress choices and behavior in public even in the absence of federal policies outlawing slacks, hot pants, and miniskirts. Community members and local leaders, through community pressure, reinterpreted such laws to push "free women" to rural areas. At the end, efforts to regulate the urban population and alter the spatial configuration of the urban terrain did not, and could not, hold up. It was the very women that residents tried to push out that had helped lay the strong economic foundation from which their cities' urban economies rested upon. Yet, the Anglophone Cameroonian urban elites' attempt to control space and mobility in towns reflected a deeper social and political struggle over preserving ideal cultural values, endeavors that would continue past the time when Ahidjo dissolved the federal structure in 1972.

CONCLUSION

Takumbeng Unleashed

Women's Continual Collective Mobilization in Anglophone Nationalism

"I was not a politician. I did my work as [a] housewife and they did theirs as politicians." Anna Foncha made this statement in 2014 to the *Cameroun Tribune*, a French-language, government-owned newspaper. The interview focused on her husband's role in the 1961 union of British Southern Cameroons with then newly independent French Cameroun. Now in her early nineties, and a widow since 1999, she described her husband as wary of the potential marginalization of Anglophone Cameroonians after 1961: "My husband use[d] to remind [President] Ahidjo during their discussion that the Anglophones were of the minority and that had to be taken into consideration so that his people should not become slaves after reunification." She further argued that her husband "wanted a united and progressive Cameroon where good things will be taken from both sides to form one nation. All that was English was not bad [and] all that was French was not bad. I am very sure that if things were handled this way, Cameroon could have been one of the best nations in the world."

Anna Foncha's recollection of her husband's politics emphasized her apolitical status during the 1960s, maintaining that she was a housewife who simply cared for her husband to ensure that "he was strong, healthy and looked presentable especially when in public." She recalled hosting male politicians in her home, saying she was "just like their mother." She delicately balanced the description of her role: "I was a teacher and had my own interest, particularly in women and children. I was urging women not to sit behind the curtains. They should also sit in the parlor and discuss family things with their husbands. I formed social groups which were all active." While Anna Foncha mostly separates herself from her husband's active role in making political decisions, she nonetheless endorses his decision to support the 1961 union, describing the resultant Federal Republic as "two brothers [who] decided to come together to be equals."[1]

Anna Foncha's reflections suggest how many Anglophone female political elites even today distinguish Anglophone and Francophone Cameroonians. Her use of certain words illustrates the political lexicon that inscribed larger aggregated ideas on political elites' minds about the different histories, cultural heritage, and morals of Anglophone and Francophone persons. Her use of the word "slaves" and the clear statement that Cameroon was not "one of the best nations in the world" because Ahidjo's government did not integrate Anglophone social and political interests hints at how many Anglophone Cameroonians have understood themselves as marginalized, second-class citizens in the modern-day Cameroonian state. Yet in the same interview, Foncha casts herself as a mother, and the Anglophone and Francophone forces as two brothers quarreling, struggling to "come together to be equals."[2] Her tone about early postcolonial Anglophone political history resonates with *maternalist* politics that have been evident among female supporters of the Anglophone nationalist movement since the 1960s. Further, she continues to invoke an embodied nationalism by emphasizing suitable behaviors and emotional expressivities of ideal Anglophone womanhood nationally. Anna Foncha frames her accomplishments during the early postindependence period as a time in which she prioritized her domestic and maternal roles at home and within Anglophone Cameroonian nationalist endeavors. By establishing herself as a "good" woman, despite her political activities, she sought to maintain suitable gender norms within a larger patriarchal context in contemporary Cameroon. But as the interview likewise evidences, Anglophone Cameroonian women like Anna Foncha continue to play important roles in supporting the political and social cohesion of separatist movements in later postcolonial Cameroon.

FROM AHIDJO'S RULE TO BIYA'S

The struggle to achieve equality between the "two brothers" disintegrated in the late 1960s as Ahidjo's annexationist and hegemonic tendencies grew. One indicator of these tendencies was Foncha's 1965 removal as prime minister of the West Cameroon State. Up until that point, John Ngu Foncha had served simultaneously as prime minister of the West Cameroon State and vice president of the Federal Republic since 1961. The ensuing struggle over who would succeed Foncha as prime minister weakened Foncha's Kamerun National Democratic Party, which made it easier for Ahidjo to create a one-party state in 1966. Augustine Ngom Jua succeeded Foncha as prime minister; at this point Foncha retained only his post as the vice president of the federation. The creation of single-party systems was common throughout Africa's newly independent states, such as Ghana, Tanzania, and the neighboring Democratic Republic of the Congo. Thus, Foncha, like many of his political counterparts in Cameroon, initially supported Ahidjo's CNU, the one-party state's new umbrella party. In 1968 Ahidjo replaced Jua with Salomon Tandeng Muna, then made Muna vice president in Foncha's stead in 1970.[3] Foncha retired from politics at this point, and he and Anna Foncha returned to their home in Bamenda, focusing on farming and fishing. Two years later, in 1972, Ahidjo established the United Republic of Cameroon as a unitary state under his own rule.[4] Foncha remerged into public life in 1979, when Ahidjo appointed Foncha Grand Chancellor of the National Orders, a largely ceremonial post, but one with a salary.[5]

To everyone's surprise, Ahidjo resigned in November 1982, ostensibly for health reasons, but he remained the chairman of the CNU. Ahidjo's behavior soon made it clear that he believed that his successor, Paul Biya, who had been his vice president, would defer to him in most things. Consequently, a power struggle ensued, and Ahidjo fled to France in 1983. There he plotted to overthrow Biya, was tried in absentia, and was sentenced to death in 1984.[6] Biya distanced his regime from Ahidjo's by renaming the CNU the Cameroon People's Democratic Movement (CPDM) in 1985.[7]

A Francophone politician of Beti origin from the south region of Cameroon, Biya continued many of Ahidjo's repressive strategies. He also emphasized ethnic politics and a patronage system more than Ahidjo had. In 1985, Biya appointed John Foncha as the first vice president of the CPDM, a largely ceremonial position. In 1990, marking a turn toward seeking to end the marginalization of Anglophone Cameroon, Foncha resigned both this position and that of Grand Chancellor of National Orders.[8] He became a leader of the Southern Cameroons National Council (SCNC), an Angolophone Cameroonian secessionist organization.

"THE ANGLOPHONE PROBLEM": THE REEMERGENCE OF ANGLOPHONE NATIONALISM

The rise of the SCNC occurred against the backdrop of larger political changes in the 1990s in which Anglophones increasingly pushed to reinstate the federal republic or secede from the Republic of Cameroon. Piet Konings and Francis Nyamnjoh coined the term the "anglophone problem" for what they described as "a major challenge to the efforts of the post-colonial state to forge national unity and integration" in early 1990s Cameroon.[9] During this time period, the Social Democratic Front (SDF), the main Anglophone opposition party of Cameroon, attracted many Anglophones to oppose their marginalization within the Francophone state.[10] Subsequently, Biya was successful in liberalizing some state policies in an effort to end the Anglophone issue. In 1990 he overturned Ahidjo's 1966 law against competing political parties and allowed a limited "degree of freedom of mass communication . . . including the right to hold public meetings and demonstrations."[11]

But Biya's regime moved to squelch Anglophone separatism as early as the 1990s, increasing its efforts after 2000. Activists have been beaten, arrested, imprisoned, and forced into exile since the mid-1990s.[12] By the late 1990s, Anglophone opposition had gotten more forceful. The SCNC officially declared English-speaking regions independent and declared the area to be an independent Republic of Ambazonia on December 30, 1999.[13] The Francophone-dominated government declared the SCNC illegal in 2001.

Scholarly studies support the charge of separatists and secessionists that the resulting Francophone-dominated government marginalizes Anglophone Cameroonians. Anglophones have had disproportionately few representatives in ministerial positions, senior- and middle-level administrative positions, the military, and parastatals since the 1960s.[14] Nor are there signs of improvement; scholars argue that the commercial discovery of more oil in the Northwest Region in 2012 led the Cameroonian government to tighten its grip on Anglophone regions. Thus, the situation resembles that of Sudan, where oil was discovered in 1979 in the southern regions of the country, leading to civil war in 1983. It seems possible that Anglophone Cameroonians will take a path to secessionism and independence similar to that of the activists who created the Republic of South Sudan.[15]

Anglophone Cameroonian separatism and secession movements are not all monolithic, which contributes to the difficulties they face on the road to political independence. Groups differ as to whether they want complete secession or a return to federalism. Some SCNC members assert that after independence, Anglophone regions of Cameroon must reunify with the former regions of the British Northern Cameroons, currently part of Nigeria.[16] Ethnic and political divisions also hinder a unified monolithic Anglophone separatist and secessionist movement. Many Anglophones blame Anglophone politicians involved in the government for being complicit in this marginalization, charging that, starting with John Foncha, they have allowed the government to co-opt them by appointing them as cabinet ministers and government bureaucrats. Scholar and activist Walters Samah calls many of these Anglophone political elites "yes-men"; he asserts that they defend the government out of fear of losing their posts, downplaying the existence of an Anglophone community that is poorly integrated into Cameroon.[17] Ethnic and regional divisions also divide Anglophone Cameroonians, which is a key reason the Anglophone opposition did not emerge earlier than the late 1980s. The economic strength of the Northwest, combined with ethnic differences, fostered tensions between political leaders in the Southwest Region and in the Northwest Region.[18] Consequently, in the early 1990s the SDF "was far more popular in the North West than the South West Province [Region], for language affiliation there did not preclude economic and ethnic rivalry."[19] The problem of the Cameroonian state to establish a unified nation is much deeper than an "anglophone problem."

#TAKUMBENGUNLEASHED IN #AMBAZONIA: WOMEN'S MOBILIZATION ON THE GROUND AND IN SOCIAL MEDIA

Women have continued to play a role in supporting Anglophone nationalism in contemporary Cameroon. Anglophone nationalist movements continue to mobilize women's actions as they did in the late 1950s and in the federal period. For instance, the Takumbeng decided to back John Fru Ndi, a viable Anglophone Cameroonian presidential candidate and the leader of the SDF, for the first presidential election after the legalization of the multiparty system in 1992. The Takumbeng are a rural-based traditional women's secret society of postmenopausal women from the Northwest Region of Cameroon. Biya won the 1992 presidential elections; Fru Ndi deemed the elections fraudulent and sought unsuccessfully to have it annulled by the country's supreme court.

Violence broke out in the Northwest Region, the area where Fru Ndi had won significant support. Biya's administration placed Fru Ndi under house arrest and sought to formally arrest him, but the Takumbeng women blocked them with a measure that recalls the Anlu's treatment of British administrative officials and local African men in the Bamenda Grassfields: removing their clothes and cupping their breasts when the national military came to arrest Fru Ndi in Bamenda.[20] While they were armed and carried tear gas, the military retreated; they did not want to tempt fate by disobeying their "mothers" merely to take Fru Ndi into custody, and they considered the sight of the women's vaginas to be bad luck. Reports among the people in Bamenda contend that soldiers who advanced on the Takumbeng even after they disrobed either died within hours of "staring at their nakedness" or suffered from severe ailments in the aftermath.[21] Biya's administration released Fru Ndi after a month of house arrest.

The reemergence of the Takumbeng in late 2017 demonstrates that women's participation in the Anglophone nationalism movement has both continuities and variations. Traditional women's organizations have been more visibly at the forefront of Anglophone nationalist than they were in the federal period. Takumbeng has been reinterpreted visually, and its membership crosses generational and national lines by including women who have not reached menopause and by their influence crossing the Atlantic. The Takumbeng took part in protests in the US, Canada, the UK, Germany, and South Africa in September and November 2017.[22] In Cameroon, while postmenopausal Takumbeng women go bare-breasted to stress the seriousness of their grievances, young women have also participated, donning white cloths for modesty. Takumbeng has also been reinterpreted to adjust to the social context abroad. In the United States, postmenopausal women and their younger counterparts did not disrobe when they protested outside of Biya's hotel in New York when he addressed the United Nations General Assembly in New York in September 2017, probably concerned that they would be arrested.[23] The form of protest, many of them kneeling on the concrete sidewalk, arms stretched out and wailing, are reminiscent of the varied ways in which Anglophone Cameroonian women in the 1960s openly used emotional expressivities—Women's Day rallies and collectively participating in local Cameroonian dances for example—to express beliefs about Cameroonian political ideologies and unity.

Through Takumbeng, women continue to invoke maternal power—a "public motherhood" as Meghan Healy-Clancy states it—and to make connections with Cameroonians in the diaspora, especially in South Africa, the UK, and the US, and to support each other across linguistic and national boundaries. They continue to do so using various forms of mass media such as radio and YouTube videos and social media such as Facebook and Twitter to call for support and to mobilize Cameroonian women around the globe—#Takumbengunleashed and #Ambazonia are hashtags that have circulated together in numerous Twitter posts covering the crises in Cameroon since 2017.[24] They also use new technological outlets to seek financial support such as GoFundMe accounts, which display videos, images of children harmed in the movement, and information about the marginalization of Anglophones.[25] Through various media outlets, Takumbeng "mothers" call on their "daughters" to support the movement, further tying their participation to an ideal gendered nationalism. A September 2017 Takumbeng mobilization poster in Germany states, "Mothers, Sisters and Daughters want their voices to be heard. They can no longer bear in the silence, the killings, rapes, maiming and abduction of their children and husbands." A poster rallying support in South Africa dubs Paul Biya the "killer" of Anglophone children, invoking the authority of mothers to protect their children as an element of Anglophone nationalism. In fact, in 2016, mothers, daughters, sisters, and wives participated in the SCNC's Bring Back Our Boys campaign to demand the return of young adult men active in the Anglophone nationalist movement whom they claimed the Francophone state had disappeared or imprisoned.[26] Thus, modern-day Anglophone women, like their counterparts in the federal period, continue to emphasize their roles as mothers to legitimatize their importance and participation in the Anglophone nationalist movement.

The future is unknown. But, as this book illustrates, women have distinctly shaped the political landscape in Cameroon by drawing from local and international ideas about women's political actions to drive a more radical Anglophone nationalist movement. In many ways, the prominence of traditional women's organizations speaks to the connection of the contemporary movement to Cameroon's European-ruled past. In times of crisis, traditional women's movements move to the forefront—perhaps because many formal women's organizations are affiliated with the very governments that such traditional women's organizations petition against. Although Takumbeng has been slightly reinterpreted to include younger members, the official website for the Republic of Ambazonia has an image of bare-breasted elderly post-menopausal women to invoke the political and maternal authority that their age offers. The caption reads: "well armed Takumbeng women send Biya a strong message[:] the real Takumbeng women took to the frontline. These post-menopausal group of women constitute a powerful secret society."[27] Younger women renegotiate new urban (and possibly rural) identities by overtly drawing from their power as women to exercise political power, similar to the "real" post-menopausal members of Takumbeng. Today the evidence is rife. University-aged Anglophone women in Cameroon and around the world responded to the rallying call of support from their Takumbeng "mothers" and "grandmothers" in 2017. They posted pictures on Facebook and Twitter of themselves with scowls on their faces, donning white robes or white cloth wrapped around their waists, with a branch, red lipstick, and cooking utensils such as spatulas, calling upon Anglophone Cameroonian embodied nationalism and renegotiating a (militarized) Anglophone womanhood in Cameron and in the diaspora. From this suspended moment of political crisis, Cameroonian women reshape ideal Anglophone womanhood and embodied nationalism by communicating diverse emotional expressivities and visual representations of femininity to negotiate Anglophone cultural values and political identity across their communities and in the diaspora. In this manner, self-identified Anglophone women continue to play a critical role in symbolically (re)producing and protecting a larger Anglophone "family" across Cameroon and the world. From elderly bare-breasted grandmothers protesting in the rolling Bamenda Grassfields to the diaspora where Cameroonian women protested on the vibrant streets of New York City, there is unity and power.

APPENDIX

Methods and Sources

As a trained historian, I found myself perplexed when in researching this book I sometimes drew from unconventional sources such as social media to weave the history of Anglophone Cameroonian women's nationalist activities. Yet many Africanists draw from diverse methods and approaches when creating historical narratives. As Barbara Cooper observes, "African history, perhaps more than other domains of history, has had to be inventive in its use of sources and eclectic in its approach to evidence."[1] It should come as no surprise, then, that this book relies on a myriad of research methods and sources to reconstruct Anglophone Cameroonian women's history, including oral interviews, newspapers, photos, government correspondence, press releases, published memoirs, radio and television interviews, and Twitter, Facebook, and YouTube.

The National Archives of Cameroon in Buea (NAB) and the National Archives of the United Kingdom (TNA) furnished most of the archival records for this project. Government correspondence and original photographs from TNA clarified how West Cameroon's relations with the UK stoked attempts to exercise political autonomy in the Federal Republic of Cameroon. The archives in Buea, the capital and administrative center of the federated state of West Cameroon, provided newspaper records, official correspondence between West Cameroonian government officials, government press releases, and photographs. While archival materials in NAB were relatively organized and available to the public, the condition of numerous sources posed challenges in accessing information. Pages from newspapers and government correspondence were sometimes missing or destroyed by the poor environmental conditions in the archives. Research in smaller archives and libraries—Memorial Library at the University of Wisconsin–Madison, Melville J. Herskovits Library of African Studies at Northwestern University, Sterling Memorial Library at Yale University, and the British Library in the

UK—allowed me sometimes to find duplicate copies of important archival records that had been destroyed and to follow up on relevant information.

Newspaper records in the NAB offered great insights into how literate Anglophone Cameroonians imagined a national Anglophone identity resonating on the global stage. As Stephanie Newell asserts, "newspapers provide a substantial and unique resource for research into reader reception, cultural production, and political agency in Africa."[2] But relying on newspapers as evidence for the viewpoints of urban elites presents complications. First, while newspapers in West Cameroon were privately owned, unlike many of the papers in East Cameroon, they were nonetheless susceptible to state propaganda; indeed, political parties backed them. Second, newspapers mostly privileged the voices of individuals who had ready access to newspapers in Buea and other nearby towns. Prominent English-language newspapers were mostly located in the southern region of West Cameroon, and it was sometimes difficult for individuals in distant regions, such as Bamenda, to access them on time.[3] Third, I have not been able to verify the identities of all of the women journalists whose work I analyze. Fourth, writers of letters were not identified "beyond the town where the letter originated," and it is not always clear if the people who signed the letters actually penned them. In an interview, I learned that some illiterate urban residents hired professional readers or scribers to write letters to newspapers for them.[4] Nevertheless, the process implies that the signing person endorsed the ideas in the letter even if he or she did not write it. Despite the challenges of analyzing newspapers as texts, as Karin Barber argues, they remain important sources of analysis because textual traditions can be seen "as a community's ethnography of itself."[5] Newspapers replicated public speeches word for word, and that became a key source for me. The readers of women's columns contributed significantly to their columns through letters and inquiries, and writers regularly ran reader questions and their responses, as well as responses to letters. Derek Peterson and Emma Hunter describe the influence of readers on print culture in colonial Africa, and a similar dynamic led to the creation of the women's columns in West Cameroonian newspapers.[6] For example, a 1968 letter to the editor of the *Cameroon Express* queried "Why is it that you don't publish a Women's Column? Have women been forgotten?"[7] All the newspaper editors eventually complied with the demands of these letter writers, most whom were women.

This book draws heavily from women's advice columns penned by Ruff Wanzie and Clara Manga, both of whom were particularly prolific columnists, and whose identities I know. Wanzie headed the *Cameroon Times* women's columns from around 1964 to 1973. While she wrote under her name until 1966, after Ahidjo's CNU eliminated the KNDP she became "Cousin Lizzy." She was a civil servant in the West Cameroon government; her husband, Joseph Wanzie, was secretary of state for primary education.[8] Clara Manga (later, Clara Yondo Tama) headed the women's column for the *Cameroon Champion* from around 1960 to 1963, writing as "Auntie Clara." She was a teacher and the first female journalist in the British Southern Cameroons.[9]

I focus on the writings of Wanzie and Manga in part because their papers were mouthpieces for two prominent West Cameroonian political parties of the time. John Foncha helped establish the *Cameroon Times*, which featured Wanzie's column, and the paper supported his KNDP party.[10] The paper was founded in 1959 in Victoria. At its pinnacle in the mid-1960s, the paper was a triweekly publication printing about 8,000 copies per issue. The *Cameroon Champion*, which featured Manga's column, supported the CPNC. Party founder E. M. L. Endeley founded the paper in 1959, and like its competitor it was launched in Victoria. It was printed and distributed in Victoria until 1963, when it closed due to lack of funds.[11] In spite of their distinct party affiliations, the women's columns in these newspapers displayed similar rhetoric concerning gender norms and social values, which appeared in other newspapers' similar columns as well.

I also draw on the columns of Elizabeth Nkuku Nwigwe, a freelance journalist who wrote as "Sister Dolly" for the *Cameroon Outlook*—a triweekly publication printing about 5,000 copies per issue—and as "Aunty Lizzy" in the *Cameroon Post*; she also had posts in the West Cameroon press releases. Popularly known in Buea as "Sweet Mother," Elizabeth Nkuku Nwigwe had a weekly program on Radio Buea in which she discussed various issues about women's civic lives. An online archive about the history of Saker Baptist College in Limbe (previously Victoria), the school where many of the formally educated elites I focus on in this work were educated, reveals that Nkuku Nwigwe, a former student, was formally educated, like Wanzie and Manga; she was a former teacher and later a civil servant.[12] Other columns whose authors I cannot identify—for example, "Sister Kamara" and "Sister Starengo" in the *Cameroon Voice* and "Mami Tolima," "Sister Julie," and "Sister Vivian" in the *Cameroon Observer*—nonetheless reflect distinctive and authentic authorial voices and featured detailed accounts of the meetings of local women's organizations, all of which suggest they were women.[13] Their references to conversations and encounters with people in their communities also suggest they were women.[14]

While this book focuses on the activities of women in Anglophone regions of Cameroon, it mostly privileges the voices of women in various towns in the contemporary Southwest Region, such as in Buea, Limbe (formerly Victoria), Kumba, and Tiko. While Bamenda, the capital of the Northwest Region, has been the foremost site of opposition to Anglophone marginalization since the early 1990s, I mostly focused my oral interviews in Buea, the town where leading politicians and their wives often resided during the federal period. Although oral history depends on the imperfect memories of individuals, it was also crucial because it provided the opportunity to privilege Cameroonian women's varied perspectives about past everyday lived realities. In 2011 and 2015, I conducted unstructured and semi-structured lengthy interviews, at least two hours or longer, with women in Buea who were fifty and older at the time. I focused on women who were at least eighteen years old between the years of 1960 and 1982 because they could better speak to how issues of gender had shaped their adult lives. Most of the women interviewed self-identified as Protestant Christians and had some level of formal education, either a primary or secondary education. Because of their ages, many of the women are now retired; they worked in teaching, nursing, civil service, law, and secretarial work. One woman was a former prison superintendent, and another worked for the military. Some have retirement careers as small-business owners who own bars and small produce shops. Oral interviews with family members of Anna Foncha and Gladys Silo Endeley in 2015–16 provided a closer look at the intimate daily lives of women political elites. From the interviews, I learned much about how they balanced their political endeavors with their domestic and marital obligations. Because of the nature and emphasis of my study, I interviewed mostly women, although I spoke with male former civil servants and engaged in participant observation in local bars, which were often wooden shacks with few or no women.

Contemporary political conditions shaped the oral interview process. In 2011, for example, the tense presidential election informed how interviewees responded to me and recollected past events. When I first conducted interviews on my own, some individuals were suspicious about my research agenda, fearing I might share their responses with government individuals who would seek political retribution. I assigned pseudonyms to some of these women to ensure privacy. I also mostly resolved the issue by eliciting the assistance of the "aunt" I reference in chapter 5, a close family friend who is like an aunt to me. A Francophone who lived in Buea since young adulthood, she became my assistant. She was invaluable in finding participants, and she attended interview sessions. Although I conducted most interviews in standard English, there were miscommunications, as evidenced by a woman who lamented that she did not understand my "American English" and might better understand if I spoke "British English." My friend's fluency in Cameroonian pidgin English, an English-based Creole language, was invaluable at such times. Furthermore, my assistant's age, at the time in her late fifties, gave her a measure of maternal authority and provided a familial atmosphere that put respondents at ease. A second research assistant, originally from Bamenda, conducted interviews and surveys in Bamenda and Nkambe, which allowed me to highlight the diverse voices of residents from the Northwest Region of Cameroon. My research assistants' roles as cultural liaisons and research collaborators facilitated productive interviews and expanded the network of contacts that I drew on in a subsequent research trip to Cameroon in 2015.

My position as a Francophone Cameroonian drove my research interests. Growing up, I knew very little about the history and daily lives of Anglophone Cameroonians. In fact, I had never set foot in Anglophone regions until I was conducting my dissertation research in 2011–2012. But this project has personally enlightened me about the long sociopolitical grievances of Anglophone Cameroonians. Like many Francophone persons, I am sometimes ignorant about the daily frustrations Anglophone persons face in Cameroon. For instance, while in Buea in 2015, I invited some Anglophone graduate students and senior scholars to dinner at the home of my "aunt" assistant. Before eating, she proceeded to pray in French. Almost unanimously, our Anglophone guests yelled, "Pray in English! We are in an English-speaking town!" I felt greatly embarrassed at our faux pas—especially given the topic of my research.

As a native woman ethnographer, I was both an insider and an outsider when conducting research, which shaped the topics I chose (and did not choose) to highlight. Nwando Achebe writes that when reflecting on her standpoint as an Igbo female researcher, "my relationship with Africa and Nigeria and the fact that I am Igbo shapes in a profound way what I am willing to do or not do when it comes to research. It shapes, rightly or wrongly, how I identify with my research collaborators—a fact that has a direct effect on what I choose to write about and my interpretation of data—as well as my notions of accountability."[15] This statement perfectly encapsulates how my Cameroonian identity, and connection to Cameroon, shaped my research and writing experience when deciding which topics to broach, and not to broach.

My Anglophone interviewees were at times apprehensive of my interest in Anglophone political history because of my Francophone background. I had to acknowledge that like Bridget Teboh, who reflects upon how her Moghamo/Anglophone identity shapes her research experiences, "[m]y Cameroonian identity is often challenged by existing Anglophone-Francophone problems."[16] But as I explained when conducting field research, living most of my adolescence as a person of color in the United States facilitated a connection with the social marginalization of Anglophone Cameroonians, even while our frustrations varied due to our different cultural and historical circumstances. Explaining this to my interviewees appeared to make them more relaxed and willing to participate in the discussion. Beyond shared feelings of social and political marginalization, the fact that I was Cameroon-born with active family roots throughout the country provoked women to embrace me as a "daughter." As a "daughter" I sometimes brought treats and small Cameroonian dishes, as tokens of gratitude, for women interviewees. On eating the dishes, the women became exuberant, expressing delight and nodding with approval while asserting that I would make a "good wife" one day. These interactions fostered shared efforts to embrace aspects of ideal African womanhood. To the women interviewees, I proved my African womanhood by my knowledge of Cameroonian cookery. But being in the role of the "daughter" meant that it was initially difficult to find subjects who were over age fifty to interview, a problem I resolved with the help of my "aunt," who is active in local women's groups and associations and convinced members to grant me interviews.[17]

I also faced difficulties as a woman scholar when interviewing men or interviewing women in the presence of men. The husbands of some of the women I interviewed at times interrupted their wives and shared what they believed to be the more "accurate" account. But as Kathleen Sheldon has observed about the works of other scholars in similar situations, it is important to privilege women's stories, because "women and men have distinct histories to tell because their own experiences varied by gender, and this was compounded because in retelling their stories male and female audiences heard and remembered the information differently."[18] Some men did not take my work or my objectives seriously. One man interrupted an interview I was conducting with an Anglophone political activist to inform him that *he*, and not me, should be writing the book. Ultimately, I found both elderly men and male university students willing to talk to me at length about the history of the British Southern Cameroons and about their ongoing marginalization in present-day Cameroon. Encounters with both women and men allowed me to use their vibrant stories to weave a colorful web of Anglophone (Southern) Cameroonian history during what Anthony Ndi identifies as the "Golden Age," the period he believes to be of greatest Anglophone independence and liberty.[19]

NOTES

INTRODUCTION

1. Pius Soh Bejeng, *Dr. John Ngu Foncha: The Cameroonian Statesman (A Biography)* (Bamenda, Cameroon: Centre for Social Sciences Research, 1999), 56–57.

2. Bejeng, *Dr. John Ngu Foncha*, 57. More on the biography of John Foncha is available in the biography cited above.

3. Harmony O'Rourke, "Foncha, John Ngu," in *Dictionary of African Biography*, ed. Emmanuel K. Akyeampong and Henry Louis Gates, Jr. (New York: Oxford University Press, 2012), 379–80.

4. O'Rourke, "Foncha, John Ngu," 380.

5. Ibid.

6. Mark Dike DeLancey, Rebecca Neh Mbuh, and Mark W. DeLancey, *Historical Dictionary of the Republic of Cameroon*, 4th ed. (Lanham, MD: Scarecrow Press, 2010), 176–77.

7. O'Rourke, "Foncha, John Ngu," 381.

8. Bejeng, *Dr. John Ngu Foncha*, 6, 66.

9. Martin Jumbam, "Fiftieth Anniversary of Cameroon's Reunification: The Summit Magazine Story," *MartinJumbam.net*, May 24, 2014. https://www.martinjumbam.net/2014/05/fiftieth-anniversary-of-cameroons-reunification-the-summit-magazine-story.html#sthash.DHGlk0fB.dpuf

10. Pamela Feldman-Savelsberg, *Mothers on the Move: Reproducing Belonging between Africa and Europe* (Chicago: University of Chicago Press, 2016), 6, 11.

11. Nicodemus Fru Awasom, "Towards Historicizing the Ossification of Colonial Identities in Africa: The Anglophone/Francophone Divide in Postcolonial Cameroon," in *Society, State, and Identity in African History*, ed. Bahru Zewde (Addis Ababa, Ethiopia: Forum for Social Studies, 2008), 47, 55. Piet Konings and Francis Beng Nyamnjoh mention the Francophone dominated state's excessive use of violence against Anglophone Cameroonian activists. See Piet Konings and Francis Beng Nyamnjoh, *Negotiating an Anglophone Identity: A Study of the Politics of Recognition and Representation in Cameroon* (Leiden, Netherlands: Brill, 2003), 79, 103.

12. For a broader discourse on ethnonationalism, see Daniele Conversi, ed., *Ethnonationalism in the Contemporary World: Walker Connor and the Study of Nationalism* (New York: Routledge, 2004), 2.

13. Jan Bender Shetler, ed., *Gendering Ethnicity in African Women's Lives* (Madison: University of Wisconsin Press, 2015), 3–4.

14. Jacqueline-Bethel Tchouta Mougoué, "The Anlu Rebellion," in *The Oxford Research Encyclopedia of African History*, ed. Thomas Spear (New York: Oxford University Press, February 2018). https://doi.org/10.1093/acrefore/9780190277734.013.273. Emmanuel Konde, *African Women and Politics: Knowledge, Gender, and Power in Male-Dominated Cameroon* (Lewiston, NY: Edwin Mellen Press, 2005), 50.

15. See the following for additional information about how West Cameroonian female political elites increased women's access to organized sports: Jacqueline-Bethel Tchouta Mougoué, "'Where Are All the Women Who Used to Be Good Athletes in Their School Days?': Sports and Gendered Leisure in Anglophone Cameroon in the 1960s and 1970s," in *Africa Every Day: Fun, Leisure, and Expressive Culture on the Continent*, ed. Oluwakemi Balogun, Lisa Gilman, Melissa Graboyes, and Habib Iddrisu (Athens: Ohio University Press), forthcoming.

16. Benedict Anderson, *Imagined Communities: Reflections on the Origin and Spread of Nationalism* (London: Verso, 2006), 4.

17. "My Husband Stopped Maintaining Me So I Beat Up His Girl," *Cameroon Times*, August 1, 1967, 2; Ndimolo C. Vincent, "Free Girls, Their Parents Versus Moral Society," *The Hero*, September 13, 1971, 3; Mougoué, "'Where Are All the Women Who Used to Be Good Athletes in Their School Days?,'" original from "Boxing Sensation: Woman Licks Male Opponent," *Cameroon Times*, October 6, 1964, 1.

18. Barry Wellman and Keith Hampton, "Living Networked On and Offline," *Contemporary Sociology* 28, no. 6 (1999): 651.

19. From 1959 to 1961, Josepha Mua succeeded Dorcas Idowu, who had served from 1957 to 1959 as the special member for women's interests in the Southern Cameroons House of Assembly. In 1961, Gladys Difo was appointed in that position by the Kamerun National Democratic Party (KNDP). Mua was a teacher at the Catholic Mission School in Wum and a member of the KNDP. Mua in the 1970s also performed duties as a Cameroon National Union (CNU) parliamentarian in the United Republic of Cameroon. Josepha Mua, "Women Are an Important Factor," *Cameroon Times*, February 8, 1964, 3; Konde, *African Women and Politics*, 121, 143. For more on the biography of Josepha Mua see Tricia Efange Oben, *Women of the Reunification* (Mumbai, India: New Media Communication, 2011), 39–48.

20. Josepha Mua, "Women Are an Important Factor," *Cameroon Times*, February 8, 1964, 3.

21. See examples in various memoirs by Anglophone male political elites and male-authored letters to English-language Cameroonian papers: Nerius Namaso Mbile, *Cameroon Political Story: Memories of an Authentic Eye Witness* (Bamenda, Cameroon: Langaa RPCIG, 2011); Albert W. Mukong, *Prisoner Without a Crime: Disciplining Dissent in*

Ahidjo's Cameroon (Bamenda, Cameroon: Langaa RPCIG, 2009); B. Waha, "Authorities Should Intervene," *Cameroon Champion*, December 19, 1961; I. Nagam, "We Want True Freedom," *Cameroon Champion*, August 14, 1962, 3.

22. For example, see Denis Atemnkeng, "British Southern Cameroons' Nationalism and the African Unity Argument," in *British Southern Cameroons Nationalism and Conflict in Postcolonial Africa*, ed. Fonkem Achankeng (Victoria, Canada: FriesenPress, 2014), 74.

23. Fonkem Achankeng, "Introduction," in *British Southern Cameroons Nationalism and Conflict in Postcolonial Africa*, ed. Fonkem Achankeng (Victoria, Canada: FriesenPress, 2014), viii.

24. Brian Girvin, "Democracy, Separatism and Secession," Secessionism and Separatism Monthly Series, January 20, 2016, https://networks.h-net.org/node/3911/discussions/107684/secessionism-and-separatism-monthly-series-democracy-separatism

25. Achankeng, "Introduction," viii.

26. B. Waha, "Authorities Should Intervene," *Cameroon Champion*, December 19, 1961.

27. Miles Larmer and Baz Lecocq, "Rethinking Nationalism, Ethnicity and Separatism in African Studies," Secessionism and Separatism Monthly Series, September 20, 2016, https://networks.h-net.org/node/3911/discussions/144633/secessionism-and-separatism-monthly-series-%E2%80%9Crethinking-nationalism

28. Meredith Terretta, *Nation of Outlaws, State of Violence: Nationalism, Grassfields Tradition, and State Building in Cameroon* (Athens: Ohio University Press, 2014), 4.

29. As Nantang Jua and Piet Konings contend, Anglophone nationalism is not new to contemporary Cameroon and has roots predating the postcolonial era. Nantang Jua and Piet Konings, "Occupation of Public Space: Anglophone Nationalism in Cameroon," *Cahiers d'Études Africaines* 44, no. 175 (2004): 611.

30. Moris N. Namata, "Unitary System Suitable for Cameroon," *Cameroon Champion*, July 24, 1962, 5.

31. Ephraim N. Ngwafor, *Ako-Aya: A Cameroonian Pioneer in Daring Journalism and Social Commentary* (Bamenda, Cameroon: Langaa RPCIG, 2010), 13, 156–57, original from Ako Aya, "Ah Glad Plenty," *Cameroon Outlook*, October 1, 1971; Ako Aya, "I Wept," *Cameroon Outlook*, September 3, 1971.

32. For examples on Anglophone nationalism and political history, see the works of Konings and Nyamnjoh, *Negotiating an Anglophone Identity*; Piet Konings and Francis Beng Nyamnjoh, "The Anglophone Problem in Cameroon," *Journal of Modern African Studies* 35, no. 2 (1997): 207–29; Mufor Atanga, *The Anglophone Cameroon Predicament* (Bamenda, Cameroon: Langaa RPCIG, 2011); Carlson Anyangwe, *Betrayal of Too Trusting a People: The UN, the UK and the Trust Territory of the Southern Cameroons* (Bamenda, Cameroon: Langaa RPCIG, 2009); and Joseph Lon Nfi, *The Reunification Debate in British Southern Cameroons: The Role of French Cameroon Immigrants* (Bamenda, Cameroon: Langaa RPCIG, 2014).

33. Jill Vickers, "Gendering Secession," Secessionism and Separatism Monthly Series, March 20, 2016, https://networks.h-net.org/node/116427/pdf

34. Frank Stark asserted in 1976 that when Ahidjo turned the Federal Republic into a single party state in the mid-1960s, "[a] little more of the shadow of West Cameroon's 'federal' nature had slipped from its grasp." Stark went as far as to argue that because "Anglophone leaders of West Cameroon long before had given up hope of any political or economic power for their state [that] [t]here was little opposition to the event among these minority leaders and even relief among many." Later, in 2014, Andreas Mehler contended that "it was the abolishment of federalism that had the long-term effect of fostering secessionism when oil was detected and a political crisis later unfolded in the course of a flawed democratization process." Frank M. Stark, "Federalism in Cameroon: The Shadow and the Reality," *Canadian Journal of African Studies* 10, no. 3 (1976): 423, 436; Andreas Mehler, "Why Federalism Did Not Lead to Secession in Cameroon," *Ethnopolitics* 13, no. 1 (2014): 48.

35. Sugam Pokharel, "Miss Tibet Wins Crown for Most Controversial Beauty Pageant," *CNN*, June 5, 2017, https://www.cnn.com/2017/06/05/asia/tibet-beauty-pageant/index.html

36. Oyèrónkẹ́ Oyěwùmí, *Gender Epistemologies in Africa: Gendering Traditions, Spaces, Social Institutions, and Identities* (New York: Palgrave Macmillan, 2011), 1.

37. Nira Yuval-Davis, *Gender and Nation* (London: Sage Publications, 1997), 45.

38. Ibid., 2.

39. Meredith Terretta, "A Miscarriage of Revolution: Cameroonian Women and Nationalism," *Stichproben* 12, no. 7 (2007), 65.

40. Ibid., 78. See the following for more on the history of the Union Démocratique des Femmes Camerounaises (UDEFEC): Meredith Terretta, *Petitioning for our Rights, Fighting for our Nation: The History of the Democratic Union of Cameroonian Women, 1949–1960* (Bamenda, Cameroon: Langaa RPCIG, 2013).

41. Terretta argues that "women had long negotiated their power and place in society through the idiom of fertility," by blaming local leaders when fertility rates fell and establishing financial autonomy through agriculture. Terretta, "A Miscarriage of Revolution," 74.

42. British officials asked women farmers to employ horizontal contour cultivation, the practice of horizontally planting across inclined land. Mougoué, "The Anlu Rebellion." For more on the Anlu Rebellion, see Shirley Ardener, "Sexual Insult and Female Militancy," in *Perceiving Women*, ed. Shirley Ardener (London: Malaby Press, 1975), 29–53; Henry Kam Kah, "Women's Resistance in Cameroon's Western Grassfields: The Power of Symbols, Organization, and Leadership, 1957–1961," *African Studies Quarterly* 12, no. 3 (2011): 67–91; Henry Kam Kah, "'Our Gowns for Your Trousers': Sexuality and Women Revolt in Colonial Laimbwe Land, Cameroon," *Epasa Moto: A Multidisciplinary Journal of Arts, Letters and the Humanities of the University of Buea* 1, no. 2 (2014): 103–22; Paul Nchoji Nkwi, "Traditional Female Militancy in a Modern Context," in *Femmes du Cameroun: Mères Pacifiques Femmes Rebelles* [Women of Cameroon: Pacific Women Rebels], ed. J. C. Barbier (Paris: Karthala, 1985), 181–93; Robert E. Ritzenthaler, "Anlu: A Women's Uprising in the British Cameroons," *African Studies* 19, no. 3 (1960): 151–56;

Eugenia Shanklin, "Anlu Remembered: The Kom Women's Rebellion of 1958–61," *Dialectical Anthropology* 15, nos. 2/3 (1990): 159–81.

43. Mougoué, "The Anlu Rebellion."

44. Women in French Cameroun similarly disrobed to mock and protest European (French) administrative rule. For an example, see Terretta, *Nation of Outlaws*, 134.

45. Oyèrónkẹ́ Oyěwùmí and Filomina Chioma Steady have shown in their work that motherhood, literally and figuratively, has served as an important social and political power base for African women. Oyèrónkẹ́ Oyěwùmí, *The Invention of Women: Making an African Sense of Western Gender Discourses* (Minneapolis: University of Minnesota Press, 1997); Filomina Chioma Steady, *Women and Leadership in West Africa: Mothering the Nation and Humanizing the State* (New York: Palgrave Macmillan, 2011).

46. Ifi Amadiume, *Re-Inventing Africa: Matriarchy, Religion and Culture* (London: Zed Books, 1997), 198.

47. Meghan Healy-Clancy, "The Family Politics of the Federation of South African Women: A History of Public Motherhood in Women's Antiracist Activism," *Signs: Journal of Women in Culture and Society* 42, no. 4 (2017): 844.

48. To be clear, the matter of Islamic traditions of marriage and divorce was pertinent in many of these cases. For specific examples, see Susan Geiger, *TANU Women: Gender and Culture in the Making of Tanganyikan Nationalism, 1955–1965* (Portsmouth, NH: Heinemann, 1997), 101–3; Elizabeth Schmidt, *Mobilizing the Masses: Gender, Ethnicity, and Class in the Nationalist Movement in Guinea, 1939–1958* (Portsmouth, NH: Heinemann, 2005), 9, 141.

49. Shanklin, "Anlu Remembered," 164; Kah, "Women's Resistance in Cameroon's Western Grassfields," 67, 72, 76, 79–80.

50. Filomina Chioma Steady, *Women and Collective Action in Africa: Development, Democratization, and Empowerment* (New York: Palgrave Macmillan, 2006), 31, 64.

51. Shireen Hassim, *Women's Organizations and Democracy in South Africa: Contesting Authority* (Madison: University of Wisconsin Press, 2006), 7.

52. Ibid., 9.

53. Catherine M. Cole, Takyiwaa Manuh, and Stephan F. Miescher, "Introduction: When Was Gender?," in *Africa after Gender?*, ed. Cole, Manuh, and Miescher (Bloomington: Indiana University Press, 2007), 3.

54. Juliana Makuchi Nfah-Abbenyi, *Gender in African Women's Writing: Identity, Sexuality, and Difference* (Bloomington: Indiana University Press, 1997), 11.

55. Amina Mama, "Feminism or Femocracy? State Feminism and Democratisation in Nigeria," *Africa Development* 20, no. 1 (1995): 41; Hussaina Abdullah, "Wifeism and Activism: The Nigerian Women's Movement," in *The Challenge of Local Feminisms: Women's Movements in Global Perspectives*, ed. Amrita Basu (New York: Routledge, 2018), 213.

56. Mougoué, "Housewives at Husbands' Throats," 415; Valentine M. Moghadam, *Globalization and Social Movements: Islamism, Feminism, and the Global Justice Movement* (Lanham, MD: Rowman & Littlefield, 2012), 134, originally cited by Valerie Sper-

ling, Myra Marx Ferree, and Barbara Risman, "Constructing Global Feminism: Transnational Advocacy Networks and Russian Women's Activism," *Signs: Journal of Women in Culture and Society* 26, no. 4 (2001): 1158.

57. Michael Billig, *Banal Nationalism* (Thousand Oaks, CA: Sage, 1995), 5–6.

58. As Cusack argues, banal nationalism also involves national cuisines because "[t]he development of a national cuisine will involve the summoning of a variety of dishes into the ambit of the discourse of the nation, and the very mention then of some national dish will quietly flag the nation." Igor Cusack, "African Cuisines: Recipes for Nation-Building?" *Journal of African Cultural Studies* 13, no. 2 (2000): 209.

59. Although several scholars have referenced the phrase, or notion of, "embodied nationalism," I expand understandings of the term, providing a more concrete definition that concurrently emphasizes emotional expression, affectional bonds, and visual representation. Oluwakemi Balogun links understandings of embodied nationalism to how female contestants in contemporary Nigerian beauty pageants "embodied representations of the nation in divergent ways." Joan Elayne Huckstep's understanding of embodied nationalism is connected to "Animation Politique . . . a nationally observed, compulsory, daily dance activity, practiced" in Mobutu Sese Seko's Zaire (modern-day Democratic Republic of Congo). Tamar Mayer connects understandings of "[e]mbodied [n]ationalisms" to political geography in a 2004 work, asserting that the aim is to "prob[e] the connection between nation and gender . . . focusing on the spatiality of power." Tamar Mayer, "Embodied Nationalisms," in *Mapping Women, Making Politics: Feminist Perspectives on Political Geography*, ed. Lynn Staeheli, Eleonore Kofman, and Linda Peake (New York: Routledge, 2004), 153–54; Oluwakemi M. Balogun, "Cultural and Cosmopolitan: Idealized Femininity and Embodied Nationalism in Nigerian Beauty Pageants," *Gender and Society* 26, no. 3 (2012): 364; Joan Elayne Huckstep, "Embodied Nationalism 'Animation Politique' (Political Dance) in Zaire: A Case Study of the Dimensionality and Agency of Dance as the Spirit of Individual, Community, and National Identity" (PhD dissertation, Temple University, PA, 2005), iii.

60. Elisabeth Militz and Carolin Schurr, "Affective Nationalism: Banalities of Belonging in Azerbaijan," *Political Geography* 54 (2016): 54.

61. Evelyn Brooks Higginbotham, *Righteous Discontent: The Women's Movement in the Black Baptist Church, 1880–1920* (Cambridge, MA: Harvard University Press, 1993), 14.

62. James C. McCann, *Stirring the Pot: A History of African Cuisine* (Athens: Ohio University Press, 2009), 63.

63. Pamela Feldman-Savelsberg, *Plundered Kitchens, Empty Wombs: Threatened Reproduction and Identity in the Cameroon Grassfields* (Ann Arbor: University of Michigan Press, 1999), 4.

64. Heather Marie Akou, *The Politics of Dress in Somali Culture* (Bloomington: Indiana University Press, 2011), 9.

65. Marie Grace Brown, *Khartoum at Night: Fashion and Body Politics in Imperial Sudan* (Stanford: Stanford University Press, 2017), 10.

66. For examples outside of Africa, see Katrina Gulliver, *Modern Women in China*

and Japan: Gender, Feminism and Global Modernity between the Wars (London: I. B. Tauris, 2012); Nhung Tuyet Tran, "Woman as Nation: Tradition and Modernity Narratives in Vietnamese Histories," *Gender & History* 24, no. 2 (2012): 411–30.

67. Tanya Lyons, *Guns and Guerilla Girls: Women in the Zimbabwean National Liberation Struggle* (Trenton, NJ: Africa World Press, 2004), 222.

68. As an example, Stephanie Newell argues in her work based on colonial West African literature that newspapers were a significant source for unique perspectives into the ideologies of the reader, cultural developments, and political scenarios in the African continent. Newell mentions that editors frequently used newspapers as a platform to engage in public discourse going beyond the realms of simple communication of information or editorial beliefs, as seen throughout the postcolonial period in Africa. Derek Peterson and Emma Hunter argue that during colonial rule in Africa, newspapers functioned as power houses that established unified political ideologies because they spearheaded campaigns and provided impetus to activities; this view applies to the early period of post-independent Anglophone Cameroon. Stephanie Newell, *The Power to Name: A History of Anonymity in Colonial West Africa* (Athens: Ohio University Press, 2013), 2, 5; Derek Peterson and Emma Hunter, "Print Culture in Colonial Africa," in *African Print Cultures: Newspapers and Their Publics in the Twentieth Century*, ed. Derek Peterson, Emma Hunter, and Stephanie Newell (Ann Arbor: University of Michigan Press, 2016), 1.

69. Anderson, *Imagined Communities*, 46.

70. Ngwafor, *Ako-Aya*.

71. Susan Z. Andrade, *The Nation Writ Small: African Fictions and Feminisms, 1958–1988* (Durham: Duke University Press, 2011), 5–6.

72. *The West African Pilot*, a newspaper published in Lagos, Nigeria, was established in 1937 by Nnmadi Azikiwe. It soon become one of the most prominent newspapers in the West African region and is still published today. Toyin Falola and Ann Genova, *Historical Dictionary of Nigeria* (Lanham, MD: Scarecrow Press, 2009), 249, 363. See the following for examples of Anglophone Cameroonian political elites who discuss their experiences reading Nigerian newspapers: Mbile, *Cameroon Political Story*, 10; S. N. Ejedepang-Koge, *In the Service of People: My Roots—An Autobiography* (Bloomington: Xlibris, 2013), 411.

73. Stephanie Newell, *West African Literatures: Ways of Reading* (Oxford: Oxford University Press, 2006), 21.

74. Jan Whitt, *Women in American Journalism: A New History* (Champaign: University of Illinois Press, 2008), 40. Also cited in Jacqueline-Bethel Tchouta Mougoué, "Intellectual Housewives, Journalism, and Anglophone Nationalism in Cameroon, 1961–72," *Journal of West African History* 3, no. 2 (October 2017): 73.

75. Whitt, *Women in American Journalism*, 40. Also cited in: Mougoué, "Intellectual Housewives," 73.

76. Whitt, *Women in American Journalism*, 40.

77. Kenda Mutongi, "Dear Dolly's Advice on Love and Courtship," *International Journal of African Historical Studies* 33, no. 1 (2000): 3–4.

78. Ibrahim Seaga Shaw, "Towards an African Journalism Model: A Critical Historical Perspective," *International Communication Gazette* 71, no. 6 (2009): 491.

79. For example, see: Jean-Philippe Marcoux, *Jazz Griots: Music as History in the 1960s African American Poem* (Lanham, MD: Lexington Books, 2012).

80. Marie-Soleil Frère, "The Journalist and the Griot: Traces of Orality in the African Written Press," *Afrika Focus* 15, nos. 1–2 (1999): 13–14.

81. Thomas A. Hale, *Griots and Griottes: Masters of Words and Music* (Bloomington: Indiana University Press, 1998), 218.

82. Karin Barber, "Views of the Field: Introduction," in *Readings in African Popular Culture*, ed. Karin Barber (Bloomington: Indiana University Press, 1997), 2.

83. For examples, see Michael Eyango, "Sister Dolly, You Are Wrong, Women Are Not Tougher," *Cameroon Outlook*, December 29, 1969, 3, 4; Bob Robertson Tayong, "Sister Dolly under Fire," *Cameroon Outlook*, March 20, 1970, 3; J. E. Ebaima, "Sister Dolly's Blunder," *Cameroon Outlook*, April 1, 1970, 3, 4.

84. "Address Delivered by her Excellency Madam J. N. Foncha on the Occasion of the Inauguration of Women's Day and the Launching of the Council of Women's Institute's Newsletter: Wednesday 31st, March 1965," West Cameroon press release no. 3864, March 31, 1965; "Women's Day Born," *Cameroon Times*, April 1–2, 1965, 3.

CHAPTER 1

1. Oben, *Women of the Reunification*, 72. For more information about the structure of the Federal National Assembly, the legislative structure of the Federal Republic of Cameroon from 1961 to 1972, see DeLancey, Mbuh, and DeLancey, *Historical Dictionary of the Republic of Cameroon*, 162.

2. Oben, *Women of the Reunification*, 72.

3. Konde, *African Women and Politics*, 158.

4. Ibid., 155. Oben, *Women of the Reunification*, 68.

5. *Cameroon Studies in English & French*, vol. 1 (Yaoundé, Cameroon: Department of English, University of Yaoundé, 1976), 52.

6. Ian F. Hancock et al., eds., *Readings in Creole Studies* (Ghent, Belgium: E. Story-Scientia, 1979), 290.

7. Konde, *African Women and Politics*, 159.

8. Gwendoline's mother was Hannah Steane, the daughter of Carl Makangai Steane. Gwendoline's sisters were educated as follows: Grace went to secondary school in Nigeria, then nursing school in the UK. Gladys went to a missionary girl's school in Lagos and St. Anne's College in Ibadan, Nigeria and obtained a Bachelor of Medicine at the University of Ibadan; she later earned a Bachelor of Surgery from the University of London and a postgraduate degree in Children's Health from the Conjoint Board of England and Wales. She also earned a master's degree in Public Health from Harvard University. Divina went to secondary school in Ibiaku, Nigeria, and went to the UK to earn a degree in Secretarial and Administration Studies. Irene's secondary education

was in Nigeria, and she attended college in the United States. Pamela also obtained her secondary school education in Nigeria. She earned her undergraduate degree at the University of Ibadan and the University of London and an advanced degree in Literature and Theater Arts at Colorado State University. V. E. Mukete, *My Odyssey: The Story of Cameroon Reunification with Authentic Letters of Key Players* (Yaoundé, Cameroon: Eagle Publishing, 2013), 458–59.

9. Gwendoline attended the Christian Missionary Society Secondary School and King's College, both located in Lagos, Nigeria. Mukete, *My Odyssey*, 458. Oben, *Women of the Reunification*, 68.

10. Konde, *African Women and Politics*, 155.

11. Oben, *Women of the Reunification*, 69. Emmanuel Konde, *Cameroon: Traumas of the Body Politic* (Bloomington, IN: Xlibris Corporation, 2015), 76.

12. Oben, *Women of the Reunification*, 70.

13. Gwendoline was initially given the position of administrative officer in 1961 and promoted to senior administrative officer in 1963. By 1968 she had become principle administrative officer. She also performed duties as principle at the Clerical School in Buea and secretary for the Public Service Commission for the West Cameroon government. Konde, *African Women and Politics*, 155; Oben, *Women of the Reunification, 70.*

14. Oben, *Women of the Reunification*, 73.

15. Ibid., 70.

16. Ibid., 71.

17. Mukete, *My Odyssey*, 458.

18. Konde, *African Women and Politics*, 157.

19. Oben, *Women of the Reunification*, 71.

20. Ibid., 73–74.

21. Gary F. Simons and Charles D. Fennig, eds., *Ethnologue: Languages of the World*, 21st ed. (Dallas: SIL International, 2018), http://www.ethnologue.com

22. DeLancey, Mbuh, and DeLancey explain that British Southern Cameroons "was initially attached to the Southern Provinces [of Nigeria] and later to the Eastern Provinces of Nigeria. It was supervised by a British resident who received orders from the lieutenant governor in Enugu. Officially, the British named Southern Cameroons as the 'Cameroons Province.'" DeLancey, Mbuh, and DeLancey, *Historical Dictionary of the Republic of Cameroon*, 14, 350; O'Rourke, "Foncha, John Ngu," 380, 350.

23. Martin Atangana, *The End of French Rule in Cameroon* (Lanham, MD: University Press of America, 2010), 97–126. For additional information on French resistance in Cameroun, see J. Achille Mbembe, *La Naissance Du Maquis Dans Le Sud-Cameroun, 1920–1960: Histoire Des Usages De La Raison En Colonie* [The Birth of the Maquis in South Cameroon, 1920–1960: History of the Uses of Reason in Colony] (Paris: Karthala, 1996).

24. For more information regarding the events leading to the 1961 reunification see: Nicodemus Fru Awasom, "Negotiating Federalism: How Ready were Cameroonian Leaders before the February 1961 United Nations Plebiscites?" *Canadian Journal of Afri-*

can Studies 36, no. 3 (2002): 425–59; Nicodemus Fru Awasom, "The Reunification Question in Cameroon History: was the Bride an Enthusiastic or a Reluctant One?" *Africa Today* 47, no. 2 (2002): 91–119.

25. Some Anglophone Cameroonian political elites have claimed in their biographies that the French played an important role in rigging the 1961 plebiscite votes in Southern Cameroons in favor of recently independent French Cameroun. For an example see Prince Kofi Itiat, *Isong Urua Adiakod: The Untold Story and the Politics of Bakassi Handover* (Bloomington, IN: Xlibris Corporation, 2012), 82.

26. As Mélanie Torrent's work illustrates, there is clear evidence that the decisions of the French and British were based on their own interests. Both countries had clear intentions for the future of Cameroon following administrative rule and its influence in the region. The British Colonial Office and Foreign Office firmly believed that Southern Cameroons would not be economically viable independently. Hence, British officials urged for a pro-Nigerian approach to this problem, which also appeased the political leaders of Nigeria. The French identified Ahidjo as a means of establishing French influence in the region. John Foncha was told by officials of both parties, the French and the British, to appeal to the United Nations General Assembly to obtain the option of full independence on the plebiscite. Due to numerous political rivalries in Southern Cameroons, this did not materialize because there was not enough agreement about the independence option on the plebiscite. It was evident that Foncha had considerably less influence in the United Nations than Britain or France. Southern Cameroons was politically divided to the extent that successfully advocating for the independence option was virtually impossible. Mélanie Torrent, *Diplomacy and Nation-Building in Africa: Franco-British Relations and Cameroon at the End of Empire* (London: I. B. Tauris, 2012), 23–27, 29.

27. Atanga, *The Anglophone Cameroon Predicament*, 3; The numbers for West Cameroon were approximately one million individuals in 1964 according to the findings of a 1964 demographic survey of West Cameroon. Ministry of Economic Affairs and Planning, Department of Statistics, *The Population of West Cameroon, Main Findings of the Demographic Sample Survey, 1964* (Paris: Société d'Études pour le Développement Économique et Social, January 1966), 53. See the following for additional population figures: Ministère des Affaires Économiques et du Plan, *La Population du Cameroun Occidental: Résultat de l'Enquête Démographique de 1964* [The Population of West Cameroon: Results of the 1964 Demographic Survey] (Paris: Secrétariat d'État aux Affaires Étrangères, I.N.S.E.E., Département de la Coopération, 1969).

28. O'Rourke, "Foncha, John Ngu," 379; Piet Konings, *Neoliberal Bandwagonism: Civil Society and the Politics of Belonging in Anglophone Cameroon* (Bamenda, Cameroon: Langaa RPCIG; Leiden, the Netherlands: African Studies Centre, 2009), 21.

29. Konings, *Neoliberal Bandwagonism*, 21.

30. The majority of the KNDP leaders were originally members of the KNC, including Salomon T. Muna and Augustine Jua. The KNC was originally established in May 1949 under the name of Cameroons National Federation (CNF). Foncha was responsible

for the KNDP breaking away from the KNC in 1955. DeLancey, Mbuh, and DeLancey, *Historical Dictionary of the Republic of Cameroon*, 90–91, 215–16.

31. Martin Ayong Ayim, *Former British Southern Cameroons Journey Towards Complete Decolonization, Independence, and Sovereignty: A Comprehensive Compilation of Efforts and Historical Documentation*, vol. 1 (Bloomington, IN: AuthorHouse, 2010), 16–17; Nfi, *The Reunification Debate in British Southern Cameroons*, 193; Konings and Nyamnjoh, *Negotiating an Anglophone Identity*, 38.

32. Konings and Nyamnjoh, *Negotiating an Anglophone Identity*, 38.

33. Ibid., 31–34; Torrent, *Diplomacy and Nation-Building in Africa*, 24; Ayim, *Former British Southern Cameroons Journey Towards Complete Decolonization, Independence, and Sovereignty*, 16–17; Nfi, *The Reunification Debate*, 193–94.

34. DeLancey, Mbuh, and DeLancey, *Historical Dictionary of the Republic of Cameroon*, 337.

35. Ibid., 176–77.

36. Mbile, *Cameroon Political Story*, 137.

37. Fonkem Achankeng, "'The Foumban Constitutional Talks' and Prior Intentions of Negotiating: A Historico-Theoretical Analysis of a False Negotiation and the Ramifications for Political Developments in Cameroon," *Journal of Global Initiatives: Policy, Pedagogy, Perspective* 9, no. 2 (2015): 134.

38. Jua and Konings, "Occupation of Public Space," 613, original from P. Messmer, *Les Blancs s'en Vont: Récits de Décolonisation* [The Whites are Leaving: Decolonization Stories] (Paris: Albin Michel, 1998), 134–35; Achankeng, "'The Foumban Constitutional Talks' and Prior Intentions of Negotiating," 135.

39. DeLancey, Mbuh, and DeLancey, *Historical Dictionary of the Republic of Cameroon*, 176–77.

40. Anthony Ndi, *Southern West Cameroon Revisited (1950–1972): Unveiling Inescapable Traps*, vol. 2 (Bamenda, Cameroon: Langaa RPCIG, 2014); 172, 176–79; Jumbam, "Fiftieth Anniversary of Cameroon's Reunification."

41. Konings and Nyamnjoh, "The Anglophone Problem in Cameroon," 212, original from Francis K. Wache, "The Plebiscite: Thirty Years After. The Choice between Fire and Deep Water," *Cameroon Life* 1, no. 8 (1991): 10.

42. For example, see "CNPC Unearths KNDP Sins," *Cameroon Champion*, December 5, 1961, 2.

43. Terretta, *Nation of Outlaws*, 4, 178, 180, 219.

44. Carlson Anyangwe, *Revolutionary Overthrow of Constitutional Orders in Africa* (Bamenda, Cameroon: Langaa RPCIG, 2012), 116. For more on the UPC see Richard Joseph, *Radical Nationalism in Cameroun: Social Origins of the U.P.C. Rebellion* (Oxford: Clarendon Press, 1977); Richard A. Joseph, "Ruben Um Nyobé and the 'Kamerun' Rebellion," *African Affairs* 73, no. 293 (1974): 428–48; Richard Joseph, "National Politics in Postwar Cameroun: The Difficult Birth of the UPC," *Journal of African Studies* 2, no. 2 (1975): 201–29.

45. Peter Tse Angwafo, *Cameroon's Predicaments* (Bamenda, Cameroon: Langaa RP-

CIG, 2014), x. See the following for more information on Ahidjo and (violent) political oppression: Mbembe, *La Naissance Du Maquis*; Achille Mbembe, "Introduction: L'État-Historien" [Introduction: The State Historian] in Ruben Um Nyobé, ed., *Écrits Sous Maquis* (Paris: Editions L'Harmattan, 1989), 10–42; Richard Joseph, ed., *Gaullist Africa: Cameroon under Ahmadu Ahidjo* (Enugu, Nigeria: Fourth Dimension Publishing, 1978).

46. The bloody massacre of Bamiléké by the indigenous Bakossi mob in the majority Bakossi Tombel town occurred on December 31, 1966 as a severe retaliation for the Christmas robbery and murder of four Bakossi allegedly by Bamiléké individuals. The main reason for the ongoing tension was loss of land and business to the Bamiléké migrants, who migrated to the Bakossi area and took up critical positions in the field of commerce. This caused suspicion and resentment among the Bakossi. Consequently, "over 230 Bamiléké were reportedly killed in the massacre, and a military tribunal sentenced 140 Bakossi to various prison terms in a bid to quell the disorder. It is believed that many Bakossi died as a result of government violence." DeLancey, Mbuh, and DeLancey, *Historical Dictionary of the Republic of Cameroon*, 365–66.

47. Anthony Yana Zumafor, interview by author, Buea, July 30, 2015.

48. Nkwi writes that "the Gendarmerie in West Cameroon were introduced because the British and Nigerian Police Force had been withdrawn [due to the independence of the Southern Cameroons] and also because it was thought wise to harmonise federal structures." A 1969 source from the British Archives (TNA) reveals that "West Cameroon retains its own police force and mobile wing. This has lessened the need to bring in the Federal Gendarmerie. But brigade groups (8–10 men) exist in each division of West Cameroon. Each group has one, but only one, local man familiar with the area. The Gendarmerie are disliked in West Cameroon partly because they are 'foreigners' and because of their police powers." Walter Gam Nkwi, "Security or Insecurity: The Gendarmerie and Popular Reaction in West Cameroon, 1961–1964," *African Nebula* 7 (2014), 53, 58; B. Waha, "Authorities Should Intervene," *Cameroon Champion*, December 19, 1961; A. J. Edden, "Constitution of Federal Republic of West and East Cameroon," July 5, 1969, FCO 65/47 TNA Subject: Constitution of Federal Republic of West and East Cameroon.

49. B. Waha, "Authorities Should Intervene," *Cameroon Champion*, December 19, 1961.

50. Konings and Nyamnjoh, *Negotiating an Anglophone Identity*, 55.

51. Richard Joseph, "The Gaullist Legacy: Patterns of French Neo-Colonialism," *Review of African Political Economy* no. 6 (May–Aug. 1976): 4, 7.

52. "President Ahidjo Flies Home after a Successful Visit," West Cameroon press release no. 911, July 19, 1960.

53. Konings and Nyamnjoh, *Negotiating an Anglophone Identity*, 55.

54. Joseph, "The Gaullist Legacy," 7–9.

55. Ibid., 11.

56. DeLancey, Mbuh, and DeLancey, *Historical Dictionary of the Republic of Cameroon*, 27; Joseph, "The Gaullist Legacy," 11–12.

57. Joseph, "The Gaullist Legacy," 12.

58. Torrent, *Diplomacy and Nation-Building*, 90. Edwin Ardener points out that other factors contributed to the UK's decision, such as objections to Cameroon's preferential status among West Indian banana-growers. Edwin Ardener, *Kingdom on Mount Cameroon: Studies in the History of the Cameroon Coast, 1500–1970* (Oxford: Berghahn Books, 1996), 304.

59. Ardener, *Kingdom on Mount Cameroon*, 304.

60. See Emmanual Chiabi, "Redressing Regional Imbalance in Cameroon: The Lessons from the Past," in *Regional Balance and National Integration in Cameroon: Lessons Learned and the Uncertain Future*, ed. Paul Nchoji Nkwi and Francis Beng Nyamnjoh (Bamenda, Cameroon: Langaa RPCIG, 2011), 47–48. Chiabi cites Jacque Benjamin's work as evidence to buttress his argument about low industrialization in West Cameroon. See Benjamin's original findings here: Jacques Benjamin, "The Impact of Federal Institutions on West Cameroon's Economic Activity," in *An African Experiment in Nation Building: The Bi-lingual Cameroon Republic since Reunification*, ed. Ndiva Kofele-Kale (Boulder: Westview Press, 1980), 191–92.

61. Patterson A. Nji, "West Cameroon Denied the Wet Blanket?" *Cameroon Telegraph*, March 19, 1969, 2.

62. The three major parties of West Cameroon were disintegrated: the KNDP, Cameroon People's National Convention (CPNC), and the Cameroon United Congress (CUC). DeLancey, Mbuh, and DeLancey, *Historical Dictionary of the Republic of Cameroon*, 27.

63. President Paul Biya legalized the multiparty system in December 1990. DeLancey, Mbuh, and DeLancey, *Historical Dictionary of the Republic of Cameroon*, 126; Konings and Nyamnjoh, *Negotiating an Anglophone Identity*, 74.

64. Konings and Nyamnjoh, *Negotiating an Anglophone Identity*, 61, 64.

65. Henry Muluh and Bertha Ndoh, "Evolution of the Media in Cameroon," in *Journalism and Mass Communication in Africa: Cameroon*, ed. Festus Eribo and Enoh Tanjong (Lanham, MD: Lexington Books, 2002), 5. Prior to this, as Victor T. Levine pointed out in his work on the early history of the Federal Republic of Cameroon, the press "while not altogether controlled, [was] officially restrained." William Jong-Ebot contends that in addition to strict press laws, debt and poor management also led to the closure of some private newspapers. Victor T. LeVine, *The Cameroon Federal Republic* (Ithaca: Cornell University Press, 1963), 77; William Jong-Ebot, "The Mass Media in Cameroon: An Analysis of Their Post-Colonial Status" (PhD dissertation, University of Wisconsin–Madison, 1989), 178, 180.

66. Carlson Anyangwe, *Imperialistic Politics in Cameroun: Resistance and the Inception of the Restoration of the Statehood of Southern Cameroons* (Bamenda, Cameroon: Langaa RPCIG, 2008), 15. Further evidence of censorship is apparent in foreign reports. A 1979 report by a journalist working for the *Washington Post* in the US, for example, attested that although Cameroonian "citizens talking to a stranger in public are not afraid to criticize the government," "blank spaces in the newspapers" "attest to the censorship" and to Ahidjo's "tight rein on the country's press." United States Department of State Bu-

reau of African Affairs, *AF Press Clips* (1979), 68, original from Leon Dash, "Cameroon, Despite Turbulent Makings, Achieves Stability," *Washington Post*, August 30, 1979.

67. DeLancey, Mbuh, and DeLancey, *Historical Dictionary of the Republic of Cameroon*, 28.

68. Konings and Nyamnjoh, *Negotiating an Anglophone Identity*, 64.

69. Ibid.

70. Perhaps Ahidjo's fears were founded as Konings and Nyamnjoh point out: "Anglophones tended to sympathise with the breakaway Eastern Region of Nigeria that had established itself as the independent Republic of Biafra." Ibid., 64–65.

71. Ibid., 65–66.

72. Anthony Ndi, *The Golden Age of Southern (West) Cameroon: Impact of Christianity* (Bamenda, Cameroon: Langaa RPCIG, 2005), 9.

73. Ibid., 4.

74. Konings, *Neoliberal Bandwagonism*, 21.

75. Ibid., 21–22.

76. Konings and Nyamnjoh, *Negotiating an Anglophone Identity*, 27.

77. Jong-Ebot, "The Mass Media in Cameroon," 140.

78. Ibid., 140–41.

79. Ndi, *The Golden Age of Southern (West) Cameroon*, 4.

80. Zumafor, interviewed by author. Other papers available in the British Southern Cameroons were *Eastern Nigerian Outlook* and *Daily Service*. William Jong-Ebot, "The Mass Media in Cameroon," 140.

81. "Milady's Bower," the women's column in Nnamdi Azikiwe's *West African Pilot*, was published from 1937 to the 1950s. "Miss Silva," the anonymous writer of the column, wrote "several articles on various aspects of relationships and offered advice to lovers." Saheed Aderinto, "Modernizing Love: Gender, Romantic Passion and Youth Literary Culture in Colonial Nigeria," *Africa: Journal of the International African Institute* 85, no. 3 (2015): 480.

82. Zumafor, interviewed by author.

83. Peterson and Hunter contend that "readers could set the agenda, too, by sending letters, asking questions of editors, and contributing their poems and stories. And if they were unhappy with the direction an editor took, they lost no time in making their voices heard." Peterson and Hunter, "Print Culture in Colonial Africa," 13.

84. Ruff Wanzie, "More for You," *Cameroon Times*, February 4, 1964, 1.

85. Ruff Wanzie, "Women's Special," *Cameroon Times*, February 8, 1964, 3.

86. J. N. Mua, "Women Are an Important Factor," *Cameroon Times*, February 8, 1964, 3. Gladys Tombise Difo, the women's special representative in the West Cameroon Legislative Assembly, also shared her gratitude for the reintroduction of the women's page in the *Cameroon Times*. Gladys Tombise Difo, "Calling All Women," *Cameroon Times*, March 21, 1964, 5. See the following for an additional example of a female political elite who openly supported the creation of women's columns: L. Effiom, "Encourage our Native Dances," *Cameroon Times*, February 29, 1964, 3.

87. Vicky Queenta, "Give Us a Women's Column," *Cameroon Telegraph*, December 13, 1968, 2.

88. Mathias Ndifor, "Create Women's Column," *New Cameroon*, September 25, 1970, 2.

89. S. E. Abia, "What Readers Say," *Cameroon Champion*, September 18, 1962, 2. For examples of newspaper editors compiling to readers' requests for the creation of women's columns, see: Sister Starengo, "Women's Column," *Cameroon Voice*, September 14, 1968, 3–4; Ruff Wanzie, "More for You," *Cameroon Times*, February 4, 1964, 5; Ruff Wanzie, "Women's Column," *Cameroon Times*, February 8, 1964, 3,

90. In 1964, Ruff Wanzie guest featured a column by a S. N. Wadhwani, an Indian woman whose husband worked for Cameroon Bank in Buea. Also a journalist, Wadhwani penned a lengthy column about women's lives in India, highlighting the marital, economic and political plight of women. S. N. Wadhwani, "She Meets with Real Friends," *Cameroon Times*, September 12, 1964, 3.

91. Callaci also asserts in her work on urban cultural production in mid- to late twentieth-century Dar es Salaam, Tanzania that "the expansion of networks of communication and media and the concurrent dramatic rise of literacy rates made it possible for people to communicate their urban visions to a wide audience." She contends that "[t]he creation of distinctly female reading publics was linked with the attempts of reformers to make spaces of respectability." Emily Callaci, *Street Archives and City Life: Popular Intellectuals in Postcolonial Tanzania* (Durham: Duke University Press, 2017), 9, 15.

92. Konde, *African Women and Politics*, 122–23.

93. Ibid., 120–22.

94. Ibid., 121.

95. Ibid., 120.

96. Oben, *Women of the Reunification*, 46.

97. Konde, *African Women and Politics*, 86–87, 117, 167, 184.

98. Melinda Jane Adams, "Negotiating the Boundaries of Political Action: Transnational Linkages, Women's Organizations, and the State in Cameroon" (PhD dissertation, University of Wisconsin–Madison, 2004), 70.

99. Modupe Labode, "From Heathen Kraal to Christian Home: Anglican Mission Education and African Christian Girls, 1850–1900," in *Women and Missions: Past and Present: Anthropological and Historical Perceptions*, ed. Fiona Bowie, Deborah Kirkwood, and Shirley Ardener (Oxford: Berg, 1993), 126–44; Fiona Bowie, "The Elusive Christian Family: Missionary Attempts to Define Women's Roles: Case Studies from Cameroon," in *Women and Missions*, ed. Bowie, Kirkwood, and Ardener, 145–64; Tabitha Kanogo, "Mission Impact on Women in Colonial Kenya," in *Women and Missions*, ed. Bowie, Kirkwood, and Ardener, 165–86; Melinda Adams, "Colonial Policies and Women's Participation in Public Life," *African Studies Quarterly* 8, no. 3 (Spring 2006): 6; Michael Kpughe Lang, "Women and Christianity in Cameroon: The Case of the Presbyterian Church in Cameroon Since the Basel Mission Era, 1886–2010," *Afro Asian Journal of Social Sciences* 7, no. 4 (2016): 1–24.

100. Tabitha Kanogo, *African Womanhood in Colonial Kenya, 1900–1950* (Oxford: James Currey; Athens: Ohio University Press, 2005), 203.

101. Nakanyike B. Musisi, "Colonial and Missionary Education: Women and Domesticity in Uganda, 1900–1945," in *African Encounters with Domesticity*, ed. Karen Tranberg Hansen (New Brunswick, NJ: Rutgers University Press, 1992), 172, 174.

102. Nancy Wood Folkerts, interview by Lisa M. Moscati, November 7 and 14, 1984, Billy Graham Center, Wheaton College. Collection 283, Billy Graham Center Archives, Wheaton College, Wheaton, IL.

103. During German rule, the Pallotine Mission, which consisted of mostly German and Swiss individuals, began their activities in 1880. In 1912, the Sacred Heart missionaries began work in Kumbo, a town located in the modern-day Northwest Region. DeLancey, Mbuh, and DeLancey, *Historical Dictionary of the Republic of Cameroon*, 93. See the following for a brief overview of female-led Catholic missionaries in Bamenda, located in the modern-day Northwest Region: Linda Ankiambom Lawyer, "Female Missionary Activities and the Redefinition of Gender Roles in the Bamenda Grassfields of Cameroon, 1904–2006," *International Journal of Liberal Arts and Social Science* 5, no. 3 (2017): 86–101.

104. Charlotte Walker-Said, "Christian Marriage between Tradition and Modernity: Catholic and Protestant Women and Marriage Education in Late Colonial Cameroon, 1939–1960," *Gender & History* 29, no. 3 (2017): 550.

105. Coquery-Vidrovitch, *African Women*, 144; Kenneth J. Orosz, "The 'Affaire des Sixas' and Catholic Education of Women in French Colonial Cameroon, 1915–1939," *French Colonial History* 1, no. 1 (2002): 35, 38; Adams, "Colonial Policies and Women's Participation in Public Life," 5.

106. Mougoué, "African Women Do Not Look Good in Wigs," 10. For additional robust analysis about gender throughout Cameroon, see Miriam Goheen, *Men Own the Fields, Women Own the Crops: Gender and Power in the Cameroon Grassfields* (Madison: University of Wisconsin Press, 1996); Feldman-Savelsberg, *Plundered Kitchens, Empty Wombs*; Jennifer Johnson-Hanks, *Uncertain Honor: Modern Motherhood in an African Crisis* (Chicago: University of Chicago Press, 2006); Emmanuel Yenshu Vubo, *Gender Relations in Cameroon: Multidisciplinary Perspectives* (Bamenda, Cameroon: Langaa RPCIG, 2012); Phyllis Mary Kaberry, *Women of the Grassfields: A Study of the Economic Position of Women in Bamenda, British Cameroons* (London: Her Majesty's Stationery Office, 1952).

107. Karen Tranberg Hansen, "Introduction," in *African Encounters with Domesticity*, ed. Karen Tranberg Hansen (New Brunswick, NJ: Rutgers University Press, 1992), 2.

108. Kanogo, *African Womanhood in Colonial Kenya, 1900–1950*, 2.

109. Nancy Rose Hunt, *A Colonial Lexicon: Of Birth Ritual, Medicalization, and Mobility in the Congo* (Durham: Duke University Press, 1999), 10.

110. Adams, "Colonial Policies and Women's Participation in Public Life," 3.

111. Additional examples include the Ndola Bitu Women's Fellowship and the Ladies Glee Club in Mamfe. Konde, *African Women and Politics*, 93.

112. The UFC changed its name to *L 'Association des Femmes Camerounaises* (AFC) in 1953 as a means of distancing itself from the more radical UDEFEC. Adams, "Negotiating the Boundaries of Political Action," 73–75.

113. Shanklin, "Anlu Remembered," 164; Kah, "Women's Resistance in Cameroon's Western Grassfields," 73; S. Ardener, "Sexual Insult and Female Militancy," 436.

114. DeLancey, Mbuh, and DeLancey, *Historical Dictionary of the Republic of Cameroon*, 357; Konde, *African Women and Politics*, 50. Also cited in Mougoué, "The Anlu Rebellion." See the following for a brief overview of women's shaming practices in Africa: Kathleen Sheldon, *Historical Dictionary of Women in Sub-Saharan Africa* (Lanham, MD: Rowman & Littlefield, 2016), 265.

115. Yuval-Davis, *Gender and Nation*, 24.

116. Adams, "Colonial Policies and Women's Participation in Public Life," 8–9.

117. Oben, *Women of the Reunification*, 54.

118. Konde, *African Women and Politics*, 144.

119. Fadimatou Abdoulayé was the first female politician from the predominately Muslim Far North Region, serving from 1973 to 1988. Konde, *African Women and Politics*, 118. See the following historical overview about female parliamentarians in Cameroon: Henry Kam Kah, "Cameroonian Women in Political Leadership, 1960–2015," *Afro Asian Journal of Social Sciences* 9, no. 2 (2016): 1–25.

120. World Bank, United Nations Population Division, "World Urbanization Prospects: 2018 Revision: Urban Population (% of total)," accessed December 14, 2018, https://data.worldbank.org/indicator/SP.URB.TOTL.IN.ZS?locations=CM

121. Ministry of Economic Affairs and Planning, Department of Statistics, *The Population of West Cameroon, Main Findings of the Demographic Sample Survey, 1964*, 59.

122. 55.7 percent of the total population of West Cameroon, that is 574,164 individuals, lived in northern West Cameroon, where Bamenda is located, whereas 44.3 percent lived in southern West Cameroon, where Buea is located. Ibid., 59–60.

123. L'OFUNC, *Visages de la Femme Camerounaise* [Faces of the Cameroonian Woman] (Yaoundé, Cameroon: Ateliers Graphiques du Cameroun, 1975), 66, 72.

124. But as DeLancey, Neh Mbuh, and DeLancey document, the activities of the CDC "were initially concentrated in the South West but later expanded into the North West with a tea estate at Ndu" (*Historical Dictionary of the Republic of Cameroon*, 6, 83); Ministry of Economic Affairs and Planning, Department of Statistics, *The Population of West Cameroon, Main Findings of the Demographic Sample Survey, 1964*, 60.

125. Piet Konings, *Gender and Plantation Labour in Africa: The Story of Tea Pluckers' Struggles in Cameroon* (Bamenda, Cameroon: Langaa RPCIG; Leiden, the Netherlands: African Studies Centre, 2012); Piet Konings, *Gender and Class in the Tea Estates of Cameroon* (Leiden, the Netherlands: African Studies Centre, 1995); Virginia H. Delancey, "The Relationship between Female Wage Employment and Fertility in Africa: An Example from Cameroon" (PhD dissertation, University of South Carolina, 1981).

126. L'OFUNC, *Visages de la Femme Camerounaise* [Faces of the Cameroonian Woman], 72.

127. Statistics from December 1962 show that women worked in various sectors of the professional workforce: there were approximately 325 female teachers and tutors, one radiographer, one doctor, eight administrative officers, and eight education officers.

L'OFUNC, *Visages de la Femme Camerounaise* [Faces of the Cameroonian Woman], 72. Dorothy Gwan-Nula, "Our Women's Roles in Family and Society: Part Two," *Cameroon Times*, May 2, 1964, 5. Ministry of Economic Affairs and Planning, Department of Statistics, *The Population of West Cameroon, Main Findings of the Demographic Sample Survey, 1964*, 165–66.

128. More detailed 1964 statistics show that in the large towns of Bamenda, Mamfe, Kumba, Tiko, Buea, and Victoria, 33 percent of women fifteen and older engaged in traditional agriculture for income, 16.2 percent engaged in trade and crafts, 2.3 percent in the administrative sector, 0.3 percent in domestic service, and a negligible number in the armed forces and police. Ministry of Economic Affairs and Planning, Department of Statistics, *The Population of West Cameroon, Main Findings of the Demographic Sample Survey, 1964*, 164, 166, 177.

129. Rebecca Mbuh, "African Women's Quest for Equality: The Case of Cameroon," in *Women in the New Millennium: The Global Revolution*, ed. Anne R. Breneman and Rebecca N. Mbuh (Lanham, MD: Hamilton Books, 2006), 77.

130. There are no corresponding statistics offered for the West Cameroon State. L'OFUNC, *Visages de la Femme Camerounaise* [Faces of the Cameroonian Woman], 64.

131. Ministry of Economic Affairs and Planning, Department of Statistics, *The Population of West Cameroon, Main Findings of the Demographic Sample Survey, 1964*, 148.

132. Jude Fokwang reports that "[h]igher education started in Cameroon in 1961, following the establishment of the National Institute for University Studies in Yaoundé. In 1962, the Institute was renamed the Federal University of Cameroon." Jude Fokwang, "Student Activism, Violence and the Politics of Higher Education in Cameroon: A Case Study of the University of Buea (1993–2003)," in *Youth and Higher Education in Africa. The Cases of Cameroon, South Africa, Eritrea and Zimbabwe*, ed. Donald P. Chimanikire (Dakar, Senegal: Council for the Development of Social Science Research in Africa, 2009), 11; L'OFUNC, *Visages de la Femme Camerounaise* [Faces of the Cameroonian Woman], 66.

133. Fidelia Ngum (pseud.), interview by author, Buea, November 4, 2011.

134. For examples see Ruff Wanzie, "Which Is Your Perfect Wife?" *Cameroon Times*, August 15, 1964, 3; Ruff Wanzie, "Which Is Your Perfect Wife? (2)," *Cameroon Times*, August 22, 1964, 3; Cousin Lizzy, "A Wife Can Help Her Husband to the Top," *Cameroon Times*, August 24, 1972, 2.

135. Ruff Wanzie, "Behave Well, Women," *Cameroon Times*, August 8, 1964, 3.

136. Asong Martha Ebey, interview by author, Buea, Cameroon, November 8, 2011.

137. Bekene Eyambe (pseud.), interview by author, Buea, Cameroon, November 8, 2011; Ebey, interview by author. To learn more about the kabba dress, see Flavius Mokake, "The Kabba Dress: Identity and Modernity in Contemporary Cameroon," in *Marginality and Crisis: Globalization and Identity in Contemporary Africa*, ed. Akanmu G. Adebayo, Olutayo Adesina, and Rasheed O. Olaniyi, 71–80 (Lanham, MD: Lexington Books, 2010).

138. Ebey, interview by author.

139. Awasom, "Towards Historicizing the Ossification of Colonial Identities in Africa," 58.

140. Ndi, *The Golden Age of Southern (West) Cameroon*, 4, 7.

141. Ndi, *The Golden Age of Southern (West) Cameroon*, 4–5. Although East Cameroon did have two influential private French-language papers, most notably *La Presse du Cameroun* and the Catholic paper *L'Effort Camerounaise*, both papers may have survived during the federal period "because they avoided the trappings politics." The *Cameroun Tribune*, today the official government newspaper, eventually replaced *La Presse du Cameroun*. Muluh and Ndoh, "Evolution of the Media in Cameroon," 4.

142. Ministry of Economic Affairs and Planning, Department of Statistics, *The Population of West Cameroon, Main Findings of the Demographic Sample Survey, 1964*, 59. See the following for additional information about the urban development of Victoria and Buea: Thomas Ngomba Ekali, "The Fluctuating Fortunes of Anglophone Cameroon Towns: The Case of Victoria, 1858–1982," in *African Urban Spaces in Historical Perspective*, ed. Steven J. Salm and Toyin Falola (Rochester, NY: University of Rochester Press, 2005), 320–39; Georges Courade, "The Urban Development of Buea: An Essay in Social Geography," paper presented to the International Colloquium of the Centre National de la Recherche Scientifique -Social Science on "Urban Growth in Black Africa and Madagascar," September 29th to October 2nd 1970, Centre d'Études de Geographie Tropicale, Bordeaux, France (Yaoundé, Cameroon: ORSTOM, 1970), horizon.documentation.ird.fr/exl-doc/pleins_textes/pleins_textes_7/carton04/02655.pdf

143. Makossa, which began in the 1950s, originated in Douala, Cameroon. In the Duala language the word means, "make me dance." The urban musical style has prominent bass rhythms. DeLancey, Mbuh, and DeLancey, *Historical Dictionary of the Republic of Cameroon*, 129–30, 235, 258; John Mukum Mbaku, *Culture and Customs of Cameroon* (Westport, CT: Greenwood Press, 2005), 200.

144. Ebey, interview by author.

145. Piet Konings, "The Anglophone Cameroon-Nigeria Boundary: Opportunities and Conflicts," *African Affairs* 104, no. 415 (2005): 275–301.

146. Ben West, *Cameroon* (Chalfont St. Peter, UK: Bradt Travel Guides Ltd., 2011), 130; Nfi, *The Reunification Debate in British Southern Cameroons*, 39–40. See the following for a fuller history of the Bakweri people: Ardener, *Kingdom on Mount Cameroon*, vii, 261.

147. "Cameroonian Lady Made Manageress," West Cameroon press release no. 4712, Jan. 7, 1966; "First Lady Doctor for the Cameroon, How does this Help the Doctors?" *Cameroon Champion*, November 30, 1962, 3.

148. Ndi, *The Golden Age of Southern (West) Cameroon*, 5–6.

CHAPTER 2

1. G. M. N. Lisinge, "Sluggish Women," *Cameroon Times*, July 11, 1964, 3.

2. Rukhsana A. Siddiqui, ed., *Sub-Saharan Africa in the 1990s: Challenges to De-*

mocracy and Development (Westport, CT: Praeger, 1997), 165; Iris Berger and E. Frances White, *Women in Sub-Saharan Africa: Restoring Women to History* (Bloomington: Indiana University Press, 1999), 57.

3. "The Role of Women in Our Modern Society," *Cameroon Champion*, November 27, 1962, 3.

4. Oben, *Women of the Reunification*, 54.

5. Benedict Anderson, *Imagined Communities*, 5–6.

6. Bejeng, *Dr. John Ngu Foncha*, 7.

7. Anna Atang Foncha, interview by Walter Gam Nkwi, Bamenda, March 5, 2011.

8. St. Joseph's Mission is the present-day Cathedral Parish and seat of the archdiocese of Bamenda. Bejeng, *Dr. John Ngu Foncha*, 6; Ndi, *Southern West Cameroon Revisited (1950–1972)*, 218.

9. Bejeng, *Dr. John Ngu Foncha*, 7–9.

10. Ibid., 6.

11. As the biographer writes, Anna Foncha's father stated "that he had been told that women who studied up to her level tended to end up not getting married." Ibid., 8.

12. Ibid., 9.

13. Bejeng, *Dr. John Ngu Foncha*, 9; O'Rourke, "Foncha, John Ngu," 379.

14. Oben, *Women of the Reunification*, 22.

15. Foncha, interview by Walter Gam Nkwi; "Madam Foncha Lays Foundation Stone for the Buea Nursery School," West Cameroon press release no. 3124, April 24, 1964; "Federation of Women's Social Clubs Thank Donators," West Cameroon press release no. 3182, May 20, 1964; "Nursery School to Be Formally Opened," West Cameroon press release no. 3912, April 29, 1965; "Address by Madam A. A. Foncha on the Occasion of the Formal Opening of the Buea Nursery School 3rd May 1965," West Cameroon press release no. 3922, May 5, 1965; "1.5 m Francs Nursery School Opens in Buea Soon," *Cameroon Times*, September 19, 1964, 3.

16. Anna Foncha, "My Life as the P.M.'s Wife," *Cameroon Times*, February 8, 1964, 3–4.

17. Ruff Wanzie, "When Madam Foncha Toured Overseas Countries," *Cameroon Times*, July 18, 1964, 3.

18. Adams, "Negotiating the Boundaries of Political Action," 101.

19. Foncha, interview by Walter Gam Nkwi. I also spoke at length about Anna Foncha's CWA activities with one of her granddaughters. Marie Thérèse Guessou, interview by author, via Skype, February 26, 2016.

20. Wanzie, "When Madam Foncha Toured Overseas Countries," 3.

21. Konde, *African Women and Politics*, 121, 143.

22. Konde, *African Women and Politics*, 191; Asheri Jedida, *Promise* (Lagos, Nigeria: African University Press, 1969).

23. Oben, *Women of the Reunification*, 54–56.

24. As Endeley's biographer explains about her father, he "believed that there were no two measures in education. . . . and so for his family, education was a given." Ibid.,

50. Gladys's sisters were educated as follows: Hannah and Sarah were the first girls to attend Normal College, located in Buea, during the 1930s. The college was the highest educational institution in the British Cameroons at the time. Priscilla attended a Teacher's Training College in Nigeria and earned a diploma in education in the UK. Kate, later Kate Idowu, or "Auntie Kate," went on to become a prominent domestic science teacher (see chapter 3 for more on her biography). Maria attended nursing school in Nigeria. Mukete, *Cameroon Reunification*, 456–57.

25. In fact, according to her biographer, Endeley's presence in the north paved the way for Yaou Aïssatou, a Muslim woman politician from the north. Oben, *Women of the Reunification*, 52–53.

26. Ibid., 50.

27. Ibid.

28. Ibid., 51.

29. Ibid.; "[Obituary] Samuel Moka Liffafa Endeley (1923–2015): Pharmacist, Barrister-at-Law, Chief Justice, Paramount Chief of Buea, *Bakwerirama*, July 9, 2015, https://www.bakweri.com/2015/07/obituary-sml-endeley.html; Oben, *Women of the Reunification*, 51.

30. Oben, *Women of the Reunification*, 51.

31. Ibid., 56.

32. Ibid., 52–54. Konde, *African Women and Politics*, 118, 125, 138. See the following interview with Delphine Tsanga for additional information on how her novels highlight issues of gender in Cameroonian society: Delphine Tsanga, interview by David Ndachi Tagne, Yaoundé, August 1996. http://aflit.arts.uwa.edu.au/intDNTzanga.html

33. Oben, *Women of the Reunification*, 51.

34. Ibid.

35. Gladys Silo Endeley's daughter, Mariana Mojoko Endeley-Matute, currently a pharmacist in the United States, spoke with me in 2015. Mariana Endeley-Matute, interview by author on May 30, 2015, via Skype. Digital audio file. Institute for Oral History, Baylor University, Waco, TX.

36. Elvis Tah, "Endeley Buries Wife," *Cameroon Postline*, April 12, 2010, http://www.cameroonpostline.com/endeley-buries-wife/

37. Adams, "Negotiating the Boundaries of Political Action," 82. Adams notes, for instance, that "[i]n 1962, Francophone and Anglophone women activists attempted unsuccessfully to form a national organization" (79).

38. Adams, "Negotiating the Boundaries of Political Action," 100.

39. See the following work by Stephanie Newell for an example of such discussions: Newell, *West African Literatures: Ways of Reading*, 149–50.

40. For an example of such a debate, see Moghadam, *Globalization and Social Movements*, 134, originally cited by Sperling, Ferree, and Risman, "Constructing Global Feminism: Transnational Advocacy Networks and Russian Women's Activism," 1158; Ferree argues that "feminism and women's movements dynamically affect each other." Ferree,

"Globalization and Feminism: Opportunities and Obstacles for Activism in the Global Arena," 8.

41. Mama, "Feminism or Femocracy?" 41.

42. My research indicates that by March 1964, the WSCA started to go by the name CWI, coincidentally coinciding with the first observation of Women's Day on March 31, 1964. Thereafter, Anna Foncha started to be referenced as the president of the CWI (not WSCA). "Women to Observe March 31 as Women's Day," West Cameroon press release no. 3267, November 20, 1964; "Madam Foncha Visits Bafreng," West Cameroon press release no. 3628, November 20, 1964.

43. Women's social clubs were invited to register their clubs with WSCA in May 1962. "West Cameroon Federation of Women Social Club to Hold Council Meeting in Bamenda," West Cameroon press release no. 2495, June 27, 1963; "Calling All Women's Social Clubs," West Cameroon press release no. 1844, May 7, 1962.

44. References to the KNDP women's wing can be found here: "Madam Foncha Receives Party Women," *Cameroon Times*, February 9, 1965, 1.

45. "Madam Foncha Opens Leadership Training Course for Leaders of Women Social Clubs," West Cameroon press release no. 3856, March 30, 1965; "Women's Institutes Get Award," *Cameroon Times*, February 14, 1967, 2; "Women's Leadership Course Opened," *Cameroon Times*, April 3, 1965, 1, 4.

46. Konde, *African Women and Politics*, 157; Adams, "Negotiating the Boundaries of Political Action," 103; "Cameroon Admitted into Women's World Organisation," West Cameroon press release, November, 13, 1968; "President of World Associated Country Women Visits Cameroon," West Cameroon press release no. 295, March 25, 1967; Noelle A. Baker, ed., *Stanton in Her Own Time: A Biographical Chronicle of Her Life, Drawn from Recollections, Interviews, and Memoirs by Family, Friends, and Associates* (Iowa City: University of Iowa Press, 2016), 135.

47. The WCNU secured affiliation with the International Council of Women in the early 1970s. Adams, "Negotiating the Boundaries of Political Action," 103.

48. Samgena Galega and Martha Tumnde, "Reversing Decades of Gender Injustice in Cameroon," in *The Leadership Challenge in Africa: Cameroon under Paul Biya*, ed. John Mukum Mbaku and Joseph Takougang (Trenton, NJ: Africa World Press, 2004), 238. Germaine Ahidjo gave a speech in 1965 to National Council of Cameroonian Women (NCCW) members in which she emphasized the apolitical status of the NCCW. She is quoted as asserting: "Le Conseil n'est pas une formation politique. Son principal objectif, c'est l'éducation et l'amélioration de la condition de la femme Camerounaise" ["The Council is not a political party. Its main objective is the education and the improvement of the condition of the Cameroonian woman"]. "Femmes Camerounaises, au Travail dans le Paix et l'Union" [Cameroonian Women, Working in Peace and Union], *L'Effort Camerounais*, March 7 1965, 1.

49. A WCNU leader had to publicly refute claims that women's organization were solely for women who underwent formal education. Angela L. Yesi, president of the

subsection of the WCNU-Ndop, stated publicly in a 1967 WCNU conference that the WCNU was open to women of all educational backgrounds. She submitted a statement to the *Cameroon Times* condemning women who did not want to participate in the WCNU because they felt that they were not educated enough. She asserted that all "women have a big part to play in the building of a nation," irrespective of their educational status. "W.C.N.U. not for Educated Women Only," *Cameroon Times*, October 12, 1967, 4. Yet, my informants often implied that mostly formally educated women participated in women's organizations. For example: Christina Ambe Manka, survey conducted by Nevian Fonkwa, Bamenda, November 17, 2011.

50. As Samgena Galega and Martha Tumnde argue, "Instead of encouraging women to increase their participation in entrepreneurial activities and the professions, the new party [the CNU] chose to emphasize traditional roles for women. Thus, women were encouraged to become good housewives and engage in such domestic activities as knitting, sewing, cooking and taking care of the household." Galega and Tumnde, "Reversing Decades of Gender Injustice in Cameroon," 237–79.

51. For example, in 1962 journalist Clara Manga shared news that in March of that year, women delegates from East and West Cameroon held a 2-day conference at the Victoria Community Hall in Victoria and the Buea Mountain Club in Buea; many of the attendees appeared to be leaders of women's organizations. Anna Foncha gave a welcome address that was translated in French for the Francophone female delegates and the Secretary General of the Francophone delegate gave a thank you speech that was translated in Cameroonian pidgin English for the Anglophone female delegates. In a second example, Adams writes that in 1964, CWI representatives traveled to Yaoundé "for a conference on women in agriculture and prostitution and juvenile delinquency." In a third example, although they did so rarely, Anna Foncha and President Ahidjo's wife, Germaine Ahidjo, also communicated about West Cameroonian women's organizations, such as during the reunification celebrations that occurred in West Cameroon in 1964. At this event, Anna Foncha introduced Germaine Ahidjo to the leaders of a women's group on Germaine's arrival at the Tiko Airport. Auntie Clara, "Women's Column," *Cameroon Champion*, April 3, 1962, 3; "Mrs. Ahidjo in West Cameroon," *Cameroon Times*, October 1, 1964, 3; Ruff Wanzie, "Cheers for the Women," *Cameroon Times*, October 6, 1964, 3. Adams, "Negotiating the Boundaries of Political Action," 83.

52. Adams, "Negotiating the Boundaries of Political Action," 87.

53. Aili Mari Tripp, *Women and Politics in Uganda* (Madison: University of Wisconsin Press, 2000), 8.

54. Ruff Wanzie, "Madam Foncha's Place Among Women," *Cameroon Times*, October 24, 1964, 3.

55. "Madam Foncha Receives Party Women," *Cameroon Times*, February 9, 1965, 1.

56. "Council of Women's Institutes Executive Meet," West Cameroon press release no. 4526, November 18, 1965.

57. "W.C.N.U. Calls for Merger with Women's Institutes," West Cameroon press release no. 848, October 18, 1967; "WCNU Bamenda wants Merger with Council of Women's Institutes," *Cameroon Times*, October 18, 1967, 4.

58. For an additional example of male politicians "observing" the meetings of women's organizations see "Community Development Starts from the House—Women Told," *Cameroon Scope*, July 25, 1970, 2; "'Our Problem Is Knowing What to Discard' - Lafon," West Cameroon press release no. 438, May 26, 1967.

59. Female politicians such as Burnley displayed their sensitivity to this dynamic when they invoked conservative politics by encouraging men to support their wives in nationalist activities by "[h]old[ing] the hands of their wives, in the race" to raise the standards of living in their communities and the country as a whole. "Show [me the] women of the country and I know what the men are," she said to men and women at a Community Development Training Center in Kumba, implying that women's empowerment is a barometer of national development. By inferring that women are the markers of national progress, Burnley strove to emphasize women's social importance, thus legitimizing their nationalist activities just as her counterparts across Africa did during the era of decolonization and nationalist politics in the mid- to late twentieth century. "Show Me the Women and I Know What the Men Are," *Cameroon Voice*, September 23, 1968, 1. For examples of women's nationalist activities in twentieth-century Africa, see Corrie Decker, *Mobilizing Zanzibari Women: The Struggle for Respectability and Self-Reliance in Colonial East Africa* (New York: Palgrave Macmillan, 2014); Laura Bier, *Revolutionary Womanhood: Feminisms, Modernity, and the State in Nasser's Egypt* (Stanford: Stanford University Press, 2011).

60. In June 1966, the *Cameroon Times* posted a retraction to previous claims that Anna Foncha had asked the CWI to have their "hands off politics" after she submitted a letter of complaint. In her letter she denied the assertion, writing that "women have a specific contribution to make, not only as efficient home manageress, but we must also take an active part in the political life of our country as well as in its social and economic development." "Madam Foncha Denies Report," *Cameroon Times*, June 28, 1966, 3.

61. Anna Foncha's dedication to spreading messages about the importance of women's organizations extended to female Cameroonian students studying abroad. In October 1965, during a three-week tour of England and Ireland, she toured several cities, had tea with Mary Wilson, wife of the UK prime minister at the time, and visited the Cameroon embassy. A speech she gave at the time for Cameroonian female university students at the British Cameroon embassy praises the significance of the CWI and asserts that "no nation could advance properly if the womenfolk were left behind." Yet she argued, "men in Cameroon had advanced much further than the women," and she described women's organizations as the way to catch up. She instructed the university students to remember that they were ambassadors of Cameroon and that their behaviors and attitudes might "make or mar Cameroon['s] reputation in Britain," suggesting the need to adhere to moral standards across national borders. "Madam Foncha Returns Home," West Cameroon press release no. 4422, October 18, 1965.

62. Modeka and Missellele are towns in southwest Cameroon. "Madam Foncha Visits Modeka and Missellele Women," West Cameroon press release no. 35341, October 14, 1964.

63. Kumba is a city located in southwest Cameroon. "Madam Foncha Completes Tour of Kumba Division," West Cameroon press release no. 3581, November 4, 1964; "Madam Anna Foncha Completes Tour of Bamenda Province," West Cameroon press release no. 3630, November 23, 1964.

64. L. Effiom, "Encourage our Native Dances," *Cameroon Times*, February 29, 1964, 3.

65. Ruff Wanzie, "Prestige of Women," *Cameroon Times*, August 1, 1964, 3; Ruff Wanzie, "Ekona Women Entertained Mrs. Foncha and her Escorts with Various Native Dances," *Cameroon Times*, October 31, 1964, 4.

66. Militz and Schurr, "Affective Nationalism," 54–55.

67. Ruff Wanzie, "Women's Day Celebrations," *Cameroon Times*, March 12, 1966, 3.

68. "Women to Observe March 31 as Women's Day," West Cameroon press release no. 3627, November 20, 1964.

69. Ruff Wanzie, "Women's Day Celebrations," *Cameroon Times*, March 12, 1966, 3.

70. "Address Delivered by her Excellency Madam J. N. Foncha on the Occasion of the Inauguration of Women's Day and the Launching of the Council of Women's Institute's Newsletter: Wednesday March 1965," West Cameroon press release no. 3864, March 31, 1965; "Women's Day Born," *Cameroon Times*, April 1–2, 1965, 1, 3.

71. "Address by the Secretary of State for Education and Social Welfare to the Women's Day Rally, Wednesday 31st March, 1965," West Cameroon press release no. 3863, March 31, 1965.

72. "Women Celebrate Their Day," West Cameroon press release no. 4978, April 4, 1966; "Madame Muna Calls on West Cameroon to Unite," West Cameroon press release, April 10, 1968.

73. For instance, Ruff Wanzie revealed information about a CWI meeting when she exalted the important roles of women's organizations in developing the nation in a July 1964 article titled "Women Step Forward." She asserts that "[w]omen's clubs in the young nation of West Cameroon are really working very hard to contribute economically, educationally and socially to the building of the nation." She explains that during one CWI council meeting, women decided to send a collective letter to the government outlining their "grievances over immoral practices in the community, juvenile delinquency, and disrespect for the prestige of women," thus "appealing to the government to look into these points and remedy the situation." She discloses that Gladys Tombise Difo, the women's special representative in the West Cameroon Legislative Assembly, would forward the letter to the government. Wanzie, "Women Step Forward," *Cameroon Times*, July 18, 1964, 3.

74. Clara Manga, originally from the coast of West Cameroon, lived in Lagos, Nigeria, for many years with her first husband, Joki Manga. Zumafor, interview by author.

75. Auntie Clara, "Women's Clubs and Organisations," *Cameroon Champion*, February 27, 1962, 3.

76. Ibid., 4.

77. Ruff Wanzie, "Our Women in the Home and Office," *Cameroon Times*, October 16, 1966, 3; Thomas Hale, "Griottes: Female Voices from West Africa," *Research in African Literatures* 25, no. 3 (1994): 78.

78. "Duties of the Woman Representative," *Cameroon Times*, September 26, 1964, 4.

79. Peterson and Hunter, "Print Cultures in Colonial Africa," 5.

80. Ruff Wanzie, "Our Women in the Home and Office," *Cameroon Times*, October 16, 1966, 3.

81. Auntie Clara, "Women's Column," *Cameroon Champion*, February 6, 1962, 3–4. As Nji writes: "[t]he brief descriptions that follow are in broad strokes. . . . [But] [i]n all Cameroon's sub-cultures, women are considered subject to male authority. Male characteristics are considered central to the decision making process at family, community and national levels. Cultural prescriptions that subject women to male authority include rules of inheritance, births and deaths, work, childcare, sex and reproduction, and a host of traditional rites, too many and varied, to list here." Ajaga Nji, "Socio-Cultural Determinants of the Status of the Cameroonian Woman: Implications for the Family in the 21st Century," in *The Anthropology of Africa: Challenges for the 21st Century*, ed. Paul Nchoji Nkwi (Bamenda, Cameroon: Langaa RPCIG, 2015), 322–23.

82. Auntie Clara, "Women's Column," *Cameroon Champion*, February 6, 1962, 3–4.

83. In April 1966, Anna Foncha explained that her visit to women in Bamenda was a "family visit." During her visit she urged women "to unite and organize dynamic social clubs for the growth of the nation." "Madam Foncha Meets Bamenda Women," West Cameroon press release no. 5031, May 12, 1966.

84. Wanzie, "Women Can Now Be Proud," *Cameroon Times*, December 5, 1964, 3.

85. Cristina Devereaux Ramírez, *Occupying Our Space: The Mestiza Rhetorics of Mexican Women Journalists and Activists, 1875–1942* (Tucson: University of Arizona Press, 2015), 63.

86. For an example, see Gwendoline Burnley's statement in the *Cameroon Times*, "Do Not Make Me Dumb in Parliament," *Cameroon Times*, May 1, 1968, 7.

87. Auntie Clara, "Women's Column," *Cameroon Champion*, July 27, 1962, 3.

88. Gladys Difo, "Calling All Women," *Cameroon Times*, March 21, 1964, 5.

89. Lilian Lem Atanga and Alexandre T. Djimeli, "Women in Politics and the Media: The Discursive Construction of Collaboration for Female Leadership in Cameroon," in *Discourse, Politics and Women as Global Leaders*, ed. John Wilson and Diana Boxer (Amsterdam: John Benjamins, 2015), 169–91.

90. Atanga and Djimeli, "Women in Politics and the Media," 181.

91. See, for example, Jean Marie Allman, "'Let Your Fashion Be in Line with Our Ghanaian Costume': Nation, Gender, and the Politics of Clothing in Nkrumah's Ghana," in *Fashioning Africa: Power and the Politics of Dress*, ed. Jean Marie Allman (Bloomington: Indiana University Press, 2004), 144–65.

92. Marie Grace Brown, "Fashioning Their Place: Dress and Global Imagination in Imperial Sudan," in *Gender, Imperialism and Global Exchanges*, ed. Stephan F. Miescher, Michele Mitchell, and Naoko Shibusawa (West Sussex, UK: Wiley-Blackwell, 2015), 115; Allman, "'Let Your Fashion Be in Line with Our Ghanaian Costume,'" 144–65.

93. The designer of the winning costume would receive 10,000 Central African francs as their prize. Auntie Clara, "West Cameroon Federation of Women Social Clubs and Associations Announce a 'National Costume for Women' Competition," *Cameroon Champion*, August 10, 1962, 3; "West Cameroon Federation of Women Social Club to hold Council Meeting in Bamenda," West Cameroon press release no. 2495, June 27, 1963; Auntie Clara, "Women's Column," *Cameroon Champion*, July 27, 1962, 3.

94. Ruff Wanzie, "Cameroon Women's National Costume," *Cameroon Times*, February 29, 1964, 3.

95. Ruff Wanzie, "West Cameroon Women's National Costume," *Cameroon Times*, August 15, 1964, 3; Ruff Wanzie, "Women's National Costume," *Cameroon Times*, August 29, 1964, 3.

96. Zumafor, interview by author. For more on the history of varied cloths in the Bamenda Grassfields, see Elizabeth M. Chilver, "Nineteenth Century Trade in the Bamenda Grassfields, Southern Cameroons," *Afrika und Übersee* 45, no. 4 (1961): 233–58.

97. J. A. Kisob, "An Appreciation of Bamenda Traditional Costume," *Abbia: Revue Culturelle Camerounaise* 3 (1963): 64; Ruff Wanzie, "Cameroon Women's National Costume," *Cameroon Times*, February 29, 1964, 3.

98. Kisob, "An Appreciation of Bamenda Traditional Costume," 65.

99. Anna Foncha, "Our Women Should Accept and Use Our National Dress," *Cameroon Times*, March 14, 1964, 3.

100. Anna Foncha continued to urge people to wear the West Cameroonian costume to a beauty contest in Buea in February 1964, which according to my interviews led women from across social classes to obtain such a costume; in December 1964 Ruff Wanzie described "[l]ocal designers bend[ing] their heads everyday on designing materials for the West Cameroon women's costume" in anticipation of Christmas. By late 1964, use of the costume had increased. Ibid.; Ebey, interview by author; Ruff Wanzie, "The Grand Occasion of Christmas," *Cameroon Times*, December 12, 1964, 3.

101. Today, many Anglophone Cameroonians continue to wear the Bamenda cloth for traditional weddings and other formal occasions as well as feasts and festivals. The nation-building endeavors of Anglophone women in the federal period continue to resonate in the contemporary era. For examples, see Comfort Mussa, "Cameroon's Fashion Designers Modernize Cultural Attire for the Catwalk," *Global Press Journal*, July 13, 2013, https://globalpressjournal.com/africa/cameroon/cameroon-s-fashion-designers-modernize-cultural-attire-for-the-catwalk/; "Cameroon: Designer finds Fashionable ways to Promote Ancient Toghu Cloth," *Africa News*, November 25, 2017, https://www.africanews.com/amp/2017/11/25/cameroon-designer-finds-fashionable-ways-to-promote-ancient-toghu-cloth/

102. The two other smaller political parties were the Cameroon United Congress

(CUC) and the Cameroon People's Convention (CPNC). Female political elites extolled the merger by trying to convince female KNDP supporters to support the merging of West Cameroonian political parties. For instance, in a 1966 address to women in Muyuka, Natalia Jua "called on them to support the KNDP/CPNC merger. She asked them to forget political differences and said that nothing could be achieved without unity." "Madam Jua Addresses Muyuka KNDP Women's Executive," West Cameroon press release no. 4805, Feb. 12, 1966; DeLancey, Mbuh, and DeLancey, *Historical Dictionary of the Republic of Cameroon*, 27.

103. "Women's CNU Sub-Sections Celebrate CNU Anniversary," West Cameroon press release no. 735, September 5, 1967.

104. "WCNU Bamenda Wants Merger with Council of Women's Institutes," *Cameroon Times*, October 18, 1967, 4; "Madam Foncha Clears the Air," *Cameroon Times*, November 1, 1967, 1, 4, 8.

105. "Hands on Deck, Women!" *Cameroon Times*, April 11, 1968, 1.

106. "Madam Foncha Clears the Air," *Cameroon Times*, November 1, 1967, 4.

107. A fuller transcription of Foncha's speech reads thus: "[A] woman who is a member of our Party [CNU] must not, at the same time, belong to any other organization which is subject to or controlled and supported by another political party. Thus, women who are both members of our Party [CNU] and of the CWI have a duty to the Party. This duty is to report and to discontinue their membership of the CWI at any moment they find that the CWI is influenced by or subject to the authority of another political party or is working against our Party [CNU]. . . . Since most or all members of the CWI are also members of the WCNU, the two should have no difficulty to work in harmony." Ibid.

108. Adams, "Negotiating the Boundaries of Political Action," 26, 102.

109. "Madam Foncha Thanked for Clarifying CWI-WCNU Membership," *Cameroon Times*, November 11, 1967, 4.

110. Ibid.

111. Further, they were to avoid "provocation, abusive language and character assassination," which were vices Gladys Difo did not want associated with the WCNU. "CNU Is New Hope for All," *Cameroon Times*, November 15, 1967, 4.

112. See the following pages for definitions of the term: Michael Schatzberg, *Political Legitimacy in Middle Africa: Father, Family, Food* (Bloomington: Indiana University Press, 2001), 15, 20.

113. Ibid., 1, 25.

114. Carol Delaney demonstrates "the role that the symbolism of mother and father play in the conception of the nation" in her gendered analysis of the birth of modern Turkey. Further, Delaney asserts, in a similar fashion to Schatzberg, that the imagery of the "Father State epitomized Ottoman rule. The state was both patriarchal and paternalistic, and the people . . . were dependent on its benevolence and its protection." Carol Delaney, "Father State, Motherland, and the Birth of Modern Turkey," in *Naturalizing Power: Essays in Feminist Cultural Analysis*, ed. Sylvia Yanagisako and Carol Delaney (New York: Routledge, 1995), 178–79.

115. For examples, see "Bring Down Barriers Raised Between Tribes," *Cameroon Telegraph*, March 19, 1969, 4–5; "Cameroon Operates On a Unified not Unitary Party System—Ahidjo," West Cameroon press release, February 4, 1969.

116. Schatzberg, *Political Legitimacy in Middle Africa*, 25.

117. Achille Mbembe, *On the Postcolony* (Berkeley: University of California Press, 2001), 120.

118. Salomon Tandeng Muna, "Make Cameroon a Nation to Live with Dignity," *Cameroon Telegraph*, July 1969, 4.

119. Ney is a retired regional inspector of bilingualism. Poubom Lamy Ney, interview by Annie Kamani, Buea, April 18, 2016. Kevin Djomo, a Cameroon Radio Television journalist in Buea, provided Poubom with additional relevant information on the identity of West Cameroonian female journalists; Kamani did not personally interview or meet with Djomo.

120. For example, see Organisation des Femmes de l'Union Nationale Camerounaise, *L'OFUNC en Marché* [The WCNU on the Move] (Douala, Cameroun: Agence Camerounaise d'Information, 1980); Organisation des Femmes de l'Union Nationale Camerounaise, *La Femme Camerounaise* [The Cameroonian Woman] (Paris: EDICEF, 1972).

121. Adams writes that the construction of "Women's Houses" in the 1970s and early 1980s "provided an organizational space for WCNU activities, particularly domestic science classes. Many of the Houses held domestic science courses for girls whose formal education had ended." Adams, "Negotiating the Boundaries of Political Action," 122.

122. Endeley-Matute, interview by author.

123. See the following surveys and interviews: Gerhard Mey and Hermann Spirik, *La Famille Africaine en Milieu Africain* [The African Family in Africa] (Yaoundé, Cameroon: 1975); Theresa Ndongko. "Tradition and the Role of Women in Africa," *Presence Africaine*, no. 99/100 (1976): 143–54; Jacques Noah Zingui, *"L'Homme et la Femme dans le Cameroun d'Hier et d'Aujourd'hui"* [Man and Women in Cameroon of Yesterday and Today], *Memo*, n.d.; *Séminaire d'Animation et la Formation de la Femme Camerounaise: Les Actes du Séminaire Féminine* [Seminar of Animation and Training of Cameroonian Women: Proceedings of the Women's Seminar] (Yaoundé, Cameroon: March 1975).

124. Organisation des Femmes de l'Union Nationale Camerounaise, *Integration de la Femme Camerounaise dans le Processus de Développement Economique: L'OFUNC en Marché* [Integration of the Cameroonian Woman into the Economic Development Process: The WCNU on the Move]. (Yaoundé, Cameroon: OFUNC, 1982), 113.

125. The WCNU's rhetoric of women's political importance was continuous with that of the CWI. A government press release quoted the regional president of the WCNU chapter in Nguti, a town in southwest Cameroon, saying that "the world of today was not the world of the past where men had to do more than women. Men and women have equal opportunities and as such women should not sit back and allow men [to] 'die alone in the task of nation-building.'" Calling WCNU members "educated militants," the president, whom sources identify only by the last name Nsange, implored them "to forget all political discrimination which existed in the past" and to cooperate with the

CNU to promote "peace, order, and unity for the development" of their community. "Men and Women Have Equal Opportunities of Service President W.C.N.U Nguti Says," West Cameroon press release no. 907, November 7, 1967.

126. "Women's Wing of Party Hold Confad [*sic*]," West Cameroon press release, December 4, 1970.

127. While scholars have mostly recognized *Promise* as a fictional novel about a young woman coming of age in Bamenda during British rule, firsthand knowledge from British anthropologist Shirley Ardener—who typed the book, illustrated it, and facilitated its publication process—clarifies that the "novel" was actually a memoir, mostly based on Prudencia Chilla's actual life. As Ardener shared in an email exchange, "Mrs. Chilla turned up one day with a few handwritten pages—the first pages of what became her book. I typed them for her, and urged her to continue. From then on, she would turn up with more handwritten text, which I typed up as we went along. She had not envisaged publishing it when she started. She was concerned about her references to her brother and other people, and especially what the Catholics would think of it. She insisted on using another name. At the time I was very enthusiastic about her book, but actually found it difficult to find a publisher for her. It was finally published by the African Universities Press, a branch of the publisher Gregg. I think they agreed because I met Deborah Manley, who had lived in Cameroon, and also then had a connection with the AUP; she backed me up. I agreed to provide a few illustrations as without them they would not publish. I understood that The African Universities Press distributed the book in Cameroon. I think it was on sale in Pressbook, and was used in the schools. She did write some further paragraphs, but not a full text. I don't know where they are." Ardener later reaffirmed that the novel was actually Chilla's memoir: "So it is a memoir, with names changed. Her concern was that some mild comments on her experience of the Catholics, might offend the nuns, and she deleted some words accordingly. She insisted on not using her own name, but I guess it was soon recognized as hers." Shirley Ardener, email message to author, May 6, 2018; Shirley Ardener, email message to author, October 9, 2018; Jedida, *Promise*.

128. Joyce Ashuntantang, "Anglophone Cameroon Literature 1959–90: A Brief Overview," *Tydskrif Vir Letterkunde* 53, no. 1 (2016): 114.

129. Lilian Lem Atanga, *Gender, Discourse and Power in the Cameroonian Parliament* (Bamenda: Langaa RPCIG, 2010), 1.

130. Konde, *African Women and Politics*, 125, 138, 158.

131. Nfah-Abbenyi, *Gender in African Women's Writing*, 75.

132. Konde, *African Women and Politics*, 151.

133. Galega and Tumnde, "Reversing Decades of Gender Injustice in Cameroon," 238.

134. Ibid., 158; "Mrs. Chilla Urges Unity of Women," West Cameroon press release, October 16, 1970.

135. Konde, *African Women and Politics*, 218.

136. Judy C. Bryson, *Women and Economic Development in Cameroon* (Washington, DC: Agency for International Development, 1979), 96, original from Ahmadou Ahidjo,

"Speech to the Nation on the Occasion of International Women's Year," *Cameroon Tribune*, July 19–20, 1975, 2; United Nations, *Report of the World Conference of the International Women's Year, Mexico City, 19 June–2 July 1975* (New York: UN, 1976).

137. However, as Atanga argues, "the Cameroon government did not take any serious measures and the Convention hardly benefited women in actual fact. Equal access to jobs and positions of responsibility by women was not achieved by this convention, for example, access to leadership positions such as provincial governors. This convention had little impact on the number of women represented in key political circles and in the parliament." Atanga, *Gender, Discourse and Power in the Cameroonian Parliament*, 11–12.

138. Alicia C. Decker, *In Idi Amin's Shadow: Women, Gender, and Militarism in Uganda* (Athens: Ohio University Press, 2014), 113.

139. Bryson, *Women and Economic Development in Cameroon*, 96.

140. Decker, *In Idi Amin's Shadow*, 113.

141. Mabel Murphy Smythe, interview by Ruth Stutts Njiiri, *Frontline Diplomacy: The Foreign Affairs Oral History Collection of the Association for Diplomatic Studies and Training*, June 2, 1981, http://memory.loc.gov/ammem/collections/diplomacy

CHAPTER 3

1. "Madam Jua Congratulates Domestic Science Organizers," West Cameroon press release no. 4645, December 23, 1965.

2. Natalia Jua was born in 1928 in Njinikom, a town in the Northwest Region of Cameroon. She graduated from St. Anthony Catholic School in Njinikom in 1943 and from St. Francis College in Kumba in 1949, earning a teaching degree in 1952. She started teaching at her alma mater, St. Anthony. She married Augustine Ngom Jua in August 1951; they had five children. Kini Nsom, "Cardinal Tumi Delivers Late PM's Widow to Eternity," *Up Station Mountain Club*, May 7, 2007, http://www.postnewsline.com/2007/05/cardinal_tumi_d.html

3. For example, Jua encouraged women to participate in nation-building endeavors during the Council of Women's Institutes' Women's Day rallies in 1966. "Women Celebrate Their Day," West Cameroon press release no. 4978, April 4, 1966.

4. "Madam Jua Congratulates Domestic Science Organizers," West Cameroon press release no. 4645, December 23, 1965.

5. Ibid.

6. McCann, *Stirring the Pot*, 63.

7. Cusack, "African Cuisines," 209.

8. Mary Ghanghi, survey conducted by Nevian Fonkwa, Bamenda, October 11, 2011; Ngum Magdalene Beghang, survey conducted by Nevian Fonkwa, Bamenda, October 9, 2011.

9. Iris Berger, *Women in Twentieth-Century Africa* (Cambridge: Cambridge University Press, 2016), 50.

10. Gladys Ejomi Martin, "Aunty Kate: The Book, the Cook, the Educator and

Homemaker," *Success Story Magazine* no. 11 (2008): 18–19, accessed December 27, 2018, https://www.successstorymagazine.info/past_issues/

11. Anthony Yana Zumafor, interview by author.

12. Initially a dish only eaten by wealthy families, at present it is consumed by many Cameroonians. Poulet DG is regarded as one of the signature dishes of Cameroon with numerous regional modifications. The dish initially originated in the western (Francophone) region of Cameroon in the 1980s. Jeanne Jacob and Michael Ashkenazi, *The World Cookbook: The Greatest Recipes from Around the Globe*, 2nd ed., vol. 1 (Santa Barbara, CA: ABC-CLIO, 2014), 217; Vera Abitbol, "Cameroon: Poulet DG (Chicken Executive Officer)," *196 Flavors,* 196flavors.com/cameroon-poulet-dg/

13. Jacqueline-Bethel Tchouta Mougoué, "How I Increased My Bride Price and Other Insights from My Dissertation Field Research," *African Studies Association News*, September 2012.

14. Mbotu started his Africanization program, called the Authenticity Campaign, during the 1970s and changed the name of Zaire to the Democratic Republic of the Congo. He also took up the new name Mbotu from Joseph-Désiré Mobutu. Emizet Francois Kisangani, *Historical Dictionary of the Democratic Republic of the Congo* (Lanham, MD: Rowman & Littlefield, 2016), xv, 54, 148, 440, 634.

15. Mark W. DeLancey, *Cameroon: Dependence and Independence* (Boulder, CO: Westview Press, 1989), 61; "Private Sector Asked to Intensify Cameroonisation Policy," *Cameroon Times*, January 31, 1968, 1.

16. Caroline Durand, "Rational Meals for the Traditional Family: Nutrition in Quebec School Manuals, 1900–1960," in *Edible Histories, Cultural Politics: Towards a Canadian Food History*, ed. Franca Iacovetta, Valerie J. Korinek, and Marlene Epp (Toronto: University of Toronto Press, 2012), 109–27.

17. Mbaku, *Culture and Customs of Cameroon*, 121.

18. Eric Ebolo Elong, "The Anglophone Problem and the Secession Option in Cameroon," in *Bondage of Boundaries and Identity Politics in Postcolonial Africa: The "Northern Problem" and Ethno-Futures*, ed. Sabelo J. Ndlovu-Gatsheni and Brilliant Mhlanga (Pretoria: Africa Institute of South Africa, 2013), 148.

19. Coquery-Vidrovitch, *African Women*, 144; Adams, "Colonial Policies and Women's Participation in Public Life," 4, 5–6. Burke similarly writes that in settler-colonial Zimbabwe, domestic courses for African women in the early 1900s "stressed the responsibility of the female pupils for maintaining the cleanliness of their children, their adult relatives, their homes, and their villages." Timothy Burke, *Lifebuoy Men, Lux Women: Commodification, Consumption, and Cleanliness in Modern Zimbabwe* (Durham: Duke University Press, 1996), 46. For additional information on the establishment and development of Christian-missionary-driven domestic science programs in other areas of colonial Africa, such as in Kenya and the Democratic Republic of the Congo, see Hunt, *A Colonial Lexicon*; Kanogo, *African Womanhood in Colonial Kenya 1900–1950*; Nancy Rose Hunt, "Colonial Fairy Tales and the Knife and Fork Doctrine in the Heart of Africa," in *African Encounters with Domesticity*, ed. Karen Tranberg Hansen (New Brunswick, NJ: Rutgers University Press, 1992), 143–71.

20. Berger, *Women in Twentieth-Century Africa*, 50.

21. Adams, "Colonial Policies and Women's Participation in Public Life," 6.

22. In June 1977, the Ministry of National Education in Cameroon organized the GCE examination for the first time for secondary and postsecondary students in Anglophone Cameroon. DeLancey, Mbuh, and DeLancey, *Historical Dictionary of the Republic of Cameroon*, 190. See the following for a fuller history of the GCE in Cameroon: Francis Beng Nyamnjoh and Richard Fonteh Akum, eds., *The Cameroon GCE Crisis: A Test of Anglophone Solidarity*, 2nd ed. (Bamenda, Cameroon: Langaa RPCIG, 2008). See the following for additional information on education in Anglophone Cameroon during the federal period: Christiane Courade and Georges Courade, *Education in Anglophone Cameroon, 1915–1975* (Yaoundé, Cameroon: National Office for Scientific and Technical Research, Institute of Social Sciences, National Geographical Centre, 1977).

23. "Madam Anna Foncha Opens Domestic Science Centre Open Day," West Cameroon press release no. 3414, August 12, 1964.

24. Ruff Wanzie, "Alarming Letters I Receive from Parents," *Cameroon Times*, October 24, 1964, 3.

25. "Mrs. Difo Addresses Okoyong Students," West Cameroon press release no. 3598, November 11, 1964.

26. Women's Day was also celebrated as an annual holiday in other African countries during the late 1950s and 1960s, such as Guinea (February 9) and South Africa (August 9). Women's Day is not to be confused with the present-day celebration of International Women's Day (IWD) in Cameroon (and around the world), which has been celebrated on March 8 of every year since 1986. IWD was established in Europe and the United States in the early 1900s. It became a popular global celebration in the late 1970s following a United Nations General Assembly invitation to proclaim March 8 as a day for women's rights and world peace. Kathryn Cullen-DuPont, *Encyclopedia of Women's History in America*, 2nd ed. (New York: Facts on File, 2000), 127; Catherine Coquery-Vidrovitch, *African Women: A Modern History* (Boulder, CO: Westview Press, 1997), 183, 195. "Women to Observe March 31 as Women's Day," West Cameroon press release no. 3627, November, 20, 1964.

27. Ruff Wanzie, "Women's Day Celebrations," *Cameroon Times*, March 12, 1966, 3. See the following for additional activities that took place on Women's Day: Ruff Wanzie, "Women Prepare for their Day," *Cameroon Times*, March 26, 1966, 3; "Women's Day Celebration—March 31," West Cameroon press release no. 292, March 25, 1967.

28. "Domestic Science Courses," West Cameroon press release no. 3003, February 19, 1964.

29. "Cameroon Women Students Find Friendliness in Britain," West Cameroon press release no. 3775, February 19, 1965.

30. Ruff Wanzie, "Women Study House Keeping," *Cameroon Times*, October 24, 1964, 3.

31. Helen M. Schneider, *Keeping the Nation's House: Domestic Management and the Making of Modern China* (Vancouver, Canada: University of British Columbia Press, 2011), 2–3.

32. Ibid., 4.

33. Carl J. Dahlman, Douglas Zhihua Zeng, Shuilin Wang, *Enhancing China's Competitiveness Through Lifelong Learning* (Washington, DC: World Bank, 2007), 142.

34. Oben, *Women of the Reunification*, 41.

35. Ibid., 62, 64.

36. Ibid., 60–61.

37. Ibid., 63–64.

38. Ibid.

39. Martin, "Aunty Kate."

40. Ibid.

41. Zumafor, interview by author.

42. Martin, "Aunty Kate."

43. Although the book was first published in 1976, efforts toward compiling recipes for the book began in December 1965, when Idowu supervised the group of domestic science teachers who experimented with local diverse cuisine in the Government Domestic Science Center in Buea.

44. Cusack, "African Cuisines," 215.

45. Ibid., 215.

46. Kate Ebenye Idowu, *Auntie Kate's Cookery Book*, 3rd. ed. (London: MacMillan, 1985), 9.

47. Feldman-Savelsberg, *Mothers on the Move*, 6.

48. Idowu, *Auntie Kate's Cookery Book*, 8.

49. Karin Barber, *The Anthropology of Texts, Persons, and Publics: Oral and Written Culture in Africa and Beyond* (Cambridge: Cambridge University Press, 2007), 2.

50. Idowu, *Auntie Kate's Cookery Book*, 8.

51. Ministry of Economic Affairs and Planning, Department of Statistics, *The Population of West Cameroon, Main Findings of the Demographic Sample Survey 1964*, 148.

52. Sarah W. Walden, *Tasteful Domesticity: Women's Rhetoric and the American Cookbook, 1790-1940* (Pittsburgh: University of Pittsburgh Press, 2018), 29.

53 . Idowu, *Auntie Kate's Cookery Book*, 9.

54. Ibid., 9, 106, 117.

55. Barber, *The Anthropology of Texts, Persons, and Publics*, 4.

56. Idowu, *Auntie Kate's Cookery Book*, 4.

57. Another kitchen prayer can be found on page 136. Idowu, *Auntie Kate's Cookery Book*, 20.

58. Ibid., 54, 72, 80, 115, 132, 142, 166.

59. Ibid., 57.

60. Ibid., 103.

61. Ibid., 148.

62. Barber, *The Anthropology of Texts, Persons, and Publics*, 4.

63. Emmanuel Obiechina, *An African Popular Literature: A Study of Onitsha Market Pamphlets* (Cambridge: Cambridge University Press, 1973), 107.

64. Shameem Black, "Recipes for Cosmopolitanism: Cooking Across Borders in the South Asian Diaspora," *Frontiers: A Journal of Women's Studies* 31, no. 1 (2010): 1.

65. Marie-Soleil Frère, "Le Journaliste et le Griot: les Traces de l'Oralité dans la Presse Écrite Africaine" [The Journalist and the Griot: Traces of Orality in the African Written Press] *Afrika Focus* 15, no. 1–2 (1999): 14.

66. Hale, *Griots and Griottes*, 5.

67. Martin, "Aunty Kate."

68. Ibid.

69. Ibid.

70. Weber asserts that the improper use of time is one of the worst sins according to his research on the Protestant work ethic. Max Weber, *The Protestant Ethic and the Spirit of Capitalism* (New York: Charles Scribner's Sons, 1958), 157–58.

71. Jeremy Rich, *A Workman Is Worthy of His Meat: Food and Colonialism in the Gabon Estuary* (Lincoln: University of Nebraska Press, 2007), xiii.

72. Rich, *A Workman Is Worthy of His Meat,* xiii–xiv. For more discourse on changing culinary and food consumption patterns in colonial and postcolonial Africa, see Elias Coutinho Mandala, *The End of Chidyerano: A History of Food and Everyday Life in Malawi, 1860–2004* (Portsmouth, NH: Heinemann, 2005); Jane I. Guyer, *ed. Feeding African Cities: Studies in Reginal Social History* (Manchester: Manchester University Press, 1987); Megan Vaughan, *The Story of an African Famine: Gender and Famine in Twentieth-Century Malawi* (Cambridge: Cambridge University Press, 1987); Diana Wylie, *Starving on a Full Stomach: Hunger and the Triumph of Cultural Racism in Modern South Africa* (Charlottesville: University of Virginia Press, 2001).

73. Beignets are French doughnuts that are also called "puff-puff" by English-speaking Cameroonians. Puff-puffs are made of dough containing flour, yeast, sugar, butter, salt, water, and oil and deep fried in vegetable oil until golden brown.

74. Auntie Clara, "Our Native Dishes," *Cameroon Champion*, September 1, 1961, 3. See the following for an additional example of another Anglophone Cameroonian female journalist who shares local Cameroonian recipes, admitting that she "may not be perfect in all that [she] may say through this page [her women's column]": Maria Ejang, "Cameroon Recipes," *Cameroon Telegraph*, Aril 26, 1969, 7.

75. Fufu is a dish made from pounded cassava, pounded yams, pounded plantains, or corn meal. Cited in Mougoué, "Intellectual Housewives," 90; original from Auntie Clara, "The Housewife Hostess," *Cameroon Champion*, September 18, 1962, 3.

76. Examples include Cusack, "African Cuisines"; Cusack, "Pots, Pens and 'Eating out the Body': Cuisine and the Gendering of African Nations," *Nations and Nationalism* 9, no. 2 (2003): 277–96.

77. Cited in Mougoué, "Intellectual Housewives," 75. For an example, see Auntie Clara, "Continuing our Native Dishes," *Cameroon Champion*, September 22, 1961, 2.

78. Cited in Mougoué, "Intellectual Housewives," 75, original from Anderson, *Imagined Communities*, 5-6.

79. Cited in Mougoué, "Intellectual Housewives," 75, original from Auntie Clara, "The Housewife Hostess," *Cameroon Champion*, September 18, 1962, 3.

80. Cited in Mougoué, "Intellectual Housewives," 75, original from Audrey Gadzekpo, "Public but Private: A Transformational Reading of the Memoirs and Newspaper Writings of Mercy Ffoulkes-Crabbe," in *Africa's Hidden Histories: Everyday Literacy and Making the Self*, ed. Karin Barber (Bloomington: Indiana University Press, 2006): 334.

81. Rich, *A Workman Is Worthy of His Meat.*

82. Ndolé is a creamy casserole made with bitter leaves; koki is a thick pudding made with ground black-eyed beans, egusi is a stew made from the grounded seeds of melons or squash; achu is a yellow soup made with palm oil and ground limestone. Victorine Folefo, survey conducted by Nevian Fonkwa, Bamenda, October 19, 2011; Ghanghi, survey conducted by Nevian Fonkwa; Margaret Ngala, survey conducted by Nevian Fonkwa, Nkambe, November 16, 2011; Beghang, survey conducted by Nevian Fonkwa; Agnes Nsotaka Shillie, survey conducted by Nevian Fonkwa, Kumba, October 9, 2011; Christina Ambe Manka, survey conducted by Nevian Fonkwa, Bamenda, November 17, 2011; Loveline Metamo, survey conducted by Nevian Fonkwa, Bamenda, October 20, 2011; Amina Mbah, survey conducted by Nevian Fonkwa, Bamenda, October 17, 2011; Charlotte Neba, survey conducted by Nevian Fonkwa, Bamenda, October 25, 2011; Aisha Bouba, survey conducted by Nevian Fonkwa, Bamenda, November 15, 2011; Constance Tah, survey conducted by Nevian Fonkwa, Yaoundé, November 30, 2011; Margaret Ngalim, survey conducted by Nevian Fonkwa, Bamenda, December 10, 2011; Tita Agnes, survey conducted by Nevian Fonkwa, Bamenda, October 23, 2011.

83. Ngum (pseud.), interview by author.

84. Ibid.

85. Mbaku, *Culture and Customs of Cameroon*, 174.

86. According to Charles Endeley, he had trouble passing various security check points when he "had a mission at the presidency" in 2010. However, his mission became easier after one gendarme realized he was Gladys Silo Endeley's son. The gendarme had once eaten in Gladys Endeley's home in Buea with Ahidjo. The gendarme recalled "that in all his career, in all his life as a military officer, he had never been fed so well as the one time they were in Buea with the President Ahidjo." Endeley's exceptional culinary skills loomed large. Oben, *Women of the Reunification*, 53.

87. Endeley-Matute, interview by author.

88. Ngum (pseud.), interview by author.

89. Konings and Nyamnjoh, *Negotiating an Anglophone Identity*, 55.

90. Ibid. See the following for more information on the decrease of economic activity in West Cameroonian port cities: Ekali, "The Fluctuating Fortunes of Anglophone Cameroon Towns," 334.

91. For example, see Chiabi, "Redressing Regional Imbalance in Cameroon," 47.

92. "French Bread Now Popular in West Cameroon," *New Standard*, October 25, 1969, 6.

93. Ngum (pseud.), interview by author; Bouba, survey conducted by Nevian Fonkwa. Bouba was the only self-identified Muslim that completed a survey.

94. Although rice was new, scarce, and expensive in the 1960s, today's elite urbanite Cameroonians generally consider rice a poor man's food. The first documented tests of rice cultivation in Cameroon dates at least as far back as the 1930s, but it was insignificant until 1953, when production shifted from the country's far north to the bank of the Logone River in northern Cameroon and southern Chad, which could support its water needs. By 1960, tall varieties covered the entire bank and production had increased tenfold from 1953, to 3,205 tons a year. The post-independence era saw a large boom in rice production because of government encouragement, and it was no longer considered a marker of wealth among Cameroonians, who began to eat it daily. Today, much of the rice eaten in Cameroon is imported. Cameroon's rice production reached 72,000 tons between 2007 and 2008, but the country imported 373,536 tons of rice in 2009, mainly from Asia. Piebiep Goufo, "Rice Production in Cameroon: A Review," *Research Journal of Agriculture and Biological Sciences Research* 4, no. 6 (2008): 747. Marcela Rondon, *2013 Exporting to Cameroon* (USDA Foreign Agricultural Service, 2014).

95. Vanessa Yonkeu (pseud.), interview by author, Buea, September 24, 2011.

96. Chin-chin is a fried sweet cookie or mini doughnut made from wheat flour and eggs; it can be made in different shapes and sizes. Juliana Muhnjuh and Nesah Tabot (pseud.), interview by author, Buea, November 5, 2011; Bekene Eyambe (pseud.), interview by author.

97. Rich, *A Workman Is Worthy of His Meat*, x.

98. Feldman-Savelsberg similarly observes that in the francophone Bangangté kingdom of the western Grassfields of Cameroon, food and women's cookery symbolically and literally brought married individuals together to procreate and reproduce, thereby helping to sustain dominant ideas about gender relations in marriages. Feldman-Savelsberg, *Plundered Kitchens, Empty Wombs*, 4, 71, 73.

99. Eyambe (pseud.), interview by author.

100. The advice connecting cooking and marital happiness that women journalists offered female readers is reminiscent of similar guidance in advice columns and manuals for housewives published in the United States from the 1940s to the 1960s. For example, see Tracey Deutsch, *Building a Housewife's Paradise: Gender, Politics, and American Grocery Stores in the Twentieth Century* (Chapel Hill: University of North Carolina Press, 2010), 196.

101. Auntie Clara, "Our Sunday Special," *Cameroon Champion*, August 7, 1962, 3; Auntie Clara, "Serviceable Measures," *Cameroon Champion*, November 27, 1962, 2.

102. Ruff Wanzie, "Cooking," *Cameroon Times*, April 18, 1964, 5.

103. Ruff Wanzie, "Which Is Your Perfect Wife? (2)," *Cameroon Times*, August 22, 1964, 3.

104. Beckley Sammy and Signals Victoria, "You Can Knock a Husband Off His Feet," *Cameroon Times*, August 19, 1972, 2.

105. Ruff Wanzie, "Cooking," *Cameroon Times*, April 18, 1964, 5.

106. John Mukum Mbaku, "Cameroon, Republic of," in *Africa: An Encyclopedia of Culture and Society*, vol. 1, ed. Toyin Falola and Daniel Jean-Jacques (Santa Barbara, CA: ABC-CLIO, 2016), 156.

107. Endeley-Matute, interview by author.

108. For research documenting similar trends in Uganda, see Grace Bantebya-Kyomuhendo and Marjorie Keniston McIntosh, *Women, Work and Domestic Virtue in Uganda, 1900–2003* (Oxford: James Currey, 2006).

109. Conversely, a man insults his wife when he declines to eat food cooked by her. In certain ethnic groups of the Western Highlands, whenever a wife is insulted in such a fashion, she has the right to return to her parents' homes; the offender must offer considerable amounts of gifts to win her back. Mbaku, "Cameroon, Republic of," 156.

CHAPTER 4

1. Cousin Lizzy, "West Miss Africa Cup-Who is She?" *Cameroon Times*, March 2, 1972, 3.

2. Ibid.

3. Ibid.

4. Ibid.

5. As Schulz asserts in her work on beauty pageants in contemporary Mali: "Beauty contests provide a useful entry into the investigation of these questions, because they allow the allegorization of womanhood and new ideals of femininity to be studied at the intersection of local, national, and international processes and influences." Dorothea E. Schulz, "Mesmerizing 'Missis,' Nationalist Musings: Beauty Pageants and the Public Controversy over 'Malian' Womanhood," *Paideuma: Mitteilungen Zur Kulturkunde* bd.46 (2000): 113.

6. For examples, see Saheed Aderinto, *When Sex Threatened the State: Illicit Sexuality, Nationalism, and Politics in Colonial Nigeria, 1900–1958* (Urbana: University of Illinois Press, 2015); Abosede George, *Making Modern Girls: A History of Girlhood, Labor, and Social Development in Colonial Lagos* (Athens: Ohio University Press, 2014); Emily Callaci, "Dancehall Politics: Mobility, Sexuality, and Spectacles of Racial Respectability in Late Colonial Tanganyika, 1930s–1961," *Journal of African History* 52, no. 3 (2011): 365–84.

7. Callaci, *Street Archives and City Life*, 64.

8. Oluwakemi M. Balogun and Kimberly Kay Hoang, "Refashioning Global Bodies: Cosmopolitan Femininities in Nigerian Beauty Pageants and the Vietnamese Sex Industry," in *Global Beauty, Local Bodies*, ed. Erynn Masi de Casanova and Afshan Jafar (New York: Palgrave Macmillan, 2013), 1.

9. For additional sources on beauty contests in colonial and postcolonial Africa, see Oluwakemi M. Balogun, *Beauty Diplomacy: Embodying an Emerging Nation* (Palo Alto, CA: Stanford University), forthcoming; Lynn Thomas, "The Modern Girl and Racial

Respectability in 1930s South Africa," *Journal of African History* 47, no. 3 (2006): 461–90; Carolyn Behrman, "'The Fairest of Them All': Gender, Ethnicity and a Beauty Pageant in the Kingdom of Swaziland," in *Dress and Ethnicity: Change Across Space and Time*, ed. Joanne Bubolz Eicher (Oxford: Berg, 1995): 195–206.

10. Scholarship suggests that beauty pageants provide avenues for upward mobility for young women in varied socioeconomic positions. See the following works for examples: Meeta Rani Jha, *The Global Beauty Industry: Colorism, Racism, and the National Body* (New York: Routledge, 2016); Rochelle Rowe, *Imagining Caribbean Womanhood: Race, Nation and Beauty Competitions, 1929–70* (Manchester, UK: Manchester University Press, 2013); Maxine Leeds Craig, *Ain't I a Beauty Queen?: Black Women, Beauty, and the Politics of Race* (Oxford: Oxford University Press, 2002).

11. Thomas, "The Modern Girl and Racial Respectability," 475.

12. Ibid., 471.

13. Ibid., 472.

14. Catherine Coquery-Vidrovitch, *African Women: A Modern History* (Boulder, CO: Westview Press, 1997), 229.

15. Dag Henrichsen, *A Glance at Our Africa: Facsimile Reprint of Southwest News—Suidwes Nuus, 1960* (Basel, Switzerland: Basler Afrika Bibliographien, 1997), 24.

16. Adams, "Colonial Policies and Women's Participation in Public Life," 12.

17. Bota is a section of Limbe (previously Victoria), where many expatriates associated with the British colonial administration resided.

18. Adams, "Colonial Policies and Women's Participation in Public Life," 12.

19. "Miss Emma Eko wins 'Miss Victoria' Title," West Cameroon press release no. 656, February 8, 1960; "Miss Southern Cameroons Beauty Contest," *Cameroon Champion*, September 15, 1961, 3.

20. "Cameroon Champion Beauty Contest," *Cameroon Champion*, October 6, 1961, 3.

21. Richard Wilk, "The Local and the Global in the Political Economy of Beauty: From Miss Belize to Miss World," *Review of International Political Economy* 2, no. 1 (1995): 118.

22. The Miss Nigeria 1959 contest was sponsored by the *Daily Times*, a local Nigerian newspaper. Etule won the competition; the prize was the opportunity to visit Harlem, New York. To this day she is the only non-Nigerian to have won the event. *Ebony*, October 1960, 32; Mbile, *Cameroon Political Story*, 253.

23. Roger Armsfield Njumbe, "Organise a 'Master Cameroon' Contest Too," *Cameroon Times*, July 6, 1967, 2; O. S. Mathias, "There Must Be a 'Master' to Match a 'Miss Cameroon,'" *Cameroon Times*, July 18, 1967, 2.

24. Colleen Ballerino Cohen, Richard Wilk, and Beverly Stoeltje, "Introduction," in *Beauty Queens on the Global Stage: Gender, Contests, and Power*, ed. Colleen Ballerino Cohen, Richard Wilk, and Beverly Stoeltje (New York: Routledge, 1996), 14–15.

25. "Hello Women," *Cameroon Outlook*, August 1, 1969, 1; "Beauty Contest not only for Free Girls," *Cameroon Outlook*, August 8, 1969, 4.

26. "Victoria to Select 'Beauty Queen' on June 28," *Cameroon Times*, June 22, 1967, 8.

27. "Miss Bamenda Wins," *Cameroon Times*, February 11, 1964, 3.

28. "Victoria to Select 'Beauty Queen' on June 28," *Cameroon Times*, June 22, 1967, 8.

29. Wilk, "The Local and the Global," 128.

30. "Beauty Contest not only for Free Girls," *Cameroon Outlook*, August 8, 1969, 4.

31. M. Cynthia Oliver, *Queen of the Virgins: Pageantry and Black Womanhood in the Caribbean* (Jackson: University Press of Mississippi, 2009), 82.

32. Auntie Clara, "That Great Day," *Cameroon Champion*, May 18, 1962, 3.

33. Ardener, *Kingdom on Mount Cameroon*, 308.

34. "Mrs. Chilla Crowns Miss. WCNU," *Cameroon Outlook*, September 4, 1970, 1.

35. "3 Beauty Queens Selected in Victoria, Kumba on New Year's Day," *Cameroon Outlook*, February 7, 1972, 3.

36. Oliver describes a similar dynamic in her research on beauty pageants in the U.S. Virgin Islands during the colonial and postcolonial period. Oliver, *Queen of the Virgins*, 4.

37. "3 Beauty Queens Selected in Victoria, Kumba on New Year's Day," *Cameroon Outlook*, February 7, 1972, 3.

38. "Teacher Wins 'Miss Kumba' Contest," *Cameroon Times*, June 28, 1967, 6.

39. Auntie Clara, "Miss West Cameroon Sails," *Cameroon Champion*, September 4, 1962, 3.

40. Auntie Clara, "Beauty Queen Chosen at Last," *Cameroon Champion*, June 5, 1962, 3.

41. Cohen, Wilk, and Stoeltje, "Introduction," 2.

42. As attested in the report, a copy of the letter was handed to the *Cameroon Outlook*. "Protest: Is Kate the Right Choice?" *Cameroon Outlook*, November 28, 1969, 1, 4.

43. Ibid.

44. Richard Wilk, "Connections and Contradictions: From the Crooked Tree Cashew Queen to Miss World Belize," in *Beauty Queens on the Global Stage: Gender, Contests, and Power*, ed. Colleen Ballerino Cohen, Richard Wilk and Beverly Stoeltje (New York: Routledge, 1996), 217.

45. Wilk argues that Belizean beauty pageants symbolize larger political processes: "On the one hand there is a respectable public contest of open democracy, where there is open expression of opinions, and expert representatives (judges) vote on contestants according to their objective merit (judges are supposed to stand above the contest). On the other hand there is a hidden, covert process of the exercise of power and privilege based on wealth and personal ability, where factions scheme and manoeuvre for advantage and influence in ways the public can only imagine or gossip about (they often attack the putative objectivity of the judges)." Richard Wilk, "Learning to Be Local in Belize: Global Systems of Common Difference," in *Worlds Apart: Modernity Through the Prism of the Local*, ed. Daniel Miller (London: Routledge, 1995), 123.

46. Scholars have proven that this phenomenon was common in colonial and postcolonial Africa. For instance, Kenneth Little, *African Women in Towns: An Aspect of*

Africa's Social Revolution (Cambridge: Cambridge University Press, 1973); Luise White, *The Comforts of Home: Prostitution in Colonial Nairobi* (Chicago: University of Chicago Press, 1990); Jean Marie Allman, "Rounding Up Spinsters: Gender Chaos and Unmarried Women in Colonial Asante," *Journal of African History* 37, no. 2 (1996): 195–214; Paula Jean Davis, "On the Sexuality of 'Town Women' in Kampala," *Africa Today* 47, no. 3/4 (2000): 29–60; Saheed Aderinto, "Prostitution and Urban Social Relations," in *Nigeria's Urban History: Past and Present*, ed. Hakeem Ibikunle Tijani (Lanham, MD: University Press of America, 2006), 75–89.

47. Joseph Bimi, "Free Women Should Pay Tax," *Cameroon Times*, December 5, 1964, 3.

48. Mougoué, "African Women Do Not Look Good in Wigs," 10. For examples, see Martin S. Ngafor, "Women of Pleasure," *Cameroon Times*, September 5, 1964, 3; Vincent C. Ndimolo, "Free Girls, Their Parents Versus Moral Society," *The Hero*, September 13, 1971, 3–4.

49. Thomas, "The Modern Girl and Racial Respectability," 478.

50. Balogun and Hoang, "Refashioning Global Bodies," 2, 5.

51. "Hello Women," *Cameroon Outlook*, August 1, 1969, 1.

52. Cousin Lizzy, "West Miss Africa Cup—Who Is She?" *Cameroon Times*, March 2, 1972, 3.

53. The meeting took place in Kumba. "Cameroon May Compete in Miss Africa," *Cameroon Outlook*, June 18, 1969, 3.

54. Mami Tolma, "Every Woman Is Beautiful," *Cameroon Observer*, July 2, 1966, 3.

55. "Four African Beauty Queens," *Cameroon Times*, November 22, 1967, 1.

56. "Beauty Contest not only for Free Girls," *Cameroon Outlook*, August 8, 1969, 4.

57. "Cool and Composed Beauty Queen Smiles in Success," *Cameroon Outlook*, February 21, 1973, 4.

58. Afshan Jafar and Erynn Masi de Casanova, "Bodies, Beauty, and Location: An Introduction," in *Global Beauty, Local Bodies*, ed. Erynn Masi de Casanova and Afshan Jafar (New York: Palgrave Macmillan, 2013), xvi.

59. Balogun, "Cultural and Cosmopolitan," 359, 369, 375.

60. Karen W. Tice, *Queens of Academe: Beauty Pageantry, Student Bodies, and College Life* (New York: Oxford University Press, 2012), 169.

61. Adolf Dipoko, "How Elsie Came to the Fore-Front," *Cameroon Outlook*, March 10, 1972, 1.

62. Auntie Clara, "Beauty Contest Postponed," *Cameroons Champion*, April 10, 1962, 3.

63. "Miss West Cameroon," *Cameroons Champion*, July 4, 1967, 6; "'Miss Radio Buea' Contest Flops," *Cameroon Times*, December 27, 1967, 7.

64. Ruff Wanzie, "When Women Look at Men," *Cameroon Times*, May 23, 1964, 3.

65. Ruff Wanzie, "Shyness Causes Great Embarrassment," *Cameroon Times*, September 19, 1964, 3.

66. "Miss West Cameroon," *Cameroon Times*, July 4, 1967, 8.

67. Schulz, "Mesmerizing 'Missis,' Nationalist Musings," 123.

68. Brown, *Khartoum at Night*, 8.

69. Jacqueline-Bethel Tchouta Mougoué, "African Women Do Not Look Good in Wigs: Gender, Beauty Rituals and Cultural Identity in Anglophone Cameroon, 1961–1972," *Feminist Africa* 21 (October 2016): 13.

70. Cousin Lizzy, "West Miss Africa Cup—Who Is She?" *Cameroon Times*, March 2, 1972, 3.

71. "Venus de Milo Gets Slimming Machine," *Cameroon Times*, January 31, 1968, 2.

72. For examples of her columns, see Anne Fosah, "Every Woman with a Young and Lovely Complexion," *Cameroon Workman*, August 18, 1969, 3; Anne Fosah, "On Fashion with Mrs. Fosah," *Cameroon Workman*, September 26, 1969, 3.

73. "Hello Women," *Cameroon Outlook*, August 1, 1969, 1.

74. Atuk Maformusong, "This Week with Atuk Maformusong," *Cameroon Workman*, August 5, 1969, 7.

75. "First Cameroonian Lady Opens School of Modelling," *Cameroon Outlook*, December 22, 1979, 8, 9.

76. For instance, Timothy Burke argues in his work on commodification and consumption in colonial-settler Zimbabwe that beauty products, such as skin lightning products, infuse a mix of "promotional messages about beauty, attraction, and socioeconomic status." Burke, *Lifebuoy Men, Lux Women*, 159.

77. Elizabeth Nkuku Nwigwe, "Grumbling Aloud," *Cameroon Outlook*, October 10, 1969, 3.

78. Hale, *Griots and Griottes*, 47; SakerPride, "'Telling the Saker Story & More': The Faces & Profiles of Some Household Names in Anglophone Cameroon of the 60s, 70s & early 80s," http://www.sakerpride.com/ALMANAC.html

79. Ruff Wanzie, "What Is Beauty?" *Cameroon Times*, February 17, 1972, 2.

80. Ibid., 4.

81. See the following for a similar argument by the author: Mougoué, "African Women Do Not Look Good in Wigs," 7–22.

82. Billings states in her work on Tanzanian beauty pageants that beauty competitions shape vernacular understandings of cosmopolitanisms where "some varieties of cosmopolitanism are more mobile across scales and spaces than others." Sabrina Billings, *Language, Globalization and the Making of a Tanzanian Beauty Queen* (Bristol, UK: Multilingual Matters, 2014), 23.

83. "This is Miss. Meme," *Cameroon Outlook*, October 13, 1969, 1.

84. "Miss Meme 1969 Selected," *Cameroon Workman*, October 17, 1969, 3.

85. For instance, see Schuster's work on the New African Woman in 1970s Lusaka, the capital of Zambia. Such a woman was formally educated and "symbolize[d] modernity, achievement, the competence of black people, a new black aesthetic and pride." Consequently, she was seen as "the role model for younger girls not only in the towns but in those rural areas in contact with the cities." Lisa M. Glazer Schuster, *New Women of Lusaka* (Palo Alto, CA: Mayfield Publishing, 1979), 1.

86. For example, see "Mrs. Chilla Crowns Miss. WCNU," *Cameroon Outlook*, September 4, 1970, 1.

87. "B.I.C.I.C Picks Beauty Queen," *Cameroon Times*, November 30, 1967, 1.

88. For example, Rosette Mbinka, a native of Bassa in East Cameroon, was crowned Miss Limbe River Club 1964. "Crowned Miss Limbe River," *Cameroon Times*, March 29, 1964, 4.

89. "Girl, 16 Wins Mamfe Red Cross Beauty Crown," *Cameroon Telegraph*, November 22, 1968, 3.

90. Auntie Clara, "Beauty Queen Chosen at Last," *Cameroon Champion*, June 5, 1962, 3; Auntie Clara, "Miss West Cameroon Sails," *Cameroon Champion*, September 4, 1962, 3.

91. Torrent, *Diplomacy and Nation-Building in Africa*, 90.

92. Auntie Clara, "Beauty Queen Chosen at Last," *Cameroon Champion*, June 5, 1962, 3.

93. Hence, Monica Manga played a similar role to that identified by Oluwakemi Balogun in her work on embodied femininities in modern-day Nigeria, in which beauty pageant winners use their winning positions in beauty pageants to shed light on Nigeria and to strengthen relationships with foreign countries. Balogun and Hoang, "Refashioning Global Bodies," 14–15.

94. Auntie Clara, "Miss West Cameroon Sails," *Cameroon Champion*, September 4, 1962, 3.

95. "English Girls Impress Cameroon Beauty Queen," West Cameroon press release no. 2010, September 29, 1962.

96. Ahmed-Ghosh asserts that in contemporary India, "Beauty queens are used as symbols to 'convince' the world at large that India has 'arrived' on the global stage as a 'modern' country on its path to 'development.'" Huma Ahmed-Ghosh, "Writing the Nation on the Beauty Queen's Body: Implications for a 'Hindu' Nation," *Meridians: Feminism, Race, Transnationalism* 4, no. 1 (2003): 206.

97. "Judges for 'Miss British Week,'" *Cameroon Telegraph*, November 15, 1968, 5; "British Week Ends in Victoria," *Cameroon Telegraph*, November 18, 1968, 1.

98. The British missionary Alfred Saker of the Baptist Missionary Society of London helped establish Victoria as the first permanent British settlement on the Cameroonian coast in 1858. The city had a stronger affinity with British administration than the rest of the country because it remained under British control for the first three years of German colonization (1884 to 1887). DeLancey, Mbuh, and DeLancey, *Historical Dictionary of the Republic of Cameroon*, 228, 334.

99. "'Cambank' Girl wins British Week Crown," *Cameroon Telegraph*, November 18, 1968, 1.

100. "British Week Ends in Victoria," *Cameroon Telegraph*, November 18, 1968, 1.

101. Ardener, *Kingdom on Mount Cameroon*, 304; Torrent, *Diplomacy and Nation-Building*, 90.

102. The National Archives (TNA): April 3, 1963, FO 371/167394, Commonwealth Preference for West Cameroon Products.

103. For example, when the West Cameroon government applied to be an associated group of the Commonwealth Parliamentary Association in 1964, their application was declined. A confidential letter from the British Office explained the decline thus: "the West Cameroon House of Assemble [West Cameroon Legislative Assembly] has virtually no power. The Federal Constitution imposes extremely narrow limits on discussion within the House and you might reasonably take the view that it cannot be regarded as a body whose responsibilities would qualify its members for registration as an associated group C.P.A." The National Archives (TNA): FO 371/176879: West Cameroon Desire to Become Member of Commonwealth Parliamentary Association; "British Week Ends in Victoria," 1. See the following for additional examples of British correspondence pertaining to revoking Commonwealth preference for West Cameroon goods on September 30: TNA: CAOG 14/179, "Continuation of Commonwealth Preference for West Cameroon Goods," 13 May 1963 West Cameroons: General Correspondence (1961–1968); "Address to Yaoundé Telegram No. 104 of June 21" Telegram, From Foreign Office to Yaoundé, No. 104, June 21, West Cameroons: General Correspondence (1961–1968), CAOG 14/179.

CHAPTER 5

1. Annie Kamani, interview by author, Buea, August 1, 2015.

2. Societies across time and space have related gossip predominantly to women. For example, see Patricia Meyer Spacks, "In Praise of Gossip," *Hudson Review* 35, no. 1 (1982): 19–38; Suzannah Lipscomb, "Crossing Boundaries: Women's Gossip, Insults and Violence in Sixteenth-Century France," *French History* 25, no. 4 (2011): 408–26.

3. Luise White, *Speaking with Vampires: Rumor and History in Colonial Africa* (Berkeley: University of California Press, 2000), 59, 65.

4. Kathleen A. Feeley and Jennifer Frost, "Introduction," in *When Private Talk Goes Public: Gossip in American History*, ed. Kathleen A. Feeley and Jennifer Frost (New York: Palgrave MacMillan, 2014), 5.

5. White, *Speaking with Vampires*, 60.

6. Luise White contends in her work on rumor and history in colonial East and Central Africa that "[g]ossip publicly condemned behavior that departed from community norms." White, *Speaking with Vampires*, 60–61.

7. Eyong, "Effects of Gossiping," *Cameroon Times*, June 13, 1964, 4.

8. Clare Birchall, *Knowledge Goes Pop: From Conspiracy Theory to Gossip* (Oxford: Berg, 2006), 97; Neal M. Ashkanasy, Celeste P. M. Wilderom, and Mark F. Peterson, eds., *Handbook of Organizational Culture and Climate* (Thousand Oaks, CA: SAGE Publications, 2000), 376.

9. Weber, *The Protestant Ethic and the Spirit of Capitalism*, 157–58.

10. Ruff Wanzie, "Women's Own," *Cameroon Times*, April 30, 1966, 3; Chifor Aloys, "Men, Stop Gossiping," *Cameroon Express*, December 21, 1968, 2.

11. Yonkeu (pseud.), interview by author.

12. Ruff Wanzie, "Ill Effects of Gossiping," *Cameroon Times*, May 2, 1964, 5.

13. Ibid.

14. Ibid.

15. Molefi Kete Asante and Ama Mazama, eds., *Encyclopedia of African Religion*, vol. 1 (Thousand Oaks, CA: Sage, 2009), 133.

16. Filomina Chioma Steady, *Women and Collective Action in Africa: Development, Democratization, and Empowerment* (New York: Palgrave Macmillan, 2006), 29.

17. Ibid., 96.

18. Although the Bondo Society has no "politically explicit function," both "female chiefs and paramount chiefs" are strategic members capable of strengthening their positions by using the power reserves of Bondo. Some female chiefs, such as Madam Yako, were alleged "to have a strong influence" in Bondo, giving them the opportunity to build up "alliances through the marriage of Sande women, who are often their relatives or protégés, to prominent chiefs. This often consolidated their position and expanded their influence." Ibid., 97–98.

19. "Madam Foncha Addresses 4th Annual Meeting of the Council of Women's Institute," West Cameroon press release no. 3926, May 6, 1965.

20. See the following for a brief biography about Salomon Muna: DeLancey, Mbuh, and DeLancey, *Historical Dictionary of the Republic of Cameroon*, 255–57.

21. Originally a key KNDP leader, Salomon Muna led the breakaway from the KNDP to form the Cameroon United Congress (CUC) in 1965. DeLancey, Mbuh, and DeLancey, *Historical Dictionary of the Republic of Cameroon*, 167, 256.

22. "Madame Muna Calls for Unity among Women," *Cameroon Times*, December 20, 1968, 6.

23. "Buea WCNU Welcomes Mrs. Muna," West Cameroon press release no. 5362, August 23, 1968; "Madam Muna Urges Women to Shun Gossips," *Cameroon Times*, February 7, 1968, 4.

24. "Tiko Women Urge Madam Muna to Help Them Crush Gossip," *Cameroon Times*, February 15, 1968, 7.

25. Healy-Clancy, "The Family Politics of the Federation of South African Women," 845.

26. "Tiko Women Urge Madam Muna to Help Them Crush Gossip," *Cameroon Times*, February 15, 1968, 7.

27. Ruff Wanzie, "Ill Effects of Gossiping," *Cameroon Times*, May 2, 1964, 5.

28. "Kumba Women Receive Madam Foncha," West Cameroon press release no. 3572, October 29, 1964.

29. Ruff Wanzie, "Girls on Holidays," *Cameroon Times*, April 16, 1966, 3.

30. Ruff Wanzie, "Girls' Organisations," *Cameroon Times,* June 13, 1964, 4.

31. "Desist from Sectionalism, Gossiping and Enemity," *Cameroon Mirror,* June 1, 1968, 1.

32. Nerius Namaso Mbile was elected into the Eastern House of Assembly in Nigeria in 1951 and later served in the West Cameroon Legislative Assembly. He was minister of works (1965–67), minister of lands and survey (1968), and secretary of state for primary education (1969–72). He later became a member of the CNU. Mukete, *Cameroon Reunification,* 512–13.

33. Weber, *The Protestant Ethic,* 81.

34. Ruff Wanzie, "Women's Own," *Cameroon Times,* April 30, 1966, 3.

35. Ibid.

36. Emmanuel Akyeampong and Charles Ambler, "Leisure in African Society: An Introduction," *International Journal of African Historical Studies* 35, no. 1 (2002): 11.

37. Ruff Wanzie, "Women's Own," *Cameroon Times,* April 30, 1966, 3.

38. Akyeampong and Ambler, "Leisure in African Society," 5.

39. Chifor Aloys, "Men, Stop Gossiping," *Cameroon Express,* December 21, 1968, 2.

40. Molara Ogundipe-Leslie, *Recreating Ourselves: African Women and Critical Transformation* (Trenton, NJ: Africa World Press, 1994), 34.

41. Stella Nana-Fabu, "An Analysis of the Economic Status of Women in Cameroon," *Journal of International Women's Studies* 8, no. 1 (2006): 155, 158.

42. Elizabeth Nkuku Nwigwe, "The Cameroonian Business Woman," West Cameroon press release, December 11, 1970.

43. Baratier, "Dangers of Gossiping," *Cameroon Times,* April 4, 1968, 2.

44. Eyong, "Effects of Gossiping," *Cameroon Times,* June 13, 1964, 4.

45. "Auntie Clara's Remarks," *Cameroon Champion,* August 3, 1963, 3.

46. Ruff Wanzie, "Ill Effects of Gossiping," *Cameroon Times,* May 2, 1964, 5.

47. Eyong, "Effects of Gossiping," *Cameroon Times,* June 13, 1964, 4.

48. Chifor Aloys, "Men, Stop Gossiping," *Cameroon Express,* December 21, 1968, 2.

49. Zumafor, interview by author.

50. "A Tormented Housewife Writes Her Sorrows to the Press," *New Cameroon,* March 10, 1971, 2.

51. He explained the meaning of his name in a March 1971 response to a male letter writer's inquiry. Ngwafor, *Ako-Aya,* 119, original from Ako-Aya, "From Kumba with Love," *Cameroon Outlook,* March 23, 1971.

52. Ngwafor, *Ako-Aya,* 89.

53. Ndi, *The Golden Age of Southern (West) Cameroon,* 84.

54. Ngwafor, *Ako-Aya,* 89, original from Ako-Aya, "Returning Home," *Cameroon Outlook,* August 7, 1971.

55. Ngwafor, *Ako-Aya,* 56, original from Ako-Aya, "I Go Die Today," *Cameroon Outlook,* October 23, 1973.

56. Anderson, *Imagined Communities*, 46.

57. "Auntie Clara's Remarks," *Cameroon Champion*, August 3, 1963, 3.

58. Ruff Wanzie, "Causes of Divorce," *Cameroon Times*, March 21, 1964, 5. Writing as "Cousin Lizzy" she similarly advised in a September 1972 column: "Married couples should develop deaf ears to outside gossips. The only impartial outside intruders are the Godparents. Their duty is to advise the couples." Cousin Lizzy, "The Secrets of Successful Marriages," *Cameroon Times*, September 21, 1972, 2.

59. Ruff Wanzie, "Ill Effects of Gossiping," *Cameroon Times*, May 2, 1964, 5.

60. "A Tormented Housewife Writes Her Sorrows to the Press," *New Cameroon*, March 10, 1971, 2.

CHAPTER 6

1. William Jong-Ebot argues that the *Cameroon Times* was like most English-language Cameroonian private papers in that it relied on their correspondents located around the country for news. But, as he contends, certain correspondents "sometimes relied on neighbors for juicy crime and sensational stories." Jong-Ebot, "The Mass Media in Cameroon," 180.

2. "Housewife Won't Let Husband's Girl-Friend Out," *Cameroon Times*, April 27, 1968, 7.

3. Dorothy Hodgson and Sheryl McCurdy, "Introduction: 'Wicked' Women and the Reconfiguration of Gender in Africa," in *"Wicked" Women and the Reconfiguration of Gender in Africa*, ed. Dorothy Hodgson and Sheryl McCurdy (Portsmouth, NH: Heinemann, 2001), 6.

4. Ibid.; Dorothy Hodgson and Sheryl McCurdy, "Wayward Wives, Misfit Mothers, and Disobedient Daughters: 'Wicked' Women and the Reconfiguration of Gender in Africa," *Canadian Journal of African Studies* 30, no. 1 (1996): 3.

5. Jane L. Parpart, "'Wicked Women' and 'Respectable Ladies': Reconfiguring Gender on the Zambian Copperbelt, 1936–1964," in *"Wicked" Women and the Reconfiguration of Gender in Africa*, ed. Dorothy Hodgson and Sheryl McCurdy (Portsmouth, NH: Heinemann, 2001), 285–87.

6. Hodgson and McCurdy, "Introduction," 6.

7. Ruff Wanzie, "Bringing Up Children," *Cameroon Times*, September 19, 1964, 3.

8. See the following pages for an overview of women's changing economic positions in postcolonial Africa and how this altered relationships between wives and husbands: Berger, *Women in Twentieth-Century Africa*, 180–86.

9. For example, Ebey, interview by author; Eyambe (pseud.), interview by author.

10. Ngwafor, *Ako-Aya*, 76, original from Ako-Aya, "What a Week-End," *Cameroon Outlook*, September 22, 1971.

11. See the following two works, for example, on further information on the topic matter: Barbara Cooper, *Evangelical Christians in the Muslim Sahel* (Bloomington: Indiana University Press, 2006); Nancy Rose Hunt, "Noise Over Camouflaged Polygamy, Colonial Morality Taxation, and a Woman-Naming Crisis in Belgian Africa," *Journal of African History* 32, no. 3 (1991): 471–94.

12. Konde, *African Women and Politics*, 35–36.

13. Atanga, *Gender, Discourse and Power in the Cameroonian Parliament*, 97.

14. Bridget Angum Teboh, "Women and Change in the Cameroon Grassfields: A Social and Economic History of Moghamoland c. 1889–1960" (PhD dissertation, University of California, Los Angeles, 2002), 96.

15. Ngum (pseud.), interview by author.

16. Sister Dolly, "Women and the Crime World," *Cameroon Outlook*, July 27, 1970, 3.

17. For examples, see Usen, "I Am Worried," *Cameroon Champion*, February 2, 1962, 3; Tacitius Katty, "Which Type of Women Would You Marry?" *Cameroon Telegraph*, February 26, 1969, 2; Auntie Clara, "Women's Column by Auntie Clara," *Cameroon Champion*, December 1, 1961, 3; Sister Kamara, "Women's Column," *Cameroon Voice*, August 12, 1968, 3; P. N. G. Nasah, "Equality of Sexes—a Dangerous Myth," *Cameroon Mirror*, February 11, 1966, 3; P. N. G Nasah, "Equality of Sexes a Myth," *Cameroon Mirror*, February 14, 1966, 3.

18. Stella, "Women's World," *Cameroon Observer*, October 1963, 3.

19. Ibid.

20. See the following for a similar argument by the author: Mougoué, "Intellectual Housewives," 76.

21. Ruff Wanzie, "Exemplary or Misleading," *Cameroon Times*, March 5, 1966, 3.

22. Ephraim, *Ako-Aya*, 49, original from Ako-Aya, "My Friend's Wife," *Cameroon Outlook*, April 23, 1971.

23. Ephraim, *Ako-Aya*, 45.

24. Ako-Aya, "Those Wives Who Work," *Cameroon Outlook*, September 4, 1970, 4.

25. "The Working Housewife," *Cameroon Outlook*, September 11, 1970, 6.

26. For example, see Michael Eyango, "Sister Dolly, You Are Wrong, Women Are Not Tougher," *Cameroon Outlook*, December 29, 1969, 3.

27. Goheen, *Men Own the Fields*.

28. Nana-Fabu, "An Analysis of the Economic Status of Women in Cameroon," 154.

29. Ruff Wanzie, "House Wife's Pocket Allowance," *Cameroon Times*, December 12, 1964, 3.

30. Ruff Wanzie, "Employed Married Women's Pay-Packets," *Cameroon Times*, February 19, 1966, 5.

31. Hale, *Griots and Griottes*, 23.

32. Ibid., 24.

33. Ibid.

34. Sister Dolly, "Who Should Keep the Purse?" *Cameroon Outlook*, July 10, 1970, 3.

35. Marc Epprecht, *Heterosexual Africa? The History of an Idea from the Age of Exploration to the Age of AIDS* (Athens: Ohio University Press, 2008).

36. Ghanghi, survey conducted by Nevian Fonkwa. Rose Nyangha Nkwain, a retired nurse who lives in Bamenda, similarly replied that married women with respectable social standing had "high repute in the society and they stand for their rights and fought against most of their societal ills." Rose Nyangha Nkwain, survey conducted by Nevian Fonkwa, Bamenda, November 10, 2011.

37. Ruff Wanzie, "Which Is Your Perfect Wife? (2)" *Cameroon Times,* August 22, 1964, 3.

38. Ruff Wanzie, "A Sweet Home," *Cameroon Times,* December 23, 1965, 9.

39. John Mbabit, "Should Wife Slap First?" *Cameroon Times,* October 31, 1964, 4.

40. Ruff Wanzie, "House Wife at Husbands' Throats," *Cameroon Times,* December 16, 1965, 2.

41. Ephraim, *Ako-Aya,* 91, original from Ako-Aya, "Man Fit Die O," *Cameroon Outlook,* August 27, 1971.

42. Sister Dolly, "Housewives Reduce Your Vigilance," *Cameroon Outlook,* April 11, 1970, 3.

43. Sister Dolly, "I Frown at Women Extremists," *Cameroon Outlook,* May 29, 1970, 3.

44. Newell, *West African Literatures,* 149.

45. Oduro-Frimpong makes a similar argument in his work on political cartoons and public debates in contemporary Ghana. Oduro-Frimpong asserts that "the humor the cartoons evoke does not devalue the serious import of the topics they explore. Rather, the humor provides a space within which to further deliberate the highlighted issues." Joseph Oduro-Frimpong, "'Better Ghana [Agenda]'? Akosua's Political Cartoons and Critical Public Debates in Contemporary Ghana," in *Popular Culture in Africa: The Episteme of the Everyday,* ed. Stephanie Newell and Onookome Okome (London: Routledge, 2014), 148.

46. The World Health Organization proposes that quickly changing gender norms in low-income homes may contribute to increased gender violence. The increase in the financial strength of women has brought humiliation and emasculation to some men who feel "a sense of loss of control within their households." Thus, "[m]en's frustration and anger at not being able to fulfil their traditional roles as breadwinners often leads to increasing levels of tension and violence." T. K. Sundari Ravindran, Anjana Bhushan, Kathleen Fritsch, and Breeda Hickey, *Integrating Poverty and Gender into Health Programmes: A Sourcebook for Health Professionals: Module on Gender-Based Violence* (Manila, Philippines: World Health Organization, Western Pacific Region, 2005), 13.

47. The preceding report further shares that "[a]lthough there are no reliable statistics on domestic violence against women in Cameroon, reports indicate that it is a widespread problem in the country [and that it] is still regarded as culturally acceptable by certain sectors of society." World Organisation Against Torture, *Violence against Women in Cameroon: A Report to the Committee against Torture, 31st Session* (United Nations Publications, 2003), 132–33.

48. Paul Nchoji Nkwi, "Traditional Female Militancy in a Modern Context," in *Femmes du Cameroun: Mères Pacifiques Femmes Rebelles* [Women of Cameroon: Pacific Mothers, Women Rebels], ed. J. C. Barbier (Paris: Orstom-Karthala, 1985), 183.

49. The insult is typically a comment on the smell of a woman's genitalia. If such an allegation were made to a Bakweri woman in the presence of a witness, she was to call every female member of the village. The women collectively approach the offender to ask him to recant and for compensation. If the demands are not satisfied, the culprit is brought in front of the village head and once the accusation has been proved, he must offer a pig to the women as a fine (or the equivalent worth amount in the form of salt, fowls, or money). This should be done in the presence of all the women so the actions of the man will be seen by his wife, sisters, etc., and the man will avert his eyes in shame. Eventually, the women will accept victory and divide the pig among themselves equally. Ardener, "Sexual Insult and Female Militancy," 422–23.

50. Ibid., 423. See the following for examples on how African women and men used the colonial legal system to redefine marriage ideals in urban and rural settings: Brett Shadle, *"Girl Cases": Marriage and Colonialism in Gusiiland, Kenya, 1890–1970* (Portsmouth, NH: Heinemann, 2006); Rachel Jean-Baptiste, *Conjugal Rights: Marriage, Sexuality, and Urban Life in Colonial Libreville, Gabon* (Athens: Ohio University Press, 2014); Emily S. Burrill, *States of Marriage: Gender, Justice, and Rights in Colonial Mali* (Athens: Ohio University Press, 2015).

51. Burrill, *States of Marriage*, 5.

52. Judith Van Allen, "'Sitting on a Man': Colonialism and the Lost Political Institutions of Igbo Women," *Canadian Journal of African Studies* 6, no. 2 (1972): 170.

53. "My Husband Stopped Maintaining Me So I Beat Up His Girl," *Cameroon Times*, August 1, 1967, 2.

54. Robert N. Alah, "Married Women Should Form Unions," *Cameroon Times*, April 18, 1967, 2.

55. Sister Dolly, "These Spare Tyres," *Cameroon Outlook*, June 12, 1970, 3.

56. Cousin Lizzy, "Relief Husbands for Faithful Wives?" *Cameroon Times*, February 3, 1972, 3.

CHAPTER 7

1. Dogo, "Bravo! Auntie Clara," *Cameroon Champion*, February 27, 1962, 4.
2. Yuval-Davis, *Gender and Nation*, 45.
3. Lyons, *Guns and Guerilla Girls*, 222.
4. Parpart, "'Wicked Women' and 'Respectable Ladies,'" 287.
5. Ibid., 284.
6. Ibid., 279.
7. Sabrina Billings writes in her work on Tanzanian beauty competitions that "modern Tanzanian femininity stand[s] in a dichotomous relationship with a conception of rural Tanzanian women." She expounds that "[r]ural women have long been understood

as the locus of true, traditional and hard-working Tanzania." Sabrina Billings, *Language, Globalization, and the Making of a Tanzanian Beauty Queen* (Bristol, UK: Multilingual Matters, 2014), 80.

8. Hildi Hendrickson, "Introduction," in *Clothing and Difference: Embodied Identities in Colonial and Post-Colonial Africa*, ed. Hildi Hendrickson (Durham: Duke University Press, 1996), 13.

9. Jean Marie Allman, "Fashioning Africa: Power and the Politics of Dress," in *Fashioning Africa: Power and the Politics of Dress*, ed. Jean Marie Allman (Bloomington: Indiana University Press, 2004), 1.

10. Sheldon, *Historical Dictionary of Women in Sub-Saharan Africa*, 84.

11. For examples, see Amita Handa, *Of Silk Saris and Mini-Skirts: South Asian Girls Walk the Tightrope of Culture* (Toronto: Women's Press, 2003); Gulliver, *Modern Women in China and Japan.*

12. Andrew M. Ivaska, "'Anti-Mini Militants Meet Modern Misses': Urban Style, Gender, and the Politics of 'National Culture in 1960s Dar es Salaam, Tanzania," *Gender and History* 14, no. 3 (November 2002): 584–607; Karen Tranberg Hansen, "Dressing Dangerously: Mini-Skirts, Gender Relations, and Sexuality in Zambia," in *Fashioning Africa: Power and the Politics of Dress*, ed. Jean Marie Allman (Bloomington: Indiana University Press 2004), 166; Decker, *In Idi Amin's Shadow*, 62–63; "Mini Dressers 'Show' to Obtain Permits," *Cameroon Telegraph*, May 1, 1969, 6.

13. Andrew M. Ivaska, *Cultured States: Youth, Gender, and Modern Style in 1960s Dar Es Salaam* (Durham: Duke University Press, 2011), 61–63.

14. Ibid., 2.

15. "Times Probes the Free Women's Menace," *Cameroon Times,* October 12, 1972, 1.

16. Charles Henry Ndonwi Ngwa, "Stop the Wearing of Mini-Skirts," *Cameroon Express*, September 10, 1968, 2.

17. Decimal Charles, "Sex Delinquency 2," *Cameroon Outlook,* August 20, 1971, 3.

18. For examples, see Orlson Ayuk, "Mini-Skirts: Should They Be Banned? Readers Speaks Out," *Cameroon Express,* September 17, 1968, 2; Carolus Ngwa, "Lets Economise on Drinks, not Mini-Skirts," *Cameroon Express,* September 17, 1968, 2; Lucas Bah Mujang, "Abandon Minis," *Cameroon Express,* September 19, 1968, 2; Scott Junior, "No to Minis," *Cameroon Express,* September 21, 1968, 2; Patterson A. Nji, "Minis Hamper Social Ease," *Cameroon Express,* September 21, 1968, 2.

19. A rare letter denouncing men's clothing practices ran in 1968 in the *Cameroon Express*. Paddy Max Tekum, a resident of Victoria, complained that "[M]en have been so concerned about women's fashion that they have forgotten of theirs." A flared style of pants, locally named "patte d'éléphant" (elephant's foot) particularly drew Tekum's ire. He considered "trousers which expose their pants, [called] 'yeye,'" and pants "that make scarecrows of them, 'patte d'éléphant'" immoral and expensive. Paddy Max Tekum, "Men Manage your Trousers Too," *Cameroon Express,* September 17, 1968, 2.

20. Lyons, *Guns and Guerilla Girls*, 221.

21. As Tanya Lyons describes, male students in Zimbabwe physically assaulted female students in Harare, the capital, for wearing Western attire in the early 1990s. This incident, Lyons avows, underlined societal viewpoints that "women are not supposed to be *that* liberated after national independence; they are to remain within the limits of national (male) boundaries." Ibid., 218.

22. Mougoué, "The Anlu Rebellion."

23. Elowyn Corby, "Cameroonian Women Use Anlu for Social and Political Change, 1958–1961," Global Nonviolent Action Database, 2011. http://nvdatabase.swarthmore.edu/content/cameroonian-women-use-anlu-social-and-political-change-1958-1961

24. Kah, "'Our Gowns for Your Trousers,'" 108–9.

25. Ibid., 113–14.

26. Ibid., 117.

27. Mougoué, "The Anlu Rebellion."

28. Kah, "'Our Gowns for Your Trousers,'" 116.

29. Mougoué, "The Anlu Rebellion."

30. Amandina Lihamba, *Women Writing Africa: The Eastern Region* (New York: The Feminist Press at the City University of New York, 2007), 60.

31. Vivian Bickford-Smith, E. Van Heyningen, and Nigel Worden, *Cape Town in the Twentieth Century: An Illustrated Social History* (Claremont, South Africa: David Philip Publishers, 1999), 180.

32. Auntie Clara, "Slacks Craze," *Cameroon Champion*, February 20, 1962, 3.

33. Ruff Wanzie, "What Is Beauty?" *Cameroon Times*, February 17, 1972, 2.

34. "My Dear Dogo," *Cameroon Champion*, February 27, 1962, 4.

35. Ruff Wanzie, "When Women Wear Slacks," *Cameroon Times*, January 22, 1966, 3.

36. Dogo, "Bravo! Auntie Clara," *Cameroon Champion*, February 27, 1962, 4.

37. Author's note: Corrections were made to part of the original sentence. I make corrections for similar errors throughout the book. Part of the original sentence read: "there is still something out of the woman seen in trousers is ordinary."

38. Martha Njoka, "Mrs. Ndaka on Malnutrition," *Cameroon Outlook*, August 29, 1969, 3.

39. For an example see: Charles Henry Ndonwi Ngwa, "Stop the Wearing of Mini-Skirts," *Cameroon Express*, September 10, 1968, 2; Charles Henry Ndonwi Ngwa, "Men, Women and Fashion," *Daily Life*, February 4, 1970, 2.

40. Ngwa, "Men, Women and Fashion," *Daily Life*, February 4, 1970, 2.

41. Thomas, "The Modern Girl and Racial Respectability in 1930s South Africa," 479.

42. Anthea D. Butler, *Women in the Church of God in Christ: Making a Sanctified World* (Chapel Hill: University of North Carolina Press, 2007), 69.

43. Ibid., 69–70.

44. Ibid.

45. Sister Kamara, "Women's Column," *Cameroon Voice*, August 12, 1968, 3.

46. Cyprian Agbor, "Fashion and Africa," *Cameroon Outlook*, April 3, 1970, 3.

47. Ruff Wanzie, "When Women Wear Slacks," *Cameroon Times*, January 22, 1966, 3.

48. Gwendoline Burnley made these statements in a speech on a visit to the West Cameroon Community Development Training Center in Kumba. "Show Me the Women and I Know What the Men Are," *Cameroon Voice*, September 23, 1968, 1.

49. Ebey, interview by author.

50. Agnes, survey conducted by Nevian Fonkwa.

51. Beghang, survey conducted by Nevian Fonkwa. Agnes Nsotaka Shillie of Bamenda also identified "salamanda" footwear as symbolizing a new cosmopolitan identity during the 1960s. Shillie, survey conducted by Nevian Fonkwa.

52. Ebey, interview by author.

53. As Hansen asserts, "the subjective and social experiences of dress are not always mutually supportive but may contradict one another or collide. . . . tensions between these two experiences of dress give rise to considerable ambiguity, ambivalence, and, therefore, uncertainty and debates over dress." Such tensions, as I argue, were reflected in how individuals recounted past clothing practices in interviews I conducted. Karen Tranberg Hansen, "Introduction," in *African Dress: Fashion, Agency, Performance*, ed. Karen Tranberg Hansen and D. Soyini Madison (London: Bloomsbury, 2013), 2.

54. Decker, *In Idi Amin's Shadow*, 62–63.

55. Heather Marie Akou, "Nationalism without a Nation: Understanding the Dress of Somali Women in Minnesota," in *Fashioning Africa: Power and the Politics of Dress*, ed. Jean Marie Allman (Bloomington: Indiana University Press, 2004), 51.

56. In fact, as Jean Allman points out, the miniskirt was "never officially banned in Zambia," although Zambia's House of Chiefs adopted a motion in 1971 expressing that "women's dress above the knee should be condemned." Allman, "'Let Your Fashion Be in Line with Our Ghanaian Costume,'" 169; Ngwa, "Stop the Wearing of Mini-Skirts," 2.

57. Ebey, interview by author.

58. Ngwa, "Stop the Wearing of Mini-Skirts," 2.

59. The decree, No. 67/DF/184 of 26/4/67, gave the sub-prefect of Victoria Central Subdivision "the powers to regulate social life and activities." "Show" activities were social spaces in which young women and men might display the latest fashion trends. Nightclubs and beaches were the only places where miniskirts and short dresses were deemed suitable to wear (although the decree forbade the use of some beaches, such as "the beach along Bota Catholic Mission and CDC Premises at Bota" for beach activities). Permits were to be carried during the activity and at any time an individual was wearing an otherwise objectionable style; those not carrying the permits were fined 10,000 Central African francs. "Mini Dressers 'Show' to Obtain Permits," *Cameroon Telegraph*, May 1, 1969, 6.

60. "Indecency: Free Women Banned from Hotels," *Cameroon Outlook*, December 18, 1970, 1.

61. "Minister Demands Enforcement of Prostitution Law," *Cameroon Outlook*, October 31, 1972, 1.

62. "Mass Swoop on Free Women Begins," *Cameroon Times*, October 12, 1972, 1.

63. "Mass Swoop on Free Women Begins," *Cameroon Times*, October 12, 1972, 1; "Times Probes the Free Women's Menace," *Cameroon Times*, October 12, 1972, 1.

64. "Landlords Issue Rejection Notices to Free Girls," *Cameroon Outlook*, October 13, 1972, 1.

65. Fesse (or "Fese" as written in other column posts), "For Women Only," *Cameroon Outlook*, October 27, 1972, 3.

66. Mougoué, "African Women Do Not Look Good in Wigs," 10; Martin S. Ngafor, "Women of Pleasure," *Cameroon Times*, September 5, 1964, 3; Ngum (pseud.), interview by author.

67. Vincent C. Ndimolo, "Free Girls, Their Parents Versus Moral Society," *The Hero*, September 13, 1971, 3–4.

68. "Mass Swoop on Free Women Begins," *Cameroon Times*, October 12, 1972, 1.

69. Ibid., 1, 4.

70. Ibid., 4.

71. "Times Probes the Free Women's Menace," *Cameroon Times*, October 12, 1972, 1.

72. "5,000 Free Girls Start Journey Back Home: End of an Era," *Cameroon Outlook*, October 17, 1972, 1, 4.

73. "Landlords Issue Rejection Notices to Free Girls," *Cameroon Outlook*, October 13, 1972, 1.

74. "Mass Swoop on Free Women Begins," *Cameroon Times*, October 12, 1972, 4.

75. "5,000 Free Girls Start Journey Back Home: End of an Era," *Cameroon Outlook*, October 17, 1972, 1, 4.

76. Priya Lal, *African Socialism in Postcolonial Tanzania: Between the Village and the World* (Cambridge: Cambridge University Press, 2015), 31.

CONCLUSION

1. Lukong Pius Nyuylime, "My Husband Wanted a United, Progressive Cameroon," *Cameroon Tribune*, January 27, 2014, accessed May 26, 2016, allafrica.com/stories/201401281247.html

2. Ibid.

3. O'Rourke, "Foncha, John Ngu," 381.

4. Ibid.; DeLancey, Mbuh, and DeLancey, *Historical Dictionary of the Republic of Cameroon*, 28.

5. O'Rourke, "Foncha, John Ngu," 381; DeLancey, Mbuh, and DeLancey, *Historical Dictionary of the Republic of Cameroon*, 167.

6. President Biya altered the punishment to life sentence and dropped the case a month later. Ahidjo was accused of being the mastermind behind the abortive coup d'état of April 6, 1984. Ahidjo later spent his exile in France and Dakar, Senegal and died in November 1989. DeLancey, Mbuh, and DeLancey, *Historical Dictionary of the Republic of Cameroon*, 28–29.

7. Ibid., 30.

8. O'Rourke, "Foncha, John Ngu," 381; DeLancey, Mbuh, and DeLancey, *Historical Dictionary of the Republic of Cameroon*, 168.

9. Konings and Nyamnjoh, "The Anglophone Problem in Cameroon," 207.

10. In May 1990, the Biya regime strongly condemned a peaceful march in support of the SDF participated "by Anglophone students at the University of Yaoundé." As Piet Konings and Francis Beng Nyamnjoh point out, the Biya regime responded by calling Anglophone Cameroonians "Biafrans" and referring to them as "enemies in the house." The minister of territorial administration at the time, Ibrahim Mbombo Njoya, asked them "'to go elsewhere' if they were dissatisfied with 'national unity.'" It is this condemnation that pushed John Foncha to resign as vice president of the CPDM in 1990. Konings and Nyamnjoh, *Negotiating an Anglophone Identity*, 77.

11. Ibid., 78. For instance, public meetings included organized conferences by Anglophone activists in the 1990s such as the All Anglophone Conference in Buea in April 1993 and the follow-up conference in April–May 1994 in Bamenda. Ibid., 84–85, 89–90.

12. For instance, see Yuh Timchia, "Mass Arrests of Anglophone Cameroon Separatists," *Africa Review*, October 1, 2012, accessed May 28, 2016, http://www.africareview.com/News/Mass+arrests+of+Anglophone+Cameroon+separatists/-/979180/1522386/-/qmd6riz/-/index.html; "Cameroon" in *Political Handbook of the World 2016–2017*, ed. Thomas Lansford (Washington, DC: CQ Press, 2017) http://library.cqpress.com.ezproxy.baylor.edu/phw/phw2017_Cameroon; Amnesty International, "Annual Report: Cameroon 2013," 2013, accessed May 28, 2016, http://www.amnestyusa.org/research/reports/annual-report-cameroon-2013

13. The term originates from Ambas Bay which is located in southwest Cameroon. Limbe is located on Ambas Bay. DeLancey, Mbuh, and DeLancey, *Historical Dictionary of the Republic of Cameroon*, 36.

14. Some Francophone Cameroonians have little knowledge of the discontent Anglophone Cameroonians express. Piet Konings and Francis Beng Nyamnjoh found, at the time of their study, that many Francophones have no idea how the unified country came about and that some insist that parts of French-speaking regions are more marginalized than Anglophone ones. As Piet and Jua also discovered, some Francophone scholars and politicians claim Anglophone nationalism only reflects the existence of a few discontented elites who have never personally found a way to gain power post-1972. Konings and Nyamnjoh, *Negotiating an Anglophone Identity*, 153; Nantang Jua and Piet Konings, "Occupation of Public Space Anglophone Nationalism in Cameroon," *Cahiers d'Études Africaines* 44, no. 175 (2004): 610, 614.

15. Chevron's discovery of oil in southern Sudan (before the independence of South Sudan) in 1978 occurred simultaneously as the renewed (second) civil war between the northern and southern regions of the country. In Cameroon, China Petroleum & Chemical Corporation revealed in October 2012 that new oil and gas resources had been discovered in the Bakassi region. Piet Konings and Francis Beng Nyamnjoh, "Anglophone Secessionist Movements in Cameroon," in *Secessionism in African Politics: Aspiration, Grievance, Performance, Disenchantment*, ed. Lotje de Vries, Pierre Englebert, and Mareike Schomerus (New York: Palgrave Macmillan, 2018), 84; M.A. Mohamed Salih, *Economic Development and Political Action in the Arab World* (New York: Routledge, 2014), 80.

16. The *International Business Times* suggested in 2016 that the western African coast could further destabilize if pro-Biafrans and Southern Cameroonians unite to seek self-determination in their respective countries. Ludovica Iaccino and Sho Murakoshi, "Biafra and Southern Cameroons Might 'Join Forces to Achieve Independence,'" *International Business Times*, February 25, 2016, accessed May 28, 2016, ibtimes.co.uk/biafra-southern-cameroons-might-join-forces-achieve-independence-1545753. For additional information about the Nigerian response, see Robbie Corey-Boulet, "Nigeria Is Being Dragged into Cameroon's Anglophone Crisis: How Will It Respond?" *World Politics Review*, January 18, 2018, accessed December 27, 2018, https://www.worldpoliticsreview.com/trend-lines/24010/nigeria-is-being-dragged-into-cameroon-s-anglophone-crisis-how-will-it-respond

17. Walters Samah, "Anglophone Minority and the State in Cameroon," in *Minorities and the State in Africa*, ed. Michael U. Mbanaso and Chima J. Korieh (Amherst, NY: Cambria Press, 2010), 259.

18. Konings and Nyamnjoh, "The Anglophone Problem in Cameroon," 211–13.

19. Paul Biya, the current president of Cameroon, replaced "provinces" with "regions" in 2008. Milton Krieger, "Cameroon's Democratic Crossroads, 1990–94," *Journal of Modern African Studies* 32, no. 4 (1994): 612; DeLancey, Mbuh, and DeLancey, *Historical Dictionary of the Republic of Cameroon*, 318–19.

20. See the following for a compelling play inspired by the 1992 events: Kehbuma Langmia, *Titabet and the Takumbeng: A Play* (Bamenda, Cameroon: Langaa RPCIG, 2008); Mougoué, "Anlu Rebellion," original from Henry Kam Kah, "Women's Resistance in Cameroon's Western Grassfields," 75.

21. Pius Tangwe Tanga, "The Role of Women's Secret Societies in Cameroon's Contemporary Politics: The Case of Takumbeng," *African Journal of Cross-Cultural Psychology and Sports Facilitation* 8 (2006): 12.

22. For examples, see: Manunga Studio 2, "Takumbeng Relief 18 11 2017 London," video, 3:19, November 12, 2017, https://ambaland.com/takumbeng-relief-18-11-2017-london/; Gil Ekane, "Southern Cameroonians Women in New York Unleashed Takumbeng at Paul Biya's Hotel," video, 2:41, September 22, 2017, https://www.youtube.com/watch?v=Yw5GXmgQidI; Catherine Muring Yombo, "Takumbeng Unleash," *Southern Cameroon National Council UK*, September 23, 2017, http://ukscnc.co.uk/2017/09/23/454/

23. For examples in the news, see "Anglophones Block Biya In New York Hotel," *Bamenda Online*, September 23, 2017, http://bamendaonline.net/anglophones-block-biya-new-york-hotel/; Blaise Okie Eyong, Josiane Kouagheu, Edward McAllister, Nellie Peyton, and Kevin Liffey, "Cameroon Anglophone Protests Reignite with Separatist Tinge," *Reuters*, September 22, 2017, https://www.reuters.com/article/us-cameroon-protests/cameroon-anglophone-protests-reignite-with-separatist-tinge-idUSKCN1BX29B

24. Twitter examples: https://twitter.com/MengnjoPaulette/status/909536267754508288; https://twitter.com/search?q=%23Takumbeng; https://twitter.com/bayellef; http://ukscnc.co.uk/2017/09/23/454/; https://www.youtube.com/

watch?v=wZ85xI6OptE; http://mediablackberry.com/no-news-is-good-news-not-very-likely-for-ambazonia/; Facebook: https://www.facebook.com/takumbengs/

25. GoFundMe: https://www.gofundme.com/takumbengs

26. "Cameroon: SCNC's Bring Back Our Boys Campaign," *AllAfrica*, December 21, 2016, http://allafrica.com/stories/201612210763.html

27. Fritz Misodi Oponde, "Well Armed Takembeng Women Send Biya a Strong Message the Real Takembeng Women Took to the Frontline. These Post Menopausal Group of Women Constitute a Powerful Secret Society. In the Advent of Multipartism in the 1990's They Literally Guarded John Fru Ndi's Residence. Today, They Are the Guardian," *Ambaland* 2017, https://ambaland.com/well-armed-takembeng-women-send-biya-a-strong-message-the-real-takembeng-women-took-to-the-frontline-these-post-menopausal-group-of-women-constitute-a-powerful-secret-society-in-the-advent-of-mult/

APPENDIX

1. Barbara Cooper, "Oral Sources and the Challenges of African History," in *Writing African History*, ed. John Edward Philips (Rochester, NY: University of Rochester Press, 2005), 191.

2. Stephanie Newell, *The Power to Name: A History of Anonymity in Colonial West Africa* (Athens: Ohio University Press, 2013), 5.

3. For example, in a 1968 letter to the *Cameroon Times*, a letter-writer complains that Bamenda is isolated from ongoing events in Cameroon and that the press has a major role to play in that isolation. The writer complains that the *Cameroon Times* is distributed in Bamenda way past the publishing dates. "Letters to the Editor: You Have Failed Us," *Cameroon Times*, February 3, 1968, 2.

4. Mougoué, "African Women Do Not Look Good in Wigs," 11; Zumafor, interview by author.

5. Barber, *The Anthropology of Texts, Persons and Publics*, 4.

6. Peterson and Hunter, "Print Culture in Colonial Africa," 13.

7. Roseline Tiku, "Give Us a Women's Page," *Cameroon Express*, November 28, 1968, 2.

8. Originally from Bafut, Wanzie and her husband lived in Limbe (previously named Victoria), where she was a teacher in the Catholic Primary School. According to an oral interview, her low salary drove her to pursue a career in journalism. She approached Simon Dikuba, the editor of the *Cameroon Times* throughout the 1960s, and expressed her interest in writing for the paper. She was in her late twenties or early thirties when she started writing for *Cameroon Times*. Simon Nunka Dikuba, interview by Eileen Manka Tabuwe, Buea, June 17–18, 2016; Zumafor, interview by author.

9. Zumafor, interview by author.

10. John Foncha founded the paper along with Paul Soppo Priso, a Francophone Cameroonian who was a member of the economic elite. He was a wealthy contractor for public works and buildings who helped fund the paper; he also facilitated printing the newspaper with a printing machine he owned. Some scholars cite the date 1959 for

the founding of the *Cameroon Times*. Emmanuel Fru Doh, for instance, asserts that the paper was in circulation by 1959. Nfi, *The Reunification Debate in British Southern Cameroons*, 199; Mbaku, *Culture and Customs of Cameroon*, 84; Muluh and Ndoh, "Evolution of the Media in Cameroon," 5; Emmanuel Fru Doh, *Anglophone-Cameroon Literature: An Introduction* (Lanham, MD: Lexington Books, 2015), 6.

11. Muluh and Ndoh, "Evolution of the Media," 5; Buma Kor, "The Literature of the Hunchback," in *Anglophone Cameroon Writing*, ed. Nalova Lyonga, Eckhard Breitinger, and Bole Butake, Bayreuth African Studies Series 30 (Bayreuth, Germany: University of Bayreuth, 1993), 70. Sources indicate that Motombi Wolete established the *Cameroon Champion* in 1959; he also served as the paper's editor. Some scholars, such as Buma Kor, allege that the *Cameroon Champion* was the first newspaper established in the British Southern Cameroons, contrary to popular belief that it was the *Cameroon Times*. Kor argues that the paper was started "in 1959, at the heart of discussions for reunification with French Cameroun or joining the Federation of Nigeria. . . . Immediately following the establishment of the *Cameroon Champion* in 1959, one saw the birth in 1960 of the *Cameroon Times*. But *Cameroon Champion* did not live long to see the course its struggle was to take when Motombi Wolete died mysteriously at the Albert Nursing Home Hospital, [in] Victoria" (70).

12. Elizabeth Nkuku Nwigwe attended teacher's training courses in Abeokuta, Nigeria from 1946 to 1949. She started teaching in Buea in 1950. She attended additional teacher's training courses in Lagos, Nigeria in 1960 and graduated in 1962. In 1968 she earned a diploma "in nursery education at the Froebel Institute in Copenhagen," Denmark. Thereafter she served as the head mistress to the Government Nursery School, located in Buea, for ten years, then went on to become the south west provincial inspector for Nursery Education until 1987 (Ney, interview by Annie Kamani; Kevin Djomo, a Cameroon Radio Television journalist in Buea, provided Poubom with additional relevant information on the identity of West Cameroonian female journalists; Kamani did not personally interview or meet with Djomo); SakerPride, "'Telling the Saker Story & More': The Faces & Profiles of Some Household Names in Anglophone Cameroon of the 60s, 70s & early 80s," http://www.sakerpride.com/ALMANAC.html; Stella Anyangwe, "It's the End that Matters!" Keynote address by Dr. Stella Anyangwe, née Nwigwe, class of 1969, 50th Jubilee celebrations of Saker Baptist College, Limbe, 28 January 2012, http://www.sakerpride.com/Saker_50_speech_rev-1.pdf; for one of Elizabeth Nkuku Nwigwe's posts in a West Cameroon press release, see Elizabeth Nkuku Nwigwe, "The Cameroonian Business Woman," West Cameroon press release, December 11, 1970; Jong-Ebot, "The Mass Media in Cameroon," 181.

13. The *Cameroon Voice* was founded in Ibadan, Nigeria in 1955 by Sankie Maimo, a Southern Cameroonian who was one of the first playwriters in the Anglophone Cameroonian region. Mbaku, *Culture and Customs of Cameroon*, 93; Doh, *Anglophone-Cameroon Literature*, 6.

14. For example, in an August 1961 column, journalist Clara Manga reports that "many people stopped me on the road to tell me how displeased they were with [an] article." Auntie Clara, "Still Going on," *Cameroon Champion*, August 22, 1961, 3. In a 2015

interview, she further disclosed: "I enjoyed very much access I had to in every event that took place anywhere around me. On presenting my press card, I was given immediate entry. I was a public figure because everywhere I went hands were being pointed at me and people will be whispering my name telling others that I was a journalist. I was very proud to belong to the journalist's family" (Mbella and Ngale-Ngwang, "Meet Clara Yondo," *Success Story Magazine*, 2015).

15. Nwando Achebe and Bridget Teboh, "Dialoguing Women," in *Africa After Gender?*, ed. Cole, Manuh, and Miescher (Bloomington: Indiana University Press, 2007), 64.

16. Ibid., 65.

17. Mougoué, "How I Increased My Bride Price."

18. Kathleen Sheldon, "Writing about Women: Approaches to a Gendered Perspective in African History," in *Writing African History*, ed. John Edward Philips (Rochester, NY: University of Rochester Press, 2005), 472.

19. Ndi, *The Golden Age of Southern (West) Cameroon*, 4.

BIBLIOGRAPHY

ORAL INTERVIEWS/SURVEYS

Adi, Rose. Interview by Nevian Fonkwa, Bamenda, November 14, 2011.

Agnes, Tita. Survey conducted by Nevian Fonkwa, Bamenda, October 23, 2011.

Beghang, Ngum Magdalene. Survey conducted by Nevian Fonkwa, Bamenda, October 9, 2011.

Bouba, Aisha. Survey conducted by Nevian Fonkwa, Bamenda, November 15, 2011.

Dikuba, Simon Nunka. Interview by Eileen Manka Tabuwe, Buea, June 17–18, 2016.

Ebey, Asong Martha. Interview by author, Buea, November 8, 2011.

Endeley-Matute, Mariana. Interview by author on May 30, 2015, via Skype. Digital audio file. Institute for Oral History, Baylor University, Waco, TX.

Eyambe, Bekene (pseud.). Interview by author, Buea, November 8, 2011.

Folefo, Victorine. Survey conducted by Nevian Fonkwa, Bamenda, October 19, 2011.

Folkerts, Nancy Wood. Interview by Lisa M. Moscati on November 7 and 14, 1984, at the Billy Graham Center of Wheaton College. Collection 283. Billy Graham Center Archives, Wheaton College, Wheaton, IL.

Foncha, Anna Atang. Interview by Walter Gam Nkwi, Bamenda, March 5, 2011.

Guessou, Marie Thérèse. Interview by author, via Skype, February 26, 2016.

Ghanghi, Mary. Survey conducted by Nevian Fonkwa, Bamenda, October 11, 2011.

Kamani, Annie. Interview by author, Buea, August 1, 2015.

Manka, Christina Ambe. Survey conducted by Nevian Fonkwa, Bamenda, November 17, 2011.

Mbah, Amina. Survey conducted by Nevian Fonkwa, Bamenda, October 17, 2011.

Metamo, Loveline. Survey conducted by Nevian Fonkwa, Bamenda, October 20, 2011.

Muhnjuh, Juliana, and Nesah Tabot (pseuds.). Interview by author, Buea, November 5, 2011.

Neba, Charlotte. Survey conducted by Nevian Fonkwa, Bamenda, October 25, 2011.

Ney, Poubom Lamy. Interview by Annie Kamani, Buea, April 18, 2016.

Ngala, Margaret. Survey conducted by Nevian Fonkwa, Nkambe, November 16, 2011.

Ngalim, Margaret. Survey conducted by Nevian Fonkwa, Bamenda, December 10, 2011.

Ngum, Fidelia (pseud.). Interview by author, Buea, November 4, 2011.
Nkwain, Rose Nyangha. Survey conducted by Nevian Fonkwa, Bamenda, November 10, 2011.
Shillie, Agnes Nsotaka. Survey conducted by Nevian Fonkwa, Kumba, October 9, 2011.
Smythe, Mabel Murphy. Interview by Ruth Stutts Njiiri. *Frontline Diplomacy: The Foreign Affairs Oral History Collection of the Association for Diplomatic Studies and Training.* June 2, 1981. http://memory.loc.gov/ammem/collections/diplomacy
Tah, Constance. Survey conducted by Nevian Fonkwa, Yaoundé, November 30, 2011.
Tsanga, Delphine. Interview by David Ndachi Tagne, Yaoundé, August 1996. http://aflit.arts.uwa.edu.au/intDNTzanga.html
Yonkeu, Vanessa (pseud.). Interview by author, Yaoundé, September 24, 2011.
Zumafor, Anthony Yana. Interview by author, Buea, July 30, 2015.

UNPUBLISHED AND ARCHIVAL SOURCES

National Archives, Buea, Cameroon

Burnley, Mrs. G. E. Personal Papers. Prime Minister's Office, Buea, West Cameroon, July 27, 1961.
Endeley, Mrs. G. S. Personal Papers. Prime Minister's Office, Buea, West Cameroon, March, 15, 1959.
Foumban Conference Summary, 1961.
Ministry of Economic Affairs and Planning. Department of Statistics. *The Population of West Cameroon, Main Findings of the Demographic Sample Survey, 1964.* Paris: Société d'Études pour le Développement Économique et Social, January 1966.
Publication for the Colonial Office. *Cameroons: Under U.K. Administration. Report for the Year 1956.* No. 334. London: Her Majesty's Stationary Office, 1957.
Publication for the Colonial Office. *Cameroons: Under U.K. Administration. Report for the Year 1958.* No. 341. London: Her Majesty's Stationary Office, 1959.
Plebiscite Results for Northern and Southern Cameroons, 1961.
West Cameroon Press Releases, 1960–1970.

Newspapers

Cameroon Champion
Cameroon Mirror
Cameroon Observer
Cameroon Outlook
Cameroon Telegraph
Cameroon Times
Cameroon Voice
Cameroon Workman
The Hero

National Archives, Yaoundé, Cameroon

Bulletin d'Information. Yaoundé, Cameroon: Agence Camerounaise de Presse, 1967.

Codes and Laws of Cameroon. Yaoundé, Cameroon: Cameroon National Printing Press, September 1967.

Le Ministère des Affaires Économiques et du Plan. *La Population du Cameroun Occidental: Résultat de l'Enquête Démographique de 1964* [The Population of West Cameroon: Results of the 1964 Demographic Survey]. Paris: Secrétariat d'État aux Affaires Étrangères, I.N.S.E.E., Département de la Coopération, 1969.

Le Ministère de L'Information. *Annuaire National de la République Fédérale du Cameroun* [National Directory of the Federal Republic of Cameroon]. Yaoundé, Cameroon: Les Quatre Points Cardinaux, 1975.

Le Ministère de L'Information. *Annuaire National de la République Fédérale du Cameroun*. Yaoundé, Cameroon: Les Quatre Points Cardinaux, 1976.

Newspapers

Cameroun Tribune
L'Effort Camerounais
La Presse du Cameroun

The British Library, London, United Kingdom

Bejeng, Pius Soh. *Dr. John Ngu Foncha: The Cameroonian Statesman (A Biography)*. Bamenda, Cameroon: Centre for Social Sciences Research, 1999.

The National Archives (TNA), Kew, United Kingdom

CAOG 14/179: West Cameroons: General Correspondence.

FCO 65/47: Constitution of Federal Republic of West and East Cameroon.

FO 371/155352: National Celebrations.

FO 371/167394: Commonwealth Preference for West Cameroon Products.

FO 371/176879: West Cameroon Desire to become Member of Commonwealth Parliamentary Association.

Melville J. Herskovits Library of African Studies, Northwestern University

Organisation des Femmes de l'Union Nationale Camerounaise. *Visages de la Femme Camerounaise* [Faces of the Cameroonian Woman]. Yaoundé, Cameroon: Ateliers Graphiques du Cameroun [Graphic Workshops of Cameroon], 1975.

United Nations. *Report of the World Conference of the International Women's Year, Mexico City, 19 June–2 July 1975*. New York: United Nations, 1976.

Memorial Library, University of Wisconsin–Madison

Bot, Henneke. *Promotion Féminine au Cameroun* [Women's Promotion in Cameroon]. Yaoundé, Cameroon: E.N.S.A., 1974.

Bryson, Judy C. *Women and Economic Development in Cameroon*. Washington, DC: Agency for International Development, 1979.

Burnley, Gwen E. "Women's Work in West Cameroon." *Women Today* 6, no. 2 (1964): 34–35.

Clignet, Remi. "Quelque Remarques sur le Rôle des Femmes Africaines en Milieu Urban: le Cas du Cameroun" [Some Remarks on the Role of African Women in Urban Settings: The Case of Cameroon]. *Canadian Journal of African Studies* 6, no. 2, (1972): 303–15.

Courade, Christiane, and Georges Courade. *Education in Anglophone Cameroon, 1915–1975*. Yaoundé, Cameroon: National Office for Scientific and Technical Research, Institute of Social Sciences, National Geographical Centre, 1977.

International Women's Club of Yaoundé. *Travel Cameroon*. Yaoundé, Cameroon: 1994.

Mey, Gerhard, and Hermann Spirik. *La Famille Africaine en Milieu Africain* [The African Family in Africa]. Yaoundé, Cameroon: 1975.

Ndongko, Theresa. "Tradition and the Role of Women in Africa." *Presence Africaine* no. 99/100 (1976): 143–54.

Noah Zingui, Jacques. "L'Homme et la Femme dans le Cameroun d'Hier et d'Aujourd'hui" [Man and Woman in Cameroon of Yesterday and Today]. *Memo*, n.d.

UNICEF. Regional Office for Central and West Africa. *Children, Youth, Women and Development Plans in West and Central Africa: Cameroon, Chad, Gabon, Ivory Coast, Mali, Mauritania, Niger, Togo: Report of the Conference of Ministers Held in Lomé, Togo, May 1972*. Abidjan, Côte d'Ivoire: UNICEF, Regional Office for West and Central Africa, 1972.

Weekes-Vagliani, Winifred, Manga Bekombo, and Lynn Wallisch. *Family Life and Structure in Southern Cameroon*. Paris: Development Centre of the Organisation for Economic Co-Operation and Development, 1976.

Sterling Memorial Library, Yale University

Cameroon Collection (MS 1507). Manuscripts and Archives, Yale University Library.

SakerPride, Online Archives for Saker Baptist College, Limbe, Cameroon

Anyangwe, Stella. "'It's the End that Matters!' Keynote address by Dr. Stella Anyangwe, née Nwigwe, class of 1969." 50th Jubilee Celebrations of Saker Baptist College, Limbe, January 28, 2012. http://www.sakerpride.com/Saker_50_speech_rev-1.pdf

"'Telling the Saker Story & More': The Faces & Profiles of Some Household Names in Anglophone Cameroon of the 60s, 70s & early 80s." *SakerPride*. http://www.sakerpride.com/ALMANAC.html

PUBLISHED PRIMARY AND SECONDARY SOURCES

Abdullah, Hussaina. "Wifeism and Activism: The Nigerian Women's Movement." In *The Challenge of Local Feminisms: Women's Movements in Global Perspectives*, edited by Amrita Basu, 209–25. New York: Routledge, 2018.

Achankeng, Fonkem. "The Foumban Constitutional Talks and Prior Intentions of Negotiating: A Historico-Theoretical Analysis of a False Negotiation and the Ramifications for Political Developments in Cameroon." *Journal of Global Initiatives* 9, no. 2 (2014): 129–54.

Achankeng, Fonkem. "Introduction." In *British Southern Cameroons Nationalism and Conflict in Postcolonial Africa*, edited by Fonkem Achankeng, v–x. Victoria, Canada: FriesenPress, 2014.

Achebe, Nwando, and Bridget Teboh. "Dialoguing Women." In *Africa After Gender?*, edited by Catherine M. Cole, Takyiwaa Manuh, and Stephan F. Miescher, 63–81. Bloomington: Indiana University Press, 2007.

Adams, Melinda Jane. "Colonial Policies and Women's Participation in Public Life: The Case of British Southern Cameroons." *African Studies Quarterly* 8, no. 3 (Spring 2006): 1–22.

Adams, Melinda Jane. "Negotiating the Boundaries of Political Action: Transnational Linkages, Women's Organizations, and the State in Cameroon." PhD dissertation, University of Wisconsin–Madison, 2004.

Aderinto, Saheed. "Modernizing Love: Gender, Romantic Passion and Youth Literary Culture in Colonial Nigeria." *Africa: Journal of the International African Institute* 85, no. 3 (2015): 478–500.

Aderinto, Saheed. "Prostitution and Urban Social Relations." In *Nigeria's Urban History: Past and Present*, edited by Hakeem Tijani, 75–89. Lanham, MD: University Press of America, 2006.

Aderinto, Saheed. *When Sex Threatened the State: Illicit Sexuality, Nationalism, and Politics in Colonial Nigeria, 1900–1958*. Urbana: University of Illinois Press, 2015.

Ahmed-Ghosh, Huma. "Writing the Nation on the Beauty Queen's Body: Implications for a 'Hindu' Nation." *Meridians: Feminism, Race, Transnationalism* 4, no. 1 (2003): 205–27.

Akou, Heather Marie. "Nationalism without a Nation: Understanding the Dress of Somali Women in Minnesota." In *Fashioning Africa: Power and the Politics of Dress*, edited by Jean Marie Allman, 50–63. Bloomington: Indiana University Press, 2004.

Akou, Heather Marie. *The Politics of Dress in Somali Culture*. Bloomington: Indiana University Press, 2011.

Akyeampong, Emmanuel, and Charles Ambler. "Leisure in African Society: An Introduction." *International Journal of African Historical Studies* 35, no. 1 (2002): 1–16.

Allman, Jean Marie. "Fashioning Africa: Power and the Politics of Dress." In *Fashioning Africa: Power and the Politics of Dress*, edited by Jean Marie Allman, 1–12. Bloomington: Indiana University Press, 2004.

Allman, Jean Marie. "'Let Your Fashion Be in Line with Our Ghanaian Costume': Nation, Gender, and the Politics of Clothing in Nkrumah's Ghana." In *Fashioning Africa: Power and the Politics of Dress*, edited by Jean Marie Allman, 144–65. Bloomington: Indiana University Press, 2004.

Allman, Jean Marie. "Rounding Up Spinsters: Gender Chaos and Unmarried Women in Colonial Asante." *Journal of African History* 37, no. 2 (1996): 195–214.

Allen, Judith Van. "'Sitting on a Man': Colonialism and the Lost Political Institutions of Igbo Women." *Canadian Journal of African Studies* 6, no. 2 (1972): 165–81.

Amnesty International. "Annual Report: Cameroon 2013." 2013. http://www.amnestyusa.org/research/reports/annual-report-cameroon-2013

Anderson, Benedict. *Imagined Communities: Reflections on the Origin and Spread of Nationalism*. London: Verso, 2006.

Andrade, Susan Z. *The Nation Writ Small: African Fictions and Feminisms, 1958–1988*. Durham: Duke University Press, 2011.

Angwafo, Peter Tse. *Cameroon's Predicaments*. Bamenda, Cameroon: Langaa RPCIG, 2014.

Anyangwe, Carlson. *Betrayal of Too Trusting a People: The UN, the UK and the Trust Territory of the Southern Cameroons*. Bamenda, Cameroon: Langaa RPCIG, 2009.

Anyangwe, Carlson. *Imperialistic Politics in Cameroun: Resistance and the Inception of the Restoration of the Statehood of Southern Cameroons*. Bamenda, Cameroon: Langaa RPCIG, 2008.

Anyangwe, Carlson. *Revolutionary Overthrow of Constitutional Orders in Africa*. Bamenda, Cameroon: Langaa RPCIG, 2012.

Ardener, Edwin. *Kingdom on Mount Cameroon: Studies in the History of the Cameroon Coast, 1500–1970*, edited by Shirley Ardener. Oxford: Berghahn Books, 1996.

Ardener, Shirley. "Sexual Insult and Female Militancy." In *Perceiving Women*, edited by Shirley Ardener, 29–53. London: Malaby Press, 1975.

Asante, Molefi Kete, and Ama Mazama, eds. *Encyclopedia of African Religion*. Vol.1. Thousand Oaks, CA: SAGE Publications, 2009.

Ashkanasy, Neal M., Celeste P. M. Wilderom, and Mark F. Peterson, eds. *Handbook of Organizational Culture and Climate*. Thousand Oaks, CA: SAGE Publications, 2000.

Ashuntantang, Joyce. "Anglophone Cameroon Literature 1959–90: A Brief Overview." *Tydskrif Vir Letterkunde* 53, no. 1 (2016): 109–27.

Atanga, Lilian Lem. *Gender, Discourse and Power in the Cameroonian Parliament*. Bamenda, Cameroon: Langaa RPCIG, 2010.

Atanga, Lilian Lem, and Alexandre T. Djimeli. "Women in Politics and the Media: The Discursive Construction of Collaboration for Female leadership in Cameroon." In *Discourse, Politics and Women as Global Leaders*, edited by John Wilson and Diana Boxer, 169–94. Amsterdam: John Benjamins Publishing, 2015.

Atanga, Mufor. *The Anglophone Cameroon Predicament*. Bamenda, Cameroon: Langaa RPCIG, 2011.

Atangana, Martin. *The End of French Rule in Cameroon*. Lanham, MD: University Press of America, 2010.

Atemnkeng, Denis. "British Southern Cameroons' Nationalism and the African Unity Argument." In *British Southern Cameroons Nationalism and Conflict in Postcolonial Africa*, edited by Fonkem Achankeng, 61–79. Victoria, Canada: FriesenPress, 2014.

Awasom, Nicodemus Fru. "Negotiating Federalism: How Ready were Cameroonian

Leaders before the February 1961 United Nations Plebiscites?" *Canadian Journal of African Studies* 36, no. 3 (2002): 425–59.

Awasom, Nicodemus Fru. "The Reunification Question in Cameroon History: Was the Bride an Enthusiastic or a Reluctant One?" *Africa Today* 47, no. 2 (2002): 91–119.

Awasom, Nicodemus Fru. "Towards Historicizing the Ossification of Colonial Identities in Africa: The Anglophone/Francophone Divide in Postcolonial Cameroon." In *Society, State, and Identity in African History*, edited by Bahru Zewde, 47–72. Addis Ababa, Ethiopia: Forum for Social Studies, 2008.

Ayim, Martin Ayong. *Former British Southern Cameroons Journey towards Complete Decolonization Independence, and Sovereignty: A Comprehensive Compilation of Efforts and Historical Documentation*. Vol. 1. Bloomington, IN: AuthorHouse, 2010.

Baker, Noelle A. ed. *Stanton in Her Own Time: A Biographical Chronicle of Her Life, Drawn from Recollections, Interviews, and Memoirs by Family, Friends, and Associates*. Iowa City: University of Iowa Press, 2016.

Balogun, Oluwakemi M. *Beauty Diplomacy: Embodying an Emerging Nation*. Palo Alto, CA: Stanford University Press, forthcoming.

Balogun, Oluwakemi M. "Cultural and Cosmopolitan: Idealized Femininity and Embodied Nationalism in Nigerian Beauty Pageants." *Gender and Society* 26, no. 3 (2012): 357–81.

Balogun, Oluwakemi M., and Kimberly Kay Hoang. "Refashioning Global Bodies: Embodiment in Nigerian Beauty Pageants and the Vietnamese Sex Industry." In *Global Beauty, Local Bodies*, edited by Erynn Masi de Casanova and Afshan Jafar, 1–21. New York: Palgrave Macmillan, 2013.

Bantebya-Kyomuhendo, Grace, and Marjorie Keniston McIntosh. *Women, Work and Domestic Virtue in Uganda, 1900–2003*. Oxford: James Currey, 2006.

Barber, Karin. *The Anthropology of Texts, Persons, and Publics: Oral and Written Culture in Africa and Beyond*. Cambridge: Cambridge University Press, 2007.

Barber, Karin. "Views of the Field: Introduction." In *Readings in African Popular Culture*, edited by Karin Barber, 1–12. Bloomington: Indiana University Press, 1997.

Behrman, Carolyn. "'The Fairest of Them All': Gender, Ethnicity and a Beauty Pageant in the Kingdom of Swaziland." In *Dress and Ethnicity: Change across Space and Time*, edited by Joanne Bubolz Eicher, 195–206. Oxford: Berg, 1995.

Benjamin, Jacques. "The Impact of Federal Institutions on West Cameroon's Economic Activity." In *An African Experiment in Nation Building: The Bi-lingual Cameroon Republic since Reunification*, edited by Ndiva Kofele-Kale, 191–226. Boulder, CO: Westview Press, 1980.

Berger, Iris. *Women in Twentieth-Century Africa*. Cambridge: Cambridge University Press, 2016.

Berger, Iris, and E. Frances White. *Women in Sub-Saharan Africa: Restoring Women to History*. Bloomington: Indiana University Press, 1999.

Bickford-Smith, Vivian, E. Van Heyningen, and Nigel Worden. *Cape Town in the Twen-*

tieth Century: An Illustrated Social History. Claremont, South Africa: David Philip Publishers, 1999.

Bier, Laura. *Revolutionary Womanhood: Feminisms, Modernity, and the State in Nasser's Egypt*. Stanford: Stanford University Press, 2011.

Billig, Michael. *Banal Nationalism*. Thousand Oaks, CA: Sage Publications, 1995.

Billings, Sabrina. *Language, Globalization and the Making of a Tanzanian Beauty Queen*. Bristol, UK: Multilingual Matters, 2014.

Birchall, Clare. *Knowledge Goes Pop: From Conspiracy Theory to Gossip*. Oxford: Berg, 2006.

Black, Shameem. "Recipes for Cosmopolitanism: Cooking Across Borders in the South Asian Diaspora." *Frontiers: A Journal of Women's Studies* 31, no. 1 (2010): 1–30.

Bowie, Fiona. "The Elusive Christian Family: Missionary Attempts to Define Women's Roles: Case Studies from Cameroon." In *Women and Missions: Past and Present: Anthropological and Historical Perception*, edited by Fiona Bowie, Deborah Kirkwood, and Shirley Ardener, 145–64. Oxford: Berg Publishers, 1993.

Breneman, Anne, and Rebecca Mbuh. *Women in the New Millennium: The Global Revolution*. Lanham, MD: Hamilton Books, 2006.

Brown, Marie Grace. "Fashioning Their Place: Dress and Global Imagination in Imperial Sudan." In *Gender, Imperialism and Global Exchanges*, edited by Stephan F. Miescher, Michele Mitchell, and Naoko Shibusawa, 115–31. West Sussex, UK: Wiley-Blackwell, 2015.

Brown, Marie Grace. *Khartoum at Night: Fashion and Body Politics in Imperial Sudan*. Stanford: Stanford University Press, 2017.

Burke, Timothy. *Lifebuoy Men, Lux Women: Commodification, Consumption, and Cleanliness in Modern Zimbabwe*. Durham: Duke University Press, 1996.

Burrill, Emily S. *States of Marriage: Gender, Justice, and Rights in Colonial Mali*. Athens: Ohio University Press, 2015.

Butler, Anthea D. *Women in the Church of God in Christ: Making a Sanctified World*. Chapel Hill: University of North Carolina Press, 2007.

Callaci, Emily. "Dancehall Politics: Mobility, Sexuality, and Spectacles of Racial Respectability in Late Colonial Tanganyika, 1930s–1961." *Journal of African History* 52, no. 3 (2011): 365–84.

Callaci, Emily. *Street Archives and City Life: Popular Intellectuals in Postcolonial Tanzania*. Durham: Duke University Press, 2017.

Cameroon Studies in English & French. Vol. 1. Yaoundé, Cameroon: Department of English, University of Yaoundé, 1976.

Chiabi, Emmanual. "Redressing Regional Imbalance in Cameroon: The Lessons from the Past." In *Regional Balance and National Integration in Cameroon: Lessons Learned and the Uncertain Future*, edited by Paul Nchoji Nkwi and Francis Beng Nyamnjoh, 41–58: Bamenda, Cameroon: Langaa RPCIG, 2011.

Chilver, Elizabeth M. "Nineteenth Century Trade in the Bamenda Grassfields, Southern Cameroons." *Afrika und Übersee* 45, no. 4 (1961): 233–58.

Cohen, Colleen Ballerino, Richard Wilk, and Beverly Stoeltje. "Introduction." In *Beauty Queens on the Global Stage: Gender, Contests, and Power*, edited by Colleen Ballerino Cohen, Richard Wilk, and Beverly Stoeltje, 1–11. New York: Routledge, 1996.

Cole, Catherine M., Takyiwaa Manuh, and Stephan F. Miescher. "Introduction: When Was Gender?" In *Africa After Gender?*, edited by Catherine M. Cole, Takyiwaa Manuh, and Stephan F. Miescher, 1–14. Bloomington: Indiana University Press, 2007.

Conversi, Daniele, ed. *Ethnonationalism in the Contemporary World: Walker Connor and the Study of Nationalism*. New York: Routledge, 2004.

Cooper, Barbara. *Evangelical Christians in the Muslim Sahel*. Bloomington: Indiana University Press, 2006.

Cooper, Barbara. "Oral Sources and the Challenges of African History." In *Writing African History*, edited by John Edward Philips, 191–215. Rochester, NY: University of Rochester Press, 2005.

Coquery-Vidrovitch, Catherine. *African Women: A Modern History*. Boulder, CO: Westview Press, 1997.

Corby, Elowyn. "Cameroonian Women Use Anlu for Social and Political Change, 1958–1961." Global Nonviolent Action Database, 2011. http://nvdatabase.swarthmore.edu/content/cameroonian-women-use-anlu-social-and-political-change-1958-1961

Courade, Georges. "The Urban Development of Buea: An Essay in Social Geography." Paper presented at the International Colloquium of the Centre National De La Recherche Scientifique, Bordeaux, France, September 29 to October 2, 1970. horizon.documentation.ird.fr/exl-doc/pleins_textes/pleins_textes_7/carton04/02655.pdf

Craig, Maxine Leeds. *Ain't I a Beauty Queen? Black Women, Beauty, and the Politics of Race*. Oxford: Oxford University Press, 2002.

Cullen-DuPont, Kathryn. *Encyclopedia of Women's History in America*. 2nd ed. New York: Facts on File, 2000.

Cusack, Igor. "African Cuisines: Recipes for Nation-Building?" *Journal of African Cultural Studies* 13, no. 2 (2000): 207–25.

Cusack, Igor. "Pots, Pens and 'Eating Out the Body': Cuisine and the Gendering of African Nations." *Nations and Nationalism* 9, no. 2 (2003): 277–96.

Dahlman, Carl J., Douglas Zhihua Zeng, and Shiulin Wang. *Enhancing China's Competitiveness Through Lifelong Learning*. Washington, DC: World Bank, 2007.

Davis, Paula Jean. "On the Sexuality of 'Town Women' in Kampala." *Africa Today* 47, no. 3/4 (2000): 29–60.

Decker, Alicia C. *In Idi Amin's Shadow: Women, Gender, and Militarism in Uganda*. Athens: Ohio University Press, 2014.

Decker, Corrie. *Mobilizing Zanzibari Women: The Struggle for Respectability and Self-Reliance in Colonial East-Africa*. London: Palgrave Macmillan, 2014.

DeLancey, Mark Dike, Rebecca Neh Mbuh, and Mark W. DeLancey. *Historical Dictionary of the Republic of Cameroon*. 4th ed. Lanham, MD: Scarecrow Press, 2010.

DeLancey, Mark W. *Cameroon: Dependence and Independence*. Boulder, CO: Westview Press, 1989.

Delancey, Virginia H. "The Relationship between Female Wage Employment and Fertility in Africa: An Example from Cameroon." PhD dissertation, University of South Carolina, 1980.

Delaney, Carol. "Father State, Motherland, and the Birth of Modern Turkey." In *Naturalizing Power: Essays in Feminist Cultural Analysis*, edited by Sylvia Yanagisako and Carol Delaney, 177–99. New York: Routledge, 1995.

Deutsch, Tracey. *Building a Housewife's Paradise: Gender, Politics, and American Grocery Stores in the Twentieth Century*. Chapel Hill: University of North Carolina Press, 2010.

Doh, Emmanuel Fru. *Anglophone-Cameroon Literature: An Introduction*. Lanham, MD: Lexington Books, 2015.

Durand, Caroline. "Rational Meals for the Traditional Family: Nutrition in Quebec School Manuals, 1900–1960s." In *Edible Histories, Cultural Politics: Towards a Canadian Food History*, edited by Franca Iacovetta, Valerie J. Korinek, and Marlene Epp, 109–27. Toronto: University of Toronto Press, 2012.

Ejedepang-Koge, S. N. *In the Service of People: My Roots—An Autobiography*. Bloomington, IN: Xlibris Corporation, 2013.

Ekali, Thomas Ngomba. "The Fluctuating Fortunes of Anglophone Cameroon Towns: The Case of Victoria, 1858–1982." In *African Urban Spaces in Historical Perspective*, edited by Steven J. Salm and Toyin Falola, 320–39. Rochester, NY: University of Rochester Press, 2005.

Elong, Eric Ebolo. "The Anglophone Cameroon Problem and the Secession Option in Cameroon." In *Bondage of Boundaries and Identity Politics in Postcolonial Africa: The "Northern Problem" and Ethno-Futures*, edited by Sabelo J. Ndlovu-Gatsheni and Brilliant Mhlanga, 148–62. Pretoria, South Africa: Africa Institute of South Africa, 2013.

Epprecht, Marc. *Heterosexual Africa? The History of an Idea from the Age of Exploration to the Age of AIDS*. Athens: Ohio University Press, 2008.

Falola, Toyin, and Ann Genova. *Historical Dictionary of Nigeria*. Lanham, MD: Scarecrow Press, 2009.

Feeley, Kathleen A., and Jennifer Frost. "Introduction." In *When Private Talk Goes Public: Gossip in American History*, edited by Kathleen A. Feeley and Jennifer Frost, 1–16. New York: Palgrave MacMillan, 2014.

Feldman-Savelsberg, Pamela. *Mothers on the Move: Reproducing Belonging Between Africa and Europe*. Chicago: University of Chicago Press, 2016.

Feldman-Savelsberg, Pamela. *Plundered Kitchens, Empty Wombs: Threatened Reproduction and Identity in the Cameroon Grassfields*. Ann Arbor: University of Michigan Press, 1999.

Ferree, Myra Marx. "Globalization and Feminism: Opportunities and Obstacles for Activism in the Global Arena." In *Global Feminism: Transnational Women's Activism,*

Organizing, and Human Rights, edited by Myra Marx Ferrere and Aili Mari Tripp, 3–23. New York: New York University Press, 2006.

Fokwang, Jude. "Student Activism, Violence and the Politics of Higher Education in Cameroon: A Case Study of the University of Buea (1993–2003)." In *Youth and Higher Education in Africa: The Cases of Cameroon, South Africa, Eritrea and Zimbabwe*, edited by Donald P. Chimanikire, 9–33. Dakar, Senegal: Council for the Development of Social Science Research in Africa, 2009.

Frère, Marie-Soleil. "Le Journaliste et le Griot: Les Traces de l'Oralité dans la Presse Écrite Africaine" [The Journalist and the Griot: Traces of Orality in the African Written Press]. *Afrika Focus* 15, nos. 1–2 (1999): 13–47.

Gadzekpo, Audrey. "Public but Private: A Transformational Reading of the Memoirs and Newspaper Writings of Mercy Ffoulkes-Crabbe." In *Africa's Hidden Histories: Everyday Literacy and Making the Self*, edited by Karin Barber, 314–37. Bloomington: Indiana University Press, 2006.

Galega, Samgena, and Martha Tumnde. "Reversing Decades of Gender Injustice in Cameroon." In *The Leadership Challenge in Africa: Cameroon under Paul Biya*, edited by John Mukum Mbaku and Joseph Takougang, 235–66. Trenton, NJ: Africa World Press, 2004.

Geiger, Susan. *TANU Women: Gender and Culture in the Making of Tanganyikan Nationalism, 1955–1965*. Portsmouth, NH: Heinemann, 1997.

George, Abosede. *Making Modern Girls: A History of Girlhood, Labor, and Social Development in Colonial Lagos*. Athens: Ohio University Press, 2014.

Girvin, Brian. "Democracy, Separatism, and Secession." Secessionism and Separatism Monthly Series, January 20, 2016, https://networks.h-net.org/node/3911/discussions/107684/secessionism-and-separatism-monthly-series-democracy-separatism

Goheen, Miriam. *Men Own the Fields, Women Own the Crops: Gender and Power in the Cameroon Grassfields*. Madison: University of Wisconsin Press, 1996.

Goufo, Piebiep. "Rice Production in Cameroon: A Review." *Research Journal of Agriculture and Biological Sciences Research* 4, no. 6 (2008): 745–56.

Gulliver, Katrina. *Modern Women in China and Japan: Gender, Feminism and Global Modernity between the Wars*. London: I. B. Tauris, 2012.

Guyer, Jane I., ed. *Feeding African Cities: Studies in Reginal Social History*. Manchester, UK: Manchester University Press, 1987.

Hale, Thomas A. *Griots and Griottes: Masters of Words and Music*. Bloomington: Indiana University Press, 1998.

Hale, Thomas A. "Griottes: Female Voices from West Africa." *Research in African Literatures* 25, no. 3 (1994): 71–91.

Hancock, Ian F., et al., eds. *Readings in Creole Studies*. Ghent, Belgium: E. Story-Scientia, 1979.

Handa, Amita. *Of Silk Saris and Mini-Skirts: South Asian Girls Walk the Tightrope of Culture*. Toronto: Women's Press, 2003.

Hansen, Karen Tranberg. "Dressing Dangerously: Mini-Skirts, Gender Relations, and

Sexuality in Zambia." In *Fashioning Africa: Power and the Politics of Dress*, edited by Jean Marie Allman, 166–85. Bloomington: Indiana University Press, 2004.

Hansen, Karen Tranberg. "Introduction." In *African Dress: Fashion, Agency, Performance*, edited by Karen Tranberg Hansen and D. Soyini Madison, 1–11. London: Bloomsbury, 2013.

Hassim, Shireen. *Women's Organizations and Democracy in South Africa: Contesting Authority*. Madison: University of Wisconsin Press, 2006.

Healy-Clancy, Meghan. "The Family Politics of the Federation of South African Women: A History of Public Motherhood in Women's Antiracist Activism." *Signs: Journal of Women in Culture and Society* 42, no. 4 (2017): 843–66.

Hendrickson, Hildi. "Introduction." In *Clothing and Difference: Embodied Identities in Colonial and Post-Colonial Africa*, edited by Hildi Hendrickson, 1–16. Durham: Duke University Press, 1996.

Henrichsen, Dag. *A Glance at Our Africa: Facsimile Reprint of Southwest News—Suidwes Nuus, 1960*. Basel, Switzerland: Basler Afrika Bibliographien, 1997.

Higginbotham, Evelyn Brooks. *Righteous Discontent: The Women's Movement in the Black Baptist Church, 1880–1920*. Cambridge, MA: Harvard University Press, 1993.

Hodgson, Dorothy, and Sheryl McCurdy, eds. "Introduction: 'Wicked' Women and the Reconfiguration of Gender in Africa." In *"Wicked" Women and the Reconfiguration of Gender in Africa*, edited by Dorothy Hodgson and Sheryl McCurdy, 1–24. Portsmouth, NH: Heinemann, 2001.

Hodgson, Dorothy, and Sheryl McCurdy. "Wayward Wives, Misfit Mothers, and Disobedient Daughters: 'Wicked' Women and the Reconfiguration of Gender in Africa." *Canadian Journal of African Studies* 30, no. 1 (1996): 1–9.

Huckstep, Joan Elayne. "Embodied Nationalism 'Animation Politique' (Political Dance) in Zaire: A Case Study of the Dimensionality and Agency of Dance as the Spirit of Individual, Community, and National Identity." PhD dissertation, Temple University, 2005.

Hunt, Nancy Rose. "Colonial Fairy Tales and the Knife and Fork Doctrine in the Heart of Africa." In *African Encounters with Domesticity*, edited by Karen Tranberg Hansen, 143–71. New Brunswick, NJ: Rutgers University Press, 1992.

Hunt, Nancy Rose. *A Colonial Lexicon: Of Birth Ritual, Medicalization, and Mobility in the Congo*. Durham: Duke University Press, 1999.

Hunt, Nancy Rose. "Noise Over Camouflaged Polygamy, Colonial Morality Taxation, and a Woman-Naming Crisis in Belgian Africa." *Journal of African History* 32, no. 3 (1991): 471–94.

Idowu, Kate Ebenye. *Auntie Kate's Cookery Book*. 3rd ed. London; MacMillan, 1985.

Itiat, Prince Kofi. *Isong Urua Adiakod: The Untold Story and the Politics of Bakassi Handover*. Bloomington, IN: Xlibris Corporation, 2012.

Ivaska, Andrew M. "'Anti-Mini Militants Meet Modern Misses': Urban Style, Gender, and the Politics of 'National Culture' in 1960s Dar es Salaam, Tanzania." *Gender and History* 14, no. 3 (November 2002): 584–607.

Ivaska, Andrew M. *Cultured States: Youth, Gender, and Modern Style in 1960s Dar Es Salaam*. Durham: Duke University Press, 2011.

Jacob, Jeanne, and Michael Ashkenazi. *The World Cookbook: The Greatest Recipes from Around the Globe*. 2nd ed. Vol. 1. Santa Barbara, CA: ABC-CLIO, 2014.

Jafar, Afshan, and Erynn Masi de Casanova. "Bodies, Beauty, and Location: An Introduction." In *Global Beauty, Local Bodies*, edited by Erynn Masi de Casanova and Afshan Jafar, xi–xxv. New York: Palgrave Macmillan, 2013.

Jean-Baptiste, Rachel. *Conjugal Rights: Marriage, Sexuality, and Urban Life in Colonial Libreville, Gabon*. Athens: Ohio University Press, 2014.

Jedida, Asheri. *Promise*. Lagos, Nigeria: African University Press, 1969.

Jha, Meeta Rani. *The Global Beauty Industry: Colorism, Racism, and the National Body*. New York: Routledge, 2016.

Johnson-Hanks, Jennifer. *Uncertain Honor: Modern Motherhood in an African Crisis*. Chicago: University of Chicago Press, 2006.

Jong-Ebot, William. "The Mass Media in Cameroon: An Analysis of Their Post-Colonial Status." PhD dissertation, University of Wisconsin–Madison, 1989.

Joseph, Richard, ed. *Gaullist Africa: Cameroon Under Ahmadu Ahidjo*. Enugu, Nigeria: Fourth Dimension Publishing, 1978.

Joseph, Richard. "National Politics in Postwar Cameroun: The Difficult Birth of the UPC." *Journal of African Studies* 2, no. 2 (1975): 201–29.

Joseph, Richard. *Radical Nationalism in Cameroun: Social Origins of the U.P.C. Rebellion*. Oxford: Clarendon Press, 1977.

Joseph, Richard. "Ruben Um Nyobé and the 'Kamerun' Rebellion." *African Affairs* 73, no. 293 (1974): 428–48.

Jua, Nantang, and Piet Konings. "Occupation of Public Space: Anglophone Nationalism in Cameroon." *Cahiers d'Études Africaines* 44, no. 175 (2004): 609–33.

Kaberry, Phyllis Mary. *Women of the Grassfields: A Study of the Economic Position of Women in Bamenda, British Cameroons*. London: Her Majesty's Stationery Office, 1952.

Kah, Henry Kam. "Cameroonian Women in Political Leadership, 1960–2015." *Afro Asian Journal of Social Sciences* 9, no. 2 (2016): 1–25.

Kah, Henry Kam. "'Our Gowns for Your Trousers': Sexuality and Women Revolt in Colonial Laimbwe Land, Cameroon." *Epasa Moto: A Multidisciplinary Journal of Arts, Letters, and the Humanities of the University of Buea* 1, no. 2 (2014): 103–22.

Kah, Henry Kam. "Women's Resistance in Cameroon's Western Grassfields: The Power of Symbols, Organization, and Leadership, 1957–1961." *African Studies Quarterly* 12, no. 3 (2011): 67–91.

Kanogo, Tabitha. *African Womanhood in Colonial Kenya 1900–1950*. Oxford: James Currey; and Athens: Ohio University Press, 2005.

Kanogo, Tabitha. "Mission Impact on Women in Colonial Kenya." In *Women and Missions: Past and Present: Anthropological and Historical Perception*, edited by Fiona Bowie, Deborah Kirkwood, and Shirley Ardener, 165–86. Oxford: Berg Publishers, 1993.

Kisangani, Emizet Francois. *Historical Dictionary of the Democratic Republic of the Congo*. Lanham, MD: Rowman & Littlefield, 2016.

Kisob, J. A. "An Appreciation of Bamenda Traditional Costume." *Abbia: Revue Culturelle Camerounaise*, no. 3 (1963): 55–65.

Konde, Emmanuel. *African Women and Politics: Knowledge, Gender, and Power in Male-Dominated Cameroon*. Lewiston, NY: Edwin Mellen Press, 2005.

Konde, Emmanuel. *Cameroon: Traumas of the Body Politic*. Bloomington, IN: Xlibris Corporation 2015.

Konings, Piet. "The Anglophone Cameroon-Nigeria Boundary: Opportunities and Conflicts." *African Affairs* 104, no. 415 (2005): 275–301.

Konings, Piet. *Gender and Plantation Labour in Africa: The Story of Tea Pluckers' Struggles in Cameroon*. Bamenda, Cameroon: Langaa RPCIG; Leiden, the Netherlands: African Studies Centre, 2012.

Konings, Piet. *Neoliberal Bandwagonism: Civil Society and the Politics of Belonging in Anglophone Cameroon*. Bamenda, Cameroon: Langaa RPCIG; Leiden, the Netherlands: African Studies Centre, 2009.

Konings, Piet, and Francis Beng Nyamnjoh. "The Anglophone Problem in Cameroon." *Journal of Modern African Studies* 35, no. 2 (1997): 207–29.

Konings, Piet, and Francis Beng Nyamnjoh. "Anglophone Secessionist Movements in Cameroon." In *Secessionism in African Politics: Aspiration, Grievance, Performance, Disenchantment*, edited by Lotje de Vries, Pierre Englebert, and Mareike Schomerus, 59–89. New York: Palgrave Macmillan, 2018.

Konings, Piet, and Francis Beng Nyamnjoh. *Negotiating an Anglophone Identity: A Study of the Politics of Recognition and Representation in Cameroon*. Leiden, the Netherlands: Brill, 2003.

Kor, Buma. "The Literature of the Hunchback." In *Anglophone Cameroon Writing*, edited by Nalova Lyonga, Eckhard Breitinger, and Bole Butake, 60–75. Bayreuth African Studies Series 30. Bayreuth, Germany: University of Bayreuth, 1993.

Krieger, Milton. "Cameroon's Democratic Crossroads, 1990–4." *Journal of Modern African Studies* 32, no. 4 (1994): 605–28.

Labode, Modupe. "From Heathen Kraal to Christian Home: Anglican Mission Education and African Christian Girls 1850–1900." In *Women and Missions: Past and Present: Anthropological and Historical Perception*, edited by Fiona Bowie, Deborah Kirkwood, and Shirley Ardener, 126–44. Oxford: Berg Publishers, 1993.

Lal, Priya. *African Socialism in Postcolonial Tanzania: Between the Village and the World*. Cambridge: Cambridge University Press, 2015.

Lang, Michael Kpughe. "Women and Christianity in Cameroon: The Case of the Presbyterian Church in Cameroon Since the Basel Mission Era, 1886–2010." *Afro Asian Journal of Social Sciences* 7, no. 4 (2016): 1–24.

Langmia, Kehbuma. *Titabet and the Takumbeng: A Play*. Bamenda, Cameroon: Langaa RPCIG, 2008.

Lansford, Tom, ed. *Political Handbook of the World 2016–2017*. Washington, DC: CQ Press, 2017.

Larmer, Miles, and Baz Lecocq. "Rethinking Nationalism, Ethnicity and Separatism in African Studies." Secessionism and Separatism Monthly Series, September 20, 2016. https://networks.h-net.org/node/3911/discussions/144633/secessionism-and-separatism-monthly-series-%E2%80%9Crethinking-nationalism

Lawyer, Linda Ankiambom. "Female Missionary Activities and the Redefinition of Gender Roles in the Bamenda Grassfields of Cameroon 1904–2006." *International Journal of Liberal Arts and Social Science* 5, no. 3 (2017): 86–101.

LeVine, Victor T. *The Cameroon Federal Republic*. Ithaca: Cornell University Press, 1963.

Lihamba, Amandina. *Women Writing Africa: The Eastern Region*. New York: The Feminist Press at the City University of New York, 2007.

Lipscomb, Suzannah. "Crossing Boundaries: Women's Gossip, Insults and Violence in Sixteenth-Century France." *French History* 25, no. 4 (2011): 408–26.

Little, Kenneth. *African Women in Towns: An Aspect of Africa's Social Revolution*. Cambridge: Cambridge University Press, 1973.

Lyons, Tanya. *Guns and Guerilla Girls: Women in the Zimbabwean National Liberation Struggle*. Trenton, NJ: Africa World Press, 2004.

Mama, Amina. "Feminism or Femocracy? State Feminism and Democratisation in Nigeria." *Africa Development* 20, no. 1 (1995): 37–58.

Mandala, Elias Coutinho. *The End of Chidyerano: A History of Food and Everyday Life in Malawi, 1860–2004*. Portsmouth, NH: Heinemann, 2005.

Marcoux, Jean-Philippe. *Jazz Griots: Music as History in the 1960s African American Poem*. Lanham, MD: Lexington Books, 2012.

Martin, Gladys Ejomi. "Aunty Kate: The Book, the Cook, the Educator and Homemaker." *Success Story Magazine*, no. 11 (2008): 18–19. https://www.successstorymagazine.info/past_issues/

Mayer, Tamar. "Embodied Nationalisms." In *Mapping Women, Making Politics: Feminist Perspectives on Political Geography*, edited by Lynn Staeheli, Eleonore Kofman, and Linda Peake, 153–67. New York: Routledge, 2004.

Mbaku, John Mukum. "Cameroon, Republic of." In *Africa: An Encyclopedia of Culture and Society*, vol. 1, edited by Toyin Falola and Daniel Jean-Jacques, 139–77. Santa Barbara, CA: ABC-CLIO, 2015.

Mbaku, John Mukum. *Culture and Customs of Cameroon*. Westport, CT: Greenwood Press, 2005.

Mbaku, John Mukum, and Joseph Takougang, eds. *The Leadership Challenge in Africa: Cameroon under Paul Biya*. Trenton, NJ: Africa World Press, 2004.

Mbella, George, and Emma Ngale-Ngwang. "Meet Clara Yondo: Cameroon's First Female English-Speaking Journalist." *Success Story Magazine*. https://www.facebook.com/permalink.php?id=822827624746264&story_fbid=839160243113002

Mbembe, Achille. "Introduction: L'État-Historien [Introduction: The State Historian]." In *Écrits Sous Maquis*, edited by Ruben Um Nyobé, 10–42. Paris: Editions L'Harmattan, 1989.

Mbembe, Achille. *La Naissance Du Maquis Dans Le Sud-Cameroun, 1920–1960: Histoire Des Usages De La Raison En Colonie* [The Birth of the Maquis in South Cameroon, 1920–1960: History of the Uses of Reason in the Colony]. Paris: Karthala, 1996.

Mbembe, Achille. *On the Postcolony*. Berkeley: University of California Press, 2001.

Mbile, Nerius Namaso. *Cameroon Political Story: Memories of an Authentic Eye Witness*. Bamenda, Cameroon: Langaa RPCIG, 2011.

Mbuh, Rebecca. "African Women's Quest for Equality: The Case of Cameroon." In *Women in the New Millennium: The Global Revolution*, edited by Anne R. Breneman and Rebecca N. Mbuh, 67–92. Lanham, MD: Hamilton Books, 2006.

McCann, James C. *Stirring the Pot: A History of African Cuisine*. Athens: Ohio University Press, 2009.

Mehler, Andreas. "Why Federalism Did Not Lead to Secession in Cameroon." *Ethnopolitics* 13, no. 1 (2014): 48–66.

Messmer, Pierre. *Les Blancs s'en Vont: Récits de Décolonisation* [The Whites are Leaving: Decolonization Stories]. Paris: Albin Michel, 1998.

Militz, Elisabeth, and Carolin Schurr. "Affective Nationalism: Banalities of Belonging in Azerbaijan." *Political Geography* 54 (2016): 54–63.

Moghadam, Valentine M. *Globalization and Social Movements: Islamism, Feminism, and the Global Justice Movement*. Lanham, MD: Rowman & Littlefield, 2012.

Mokake, Flavius. "The Kabba Dress: Identity and Modernity in Contemporary Cameroon." In *Marginality and Crisis: Globalization and Identity in Contemporary Africa*, edited by Akanmu G. Adebayo, Olutayo C. Adesina, and Rasheed O. Olaniyi, 71–90. Lanham, MD: Lexington Books, 2010.

Mougoué, Jacqueline-Bethel Tchouta. "African Women Do Not Look Good in Wigs: Gender, Beauty Rituals and Cultural Identity in Anglophone Cameroon, 1961–1972." *Feminist Africa* 21 (2016): 7–22.

Mougoué, Jacqueline-Bethel Tchouta. "The Anlu Rebellion." In the *Oxford Research Encyclopedia of African History*, edited by Thomas Spear. New York: Oxford University Press, February 2018. https://doi.org/10.1093/acrefore/9780190277734.013.273

Mougoué, Jacqueline-Bethel Tchouta. "Housewives at Husbands' Throats: Recalcitrant Wives and Gender Norms in a West African Nation, 1961–72." *Gender and History* 29, no. 2 (2017): 405–22.

Mougoué, Jacqueline-Bethel Tchouta. "How I Increased My Bride Price and Other Insights from My Dissertation Field Research." *African Studies Association News*. September 2012.

Mougoué, Jacqueline-Bethel Tchouta. "Intellectual Housewives, Journalism, and Anglophone Nationalism in Cameroon, 1961–72." *Journal of West African History* 3, no. 2 (2017): 67–92.

Mougoué, Jacqueline-Bethel Tchouta. "'Where Are All the Women Who Used to Be Good Athletes in Their School Days?': Sports and Gendered Leisure in Anglophone Cameroon in the 1960s and 1970s." In *Africa Every Day: Fun, Leisure, and Expressive Culture on the Continent*, edited by Oluwakemi Balogun, Lisa Gilman, Melissa Graboyes, and Habib Iddrisu. Athens: Ohio University Press, forthcoming.

Mukete, V. E. *My Odyssey: The Story of Cameroon Reunification with Authentic Letters of Key Players*. Yaoundé, Cameroon: Eagle Publishing, 2013.

Mukong, Albert W. *Prisoner Without a Crime. Disciplining Dissent in Ahidjo's Cameroon*. Bamenda, Cameroon: Langaa RPCIG, 2009.

Muluh, Henry, and Bertha Ndoh. "Evolution of the Media in Cameroon." In *Journalism and Mass Communication in Africa: Cameroon*, edited by Festus Eribo and Enoh Tanjong, 3–16. Lanham, MD: Lexington Books, 2002.

Musisi, Nakanyike B. "Colonial and Missionary Education: Women and Domesticity in Uganda, 1900–1945." In *African Encounters with Domesticity*, edited by Karen Tranberg Hansen, 172–94. New Brunswick, NJ: Rutgers University Press, 1992.

Mutongi, Kenda. "Dear Dolly's Advice on Love and Courtship." *International Journal of African Historical Studies* 33, no. 1 (2000): 1–28.

Nana-Fabu, Stella. "An Analysis of the Economic Status of Women in Cameroon." *Journal of International Women's Studies* 8, no. 1 (2006): 148–62.

Ndi, Anthony. *The Golden Age of Southern (West) Cameroon, 1946–1972: Impact of Christianity*. Bamenda, Cameroon: Langaa RPCIG, 2005.

Ndi, Anthony. *Southern West Cameroon Revisited (1950–1972): Unveiling Inescapable Traps*. Vol.1. Bamenda, Cameroon: Langaa RPCIG, 2014.

Ndi, Anthony. *Southern West Cameroon Revisited: North-South West Nexus 1858–1972*. Vol. 2. Bamenda, Cameroon: Langaa RPCIG, 2014.

Newell, Stephanie. *The Power to Name: A History of Anonymity in Colonial West Africa*. Athens: Ohio University Press, 2013.

Newell, Stephanie. *West African Literatures: Ways of Reading*. Oxford: Oxford University Press, 2006.

Nfah-Abbenyi, Juliana Makuchi. *Gender in African Women's Writing: Identity, Sexuality, and Difference*. Bloomington: Indiana University Press, 1997.

Nfi, Joseph Lon. *The Reunification Debate in British Southern Cameroons: The Role of French Cameroon Immigrants*. Bamenda, Cameroon: Langaa RPCIG, 2014.

Ngwafor, Ephraim N. *Ako-Aya: A Cameroonian Pioneer in Daring Journalism and Social Commentary*. Bamenda, Cameroon: Langaa RPCIG, 2010.

Nji, Ajaga. "Socio-Cultural Determinants of the Status of the Cameroonian Woman: Implications for the Family in the 21st Century." In *The Anthropology of Africa: Challenges for the 21st Century*, edited by Paul Nchoji Nkwi, 317–32. Bamenda, Cameroon: Langaa RPCIG, 2015.

Nkwi, Paul Nchoji. "Traditional Female Militancy in a Modern Context." In *Femmes du Cameroun: Mères Pacifiques Femmes Rebelles* [Women of Cameroon: Pacific Mothers, Women Rebels], edited by J. C. Barbier, 181–91. Paris: Orstom-Karthala, 1985.

Nkwi, Walter Gam. "Security or Insecurity: The Gendarmerie and Popular Reaction in West Cameroon, 1961–1964." *African Nebula* 7 (2014): 53–73.

Nyamnjoh, Francis Beng, and Richard Fonteh Akum. *The Cameroon GCE Crisis: A Test of Anglophone Solidarity*. 2nd ed. Bamenda, Cameroon: Langaa RPCIG, 2008.

Oben, Tricia Efange. *Women of the Reunification*. Mumbai, India: New Media Communication, 2011.

Obiechina, Emmanuel. *An African Popular Literature: A Study of Onitsha Market Pamphlets*. Cambridge: Cambridge University Press, 1973.

Oduro-Frimpong, Joseph. "'Better Ghana [Agenda]?' Akosua's Political Cartoons and Critical Public Debates in Contemporary Ghana." In *Popular Culture in Africa: The Episteme of the Everyday*, edited by Stephanie Newell and Onookome Okome, 131–53. London: Routledge, 2013.

Ogundipe-Leslie, Molara. *Recreating Ourselves: African Women and Critical Transformation*. Trenton, NJ: Africa World Press, 1994.

Oliver, M. Cynthia. *Queen of the Virgins: Pageantry and Black Womanhood in the Caribbean*. Jackson: University Press of Mississippi, 2009.

Organisation des Femmes de l'Union Nationale Camerounaise. *La Femme Camerounaise* [The Cameroonian Woman]. Paris: EDICEF, 1972.

Organisation des Femmes de l'Union Nationale Camerounaise. *L'OFUNC en Marché* [The WCNU on the Move]. Douala, Cameroun: Agence Camerounaise d'Information, 1980.

Organisation des Femmes de l'Union Nationale Camerounaise. *Integration de la Femme Camerounaise dans le Processus de Développement Economique: L'OFUNC en Marché* [Integration of the Cameroonian Woman into the Economic Development Process: The WCNU on the Move]. Yaoundé, Cameroon: OFUNC, 1982.

Orosz, Kenneth J. "The 'Affaire des Sixas' and Catholic Education of Women in French Colonial Cameroon, 1915–1939." *French Colonial History* 1, no.1 (2002): 33–49.

O'Rourke, Harmony. "Foncha, John Ngu." In *Dictionary of African Biography*, vol. 6, edited by Emmanuel K. Akyeampong and Henry Louis Gates, Jr., 379–81. New York: Oxford University Press, 2012.

Oyěwùmí, Oyèrónkẹ́. *Gender Epistemologies in Africa: Gendering Traditions, Spaces, Social Institutions, and Identities*. New York: Palgrave Macmillan, 2011.

Oyěwùmí, Oyèrónkẹ́. *The Invention of Women: Making an African Sense of Western Gender Discourses*. Minneapolis: University of Minnesota Press, 1997.

Parpart, Jane L. "'Wicked Women' and 'Respectable Ladies': Reconfiguring Gender on the Zambian Copperbelt, 1936–1964." In *"Wicked" Women and the Reconfiguration of Gender in Africa*, edited by Dorothy Hodgson and Sheryl McCurdy, 274–92. Portsmouth, NH: Heinemann, 2001.

Paoletti, Jo Barraclough. *Sex and Unisex: Fashion, Feminism, and the Sexual Revolution*. Bloomington: Indiana University Press, 2015.

Peterson, Derek, and Emma Hunter. "Print Culture in Colonial Africa." In *African Print Cultures: Newspapers and Their Publics in the Twentieth Century*, edited by Derek Peterson, Emma Hunter, and Stephanie Newell, 1–45. Ann Arbor: University of Michigan Press, 2016.

Ramírez, Cristina Devereaux. *Occupying Our Space: The Mestiza Rhetorics of Mexican Women Journalists and Activists, 1875–1942*. Tucson: University of Arizona Press, 2015.

Ravindran, T. K. Sundari, Anjana Bhushan, Kathleen Fritsch, and Breeda Hickey. *Integrating Poverty and Gender into Health Programmes: A Sourcebook for Health Professionals: Module on Gender-Based Violence*. Manila, Philippines: World Health Organization, Western Pacific Region, 2005.

Rich, Jeremy. *A Workman Is Worthy of His Meat: Food and Colonialism in the Gabon Estuary*. Lincoln: University of Nebraska Press, 2007.

Ritzenthaler, Robert E. "Anlu: A Women's Uprising in the British Cameroons." *African Studies* 19, no. 3 (1960): 151–56.

Rondon, Marcela. *2013 Exporting to Cameroon*. USDA Foreign Agricultural Service, 2014. http://gain.fas.usda.gov/Recent%20GAIN%20Publications/2013%20Exporting%20to%20Cameroon%20_Lagos_Cameroon_3-13-2013.pdf

Rowe, Rochelle. *Imagining Caribbean Womanhood: Race, Nation and Beauty Competitions, 1929–70*. Manchester, UK: Manchester University Press, 2013.

Salih, M.A. Mohamed. *Economic Development and Political Action in the Arab World*. New York: Routledge, 2014.

Samah, Walters. "Anglophone Minority and the State in Cameroon." In *Minorities and the State in Africa*, edited by Michael U. Mbanaso and Chima J. Korieh, 243–65. Amherst, NY: Cambria Press, 2010.

Schatzberg, Michael. *Political Legitimacy in Middle Africa: Father, Family, Food*. Bloomington: Indiana University Press, 2001.

Schmidt, Elizabeth. *Mobilizing the Masses: Gender, Ethnicity, and Class in the Nationalist Movement in Guinea, 1939–1958*. Portsmouth, NH: Heinemann, 2005.

Schneider, Helen M. *Keeping the Nation's House: Domestic Management and the Making of Modern China*. Vancouver: University of British Columbia Press, 2011.

Schulz, Dorothea E. "Mesmerizing 'Missis,' Nationalist Musings: Beauty Pageants and the Public Controversy Over 'Malian' Womanhood." *Paideuma: Mitteilungen Zur Kulturkunde* 46 (2000): 111–35.

Schuster, Lisa M. Glazer. *New Women of Lusaka*. Palo Alto, CA: Mayfield Publishing, 1979.

Séminaire d'Animation et la Formation de la Femme Camerounaise: Les Actes du Séminaire Féminine [Seminar of Animation and Training of Cameroonian Women: Proceedings of the Women's Seminar]. Yaoundé, Cameroon: March 1975.

Shadle, Brett. *"Girl Cases": Marriage and Colonialism in Gusiiland, Kenya, 1890–1970*. Portsmouth, NH: Heinemann, 2006.

Shanklin, Eugenia. "Anlu Remembered: The Kom Women's Rebellion of 1958–61." *Dialectical Anthropology* 15, nos. 2/3 (1990): 159–81.

Shaw, Ibrahim Seaga. "Towards an African Journalism Model: A Critical Historical Perspective." *The International Communication Gazette* 71, no. 6 (2009): 491–510.

Sheldon, Kathleen. "Writing About Women: Approaches to a Gendered Perspective in African History." In *Writing African History*, edited by John Edward Philips, 465–89. Rochester, NY: University of Rochester Press, 2005.

Shetler, Jan Bender, ed. *Gendering Ethnicity in African Women's Lives*. Madison: University of Wisconsin Press, 2015.

Siddiqui, Rukhsana A., ed. *Sub-Saharan Africa in the 1990s: Challenges to Democracy and Development*. Westport, CT: Praeger, 1997.

Simons, Gary F., and Charles D. Fennig, eds. *Ethnologue: Languages of the World*. 21st ed. Dallas, TX: SIL International, 2017. http://www.ethnologue.com

Spacks, Patricia Meyer. "In Praise of Gossip." *Hudson Review* 35, no. 1 (1982): 19–38.

Sperling, Valerie, Myra Marx Ferree, and Barbara Risman. "Constructing Global Feminism: Transnational Advocacy Networks and Russian Women's Activism." *Signs: Journal of Women in Culture and Society* 26, no. 4 (2001): 1155–86.

Stark, Frank M. "Federalism in Cameroon: The Shadow and the Reality." *Canadian Journal of African Studies* 10, no. 3 (1976): 423–42.

Steady, Filomina Chioma. *Women and Collective Action in Africa: Development, Democratization, and Empowerment*. New York: Palgrave Macmillan, 2006.

Steady, Filomina Chioma. *Women and Leadership in West Africa: Mothering the Nation and Humanizing the State*. New York: Palgrave Macmillan, 2011.

Tanga, Pius Tangwe. "The Role of Women's Secret Societies in Cameroon's Contemporary Politics: The Case of Takumbeng." *African Journal of Cross-Cultural Psychology and Sports Facilitation* 8 (2006): 1–17.

Teboh, Bridget Angum. "Women and Change in the Cameroon Grassfields: A Social and Economic History of Moghamoland C. 1889–1960." PhD dissertation, University of California, Los Angeles, 2002.

Terretta, Meredith. "A Miscarriage of Revolution: Cameroonian Women and Nationalism." *Stichproben* 12, no. 7 (2007): 61–90.

Terretta, Meredith. *Nation of Outlaws, State of Violence: Nationalism, Grassfields Tradition, and State Building in Cameroon*. Athens: Ohio University Press, 2014.

Terretta, Meredith. *Petitioning for our Rights, Fighting for our Nation: The History of the Democratic Union of Cameroonian Women, 1949–1960*. Bamenda, Cameroon: Langaa RPCIG, 2013.

Thomas, Lynn. "The Modern Girl and Racial Respectability in 1930s South Africa." *Journal of African History* 47, no. 3 (2006): 461–90.

Tice, Karen Whitney. *Queens of Academe: Beauty Pageantry, Student Bodies, and College Life*. New York: Oxford University Press, 2012.

Torrent, Mélanie. *Diplomacy and Nation-Building in Africa: Franco-British Relations and Cameroon at the End of Empire*. London: I. B. Tauris, 2012.

Tran, Nhung Tuyet. "Woman as Nation: Tradition and Modernity Narratives in Vietnamese Histories." *Gender & History* 24, no. 2 (2012): 411–30.

Tripp, Aili Mari. *Women and Politics in Uganda*. Madison: University of Wisconsin Press, 2000.

United States Department of State Bureau of African Affairs. *AF Press Clips*. 1979.

Vaughan, Megan. *The Story of an African Famine: Gender and Famine in Twentieth-Century Malawi*. Cambridge: Cambridge University Press, 1987.

Vickers, Jill. "Gendering Secession." Secessionism and Separatism Monthly Series, March 20, 2016. https://networks.h-net.org/node/116427/pdf

Vubo, Emmanuel Yenshu. *Gender Relations in Cameroon: Multidisciplinary Perspectives.* Bamenda, Cameroon: Langaa RPCIG, 2012.

Wache, Francis K. "The Plebiscite: Thirty Years After. The Choice between Fire and Deep Water." *Cameroon Life* 1, no. 8 (1991): 6–10.

Walden, Sarah W. *Tasteful Domesticity: Women's Rhetoric and the American Cookbook, 1790–1940*. Pittsburgh: University of Pittsburgh Press, 2018.

Weber, Max. *The Protestant Ethic and the Spirit of Capitalism*. New York: Charles Scribner's Sons, 1958.

Wellman, Barry, and Keith Hampton. "Living Networked On and Off Line." *Contemporary Sociology* 28, no. 6 (1999): 648–54.

West, Ben. *Cameroon*. Chalfont St. Peter, United Kingdom: Bradt Travel Guides, 2011.

White, Luise. *The Comforts of Home: Prostitution in Colonial Nairobi*. Chicago: University of Chicago Press, 1990.

White, Luise. *Speaking with Vampires: Rumor and History in Colonial Africa*. Berkeley: University of California Press, 2000.

Whitt, Jan. *Women in American Journalism: A New History*. Champaign: University of Illinois Press, 2008.

Wilk, Richard. "Connections and Contradictions: From the Crooked Tree Cashew Queen to Miss World Belize." In *Beauty Queens on the Global Stage: Gender, Contests, and Power*, edited by Colleen Ballerino Cohen, Richard Wilk, and Beverly Stoeltje, 217–32. New York: Routledge, 1996.

Wilk, Richard. "Learning to Be Local in Belize: Global Systems of Common Difference." In *Worlds Apart: Modernity Through the Prism of the Local*, edited by Daniel Miller, 110–33. London: Routledge, 1995.

Wilk, Richard. "The Local and the Global in the Political Economy of Beauty: From Miss Belize to Miss World." *Review of International Political Economy* 2, no. 1 (1995): 117–34.

World Bank. United Nations Population Division. "World Urbanization Prospects: 2018 Revision: Urban Population (% of total)." https://data.worldbank.org/indicator/SP.URB.TOTL.IN.ZS?locations=CM

World Organisation Against Torture. *Violence against Women in Cameroon: A Report to the Committee against Torture, 31st Session*. United Nations Publications, 2003.

Wylie, Diana. *Starving on a Full Stomach: Hunger and the Triumph of Cultural Racism in Modern South Africa*. Charlottesville: University of Virginia Press, 2001.

Yuval-Davis, Nira. *Gender and Nation*. London: Sage Publications, 1997.

INDEX

Note: Page numbers in italic indicate an illustration.